# THE MISSIONARY LIFE

For Andrew MacLennan

*Also available from Longman*

# The Medieval World

General Editor: David Bates
*Professor in Medieval History, University of Glasgow*

This series provides the student, scholar and general reader with authoritative short studies of key aspects and personalities of the medieval world. The careers explored in the biographical volumes will be studied not only for their own importance, but also for the light they shed on the wider themes and processes of the time.

| | |
|---|---|
| The English Church | H R Loyn |
| Alfred the Great | Richard Abels |
| Cnut | M K Lawson |
| The Formation of English Common Law 1066–1215 | John Hudson |
| The Reign of King Stephen | David Crouch |
| The Reign of Richard Lionheart | Ralph V Turner and Ralph Heiser |
| William Marshal: Court, Career and Chivalry in the Angevin Empire 1147–1219 | David Crouch |
| The Age of Charles Martel | Paul Fouracre |
| The Friars | C H Lawrence |
| Medieval Monasticism: Forms of Religious Life in Western Europe in the Middle Ages | C H Lawrence |
| Ambrose | John Moorhead |
| Medieval Canon Law | James A Brundage |
| John of Salisbury | John Mcloughlin |
| Innocent III | Jane Sayers ✓ |
| The Age of Robert Guiscard | Graham Loud |
| The Cathars | Malcolm Barber |

# THE MISSIONARY LIFE

## Saints and the evangelisation of Europe, 400–1050

IAN WOOD

*An imprint of* **Pearson Education**

Harlow, England · London · New York · Reading, Massachusetts · San Francisco · Toronto · Don Mills, Ontario · Sydney
Tokyo · Singapore · Hong Kong · Seoul · Taipei · Cape Town · Madrid · Mexico City · Amsterdam · Munich · Paris · Milan

**Pearson Education Limited**

Edinburgh Gate
Harlow
Essex CM20 2JE
England

and Associated Companies around the world

*Visit us on the World Wide Web at*
*www.pearsoneduc.com*

---------------------

First published in Great Britain in 2001

ISBN 0 582 31213 2 PPR

*British Library Cataloging-in-Publication Data*
A catalogue record for this book can be obtained from the British Library

*Library of Congress Cataloging-in-Publication Data*
Wood, I. N. (Ian N.), 1950–
    The missionary life : saints and the evangelisation of Europe, 400–1050 / Ian Wood.
      p. cm.
    Includes bibliographical references and index.
    ISBN 0–582–31212–4 (alk. paper) — ISBN 0–582–31213–2 (pbk. : alk. paper)
    1. Missions—Europe—History—Early church, ca. 30–600.  2.
Missions—Europe—History—Middle Ages, 600–1500.  3.
Missionaries—Europe—Biography.  4. Europe—Church history.  I. Title.

BV2855.W66  2001
266′.0094′09021—dc21                                   00–061357

10 9 8 7 6 5 4 3 2 1
06 05 04 03 02 01

Typeset by 35 in 9$\frac{1}{2}$/13pt Stone Serif
Produced by Pearson Education Asia Pte Ltd.
Printed in Singapore

# CONTENTS

# LIST OF MAPS

# PREFACE

I first decided to write a book on the history of Christianisation when preparing an article which appeared in a volume edited by Geoffrey Barraclough in 1981.[1] In the course of writing that piece it struck me that the standard interpretation of the Christianisation of Europe was based on far too many assumptions, some of which I, as a very junior scholar in awe of the editor, felt obliged to repeat. Although I have returned to the topic in articles on numerous occasions since, the idea of writing a book on the subject was shelved while I focused my attention on the Merovingian kingdoms. It was not until Herwig Wolfram gave me the opportunity to teach in the Institut für Österreichische Geschichtsforschung in 1994–5 that I found time to begin an overall re-examination of my ideas in the context of a course on *Missionsgeschichte*. I also had the benefit of being surrounded by an extraordinary group of students, who discussed my ideas with me, almost every lunchtime for a period of four months, and eventually even hijacked the text of the lectures and presented me with a bound copy entitled (significantly) *The Narrators of Missionary History*.

The title was a clear recognition of the extent to which I had been influenced by the approach adopted by Walter Goffart in his *Narrators of Barbarian History*, notably in his analysis of the chain of texts which culminated in Bede's *Historia Ecclesiastica*.[2] I had come increasingly to believe that the purposes of our sources had been ignored in earlier, often pious, attempts to construct the Grand Narrative of Mission, and that those purposes could best be understood by considering the relationship between texts. Further, what interested me above all in missionary history was the way in which missionaries were depicted by their contemporaries, and what this told us about changing attitudes to mission. Indeed, it seemed to me, and still does, that one could understand mission in much greater depth, if one looked not just at the missions, but also the way in which they were represented, for this would allow one to superimpose on the straightforward narrative a history of the understanding of missionary activity. Further, since many of the sources were written by missionaries themselves, it would also allow some exploration of missionary psychology.

In 1994 there was, however, no up-to-date coverage of missionary history, and it looked as if any book which attempted to write about the presentation of missionaries in the sources – which should ideally follow the chronology of the composition of those sources, and not the chronology of the missions themselves – would simultaneously have to provide a full chronological narrative of the process of Christianisation. This would clearly have presented extremely difficult formal problems. Fortunately, help was at hand, since I was lucky enough to have the opportunity of reading in typescript, and thus some while before their publication dates, first Peter Brown's *The Rise of Western Christendom*[3] and then Richard Fletcher's *The Conversion of Europe*.[4] In the knowledge of what Peter Brown was about to put into print, I was able to embark on pursuing what for me was the great question still to be asked about missionary history: who was narrating it, when and why, and what did this tell us about mission and missionaries? *The Rise of Western Christendom* and *The Conversion of Europe* exonerated me from a task which would once have been a necessary preliminary to what I wished to consider. While I have certainly not ignored the narrative of mission or its impact in what follows, I have not felt the need to structure my discussion around those elements. Although neither Peter Brown's nor Richard Fletcher's book appears much in the footnotes of what follows, both could have been cited on almost every page – for anyone interested in Christianisation they are required reading.

If I was lucky in having the opportunity to teach in Vienna, I was every bit as fortunate the following year (1995–6) to hold a Fellowship at the Netherlands Institute for Advanced Study. I could not be more indebted to NIAS. The Institute in Wassenaar (and the library at the University of Leiden) provided near-perfect conditions for rereading almost all the major hagiographical texts, while the other fellows provided constant intellectual stimulation – and in the case of Petr Pit'ha (who provided me with a samizdat translation of his own *Cechy a Jejich Svatí*)[5] opened up an area of investigation which I had not considered at all. Quite apart from the stimulation provided by NIAS and its fellows, I was also fortunate in being able to try out my ideas on Mayke de Jong and her students in Utrecht, and, for part of the year, on old friends from Vienna, Walter Pohl and Brigitte Pohl-Resl, who were then staying in Leiden. I had the additional good fortune in having gained, through the European Science Foundation's Programme on The Transformation of the Roman World, a large number of continental friends and contacts, on whom I could test my evolving thoughts, not least through lectures and seminars which they kindly arranged for me.

Even a year at NIAS, on top of a semester at the Institut für Österreichische Geschichtsforschung, did not leave me the time I needed to complete the task I had set myself. This book would not have been finished had I not been given an additional semester's study leave by the School of History of the University of Leeds in 1999–2000. Among the many debts incurred in the course of writing this book is one to my colleagues, particularly my medieval colleagues, at Leeds.

To list by name everyone to whom I have become indebted in the course of writing this book would be impossible. Even attempting to mention some of them is invidious, and no doubt I will have forgotten – quite inexcusably – to mention friends and colleagues who should certainly be listed. I should, however, particularly like to thank Stuart Airlie, Janos Bak, Donald Bullough, Richard Corradini, Mayke de Jong, Maximilian Diesenberger, Dick Gerberding, Karl Giesriegel, Matthias Hardt, Joyce Hill, Paul Hyams (who helped to give me a vocabulary), Jörg Jarnut, Anna Kuznetsova, Graham Loud, Rob Meens, Petr Pit'ha, Walter Pohl, Brigitte Pohl-Resl, Helmut Reimitz (who came close at times to being a personal *Assistent*), Barbara Rosenwein, Peter and Bibi Sawyer, Danuta Shanzer, Adriaan Verhulst, Lutz von Padberg (not least because the bibliography to his *Mission und Christianisierung*[6] has saved me many hours of labour) and Anthony Wright.

I should also like to thank all those who offered criticism or approval after lectures or seminar papers relating to this book, which were delivered at NIAS, the Humbolt University in Berlin, the CEU in Budapest, the universities of Århus, Cornell, Glasgow, Gothenburg, Groningen, Huntsville, Kassel, Leeds, Münster, Oxford, Paderborn, Utrecht, Vienna and York, as well as the Poznan Society for the Advancement of the Arts and Sciences.

Special thanks are due to my wife, Ann, for putting up with me through all the tensions which accompany an extended piece of writing and for sacrificing precious time to help turn around the proofs. And finally, I must record my debt to Andrew MacLennan, who originally commissioned this book for Longman, and despite his retirement from the company still found time to read the text, with enormous care, and to offer his inimitable advice on how to improve a manuscript. I dedicate the final result to him.

*Ian Wood*

## Notes

1. I. N. Wood, 'The conversion of the barbarian peoples', in G. Barraclough, *The Christian World* (London, 1981), pp. 85–98.
2. W. Goffart, *The Narrators of Barbarian History (A.D. 550–800)* (Princeton, 1988).
3. P. Brown, *The Rise of Western Christendom* (Oxford, 1996): 2nd edn. (with footnotes) (Oxford, 1997).
4. R. Fletcher, *The Conversion of Europe: from Paganism to Christianity 371–1386 AD* (London, 1997).
5. P. Pit'ha, *Cechy a Jejich Svatí* (Prague, 1992).
6. L. von Padberg, *Mission und Christianisierung, Formen und Folgen bei Angelsachsen und Franken im 7. und 8. Jahrhundert* (Stuttgart, 1995).

# PART 1

## INTRODUCTORY

# Chapter 1

# THE CHRISTIANISATION OF EUROPE, 400–1000

## 1. CHRISTIANISATION AND MISSION

Matthew's Gospel ends with the appearance of Jesus to the disciples in Galilee, and with his injunction: 'Go ye therefore, and teach all nations, baptizing them in the name of the Father and of the Son, and of the Holy Ghost.' (Matthew 28, 19)[1] The conclusion of one of the four great narratives of Christ's life is, therefore, a command to evangelise. The story is continued in the Acts of the Apostles, which shows the first attempts at evangelisation by Christians outside the Holy Land. Christianity was to be a missionary religion. Mission and missionaries, real and perceived, are the prime subject of this book.

'Mission', of course, is a word which has been applied to a wide range of activities. It can be used to refer to the evangelisation of insiders as well as outsiders: there are missions to the inner cities and to seamen, as well as overseas missions. In what follows I will confine the word as far as is possible to mean mission to the pagan: that is, mission as envisaged at the end of Matthew's Gospel. Evangelisation within communities that were officially or superficially Christian I shall generally refer to using the term 'Christianisation'. 'Conversion' I shall reserve, in so far as I can, to refer to the spiritual change of an individual. By limiting my use of the word 'mission' I do not wish to imply that there is a firm divide between the evangelisation of pagans, Christianisation of an officially Christian country-side, pastoral care, and even Church reform. These belong to a single spectrum. The same may be said of missionaries to the pagans, bishops and abbots who played a role in Christianisation, and reformers. At times my subject matter will take me more towards the middle of these spectra than at others – especially when dealing with the Christianisation of the Bavarians and the Bohemians. My chief focus, however, is the history of mission to the pagans.

The reason for making at least some attempt to circumscribe my area of investigation is that there is clearly a difference between working in an area which has been officially Christianised and one that has not. At a straightforwardly practical level there is the matter of resources and backing: a

Merovingian bishop in northern Gaul might meet local opposition, but ultimately he had the power of a Christian king behind him. There was no such security in a region which had not accepted Christianity officially – indeed there was the reverse danger: that the internal patterns of authority within a pagan state were liable to be used against the missionary. Paganism itself obviously had a different status in the two regions. Although there were pagans in Christian states in the Early Middle Ages, their paganism would in most circumstances have had to be practised in private – it was, in a sense, superstition.[2] Public cult performed in a pagan political environment was a different matter.

There is another, and perhaps more important point: the further a Christian moved from a world with established churches, with their recurrent rituals and practices, the more alien were the circumstances in which he had to work. Again, the notion of a spectrum is useful: paganism directly across the border from a Christian state would have been very much more familiar than that to be found hundreds of miles removed, in a culture which had little or no direct contact with the world from which the missionary came, and which may well have belonged to a different linguistic zone.

An additional distinction may also usefully be drawn between mission and Christianisation. Mission implies a plan and individuals to carry it out. Christianisation includes this, but it also involves processes which were not deliberate, such as the steady impact of cultural and economic contacts or the effects of military conquest. Christianisation often begins before and ends after mission. In writing a history of the Christianisation of western and central Europe it is all too easy to concentrate on the missionaries, whose biographies provide us with a grand narrative,[3] rather than to emphasise the less eye-catching evidence for religious, cultural and even political seepage. Indeed, not only is the direct evidence for such influences less eye-catching, it is often negligible, and the process has to be inferred from mere traces. On the other hand, the history of missionaries is itself an important topic, and deserves consideration as something other than an accidental substitute for the history of Christianisation.

Missionaries, supposed missionaries, and the hagiography written about them are my main concerns in this book. Their role in Christianisation will be one issue, but only one. The purposes of the hagiographers, the contexts in which they were writing, and the way they responded to other hagiographical texts, will all feature more prominently. The history of Christianisation will thus be but one aspect of the argument of subsequent chapters, and at times it will be a minor one at that. For the missionary, however, Christianisation was his major task. Before turning to the history of missionaries and the way in which they are represented I shall, therefore, provide a sketch of the history of the Christianisation of western and central Europe between 400 and 1000. In so doing I shall pay most attention to those issues which do not involve missionaries – for their work will concern us at length later. This will inevitably lead to a picture which differs from the normal portrayal of the history of Christianisation in the Early Middle Ages – which is of a top-down process, where missionaries convert kings, and kings force their people, and any peoples subject to them, to accept the new religion.[4] Such a process, which was undoubtedly important in the history of mission, is one among many in the history of Christianisation. It is important to recognise this, in order to place missionaries in context.

## 2. PAGANISM

Before sketching the history of Christianisation, it is important to register the nature of the religious beliefs to which the missionaries were opposed. This is an issue to which we shall return, once we have considered the whole range of our documentation. From the start, however, it is necessary to recognise the variety within the belief systems that are lumped together as being pagan. In so far as the categorisation 'pagan' and 'Christian' implies no more than two cosmologies, it is completely inadequate. The Roman Empire had many varieties of paganism. There were the cults of the Olympian gods, and of more local deities, some of whom were equated with members of the Olympian pantheon. There were the so-called mystery religions: the cults of such figures as Mithras, Isis and the Magna Mater. Most, if not all these cults, had specially designated priests and involved sacrifice. There was also philosophy, which could fulfil spiritual functions. With all these, and especially with the mystery religions, Christianity was in competition at least until the fourth century. A more immediate problem for the Christians, however, was the imperial cult, which involved such practices as sacrifices on the emperor's birthday – though it should be noted that the emperor, technically speaking, was only deified after his death.[5] At these ceremonies one effectively expressed one's loyalty to the Empire. Not to comply with the imperial cult was tantamount to expressing opposition to the state. Christians and pagans saw sacrifice to the emperor as a religious issue, but it was religion defined in terms of civic loyalty rather than spiritual experience.

In the Germanic, Celtic and Slav worlds there appears to have been no direct equivalent to the imperial cult, although individual tribes undoubtedly had gods with whom they were particularly associated: for instance, the Lombards seem to have had a special affiliation with Wodan and the Slavonic Liutizi with Zuarasici. In the case of the Slavs there is good evidence, not just for belief in a number of deities – associated with natural forces – but also for an established priesthood, and sizeable temple complexes.[6] When Christians attempted to Christianise the Slav lands they were faced with strongly entrenched priestly interests, as well as an alien belief system.

Germanic paganism seems to have been rather different. Despite beliefs in a number of gods, some, if not all, of whom could be grouped together into a single pantheon, and despite evidence for cults dedicated to those gods, involving drinking bouts, major festivals and sacrifice, there is little evidence for temples or a priesthood.[7] When we do see figures officiating at religious ceremonies, like the casting of lots, they tend to be rulers or the heads of households. In continental Europe, at least, public cults associated with the gods collapsed early on in the conflict with Christianity – as an immediate result of conquest. Only missionaries working within pagan kingdoms or peoples would have come across public paganism. On the other hand, superstitious practices, associated with such matters as harvests and childbirth, persisted, as everywhere – and it is these which tend to be the butt of religious legislation. To speak of paganism, therefore, is to speak of a whole raft of religious issues, each of which called forth different responses from the Christians.

## 3. THE CHRISTIAN EMPIRE

Despite the model provided by the Acts of the Apostles, the history of the Christianisation of the Roman Empire is not one dominated by missionaries. There were attempts to remedy this unfortunate reality in the Early Middle Ages, by Churches intent on laying claim to apostolic origins: hence, for instance, the legend of the Seven Apostles of Gaul.[8] Such stories, however, have not found favour amongst historians of Antiquity, who have instead tended to concentrate on the spread of Christianity among particular groups: initially Jews, traders and townsmen, who found support within the social concerns of the new religion as well as solace in its spiritual and philosophical teachings.[9]

This somewhat amorphous picture of the new religion is given a certain amount of spice by the growing importance of Christian heroes, first martyrs and then holy men. The persecutions of the third and early fourth centuries, far from wiping out Christianity, had the effect of drawing attention to the heroism of the persecuted and thus of prompting some to be drawn to their religion. They would be followed, after the acceptance of Christianity as the official religion of the Empire, by holy men, who also had an impact on their contemporaries, challenging them and their religious beliefs,[10] and even impressing them by miracles.[11]

Of more widespread importance than the impact of such saints was that of Constantine, whose conversion and backing for Christianity gave the Church the opportunity and the funds to consolidate an Empire-wide institution, which increasingly had the right to intervene in the lives of individuals. Although Constantine would scarcely have converted had Christianity not achieved a certain importance before his day, it was his conversion which made possible the full Christianisation of the Empire. Nevertheless, the process of Christianisation was not simply the preserve of churchmen, backed by imperial authority. It worked through family and personal connections, which can be mapped carefully through our knowledge of Late Roman prosopography and of the spiritual circles of such men as Jerome, Pelagius and Augustine.[12]

## 4. THE BARBARIANS

To turn from the Christianisation of the Roman Empire to that of the barbarian incomers who crossed its borders in the fourth and fifth centuries, is to abandon one set of historical models for another. Though this change of model certainly reflects the different documentation for the two developments, and probably reflects distinctions between the societies involved, it nevertheless gives pause for thought: should the Christianisation of the barbarians be understood as a fundamentally different process from that of the Romans? That it should seems to be the unspoken assumption of much scholarship.

Most of the barbarian peoples who entered the Roman Empire in the course of the fourth and fifth centuries, accepted Christianity as a result.[13] Some, including the Franks, did so over a period of time, as a result of their settlement within or at least alongside an already Christian society. The Visigoths, on the other hand, seem to have accepted Christianity as part of the deal which initially allowed them to settle within the Empire,[14] although, of course, Christianisation must have take a good deal longer to achieve than the acceptance of Roman terms.

Missionaries may appear from the historical record to have been no more significant in the history of the Christianisation of those barbarian groups who entered the Roman Empire, than they were in the Christianisation of the Empire itself. There were, nevertheless, missionaries at work among the barbarians, of whom the best known is the Goth Ulfilas.[15] Having fled to the Empire, he was sent back by the imperial government to work among the Goths while they were still living north of the Danube, but he was driven out as a result of persecution. His great achievement, however, was not as a missionary, but rather as the translator of the majority of the Bible into Gothic, thus facilitating the evangelisation of his people after they entered the Empire in 376.

The fact that Ulfilas was sent to evangelise the Goths before they crossed the Danube is an indication that there was also missionary work outside the Roman Empire, even though Christianisation in the fourth and fifth centuries took place for the most part on Roman soil. In fact, without being subject to missionary work, the barbarians who lived across the *limes* were relatively well used to Christians. Those barbarians who traded with the Empire would, inevitably, have come into contact with Christianity. But Christians could also be found north of the Danube and east of the Rhine. There were Roman traders and diplomats, and there were also slaves. In the pre-migration world of the Visigoths, there was a notable group of Cappadocians who had been captured in the third century, and one of their descendents, Saba, is well known from the surviving account of his martyrdom.[16] The Visigoths had, therefore, come into contact with Christianity long before the mission of Ulfilas, or their entry into the Roman Empire in 376.

Captives taken by the barbarians might remain slaves and have little or no impact on their masters. On the other hand, at least one escaped from captivity, only to return as a missionary. Patrick, having been enslaved in Ireland, returned to evangelise the people who had held him. His own account of his work makes it clear that his mission was directed at areas which had little or no previous experience of Christianity.[17] On the other hand, there were already Christians among the Irish, for it was to them that Pope Celestine sent Palladius in 432.[18] Who these Christians were we do not know, although the chances are that they were to be found in the south-east of Ireland, outside Patrick's subsequent mission field. They have been set within a context of trading connections, for, while Ireland had never been subject to the Roman Empire, it was certainly in contact with both Britain and Gaul before the fifth century.[19] In Ireland, trading and raiding came before mission, and indeed helped to create the mission field.

Despite the fact that most tribes that settled within the Empire in the fourth and fifth centuries were Christianised once inside imperial boundaries, it is important to take note of the fact that Christianisation also took place outside what had been the Empire: north of the Danube and east of the Rhine, as well as in Ireland, even in the fifth and sixth centuries. The clearest example is that of the *Rugi*, settled on the very banks of the Danube, in what is now the Austrian *Waldviertel*. In the early sixth-century *Life* of Severinus of Noricum by Eugippius, the Rugian kingdom is clearly described as Christian, albeit belonging to the heretical Arian persuasion.[20] Since the Rugians were Arian, there is a strong possibility that they had been Christianised under the influence of the Visigoths: yet that should not lead us to ignore the fact of Christianisation beyond the bounds of the Danube frontier.

A more difficult case is that of the Thuringians, the centre of whose power lay in the region of Weimar on the River Unstrut. Because their leaders were opponents of the Carolingians in the eighth century, they were portrayed as being lenient towards paganism in that period.[21] It is certain, though, that Carolingian political propaganda is misleading here. In so far as much can be said about the Thuringians in the early sixth century, their leading family, at least, seems to have accepted Christianity by then. Radegund, a Thuringian princess, who was taken prisoner by the Franks and forcibly married to the Merovingian king, Chlothar I, but who then abandoned him to become a nun, was widely regarded as a saint both before and after her death. However, while she is the subject of two saint's *Lives* and of many comments in Gregory of Tours' *Histories*, no source stops to say she had to be converted to Christianity, which would surely have been an additional mark of her virtue. Further, a spoon of Byzantine manufacture, engraved with a name associated with Radegund's family, Basena, was found at Weimar, and although such spoons may not have been liturgical as was once thought, that is at least a possibility.[22] These straws in the wind suggest that Thuringia – or at least its ruling dynasty – may have been Christianised, even if lightly, before it was conquered by the Franks in the 530s.

## 5. ENGLAND

One group of barbarians that did not accept Christianity as a result of entry into what had been the Roman Empire was that of the Anglo-Saxons. Their religious history is the subject of Bede's monumental *Ecclesiastical History*, where it appears that they had to wait until 597, when a mission sent by Gregory the Great arrived in England, before the process of Christianisation was begun. What followed, according to Bede, was a history of evangelisation which went hand in hand with political contacts. Yet before the arrival of Augustine, except in the places of densest Germanic settlement, the English had been living next to communities of Britons – some of whom were still practising Christianity, even in the south-east of England.[23] Further west, around the River Severn, and in Wales, Cornwall and Cumbria, there was no disruption to the religion of the Christian Britons. It is highly likely, therefore, that the English came into contact with Christianity long before 597, and that this helped prepare the way for the evangelisation which followed,[24] even if, for the most part, linguistic differences between the indigenous population and the newcomers, as well as resentment of the invaders, meant that the Britons did little to convert their neighbours. It was not, however, in Bede's interest to identify a British contribution to the Christianisation of the English, since he regarded the Britons as heretical. Nor was Bede much interested in any Frankish contribution to the process,

9

even though Æthelberht had long been married to a Christian Frankish princess by the time that Augustine arrived in Kent, and despite the fact that she had in her entourage a Frankish bishop.[25] The Franks were to play a considerable role in the evangelisation of England, once they saw that it was in their political interest to do so[26] – but of this there is scarcely a word in Bede. He was intent on privileging the influence first of Rome, since that linked the English Church with the centre of Christianity, and second, and to a lesser extent, of the Irish, since they had deeply influenced the Christian style of Northumbria.

What Bede provides in the *Ecclesiastical History* is a partial account of the Christianisation of the English – and one that to some extent deals with the secondary phase of the process. In a sense Christianisation had already begun once the Germanic incomers settled alongside Britons. Mission from Rome, Ireland and Francia built on a pre-existing awareness of Christian communities. Further, Christianisation would continue as a process long after the missions described by Bede had ended.

## 6. THE BORDERS OF FRANCIA

A similar case can be made with regard to the peoples to the east of the Rhine. This was an area that the English themselves, in the late seventh and eighth centuries, thought was ripe for evangelisation. Indeed, a number of them explicitly went to work there because they thought it was their duty to bring Christianity to those peoples to whom they were related, particularly the continental Saxons and the Frisians.[27] Certainly, these two peoples were only Christianised in the course of the eighth century, and did, therefore, provide a mission field for a group of Englishmen. Other peoples did not present the English with the opportunity for mission to the pagans, although they are often thought to have been evangelised by Anglo-Saxon missionaries.

The possibility that an initial Christianisation of Thuringia had already taken place in the sixth century has already been mentioned. There may have been continuity of pagan superstitions in the region thereafter – as, famously, at Geismar in Hesse – but the ruling, ducal, dynasty of the late seventh and early eighth century was unquestionably Christian, and one of its members, Heden II, was a major benefactor of the great Frankish monastery of Echternach, in the modern state of Luxembourg.[28] Further, either Heden II or his grandfather seems to have been responsible for issuing the *Lex Ribvaria*, the most ostentatiously Christian of all the pre-Carolingian law codes.[29]

The region to the south of Thuringia presents a similar picture. Bavaria is represented in some texts as badly in need of Christianisation in the eighth century. It is highly likely that pagan superstition still existed – as it did everywhere – while it is certain that the ducal family, the Agilolfings, did not follow standard Christian teaching on marriage.[30] Nevertheless, from the late sixth century onwards, the ruling dynasty was Frankish, and had strong contacts with Lombard Italy.[31] It was certainly not pagan. Nor was its legislation.[32] Part of the duchy, notably the city of Augsburg, had a Christian past which stretched back to the Roman period, apparently with no interruption.[33] There were at the same time pockets of paganism: one possible example is the area south of the Bodensee, where the holy man Gallus settled.[34] Certainly, there were missions to Bavaria, sent by Gallus' one-time colleague, Abbot Eustasius of Luxeuil, in the period after 615.[35] There is, however, no reason to doubt that Bavaria was substantially Christianised by the eighth century. When, in the ninth century, the Church of Salzburg compiled an account of the *Conversio* of the Bavarians, and concentrated on the late seventh-century figure, Rupert of Salzburg,[36] it was not describing the initial introduction of Christianity to the region, but rather its own establishment as an ecclesiastical and diocesan centre.

In the light of such material it is not surprising that the linguistic evidence suggests that the Church east of the upper and middle Rhine was established not by Anglo-Saxons, or indeed by Irishmen, but rather by the Franks themselves.[37] Generations of unknown Frankish priests must have taken Christianity across the boundaries of Francia. When figures from the British Isles reached the region, as they did, their contribution was as holy figures in a world already partially Christianised: some were associated with the courts of rulers; others helped in the organisation of dioceses; and yet others with the establishment and leadership of monasteries. All this contributed to the deeping of Christianity in the region, but it was in no sense part of an initial phase of evangelisation.

Frisia and Saxony stand apart in this respect. The English, notably Willibrord, did play a notable part in the initial establishment of the Church in southern Frisia, and some of them worked further afield, in northern Frisia and even in Saxony. What is especially notable about a number of these figures is their initial independence of the Frankish Church. Certainly, Willibrord and those who worked alongside or with him seem from the start to have sought approval from the Pippinid rulers of Francia.[38] On the other hand, Lebuin, who was to work in the region of the River Yssel, sought permission not from the Pippinids, but from Gregory, who was charged with missionary organisation from his centre in Utrecht.[39] Even more remarkably, the Northumbrian Willehad is said by his hagiographer to have sought and been given authorisation for his mission from his native country, before going to northern Frisia.[40] He is only said to have attracted the attention of Charlemagne after he had been working for some time on the continent.[41] Although Charles Martel, Pippin III, and especially, Charlemagne promoted Christianity, pastly because of their own religious commitments, but also as an element in the annexation and conquest of Frisia and Saxony, they were by no means the chief initiators of mission. Indeed, while Pippinid backing was important in the eyes of some, others, like Lebuin, appear to have ignored it altogether.

Saints undoubtedly had an important role to play in preaching in pagan areas and then in establishing churches. One piece of hagiography, however, directs our attention away from the saints towards other issues. When dealing with the region of *Frisia Citerior*, around Utrecht, Altfrid, in his *Life of Liudger*, describes the Christianisation of the area in terms of the history of his own family. Wrrsing, the *pater familias*, was converted and baptised after he had fled from Frisia to Francia, having fallen foul of the local king, Radbod.[42] The conversion of another branch of the family is not described, although we are told that Adelburga handed over her two brothers to Willibrord, and that they became the first indigenous Frisian priests.[43] Undoubtedly, the downplaying of Willibrord in this text does not mean that missionaries were unimportant in the history of the Christianisation of Frisia – later in his *Vita Liudgeri* Altfrid makes much of his subject's contribution in northern Frisia and Saxony. But Liudger was Altfrid's uncle, and the hagiographer's interest was in the role played by his family – he was not concerned to give a dispassionate account of the history of Christianisation. The model he presents is, however, an important one: Christianisation can be read in terms of family history.

In Saxony, too, there were families with Frankish connections who were inclined to accept Christianity, or at least to support missionaries before the Christianisation of the region – as can be seen, once again, in the history of Lebuin, who received backing from the family of Folcbraht.[44] On the other hand, there were groups in Saxony who were hostile to missionaries and churches, because they were symbols of the power of the neighbouring Franks. Pagan uprisings thus broke any possibility of peaceful Christianisation in Saxony. The permanent establishment of Christianity was, ultimately, dependent on Frankish conquest, followed by a long process involving the establishment of ecclesiastical organisation and pastoral care.[45]

Something similar happened in the territory of the Avars, in what is now eastern Austria and western Hungary. It was the military collapse of the Avar state in the face of Carolingian aggression in 796 which allowed missions to enter the region: hence a flurry of activity in that and subsequent years, particularly in Salzburg, under Bishop Arno. Further, because of recent failures and successes in Saxony, the Avar mission was able to profit from the experience. The result was a painstaking history of church foundation and the provision of clergy.

# 7. THE SLAVS OF CARINTHIA, MORAVIA AND BOHEMIA

Even before the Carolingian Church turned its mind to the Christianisation of the Avars, Salzburg had become involved in that of the Carantanian Slavs – that is, the Slavs of Carinthia. The *Conversio Bagaoariorum et Carantanorum* sees their evangelisation as growing directly out of the Christianisation of Bavaria. An opportunity occurred in the 740s when the leader of the Carantanians, Boruth, sent his nephew, Hotimir, to be educated at the Bavarian monastery of Chiemsee. When the nephew returned to Carinthia he brought with him a priest.[46] Once Hotimir succeeded to his uncle's position, the way was open to the Church of Salzburg to establish churches and to appoint clergy to the region. The Christianisation of the Carantanian Slavs thus began with what was a political act: Boruth was desperate for allies against his Avar neighbours – and we may presume that the Christian education of Hotimir was a prerequisite for Bavarian support. What followed was the establishment of a Church organisation. Only occasionally can we see missionaries dealing with pagans in Carinthia, although we are told about the tactics of the priest Ingo, who invited Christian slaves to meals where they were well served, while their pagan masters were left outside to eat like dogs.[47] Whether or not the story is true, it suggests that social pressures were as important as preaching in the Christianisation of the Carantanians.

Next to the Carantanians were the Moravians, who emerge in the aftermath of the collapse of the Avar empire.[48] The establishment of a Church in Moravia depended on the activity of the bishops of Passau and, once again, of Salzburg.[49] There is also some evidence of earlier cultural influence from Italy and Dalmatia.[50] The Moravian leader, Mojmir, was probably concerned to ape the culture of his successful Frankish and Bavarian neighbours, but there also seem to have been political pressures at work. Mojmir himself may have been among a group of Moravian and Bohemian aristocrats who appeared at an imperial council at Frankfurt in 822.[51] Politics were certainly involved when Mojmir subsequently drove out Priwina, who threw himself on the mercy of the Franks, and was as a result established on the shores of Lake Balaton in western Hungary, where he played an important role in furthering the Christian cause.[52]

The mention of Bohemians in the embassy of 822 points to the importance of their contacts with the East Frankish kingdom. That these contacts were significant in the introduction of Christianity to Bohemia is confirmed by the arrival in 845 at the court of Louis the German of fourteen prominent Bohemians, who wanted to become Christian.[53] Fifty years later another Bohemian leader, Spytignev, surrendered to the East Frankish king, Arnulf.[54] He may have been the earliest Christian member of the Premyslid

13

family,[55] which was soon to establish itself as the ruling dynasty of Bohemia, with its power-centre in Prague. In time the Premyslids were to play a role in the Christianisation of Poland, for it seems to have been the marriage of Dobrava, the daughter of Boleslav I, to the Piast ruler, Miesko I, that prompted his conversion.[56]

There is, however, an alternative candidate to Spytignev, as the first Premyslid Christian. In some sources his father, Borivoj, is given this honour.[57] There is significance in this clash of traditions, since Spytignev's conversion is associated with the Greek missionary, Methodius, while Borivoj's connections would seem to link his conversion to the Bavarian Church. Neither account is secure – and that linking Spytignev to Methodius is chronologically impossible – but together they point to a development within the Slav territories: the exploitation of sources of Christianity alternative to Germany and Bavaria, with at least a partial eye on weakening the influence of the German *Reich*. This was the context for the work of Constantine, Methodius and their followers in Moravia – which marked a secondary phase in Christianisation, however important it may have been for the development of a Slavonic Church.[58]

A similar exploitation of rival Christianities was attempted at the same time by Khan Boris of Bulgaria, who appealed to Pope Nicolas I in an attempt to counterbalance the influence of the Byzantine patriarchate. The pope's response, albeit fruitless because of the proximity of Byzantine power to Bulgaria, together with his intervention in the challenges to Constantine and Methodius and his correspondence with the Danish king, Horic II, make him the most important papal figure in mission in the Early Middle Ages after Gregory I.[59]

## 8. SCANDINAVIANS

Just as the Christiansation of the Slavs began in earnest in the ninth century, so too did that of the Scandinavians.[60] Once again, politics is a major factor in much of the documentation. Interest had been expressed in evangelising the Danes by Willibrord and subsequently by Liudger in the eighth century, but the first known mission is that of Ebo of Rheims in 823. This was followed three years later by the sending of Anskar. This latter mission was prompted by the visit of the Danish king, Harald Klak, to the court of Louis the Pious, and his subsequent baptism. Harald had come in search of support from the Franks against political rivals at home, and the mission was bound up with Carolingian backing. Harald, however, did not last long; nevertheless, both Horic I and Horic II, who ruled after him, allowed and even encouraged Anskar and his disciples to continue in their work. Further,

Denmark provided a springboard for mission among the Swedes, particularly in the trading centre of Birka.

Trade, along with politics, seems to have been a major factor in the early Scandinavian mission. Birka was not the only trading centre used by missionaries. Schleswig[61] and Ribe[62] were also important emporia where churches were established. Nor had these sites attracted missionaries simply because they were centres of population. They lay at the end of trade routes, which were themselves paths by which Christian influences had already reached Scandinavia. Christian merchants traded with the Danes and the Swedes, and they needed places to perform their own religious rituals. Equally, Scandinavian merchants had already become accustomed to Christianity from seeing it at first hand, in such Frankish centres as Dorestad. Further, pagans in search of security on their homeward journeys might seek protection from the Christian God, and might as a result even undergo the initiatory ritual of prime-signing or baptism.[63] The search for divine protection was a key factor in a man's choice of gods, which continued into the tenth century, albeit sometimes in mirror image, for the Christian Helgi the Lean found it useful to invoke Thor on voyages.[64] It may well be significant that Willibrord, who was based at Utrecht, which was near to and closely associated with Dorestad, appears to have been the first to have had the idea of evangelising the Danes.[65] The Frankish emporium was very closely associated with Christian communities in Scandinavia.[66]

Trade, of course, was not the only context in which Scandinavians came into contact with Christianity. Political missions less significant than that of Harald Klak in 826, revealed the glory of Christian cult to foreigners, and this was something that Louis the Pious exploited.[67] As Notker the Stammerer recounted, the emperor used to offer visitors the option of being baptised while at court, and many took up the offer, including one Northman who was baptised some twenty times, not least to get a new set of clothes: on one occasion when the emperor only had second-hand shirts, he objected.[68] Scandinavians also saw Christianity in less favourable circumstances – when they sacked churches and took the booty back with them. In a world where victory and protection were ascribed to the power of one's god – even by Christians – the successes of the Vikings could be understood as demonstrating the limitations of the Christian God.

The growth of Viking activity effectively put an end to missionary activity within Scandinavia, and what conversions were effected in the late ninth century were principally those of Vikings who had to accept baptism as a consequence of defeat – as for instance did Guthrum, following his defeat by Alfred the Great at Edington.[69] On the other hand, once settlement had taken place in the British Isles and in Francia, the Vikings found themselves increasingly susceptible to the influence of Christianity, from the indigenous inhabitants and from the Christian rulers who put ever more pressure on them in the tenth century.[70]

Although missions to Scandinavia came to an end in the second half of the ninth century, it would be wrong to assume that the achievements of such missionaries as Ebo, Anskar and Rimbert evaporated completely. Widukind of Corvey, writing in the 960s, remarked, in the context of the conversion of Harald Bluetooth, that the Danes had long been Christian, but they had still served idols.[71] Even so, Thietmar of Merseburg, writing some fifty years later, described Danish paganism in the early part of the tenth century as involving, among other things, sacrifices of ninety-nine men, horses, dogs and chickens, annually at Lejre on the island of Sjælland.[72] Despite this picture, we should probably take Widukind's comment seriously: Harald's conversion, even though it was prompted by a priest called Poppo undergoing an ordeal wearing a heated metal glove,[73] should be set against a background of long-standing awareness of Christianity in Denmark. It should also be set against the relationship between the newly emergent ruling dynasty of the Danes and the German *Reich*. That the Christianisation of the Danes had its political aspect is clear from the fact that Harald's conversion and the associated Christianisation of Denmark are recorded alongside his unification of the region in the splendid inscription he set up at the dynastic centre of Jelling in Jutland.

Unfortunately, we know little about Poppo and his mission. He was not of great interest to the great historian of missionary activity in Scandinavia, Adam of Bremen, probably because he had not been sent by the Church of Hamburg.[74] Just as Bavarian and Slavonic traditions differ over their interpretation of the Christianisation of Moravia and Bohemia, so too there were varying interpretations of the Christianisation of Scandinavia. In both cases rival jurisdictions were at stake.[75] Adam wished to attribute the origins of Scandinavian Christianity and ecclesiastical jurisdiction over the region to Hamburg-Bremen, and even went so far as to label as pagans or apostates, Christian leaders who looked to other sources of religious influence, such as the Anglo-Saxon Church.

Denmark was Christianised in the tenth century. Norway, and Iceland soon followed suit, while Sweden had to wait rather longer. Regrettably, since neither Norway nor Iceland was evangelised from Hamburg-Bremen, neither attracted detailed consideration from Adam.[76] It is clear, however, that Christianity was adopted by a number of Norwegians as a result of their foreign contacts, notably with England and Ireland – contacts which developed directly out of Viking raids and settlement. Håkon, the son of Harald Finehair, appears to have spent some time at the court of the West Saxon king, Athelstan, whether as hostage or foster son, and he subsequently tried to promote Christianity at home – although ultimately he failed and died as an apostate. At the end of the tenth century Olaf Tryggvason linked the new religion with the expansion and exercise of his own royal power. The completion of this process fell to a royal namesake, Saint Olaf, who died in battle in 1030. Despite his limited success at home, Olaf Tryggvason's influence was not confined to Norway. Although he did not rule over Iceland, he sponsored a mission under Thangbrand to the island, and, more importantly, when that failed, the Norwegian king took a number of Icelanders hostage, while two others, Hjalti Skeggjason and Gizurr the White, were sent to persuade their compatriots to accept Christianity. This they did at a meeting of the Althing, supposedly in the year 1000, but more probably a year earlier.

Such is a political interpretation of events, and Olaf's intervention was undoubtedly crucial in determining the exact timing of the acceptance of Christianity. Yet it is possible to see the Christianisation of Iceland in more humble terms; in terms more closely akin to those of trade and cultural proximity, which we have already seen as factors in the Migration and Carolingian periods. There had long been Christians in Iceland, not least because of connections between Icelandic settlers and the Irish and other Celts: intermarriage between the groups and the importation of Celtic slaves into Iceland meant that Christianity had been a factor in the religion of the Icelanders for more than a century before the decision at the Althing.[77] Although the precise nature of the consensual acceptance of Christianity makes the case of Iceland unique, the combination of long-term influences, individual missions, and political pressures from outside can be paralleled elsewhere, even if, by Scandinavian standards, the process was remarkably peaceful.

## 9. UNFINISHED BUSINESS

By the start of the eleventh century almost the whole of the Europe had been Christianised. The Russian ruler, Vladimir, had accepted Christianity from Byzantium, along with an imperial bride, in the late 980s.[78] The southern and western Slavs had already been Christianised.[79] The Swedes were to follow suit in the course of the eleventh century. The resulting Christianity was often, admittedly, skin-deep, and pagan practices were revived in periods of crisis. The full process of Christianisation, which involved the foundation of churches, the establishment of ecclesiastical organisation, including a parish structure, and even cultural change, took centuries longer – if, indeed, it was ever completed. In any case, there remained the Wends of north Germany, and beyond them the Baltic peoples and the Finns.

The pagan Wends were the butt of combined attacks by the Germans and Poles in the 990s, but when the Emperor Henry II fell out with the Polish leader, Boleslaw Chrobry, he used a group of Wends, the Liutizi, against his Christian neighbour, a policy which prompted a diatribe from Bruno of Querfurt.[80] The policy also prompted a long excursus describing their religion in the pages of the *Chronicle* of Thietmar of Merseburg.[81] Despite their proximity to Christian territory, and despite Christian interest in the ports of the southern Baltic which they controlled, the Wends survived for a while longer. It was not to be until 1067 that the great pagan sanctuary of the Liutizi at Rethra was destroyed, and then by Bishop Burchard of Halberstadt.[82] The Wendish stronghold of the island of Rügen, however, survived further attacks, until Bernard of Clairvaux adapted the ideology of crusade to the world of the Baltic. Rügen, and its great shrine of Arkona finally fell in 1168.[83]

This still left the Balt peoples. The Prussians had already attracted the attention of the missionaries Adalbert of Prague and Bruno of Querfurt, both of whom had been martyred for their pains, the former in 997 and the latter in 1009. Despite the attraction of the ports of the eastern Baltic, and of the amber trade, which ran through Balt territory, the Prussians were not overrun until the early thirteenth century, and the Lithuanians survived as pagans for a further hundred and fifty years.[84]

## 10. THE DOCUMENTATION OF MISSIONARIES

The preceding sketch may seem surprising because of its silences. Names of saints who have traditionally been closely associated with mission – notably Boniface – are absent, as are such institutions as monasteries, which have been called 'the power houses of mission'.[85] These silences reflect what I would argue is a properly nuanced reading of the sources, but they are also deliberate: they are intended to exclude certain individuals and certain factors from the history of the evangelisation of the pagans of western and central Europe. Why those individuals have been excluded will become clear in ensuing chapters. The point, however, is that some documentation which is habitually treated as being concerned with mission, can only be so treated if a very broad definition of missionary activity is employed – one which extends to the in-depth Christianisation of officially Christian regions. Among the documentation that has traditionally been cited in discussions of Christianisation there are numerous texts which are not, strictly speaking, concerned with the history of the confrontation between the Christian and the pagan. A second – and related – point is that some sources which appear to be concerned with mission to the pagans do not provide accurate records of mission, but are rather inventions made for any one of a number of reasons.

The sources which are habitually called on to reconstruct the role of missionaries in the history of Christianisation – that is, to a large extent, the saints' *Lives* – often have very specific agendas, which need to be considered: indeed, each source needs to be assessed on its own terms. In some cases this enhances the value of the source for the history of mission, in others it radically alters it. At the same time, while each source needs to be considered separately, it will become clear that many of our sources for missionary activity are related to each other. They borrow from each other, both to uphold traditions and to subvert them. Much has rightly been made of the way Northumbrian hagiography of the early eighth century needs to be seen as a cluster of texts, which should be read in conjunction.[86] The same can be said of the continental hagiography of mission.[87] The relationship between many of our sources is such that it can even be presented 'genealogically' – and it will become clear that this 'genealogy' is important for understanding some of the concerns of the authors of our evidence. For this very reason the ordering of the discussion that follows will not be dictated by the chronology of the saints and missionaries themselves, but rather by that of the hagiography, and by the connections between the individual texts.[88]

The texts to be discussed are not a random sample, but rather the major surviving hagiographical works written about missionaries, or supposed missionaries, within two or three generations of the death of the saint described. Some *vitae* were, of course, written centuries after the lifetime of the saint with which they are concerned: for the most part these have been ignored, since they rarely provide accurate information which cannot be found elsewhere: besides, those texts written after 1050 do not contribute to our understanding of the changing representation of mission in the course of the Early Middle Ages. The *vitae* which form the subject matter for subsequent chapters thus allow as close an examination as possible of the career of the saint in question, as well as a precise study of the varying and changing attitudes to mission itself.

By drawing attention to the links between the texts and by concentrating on what one might call 'the hagiography of mission' – even though that hagiography is not always concerned with figures who actually spent much or any time evangelising pagans – I am not attempting to claim that 'missionary hagiography' is an identifiable genre. Hagiography is an infinitely flexible religious and literary form[89] and, although some texts do conform to the patterns established by earlier *vitae*, there is no overriding model, nor is there any unity of purpose, even in the case of those texts which are concerned with missionaries. Variety is a central feature.

From what follows it will become apparent that the notion of the missionary saint's *Life* – as explored here – is made up of a series of textual constructs, some of which go back to the Early Middle Ages and some of which are modern. It will also become apparent that while some texts have little to tell us about the world and actions of the missionary, others take us remarkably deeply into the experiences of Christians working in a pagan environment. Sometimes 'the missionary *Life*' will be concerned with no more than texts, sometimes it will be concerned with intellectual programmes, and on occasion it will take us close to the life envisaged, and arguably lived, by missionaries themselves. Both the intellectual programmes and the individual missionaries will take us beyond any simple narrative of the history of mission.

Edward Thompson once remarked that 'The conversion must not be studied simply or mainly as an episode in the life of the individual missionary but as an episode in the general history of the converted people.'[90] His approach has often found favour.[91] There is, however, a danger in overlooking the individual missionary and the individual hagiographer, since it is to them and their experiences that we owe what evidence we have. There is even more danger in assuming, without further thought, that the evidence for an individual can be treated as providing the basis for reconstructing the attitudes and experiences of the majority of the population. The basic outline of the Christianisation of Europe has been established by generations of scholars. In order to take the history of Christianisation beyond what has been mapped in outline, it is necessary to return to the experiences of individuals and above all to understand the perceptions of the men who evangelised pagan Europe.

## Notes

1. See also Matthew 24, 14: 'And the gospel of the kingdom shall be preached in all the world for a witness unto all nations; and then shall the end come.' For the importance of this as a starting point for early medieval mission, L. von Padberg, *Mission und Christianisierung. Formen und Folgen bei Angelsachsen und Franken im 7. und 8. Jahrhundert*, pp. 7, 32.
2. On the distinction between religion and superstition, see I. N. Wood, 'Pagan religions and superstitions east of the Rhine from the fifth to the ninth century', in G. Ausenda (ed)., *After Empire: towards an Ethnology of Europe's Barbarians* (Woodbridge, 1995), pp. 253–79.
3. See K. Schäferdiek (ed.), *Kirchengeschichte als Missionsgeschichte, 2, 1: Die Kirche des früheren Mittelalters* (Münster, 1978).
4. For example, A. Angenendt, 'The conversion of the Anglo-Saxons considered against the background of the early medieval mission', *Angli e sassoni al di qua e al di là de mare*, Settimane di studio del centro italiano di studi sull'alto medioevo 32 (Spoleto, 1986), pp. 747–92; N. Higham, *The Convert Kings* (Manchester, 1997).
5. S. Price, 'From noble funerals to divine cult: the consecration of Roman Emperors', in D. Cannadine and S. Price, *Rituals of Royalty: Power and Ceremonial in Traditional Societies* (Cambridge, 1987), pp. 56–105. For a general survey of Roman religion, P. Garnsey and R. Saller, *The Roman Empire: Economy, Society and Culture* (London, 1987), pp. 163–77.

6. See in particular, L. Slupecki, *Slavonic Pagan Sanctuaries* (Warsaw, 1994).

7. For a general survey, Wood, 'Pagan religions and superstitions east of the Rhine from the fifth to the ninth century'.

8. Gregory of Tours, *Decem Libri Historiarum* I 30, ed. B. Krusch and W. Levison, MGH, SRM 1, 1 (Hanover, 1951).

9. R. Lane Fox, *Pagans and Christians* (London, 1987): R. A. Markus, *Christianity in the Roman World* (London, 1974), pp. 13–86.

10. R. M. Price, 'The holy man and Christianisation from the apocryphal gospels to St Stephen of Perm', in J. Howard-Johnston and P. A. Hayward (eds), *The Cult of the Saints in Late Antiquity and the Early Middle Ages* (Oxford, 1999), pp. 215–38.

11. R. MacMullen, *Christianizing the Roman Empire A.D. 100–400* (Yale, 1984).

12. P. R. L. Brown, 'Aspects of the Christianization of the Roman Aristocracy', *Journal of Roman Studies* 51 (1961), pp. 1–11, reprinted in *id.*, *Religion and Society in the Age of Saint Augustine* (London, 1972), pp. 161–82.

13. E. A. Thompson, 'Christianity and the northern barbarians', in A. Momigliano (ed.), *The Conflict between Paganism and Christianity in the Fourth Century* (Oxford, 1963), pp. 56–78.

14. P. Heather, 'The crossing of the Danube and the Gothic conversion', *Greek, Roman and Byzantine Studies* 27 (1986), pp. 289–318.

15. P. Heather and J. F. Matthews, *The Goths in the Fourth Century* (Liverpool, 1991), pp. 133–5, 151–2; for evidence of other figures, *ibid.*, p. 134, n. 1.

16. P. Heather and J. F. Matthews, *The Goths in the Fourth Century*, pp. 111–17. See also E. A. Thompson, *The Visigoths in the Time of Ulfila* (Oxford, 1966).

17. Patrick, *Confessio*, ed. D. R. Howlett, *The Book of Letters of Saint Patrick the Bishop* (Blackrock, 1994).

18. Prosper, *Chronicle*, s.a. 431, ed. T. Mommsen, *Chronica Minora* 1, MGH, AA 9 (Berlin, 1892); T. M. Charles-Edwards, 'Palladius, Prosper, and Leo the Great: mission and primatial authority', in D. N. Dumville (ed.), *Saint Patrick, A.D. 493–1993* (Woodbridge, 1993), pp. 1–12.

19. C. Thomas, *Christianity in Roman Britain to A.D. 500* (London, 1981), pp. 271–4.

20. Eugippius, *Vita Severini* 5, 8, 19, 22, 31, 40, 42, 44, ed. P. Régerat, *Eugippe, Vie de saint Séverin*, Sources Chrétiennes 374 (Paris, 1991).

21. Willibald, *Vita Bonifatii* 6, ed. W. Levison, *Vitae sancti Bonifatii archiepiscopi Moguntini*, MGH, SRG 57 (Hanover, 1905).

22. I. N. Wood, 'The frontiers of Western Europe: developments east of the Rhine in the sixth century', in R. Hodges and W. Bowden (eds), *The Sixth Century. Production, Distribution and Demand* (Leiden, 1998), pp. 232, 234, with the reservations on p. 232, n. 8.

23. I. N. Wood, 'Augustine's journey', *Canterbury Cathedral Chronicle* 92 (1998), p. 34.

24. P. Sims-Williams, *Religion and Literature in Western England, 600–800* (Cambridge, 1990), pp. 54–96.

25. Bede, *Historia Ecclesiastica Gentis Anglorum* I 25, ed. C. Plummer, *Baedae Opera Historica* (Oxford, 1896).

26. J. Campbell, 'The first century of Christianity in England', *Ampleforth Journal* 71 (1971), pp. 12–29, repr. in *id.*, *Essays in Anglo-Saxon History* (London, 1986), pp. 49–67; I. N. Wood, 'The mission of Augustine of Canterbury to the English', *Speculum* 69 (1994), pp. 7–9.

27. Bede, *Historia Ecclesiastica* V 9; Boniface, ep. 46, ed. M. Tangl, *S. Bonifatii et Lulli Epistolae*, MGH, Epistolae selectae in usum scholarum 1 (Berlin, 1916).

28. *Liber Aureus Epternacensis*, 8, 26, ed. C. Wampach, *Geschichte der Grundherrschaft Echternach im Frühmittelalter* 1, 2, Quellenband (Luxembourg, 1930).

29. H. Mordek, 'Die Hedenen als politische Kraft im austrasischen Frankenreich', in J. Jarnut, U. Nonn and M. Richter (eds), *Karl Martell in seiner Zeit* (Sigmaringen, 1994), pp. 356–60.

30. Arbeo of Freising, *Vita Corbiniani* 24, ed. B. Krusch, *Arbeonis episcopi Frisingensis vitae sanctorum Haimhrammi et Corbiniani*, MGH, SRG (Hanover, 1920); see also *Passio Kiliani* 8, ed. W. Levison, MGH, SRM 5 (Hanover, 1910).

31. E. Zöllner, 'Die Herrkunft der Agilolfinger', *Mitteilungen des Instituts für Österreichische Geschichtsforschung* 59 (1951), pp. 245–64; also H. Wolfram, *Grenzen und Räume* (Vienna, 1995), pp. 281–5.

32. *Leges Baiwariorum*, ed. E. von Schwind, MGH, Leges 5, 2 (Hanover, 1926).

33. H. Wolfram, *Die Geburt Mitteleuropas* (Vienna, 1987), pp. 115–6.

34. Wetti, *Vita Galli* 4–7, ed. B. Krusch, MGH, SRM 4 (Hanover, 1902).

35. Jonas, *Vita Columbani* II 8–9, ed. B. Krusch, MGH, SRM 4 (Hanover, 1902): reprinted in B. Krusch, *Ionae Vitae Sanctorum Columbani, Vedastis, Iohannis*, MGH, SRG (Hanover, 1905).

36. *Conversio Bagoariorum et Carantanorum*, ed. F. Losek, MGH, Studien und Texte 15 (Hanover, 1997).

37. D. H. Green, *Language and History in the Early Germanic World* (Cambridge, 1998), pp. 273–356.

38. Bede, *Historia Ecclesiastica* V 10.

39. Altfrid, *Vita Liudgeri* I 13, ed. W. Diekamp, *Die Vitae Sancti Liudgeri* (Münster, 1881).

40. *Vita Willehadi* 1–2, ed. A. Poncelet, AASS, Nov 8th, Vol. 3 (Brussels, 1910), pp. 842–6.

41. *Vita Willehadi* 5.

42. Altfrid, *Vita Liudgeri* I 1–2.

43. Altfrid, *Vita Liudgeri* I 5.

44. Altfrid, *Vita Liudgeri* I 13–14.

45. I. N. Wood, 'An absence of saints? The evidence for the Christianisation of Saxony' (forthcoming).

46. *Conversio Bagoariorum et Carantanorum* 4.

47. *Conversio Bagoariorum et Carantanorum* 7.

48. For the Moravians, see H. Wolfram, *Grenzen und Räume*, pp. 315–21; for an alternative view of the siting of Moravia, C. Bowlus, *Franks, Moravians and Magyars: the Struggle for the Middle Danube 788–907* (Philadelphia, 1995).

49. *Conversio Bagoariorum et Carantanorum* 10–12; Theotmar, *Epistola*, ed. F. Losek, *Die Conversio Bagoariorum et Carantanorum und der Brief des Erzbischofs Theotmar von Salzburg*, MGH, Studien und Texte 15 (Hanover, 1997) p. 140.

50. A. P. Vlasto, *The Entry of the Slavs into Christendom* (Cambridge, 1970), pp. 23–5.

51. *Annales Regni Francorum*, s.a. 822, ed. F. Kurze, MGH, SRG (Hanover, 1895).

52. *Conversio Bagoariorum et Carantanorum* 10–12; Vlasto, *The Entry of the Slavs into Christendom*, pp. 24–5.

53. *Annales Fuldenses*, s.a. 845, ed. F. Kurze, MGH, SRG (Hanover, 1891), trans. T. Reuter, *The Annals of Fulda* (Manchester, 1992).

54. *Annales Fuldenses*, s.a. 895.

55. *Crescente Fide* (Bavarian recension), ed. J. Truhar, *Fontes rerum Bohemicarum* 1 (Prague, 1973), p. 183; Gumpold, *Passio sancti Vencezlavi martyris* 2, ed. F. J. Zoubek, *Fontes rerum Bohemicarum* 1 (Prague, 1973), pp. 146–66.

56. Thietmar, *Chronicon* IV 55, ed. W. Trillmich (Darmstadt, 1957); Vlasto, *The Entry of the Slavs into Christendom*, p. 115.

57. *Crescente Fide* 1 (Czech recension), ed. V. Chaloupecky, *Svatovaclavsky Sbornik* II 2, *Prameny X. Stoleti* (Prague, 1939); *Diffundente Sole* 4–8, ed. V. Chaloupecky, *Svatovaclavsky Sbornik* II 2, *Prameny X. Stoleti*; *Fuit in Provincia Boemorum* 1, ed. V. Chaloupecky, *Svatovaclavsky Sbornik* II 2, *Prameny X. Stoleti*; *Legenda Christiani*, ed. J. Pekar, *Die Wenzels- und Ludmila-Legenden und die Echtheit Christians* (Prague, 1906).

58. Vlasto, *The Entry of the Slavs into Christendom*, p. 48: 'They were not so much pioneers as consolidators of the second stage of Moravian Christianity.'

59. Nicolas, epp. 26, 27, 99, ed. E. Perels, MGH, Epp 6 (Berlin, 1892); R. E. Sullivan, 'Khan Boris and the conversion of Bulgaria: a case study of the impact of Christianity on a barbarian society', *Studies in Medieval and Renaissance History* 3 (1966), pp. 55–139, repr. in *id.*, *Christian Missionary Activity in the Early Middle Ages* (Aldershot, 1994).

60. I. N. Wood, 'Christians and pagans in ninth-century Scandinavia', in B. Sawyer, P. H. Sawyer and I. N. Wood (eds), *The Christianization of Scandinavia* (Alingsås, 1987), pp. 36–67.

61. Rimbert, *Vita Anskarii* 24, ed. W. Trillmich, *Quellen des 9. und 11. Jahrhunderts zur Geschichte der Hamburgischen Kirche und des Reiches* (Darmstadt, 1961).

62. Rimbert, *Vita Anskarii* 32.

63. Rimbert, *Vita Anskarii* 24, 27.

64. *Islendingabók Landnámabók*, ed. J. Benediktsson (Reykjavik, 1968), pp. 250, 253: see Wood, 'Christians and pagans in ninth-century Scandinavia', p. 54.

65. Alcuin, *Vita Willibrordi* 9, ed. W. Levison, MGH SRM 7 (Hanover, 1920).

66. Rimbert, *Vita Anskarii* 20, 24, 27.

67. Ermoldus Nigellus, *In honorem Hludovici Pii*, ll. 1882–2513, ed. E. Faral, *Ermold le Noir – Poème sur Louis le Pieux* (Paris, 1932).

68. Notker, *Gesta Karoli Magni Imperatoris* II 19, ed. H. F. Haefele, MGH, SRG 12 (Berlin, 1962).

69. *Anglo-Saxon Chronicle*, s.a. 878, ed. C. Plummer and J. Earle, *Two of the Saxon Chronicles Parallel* (Oxford, 1892–9).

70. P. H. Sawyer, 'The process of Scandinavian Christianization in the tenth and eleventh centuries', in B. Sawyer, P. H. Sawyer and I. N. Wood (eds), *The Christianization of Scandinavia* (Alingsås, 1987), pp. 68–87.

71. Widukind, *Res Gestae Saxonicae* III 65, ed. A. Bauer and R. Rau, *Quellen zur Geschichte der sächsischen Kaiserzeit* (Darmstadt, 1971).

72. Thietmar, *Chronicon* I 17.

73. Widukind, *Res Gestae Saxonicae* III 65; Thietmar, *Chronicon* II 14.

74. The mission is only covered in Scholion 20, to Adam, *Gesta Hammaburgensis Ecclesiae Pontificum* II 25 (22), ed. Trillmich, *Quellen des 9. und 11. Jahrhunderts zur Geschichte der hamburgischen Kirche und des Reiches*.

75. For Scandinavia, see B. Sawyer, 'Scandinavian conversion histories', in B. Sawyer, P. H. Sawyer and I. N. Wood, *The Christianization of Scandinavia* (Alingsås, 1987), pp. 92–4.

76. P. Sawyer, 'The process of Scandinavian Christianization in the tenth and eleventh centuries', p. 82. See also P. Meulengracht Sørensen, 'Religions old and new', in P. Sawyer (ed.), *The Oxford Illustrated History of the Vikings* (Oxford, 1997), pp. 202–24.

77. See the overview by J. Jochens, 'Late and peaceful: Iceland's conversion through arbitration in 1000', *Speculum* 74 (1999), pp. 620–55.

78. S. Franklin and J. Shepard, *The Emergence of Rus 750–1200* (London, 1996), pp. 158–66.
79. Vlasto, *The Entry of the Slavs into Christendom*.
80. Bruno, ep. to Henry; Vlasto, *The Entry of the Slavs into Christendom*, pp. 148–9.
81. Thietmar, *Chronicon* VI 23–5. On the paganism of the Slavs see Slupecki, *Slavonic Pagan Sanctuaries*.
82. Vlasto, *The Entry of the Slavs into Christendom*, p. 151.
83. Vlasto, *The Entry of the Slavs into Christendom*, pp. 152–4; see more recently K. Coblenz (ed.), *825 Jahre Christianisierung Rügens* (Altenkirchen, 1993).
84. E. Christiansen, *The Northern Crusades* (London, 1980), pp. 132–79; R. Fletcher, *The Conversion of Europe: from Paganism to Christianity 371–1386 AD*, pp. 497–507.
85. I. N. Wood, 'The conversion of the barbarian peoples', in G. Barraclough (ed.), *The Christian World*, pp. 85–98.
86. Goffart, *The Narrators of Barbarian History*, pp. 256–7.
87. See Figure 3.1 and Table 3.1.
88. A similar approach is present in the work of W. Berschin, *Biographie und Epochenstil im lateinischen Mittelalter* III, *Karolingische Biographie 750–920 n. Chr.*, Quellen und Untersuchungen zur lateinischen Philologie des Mittelalters Band X (Stuttgart, 1991), p. 62.
89. For comments on the variety of hagiography in the Late Antique and Early Medieval periods see I. N. Wood, 'The use and abuse of Latin hagiography', in E. Chrysos and I. N. Wood (eds), *East and West: Modes of Communication* (Leiden, 1999), pp. 93–109.
90. Thompson, *The Visigoths in the Time of Ulfila*, p. 129. Ironically, Thompson was at his best as a careful reader of texts.
91. See, for instance, E. Ewig, 'Die christliche Mission bei den Franken und im Merowingerreich', in D. Baker (ed.), *Miscellania Historiae Ecclesiasticae* 3 (Louvain, 1970), p. 24.

# Chapter 2

# FROM PATRICK TO BEDE

## 1. NARRATING MISSION

Despite the missionary injunction at the end of Matthew's Gospel and despite the model provided by the Acts of the Apostles, mission has not always been uppermost in the Christian tradition: indeed, evangelisation has been relatively insignificant in long periods of the history of the Church.[1] It has occurred in waves, sometimes becoming fashionable for no apparent reason, and often with no overall guiding hand. Similarly, despite the model provided by Acts, the notion of writing histories which concentrate primarily on mission has only been intermittently pursued. Even on a smaller scale, the idea of using hagiography to portray saints primarily as missionaries, as opposed to including individual anecdotes relating to the work of evangelisation in texts concerned with holy bishops or abbots, has been an idea which has only had fitful popularity. My concern in what follows is not to consider why mission has rarely been the dominant theme in historical or hagiographical writing – the Church and its history are multifaceted enough for no single ecclesiastical tradition to be dominant. Instead, I am concerned to ask when, in the Early Middle Ages, hagiography – and history – concentrated on mission to the pagans, and why.[2]

One possible answer to the absence of historical and hagiographical writing dominated by mission – that there is a direct correlation between missionary activity and missionary hagiography or history – can be dismissed immediately. Certainly, there have been periods when there has been more evangelisation than there has been at other times. Yet there have been missionaries who were the subject of saints' *Lives*, without their being portrayed as primarily involved in mission. The reverse is even true: that saints who were scarcely involved in mission, were given a missionary varnish – and this varnish has been applied by modern writers, because of their own religious commitments, just as much as it was by medieval. The relationship between mission and its portrayal is more complex than a straightforward correlation between chronicle and event.

This is nowhere more apparent than at the very start of the Middle Ages. Although evangelisation took place on a vast scale between the fourth century and the beginning of the eighth, scarcely any hagiographer thought fit to depict a saint primarily as a missionary, while no Latin historian before Bede used mission as one of the organising principles of a large-scale historical narrative.

## 2. PATRICK

In certain respects Patrick is an exception. Admittedly, no surviving hagiographical work was written about him before the middle of the seventh century.[3] The only early accounts of Patrick's career are, of course, to be found in his own work: the autobiographical *Confessio* and his *Letter* to the soldiers of Coroticus – and these by no means provide straightforward narratives, since they were written to justify Patrick's actions to specific groups of opponents, and they jump from one event in the author's life to another as he thought necessary for his argument.[4]

Patrick was born of noble and wealthy parents in the Roman province of *Britannia* – probably in the early fifth century, although his dates are open to question: he may have died in *c.* 460 or in 493.[5] His family was Christian: his grandfather, Potitus, had been a priest, and his father, Calpornius, was a local official and a deacon.[6] Despite this, he had not been well educated[7] before he was captured by Irish raiders when he was fifteen.[8] The fact of his capture suggests that his family home was somewhere near the west coast of Britain. He was taken to Ireland, where he was kept as a slave near the Forest of Foclut, by the Western Sea – neither of which can be securely identified.[9] There he came to rely much on prayer.

After six years he was told in a vision to escape, so he travelled two hundred miles across Ireland, and took ship.[10] The crossing lasted three days, after which he and his companions disembarked. They travelled for twenty-eight days without food, before seeing a herd of pigs – some of which they killed. Patrick, however, avoided eating, because the killing had been performed as a pagan sacrifice.[11] Where this took place is unclear, and while Patrick is precise about distances and times, it is probable that the desert through which he and his companions passed was in his imagination a spiritual one.

Having reached Britain, Patrick returned to his family, but while he was back at home he had a vision of a figure called Victorius, coming from the Forest of Foclut, the place of his servitude, asking him to return.[12] At the time of the vision he was still young – he is addressed as boy, *puer.*[13] How soon he responded to this appeal is unclear, but he says that he was still a youth when he returned to evangelise in Ireland.[14]

Patrick's work in Ireland lasted for a considerable time. He talks of a priest whom he had taught as a child,[15] implying that he had known the man for at least twenty years. He does so in the context of a letter addressed to the soldiers of a British warleader, Coroticus, who had taken some of his converts captive and killed others. The letter is an excommunication of Coroticus and his men for their actions. The order of events between the vision of Victorius and this moment is unclear, although Patrick scatters snippets of information throughout his writings. He had been captured again.[16] He entered the Church and became a deacon.[17] He regarded himself as a bishop, but exactly on whose authority, other than God's, is by no means clear.[18] His office was unquestionably a matter of considerable importance to him for he places a reference to it in the very centre of his work. Nevertheless, the precise nature of his jurisdiction is nowhere specified. Certainly, the British Church seems to have thought he had exceeded that jurisdiction in excommunicating Coroticus.[19] He had, however, had considerable success in evangelising – even so, despite the fact that he had given gifts to local rulers, he and his converts suffered persecution.[20]

Nor is the chronological relation between the *Letter* to the soldiers of Coroticus and the *Confessio* certain – although the two of them may not have been written far apart in time. The latter was composed in the aftermath of an accusation brought against him by the British Church. Patrick, before he was even made a deacon, had told a friend – indeed the man who had actually prophesied that he would be given episcopal office[21] – about a sin which he had committed when he was fifteen, in other words, about the time of his initial capture by Irish raiders.[22] Thirty years later – although it is not clear whether these thirty years are to be counted from the sin, or from Patrick's private confession – the one-time friend raised the issue.[23] This led to a trial, although Patrick himself refused to abandon his work in Ireland.[24] The *Confessio*, which is a justification of his position, he set down as an old man – *in senectute mea*.[25]

Unravelling Patrick's career, its chronology and its geography, with any precision or certainty is scarcely possible. What we have are two works of justification, which, indeed, we would not have, had the author not been a controversial character who needed to defend himself. The *Confessio* and the *Epistola* cast a sharp light on the work of a missionary: the dangers, from pagans and from one's fellow countrymen, the need to finance and to bribe, the teaching and baptism, and the subsequent concern for the converts. Patrick's writings also draw attention to the depth of faith needed for that work. Faith, bolstered by prayer and visions, is a recurrent theme for missionaries. It is central to Patrick's account of his work, which offers a remarkable psychological self-portrait. If we are to believe, as some do, that autobiography lapsed from the time of Augustine of Hippo until the eleventh century,[26] we should at least list Patrick alongside his great contemporary.

No one would now turn to Patrick's seventh-century hagiographers to understand the realities of his mission. In some way or other they reflect claims of authority and jurisdiction made in the context of competition between the churches of Armagh, Kildare and Iona.[27] To try to extract information on the Christianisation of Ireland from the *Lives* of Patrick is, at the least, hazardous. Yet, while those *Lives* cannot be used to understand Patrick, they do shed light on how later generations thought fit to describe the process of evangelisation. Tírechán, in particular, describes Christianisation in a way not dissimilar to that followed by at least one later writer in the Church of Salzburg, as we shall see. It is conceived of as the process of baptism, church foundation and the ordination of clergy. This was a way of registering mission which was more appropriate to some contexts than was the deeply personal, autobiographical approach of Patrick.[28]

## 3. SULPICIUS SEVERUS AND PAGANISM IN THE *VITA MARTINI*

Patrick is unusual in the fifth century, even though there does seem to have been a flurry of missionary interest, not least in the papacy at the time of Celestine (422–32) and Leo the Great (440–61).[29] If one turns to accounts of mission on the continent in this period, first, there is an absence of sources on attempts to evangelise outside the Roman Empire, although there undoubtedly were successful missions, Arian if not Catholic, for which no evidence survives. Second, even those figures who are seen by modern tradition as missionaries within the pagan world of the Roman countryside, are not represented primarily in that guise. Thus, the Christianising work of Martin, who undoubtedly did much to evangelise the Touraine, only occupies four chapters out of twenty-seven in the *Vita Martini* of Sulpicius Severus.[30] To emphasise this ratio is not to deny Martin's importance in the Christianisation of Gaul,[31] but rather to say that Sulpicius Severus was less interested in this work than in other aspects of Martin's career – as bishop and as ascetic – both of them of more immediate significance for the hagiographer than was Christianisation.[32]

Sulpicius Severus' work was well known to later writers of hagiography – as to modern historians, and his four chapters describing the saint's confrontations with pagans have, therefore, had an impact on the portrayal of mission by both medieval and modern authors.[33] Sulpicius Severus relates that once, when Martin saw what he took to be a pagan ritual, he made the sign of the cross and ordered the participants to stand still: unable to progress, they whirled around in circles. When Martin discovered that the rites were nothing other than the funeral procession of a pagan, he let the mourners continue.[34] Again, once when the saint had destroyed a temple, the locals intervened to protect their sacred tree. In the end they agreed to do the cutting themselves, if Martin would stand in the path of the tree's fall: he did so, but it twisted round and fell in the other direction.[35] He was also protected by two angels when he burnt down a temple,[36] and when attempts were made to stab him in the course of his work of destruction, his assailants were unable to strike home.[37] These stories influenced a number of subsequent descriptions of confrontations between pagans and holy men, as, for instance, when the guardian of a shrine attacked Willibrord at Walcheren.[38] Yet, despite its influence, the *Vita Martini* did not create an image of a missionary saint.

## 4. GREGORY OF LANGRES AND GREGORY OF TOURS

In the course of the fifth century the history of mission did, however, attract some interest, but essentially in the context of ecclesiastical rivalry. In particular, the Church of Arles developed the legend of the apostle Trophimus, to bolster its claims to antiquity and jurisdictional pre-eminence in Gaul.[39] By the beginning of the sixth century Trophimus had gained three companions, and shortly after the number of Gallic apostles was expanded to seven. At about the same time another legend was developed, probably under the aegis of Gregory, bishop of Langres (*c.* 507–539), which joined a whole set of stories to form the *Passio sanctorum Herenaei episcopi, Andochii presbiteri, Benigni presbiteri, Tyrsi diaconi, Felicis negotiatoris*.[40] This purported to recount the history of mission to the region of Autun, Saulieu, Langres and Dijon. Significantly, however, the narration is essentially a series of martyr acts: missionary history was conceived of as a sequence of martyrdoms. In this respect it differs little from other associated texts, notably the *Acts* of Ferreolus and Ferrucio of Besançon, and of Felix, Fortunatus and Achilleus of Valence, on which it seems to have drawn.[41] Despite the apparent ambitions of the *Passio sanctorum Herenaei episcopi, Andochii presbiteri, Benigni presbiteri, Tyrsi diaconi, Felicis negotiatoris*, its composite narrative seems to have had little impact, for it only survives in a single Farfa manuscript.

The story was, however, known to Gregory's great-grandson and namesake, the most prolific hagiographer of the sixth century, Gregory of Tours, who borrows from it in his *Liber in Gloria Martyrum*.[42] In Book One of his *Histories* Gregory also pays some attention to the legend of the evangelisation of Roman Gaul by the seven apostles, Gatianus, Trophimus, Paulus, Saturninus, Dionysius, Stremonius and Martialis.[43] Nor was Gregory simply interested in evangelisation in the distant past. The conversion of Clovis to Catholicism is a moment of major importance in the second book of the *Histories*.[44] Thereafter, however, Christianisation is rarely an issue. It marks a phase in Gregory's record of the past, but not an ongoing theme.

Gregory does, however, record a meeting he had with the deacon Vulfolaic, who lived in a monastery near Carignan. Ever avid for information, he asked Vulfolaic to give him an account of his life. Although of Lombard birth, the deacon had come to Gaul, where he became a pupil of Aredius of Limoges. Later he went to Carignan, in the Trier region, where he found a statue of Diana, and in order to dissuade the local populace from revering it, he set himself up on a nearby column, as a stylite. Eventually, he persuaded the people to pull down the idol, which they did – although the stylite was miraculously covered with sores as a result. Thereafter, he was persuaded by local bishops to give up his column for life in a monastery.[45]

There are a number of interesting features to this story. First, there is a *Life of Aredius*, which also involves the identification of a pagan shrine and the destruction of idols,[46] suggesting perhaps that Vulfolaic was copying his master in some way – or alternatively, that there is a literary connection between the *Life* and Gregory's writing. Second, the bishop of Tours purports to be quoting the stylite's own words, inserting, as it were, a short autobiographical account into his *Histories* – an unusual action for Gregory, and one which should be noted: for some reason the stylite missionary deserved to be heard in his own voice. Patrick had already provided an autobiographical account of mission, and later missionaries would follow suit – autobiographical statements seem on occasion to have been regarded as the appropriate medium for recording missionary work. How much the story tells us about paganism in Gaul is a different matter: the cult of Diana can scarcely have been more than the continuance of a local tradition.[47] On the other hand, there may have been more survival of superstitious practice in the north-east of Gaul than elsewhere. In his *Life* of his uncle Gallus, Gregory recounts that, when still a young man, the saint was attendant on King Theuderic in the Cologne region, when he discovered a temple with various votive offerings, to which he set fire. He was, says Gregory, lucky to escape from the angry idolators.[48]

The Merovingian evidence may suggest some pagan survival, particularly in the north, but it does not amount to much.[49] The kingdom of the Franks was at least officially Christian from the first quarter of the sixth century – although there was plenty of rural evangelisation required to deepen understanding of Christianity, especially in the north-east. The fact that Francia had largely been Christianised is in itself enough to account for the small number of stories relating to confrontations between saints and pagans. The stories themselves are, for the most part, freestanding anecdotes, which give no indication as to whether they reflect the general state of the region, whether they are isolated episodes, or whether, indeed, they are merely *topoi*, which allow no insight into the Christianisation of the region.

## 5. COLUMBANUS AND JONAS OF BOBBIO

In the hagiography of the seventh century there are, once again, occasional chapters on the work of Christianisation within Christian kingdoms, but no overriding emphasis on the matter. The pattern is essentially repeated in the *Life of Columbanus* by Jonas of Bobbio. Here, however, there is a significant twist. There is a recurrent tendency to see Columbanus as a missionary. Certainly, like Martin, he had an impact on the Christianisation of parts of Gaul – in his case the regions round his monastic foundations of Annegray and Luxeuil. He also thought about working among the pagan Bavarians. He himself remarks that 'It was in my wish to visit the heathen and have the gospel preached to them by us, but when x just reported their coolness he quite took my mind from that.'[50] In a sense there is good Biblical precedent for Columbanus' decision: as Christ said, 'And whosoever shall not receive you, nor hear your words, when ye depart out of that house or city, shake off the dust of your feet.' (Matthew 10, 14). On the other hand, the fact that Columbanus did forget to preach to the heathen rather undermines the picture of him as a missionary.

Columbanus was born in Leinster, in the middle of the sixth century,[51] and was taught by Sinil, before entering the religious community at Bangor.[52] In *c.* 591 he left Bangor for Gaul, and there he was supported first, it seems, by Guntram and then by Childebert II, who probably founded Luxeuil for him between 593 and 596.[53] The Merovingian kings seem to have regarded him as something of a dynastic holy man. Despite the fact that his views on monasticism and on the dating of Easter differed from those of the Gallic bishops, he was able to continue to live as he wanted at Luxeuil, until he alienated royal support, apparently by refusing to bless the bastards of Theuderic II in *c.* 610.[54] He was sent back to Ireland, but somehow managed to avoid the sentence, travelling instead to the Frankish courts of Chlothar II and Theudebert II, before setting up in Bregenz.[55] There he heard of the death of Theudebert, and travelled on to northern Italy, where he was given territory at Bobbio by King Agilulf to found a monastery.[56] He died in 615.

The first book of the *Life of Columbanus and his disciples*, which was written by Jonas of Bobbio in *c.* 641/2,[57] essentially provides an account of the saint as *peregrinus pro Christo*, a pilgrim who had abandoned his homeland for Christ, and as monastic founder,[58] issues which are amply illustrated in Columbanus' own letters. Not that there is a perfect fit between the letters and the hagiography. In the letters Columbanus spells out views on two theological issues, the Easter question and on the Tricapitoline schism,[59] views which were regarded as heretical by the Frankish Church and the papacy during his own lifetime, and by the communities of Luxeuil and Bobbio shortly afterwards. Not surprisingly, Jonas omits any discussion of these issues in his account of Columbanus.[60] Jonas' picture of Columbanian monasticism may also reflect the norms of his own day rather more exactly than the original ideas of the founder.[61] Equally important, Jonas imagines the historical context of Columbanus in Francia through the eyes of hindsight, downplaying the role of Childebert II and misrepresenting those of Theuderic II and Brunhild, not least because that branch of the Merovingian dynasty was wiped out in 613, and became a scapegoat for many of the kingdom's ills.[62]

Since the *Vita Columbani* raises complex questions involving both the lifetime of the saint and the period of the work's composition, it is not surprising that the one major chapter relating to mission in the first Book of the *vita* requires careful consideration. The issue of mission is initially raised in a discussion which supposedly took place between Columbanus and Theudebert in *c.* 611:

> Theudebert promised to find him pleasant places inside his territories offering every opportunity to the holy man, and having neighbouring nations on all sides to be preached to. To these words the holy man said: 'If you offer the support of your promise, and if the harm of falsehood does not get in the way of your recognizance, let me be allowed to stay there a little and see what may be done, sowing faith into the hearts of the neighbouring people.' The king allowed him to stay wherever he wanted, and he sought out a place for the experiment, which was pleasing to him and his followers; and they found a place of which everybody approved, within the boundaries of *Germania*, but close to the Rhine, an *oppidum*, which had once been ruined, and which they called Bregenz.[63]

The passage raises many interesting questions. The issue of mission is first raised by the king. Since Columbanus wrote the letter to the monks of Luxeuil in which he said that he had forgotten to evangelise the pagans approximately one year before his meeting with Theudebert,[64] he had already considered mission, even if he had not followed up his idea. Nevertheless, there is evidence that Brunhild and her grandsons, Theuderic II and Theudebert II, were inspired to consider a missionary policy as a result of the Augustinian mission to England in 597.[65] It would not be surprising if, having seen the (political) value of being involved in the evangelisation of Kent, the Merovingians saw advantages in sending missionaries to the peoples who bordered their kingdom in such regions as the extreme southeast: and that Bregenz was on the edge of the Merovingian kingdom is made more than clear in Jonas' description of the meeting between Columbanus and Theudebert. In this way the Christianisation of England may have contributed to the formation of a missionary ideology in Francia. Thus, although Jonas denigrates Brunhild and Theuderic, he may give a reasonable account of Theudebert at this point in his narrative. Merovingian missionary policy, one might add, did not end with Theudebert's death: it certainly continued under Dagobert I (623–39),[66] who died only two years or so before the composition of Book One of the *Vita Columbani*.

It is not merely the emphasis on Theudebert that is interesting in Jonas' account. Mission is here described as an *experimentum*: it is something new for Columbanus, and, interestingly, his success is limited. Having reached Bregenz,

> Going round the region the man of God said that he did not like it, but that he would stay there a little to sow the faith among the *gentes*. The neighbouring peoples there are Sueves. While he was there and was travelling round the inhabitants of the region, he found they wished to offer a profane sacrifice, and that they had set in the centre [of their gathering] a huge barrel, which they call *cupa* in the vernacular, and which holds more or less 20 *modia*, filled with beer. The man of God went up to it, and enquired what they were doing. They said they wanted to honour their God, Wodan by name, whom others, as they say, call Mercury. He, hearing of their evil work, blew on the barrel, and miraculously it shattered with a bang and was broken into pieces, and the beer flowed out with great force, making it clear that the devil was hidden in the barrel, and that he ensnared the minds of those offering the sacrifice through profane drink. The onlooking barbarians were astonished and said that the man of God had a very strong breath, capable of breaking a barrel bound with hoops. He criticised them with evangelical words, telling them to refrain from sacrifice, and told them to go home. Many of them at that time were converted to the faith of Christ by the blessed man's arguments and doctrine, and were baptised. Others, already baptised but held by prophane error, he led back to the cult of evangelical doctrine, as a good pastor leading them to the bosom of the Church.[67]

Despite the baptisms, the limits of Columbanus' success are indicated by the somewhat muted reaction of the Sueves, who could only comment on the strength of his breath. Nor does mission hold Jonas' attention at this point, for he instantly turns from Columbanus' dealings with the Sueves to an account of the martyrdom of Bishop Desiderius of Vienne and then to two miracles concerned with the provision of food in the Bregenz region. Further, the muted nature of Jonas' account of the reaction to Columbanus' beer miracle is highlighted by comparison with another text which has convincingly been attributed to the same hagiographer, the *Vita Vedastis*.[68] Here an almost exactly analogous miracle is performed, although this time the saint merely makes the sign of the cross over the offending barrel.[69] The audience was also more distinguished, including the Merovingian king, Chlothar I (511–61), his host, Hocin, and a mixed group of pagan and Christian guests.

> As a result [of the barrel bursting] the king was astonished by the miracle and the whole group of magnates wondered what was the cause of the event, and discussed it openly. To him the venerable man Vedast said, 'O king, glory of your Franks, you can see how great is the skill of diabolic deceit in deceiving the minds

of men. For what do you think is the intention of the demons, who attempt to subject to eternal death through this draught of beer the hearts of the unfaithful, suffocated by prevarication, although the art of the devil is now repulsed and driven away by divine strength? It is necessary for everyone to know how Christians should learn to flee to the healthy medicine of true faith and should strive as best they can to avoid these pagan superstitions.' As a result he brought many who were present to salvation, for as a result many rushed to the grace of baptism and bowed their necks to holy religion.

Jonas makes more of the immediate aftermath of Vedast's beer miracle than he does of Columbanus'. Moreover, when he does return to the question of mission at the end of the same chapter of the *Vita Columbani*, he spells out the failure of Columbanus to evangelise even more clearly.

Meanwhile he thought to travel to the frontiers of the Wends, who are also called Slavs, and illuminate with evangelical light their blind minds, and to show the way of truth to those in error from the beginning, through the times of their ancestors. And when he was ready to carry out this desire, the angel of the Lord appeared to him in a vision, and showed him the structure of the world in small scale, just as a pair of compasses can draw a circle. 'You see', said he, 'that the whole world remains a desert. Go right or left, as you choose, to eat the fruits of your labours.' And so he understood that he should not set out to expound the faith to that people, and he stayed where he was until the opportunity opened the way to Italy.[70]

Columbanus' angelic vision looks like a *post eventum* attempt to justify the saint's failure to move east from Bregenz to the Slavs. Columbanus' failure to work among the Wends has more than one cause. There is the clear indication from his letter to the monks of Luxeuil that he was not really committed to mission. Further, the growing tension and eventual civil war between Theudebert II and Theuderic II meant that support from the Merovingians became less and less likely.[71] Perhaps more important, the threat of the newly arrived Avars made work among the Slavs ever less promising. Already in *c.* 610 the Avar khagan had launched an attack on Lombard Friuli,[72] possibly as a result of an alliance with Theuderic II, in opposition to the Lombard alliance of Theudebert.[73]

Columbanus' own lack of enthusiasm for mission suggests that, far from failing to do justice to his subject's missionary work, Jonas was doing his best to give a missionary twist to the career of a man who was a *peregrinus pro Christo*, that is, a man who had abandoned his homeland in order to follow the Gospel injunction of abandoning for Christ's sake the society in which he had been brought up (e.g. Matthew 10, 37–8). That Columbanus and other such *peregrini*, not all of them Irish, did help in the Christianisation of the regions in which they settled is not at issue[74] – but there is a distinction to be drawn between such 'pilgrims' and men dedicated to mission in a pagan land, not least because the *peregrini* that we know about settled in contexts which were at least officially Christian, indeed, some of them became associated with the royal and ducal courts of the regions to which they went. As a court holy man, a *peregrinus* could be highly prized by the ruling dynasty for his charisma. If the hagiographers of *peregrini* concluded, as in the case of the authors of the *Lives* of Kilian and Emmeram, that the marital arrangements of the ducal family were unchristian, such an interpretation does not mean that their heroes were missionaries beyond the Christian frontiers – the attacks made by Kilian and Emmeram on the marital behaviour of their patrons can be paralleled with similar clerical attacks on rulers in the heart of the Frankish kingdom, not least by Columbanus himself.[75] Columbanus' disciple, Gallus, who was left behind by his master because of disobedience, almost certainly encountered more paganism in the countryside round Lake Constance, but the fragmentary *Vita Vetustissima* portrays him first and foremost as the leader of an ascetic community.[76]

## 6. JONAS, BOBBIO AND LUXEUIL

If the *Vita Columbani* had been intended to be a balanced account of Columbanus' achievement, Jonas' decision to include the mission to the Slavs would require rather more justification than Columbanus' own lack of interest in mission. To understand what Jonas was doing, it is necessary to consider his own life. He came from the Alpine city of Susa, which was then in Merovingian hands, and entered Bobbio nine years before the death of Abbot Athala,[77] in other words in 616/7, not much more than a year after the death of Columbanus himself. At Bobbio he seems to have had some charge over the archives, or at least Athala entrusted him with a letter sent by Agrestius. As he himself explains, he subsequently lost the document.[78] It was perhaps as archivist that he travelled with Abbot Bertulf to secure a papal privilege from Pope Honorius in 628.[79] One might further hypothesise that it was because he had been archivist that he was asked to write the *Life of Columbanus* by Bertulf and the community of Bobbio.[80] The *vita*, for all its historical problems, is no simple expression of piety. Much of Book I and parts of Book II can as easily be classified as history as hagiography.[81] Both books draw on liturgical and regular texts of the Columbanian movement,[82] and are aware of some legal documents.[83] In all probability Jonas knew Columbanus' letters: he would therefore have known Columbanus' own comments on mission, which he describes as something he had intended to do, but forgotten to follow up.

Before he was asked to write the *Life of Columbanus*, Jonas had, however, left the community of Bobbio. By the time he settled down to write he had visited or been in touch with a number of Columbanus' disciples. He had seen Gallus,[84] and Chagnoald, bishop of Laon,[85] and had been present at the funeral of Gibitrude at Faremoutiers.[86] As a result, he was equipped not only to write the *Life of Columbanus*, but also the *Lives* of the saint's successors, both at Bobbio and Luxeuil. When he completed the *vita* it was addressed to the abbots of both houses. The address to Luxeuil may help explain the presence of Jonas' account of Columbanus' stay at Bregenz, for while Columbanus may not have been much interested in missionary activity, his successor at Luxeuil, Eustasius, was.

The *Life of Eustasius* takes up Chapters 7 to 10 of Book II of the *Vita Columbani*. Written shortly after Book I,[87] the second book of Jonas' *magnum opus* is rather more difficult to describe. It is made up of five sections, the *Life of Athala* (cc. 1–6), that of Eustasius (cc. 7–10), the *Miracles of Faremoutiers* (cc. 11–22), the *Life of Bertulf* (*c.* 23) and two miscellaneous chapters on the monks of Bobbio (cc. 24–5). Although some manuscripts of the *Vita Columbani* contain all this material, and although Krusch edited the accounts of Columbanus' disciples as a single book – which may well have been what Jonas intended – it appears from other, earlier, manuscripts that different audiences treated the sections of Book II as separate texts, some or all of which could be appended to the *Life of Columbanus* himself, depending on the requirements of a particular monastery.[88]

Be that as it may, the first two chapters of the *Life of Eustasius* concentrate on his association with Burgundofara and Sadalberga, and thus illuminate the spread of Columbanian ideals amongst the female offspring of the Merovingian aristocracy, while the last two chapters concentrate on the conflict between Eustasius and Agrestius, and thus highlight the abbot's defence of the Columbanian tradition. Nevertheless, in the course of two of these four chapters Jonas does draw attention to Eustasius' interest in mission. In the first of these we are told that on returning from a visit to Columbanus in Bobbio,

> the venerable man Eustasius prepared to fulfil the command of the master, that the neighbouring peoples should be nourished by the food of faith. So he set out and preached to the *Warasci*, some of whom were devoted to the cult of idols, and others were stained with the heresy of Fotinus or Bonosus. Having converted them, he set out for the *Boiae*, who are now called Bavarians, and having worked hard among them, and having corrected them with the remedy of faith, he converted many of them to that faith. When he had stayed there for some while he sent wise men, who could tire themselves carrying out the work that had been begun; he took care to return to Luxeuil.[89]

The second passage is yet more important: Agrestius, one-time referendary of Theuderic, entered Luxeuil.

To set out the whole story, showing a facade of religion in the monastery, he then asked permission to preach to the heathen. The holy man long reproved him, swearing that he ought not to think himself fit for such work, as he was still untrained in religion, while the man who was preferred to such work ought to be endowed with every ecclesiastical virtue, for Jeremiah, when elevated by the choice of God, denied that he was worthy, saying, 'Ah, ah, Lord God, behold I am a child and know not how to speak.' Moses, elected by God, bore witness that he was slow of speech.

Having said those things with no avail, he allowed him to go, not being strong enough to hold him. He set out for the Bavarians and having reached them, stayed a little, yielding no fruit, like the high plane-tree shaking its noisy leaves in the winds at the quivering air, knowing no crop of fruit.[90]

Eustasius' assessment of Agrestius not being fit for mission is soon borne out by his lapsing into heresy among the Tricapitoline schismatics, and then turning against the Columbanian movement itself.[91]

Agrestius' history was undoubtedly more complicated than Jonas made out. In joining the schismatics he was, in all probability, upholding the doctrinal position of Columbanus himself.[92] Even Jonas' account of Agrestius' attack on Columbanian monasticism is probably an inaccurate representation of events: compromises may have been made by Eustasius subsequent to the conflict,[93] although Jonas prefers to depict the traditions of Luxeuil in the days of Eustasius as being those of its founder.

Considered from the point of view of the history of mission, however, the story of Agrestius provides a clear indication of a missionary movement and strategy. The strategy, whether or not it was inspired by Columbanus, was worked out by Eustasius, who took it for granted that only the most qualified ascetics could work as missionaries. Such men he sent to work in Bavaria. This may in part underlie Jonas' depiction of Columbanus as a missionary: before he preached to the pagan Sueves, Columbanus had triumphed as monk, ascetic and monastic founder and leader. By depicting Columbanus as a missionary in the last phase of his stay in the Merovingian kingdom, Jonas had portrayed his missionary ideals as being comparable to those of Eustasius.

Unfortunately, no other early source provides much detail on Eustasius' missionary work, but it was remembered, like other aspects of Columbanian tradition, at Rebais.[94] Following the *Vita Agili*, a text which was certainly written after the Merovingian period,[95] a council of bishops sent Agilus and Eustasius to evangelise neighbouring peoples. They worked among the *Warasci* and the Bavarians.[96] Since the author of the *Vita Agili* is known to have had access to Jonas' work,[97] the account of the mission among the Warasci and the Bavarians need not be an independent source. On the other hand, although Jonas refers to Agilus' association with Eustasius,[98] he makes no mention of his involvement in mission, which is recorded only in the *Vita Agili*. Further, mention of a Church council might be regarded as proving that the author of the *Life of Agilus* did indeed have access to independent evidence of Eustasius' missionary work.

Eustasius and Agilus were, moreover, not the only members of the Columbanian movement who were involved in missionary work. In some ways as important was Jonas himself, who collaborated with one of the most active missionaries of the seventh century, Amandus. Jonas records his collaboration with Amandus in his prefatory letter to the *Vita Columbani*, addressed to Waldebert and Bobolenus.

> For three years I was borne over the estuaries of the Ocean and the Scarpe, heavy with its boats, and the Scheldt wet me as I sailed along its gentle waterways, while the sticky marsh of the Elno wet my feet as I assisted the venerable Bishop Amandus who had been placed over these regions to combat the old errors of the Sicambri with the sword of the Gospel.[99]

Jonas was, therefore, a missionary, albeit within Frankish territory, and that may have encouraged him to put together what fragments he could, relating to Columbanus' somewhat half-hearted missionary work.

The interests of Eustasius and of Jonas himself explain the coverage of Columbanus' missionary attempts in the region of Bregenz. Indeed, the significance of Eustasius' work may make it surprising that Jonas has so little to say about mission in either book of the *Vita Columbani*. Here it may be important that Eustasius died in 629, more than a decade before Jonas wrote the *Life*. Further, there is little to suggest that his successor, Waldebert, had the same interest in mission. Although there is no *Vita Waldeberti*, references to him in the *Vita Columbani*,[100] the *Vita Germani Grandivallensis*[101] and the *Vita Balthildis*,[102] present him as a primarily monastic figure, while in the *Passio Aunemundi* he plays a rather more political role.[103] The political significance of Luxeuil becomes even more apparent after Waldebert's death, when the monastery served as a prison for both Ebroin and Leodegar of Autun.[104] Waldebert does not, therefore, appear to have been a man much interested in pursuing Eustasius' missionary programme.

Nor, in all probability, were the monks of Luxeuil. After Eustasius' death they seem to have wanted Gallus to be their next abbot.[105] Gallus does not seem to have been a missionary figure, despite the fact that he remained in the region of the Bodensee when Columbanus departed for Italy.[106] Although, as a *peregrinus* in the *desertum* of Steinach, Gallus had to deal with the local demons, some of whom may reasonably be associated with the survival of pagan practices,[107] there is nothing to suggest that he set out to be a missionary to the surrounding *gentes*. In this he was probably following the example of his master. Although he was excommunicated by Columbanus, the excommunication was revoked, according to the *Vita*

*Galli Vetustissima*, when the master, on his deathbed, sent his staff to his disobedient disciple.[108] Gallus, therefore, was reinstated in Columbanus' favour. His choice as abbot of Luxeuil can, as a result, be read as representing a determination to emphasise traditions associated with Columbanus himself, who does not appear to have regarded mission as a prime concern.

Further, although there may be a case for seeing Birinus, who was consecrated bishop in Genoa, and who subsequently acted as a missionary in England, as coming from Bobbio,[109] there is no strong evidence to suggest that Columbanus' Italian foundation developed the missionary interests espoused by Luxeuil in the days of Eustasius. Mission, therefore, interested Eustasius and, perhaps more important, Jonas enough to justify its coverage in the *Vita Columbani*: but it was not so central to the career of Columbanus or to the interests of the audience to justify more than a few passing references. Jonas' account of mission in the *Vita Columbani* is thus affected by the responses of three generations: of Columbanus himself, who was not firmly committed to mission; of Eustasius, who was; and of Waldebert and Bobolenus, who appear not to have been. Jonas' own ideas, however, may have been closest to those of Eustasius.

Jonas' missionary activity took place within the Frankish kingdom. It belonged to a sort of mopping-up operation, which can also be seen in the *Lives* of such north-eastern bishops as Eligius of Noyon,[110] and which Jonas himself seems to have explored in his *Life* of the sixth-century Saint Vedast. Although it was mission deliberately undertaken, it lay halfway between the missions to foreign peoples and the evangelical impact of the ordinary *peregrinus pro Christo*. To see a fully fledged Frankish missionary of the early seventh century in action, one must turn to Amandus.

## 7. AMANDUS

That Columbanus' disciples were coming increasingly to formulate a notion of mission to all peoples, and that that notion was steadily affecting hagiography might be deduced from what we know about Amandus, and about the *Lives* written about him. Nothing survives from the pen of Amandus himself, but careful detective work by Wolfgang Fritze came to the convincing conclusion that he brought together ideas of Columbanus, on the *peregrinatio pro Christo*, and Gregory the Great, particularly on the evangelisation of the English, to create a notion of mission to all nations.[111] That mission was central to his career is apparent from the hagiography which commemorates him. According to what was regarded until recently as the earliest *Life of Amandus*, the saint came from Aquitaine.[112] He joined a monastery on the Île de Yeu, before setting out first for Tours, then for Bourges and finally for Rome.[113] In Rome St Peter appeared to him, and sent him back to preach within Gaul. On his return he was forcibly consecrated as bishop, with missionary duties, albeit without a see, at the command of King Chlothar II, thus before 629.[114] This led to his work on the Scheldt, in which Jonas joined him, at some point in the 630s.[115] As bishop, he bought captives, placing them in monasteries, and they later became bishops and abbots[116] – the text does not say that they were trained to become missionaries, although in the light of what later missionaries were to do, this has been assumed to be the case. After recording a second visit to Rome,[117] the author of the *Vita Amandi* relates how the saint came across apostates in the region of Ghent, and on finding them too savage to preach to, he asked Bishop Aicharius of Noyon to secure permission from King Dagobert for forcible conversion. Even with permission to use force, he often encountered opposition from pagans, and was deserted by his companions. Living off the work of his own hands – a recurrent idea which looks back to the Epistles of St Paul (2 Thess. 3, 10) – he redeemed captives and baptised them.[118]

After this description of work among the pagans of the saint's own diocese, the hagiographer relates a tale of the revival of a hanged man,[119] followed by an account of the bishop baptising pagans, destroying temples and founding monasteries with the king's help.[120] Then, hearing that the Slavs across the Danube were pagan, he went to evangelise them, but gave up on discovering they were likely neither to listen to him nor to martyr him.[121] There may here be an echo of Columbanus' decision not to work among the Slavs, or, indeed, among the Bavarians. It appears that one reason for Amandus' attempt to work among the Slavs was a disagreement with the king, which Dagobert now patched up by asking the bishop to baptise his son in return for permission to preach where he wanted.[122] The king – perhaps no longer Dagobert – subsequently insisted that Amandus take on the see of Maastricht.[123] Thereafter the saint turned his mind to paganism among the Gascons, albeit without much success.[124] He then returned to Francia, founding monasteries at Elno and Nant.[125] Among the miracles recorded as taking place before the saint's death is one involving a blind pagan woman, who recovered her sight when she showed Amandus a tree that she had worshipped, and cut it down under his instructions.[126] The story has a parallel in a later confrontation between the Frisian missionary Liudger and a pagan ballad singer called Bernlef, who was cured after agreeing to do penance.[127]

There is in fact much in common between the account of evangelisation in the district of Ghent and the diocese of Maastricht and descriptions of later missions in Frisia and Saxony. It is unfortunate that we cannot date the earliest surviving version of the *Vita Amandi*, and thus trace its influence. Krusch, who was inclined, if anything, to underestimate the antiquity of texts, assigned the first *Life of Amandus* to the second half of the eighth century – not least because he thought he detected in it borrowings from Willibald's *Life of Boniface*.[128] It cannot be much later, since it was revised by Milo in the mid-ninth century. Others have been very much more willing to place the work earlier.[129] The discovery of a fragment of a yet earlier *Vita Amandi* seems, however, to have gone a long way towards vindicating Krusch's position, for it appears that one must now fit in this newly discovered text between the death of Amandus in *c.* 675 and what has hitherto been regarded as the first *Life of Amandus*, Krusch's *Vita Prima*.

The new fragment, which comes from an eighth-century manuscript in the Tiroler Landesmuseum Ferdinandeum in Innsbruck, is unfortunately not substantial enough for us to determine whether it was similar in its coverage to the earliest complete text that we have – since the fragment deals with little more than Amandus' failed mission to the Danubian Slavs.[130] What is apparent, however, is that the account of Amandus transcribed in the fourteenth-century *Speculum Sanctorale* of Bernard Gui[131] is closer to the earliest version of the *Life* than is Krusch's *Vita Prima*. Perhaps more interesting is the possibility that the fragment that we have belonged to a manuscript brought by the eighth-century bishop of Salzburg, Arno, who was also abbot of Amandus' monastery of Elno.[132] Arno was to play a major role in the development of mission in central Europe.

The chronological problems of the earliest complete *Vita Amandi* are important, because of the difficulty of finding supporting evidence for its account of mission. Thus, there is no evidence that forcible baptism was an issue in the last half-century of the Merovingian period, but if the *Life* were written in the later years of the eighth century, its account of Amandus asking the king for permission to baptise by force[133] would take on a very particular significance, since forcible conversion, if not forcible baptism, was very much a matter for debate in the late eighth-century Carolingian Church.[134] Over the more general question of royal interest in mission, however, the evidence for the involvement of Brunhild, Theuderic and Theudebert in the mission to England and, in Theudebert's case, in the Bregenz region, provides a plausible background to Amandus' activities. Further, Dagobert's promotion of mission in the Rhine delta is attested in a letter of Boniface, which refers to the king's gift of the *castellum* of Utrecht with its church to the bishop of Cologne, with the specific intention that the bishop should use it as a base for the evangelisation of the Frisians.[135]

Equally plausible within Merovingian tradition is the emphasis on Amandus as *peregrinus*,[136] which may well reflect the influence of Columbanus. Indeed, the very fact that the author of the *Vita Amandi* makes no reference to Columbanus or his *Life*, and that the saint's association with the Columbanian tradition has to be reconstructed from Jonas' comments, implies on the one hand that the depiction of Amandus as a *peregrinus pro Christo* reflects a genuine tradition, and on the other that it was not a tradition which derived from a literary source.

One element in the *Vita Amandi* which might seem anachronistic is the emphasis on St Peter's influence on the saint.[137] On the whole the Merovingian Church is not known for its association with Rome. Fortunately, however, Milo, in his expanded version of the *vita*, provided abundant evidence of contact with Pope Martin over the question of the Monothelete heresy.[138] The earliest surviving *Vita Amandi*, despite its probable eighth-century date, does, therefore, appear to be a text which provides a plausible image of a Merovingian missionary of the middle of the seventh century.

More important for the history of missionary hagiography, the so-called *Vita Prima* comes close to being a text in which the saint's activity as a missionary overrides his other work. If it is a text of the mid to late eighth century, it has contemporary parallels. The fragmentary nature of the earlier *Life*, on the other hand, leaves open the possibility that a hagiography which concentrated primarily on mission might have already been created for Amandus, perhaps in the late seventh century – and Amandus would not have been an inappropriate saint for such a hagiographical development.[139] Moreover, it may well be that the hagiography relating to Amandus did have some impact on subsequent saints' *Lives*. Although it has been argued that the *Vita Prima* of Amandus was influenced by Willibald's *Vita Bonifatii*,[140] it has also been suggested that it (though one might wish to say 'a' *Vita Amandi*) influenced Arbeo of Freising's *Passio Haimhrammi* as well as the *Passio Kiliani*.[141]

## 8. BEDE

While accounts of Amandus suggest that the possibility of constructing a hagiographical work around missionary activity was being grasped, and while hagiography relating to Amandus may have influenced other texts, the absence of any complete manuscript of the earliest *Life* suggests that it was not widely disseminated, and was, therefore, not hugely influential. The case is very different with the next text to concentrate on mission. Bede's *Ecclesiastical History* is, to a large extent, a history of mission, and although, strictly speaking, it is not a work of hagiography, it spends much time recounting the lives of saints, one after the other.

Having described Britain, and its conquest by the Romans, Bede turns to the legendary conversion of King Lucius.[142] He then recounts the establishment of the Wall, before dealing with Diocletian's persecution, and the martyrdom of Alban.[143] The ensuing picture of British Christianity is dominated by accounts of the various heresies that flourished, but a rather more optimistic note is also struck with the mission of Palladius to the Irish.[144] After dealing with the initial invasions by the Angles and Saxons, Bede inserts an account of Germanus of Auxerre's visits to Britain.[145] Then, following a very brief account of the collapse of the British, he embarks on a lengthy account of the mission of Augustine,[146] which is in many respects the successful counterpart to Germanus' initially successful, but ultimately fruitless, dealings with the British.[147]

Having dealt with the Christianisation of Kent, first by Augustine, and then, after a relapse, by his pupils, Laurentius and Mellitus,[148] Bede embarks on what can be read as a history of the Christianisation of the English kingdoms one by one. First there is Northumbria, with Lindsey as a pendant, initially through the agency of Paulinus and Edwin,[149] and subsequently, following the death of Edwin and a period of apostasy, through the work of Aidan and Oswald.[150] Bede then briefly casts his eye on the Christianisation of Wessex.[151] That of East Anglia, which had been interrupted by the supposed apostasy of Rædwald,[152] next attracts attention,[153] followed in quick succession by the Middle Angles,[154] East Saxons,[155] and Mercia,[156] although there was to be a brief period of apostasy among the East Saxons.[157] By the end of Book Three of the *Ecclesiastical History* most of England has been evangelised, but there are still the South Saxons[158] and the Isle of Wight[159] to be Christianised. Finally, having narrated the Christianisation of England, Bede casts his eyes further afield, and Book Five of the *Ecclesiastical History* actually extends the notion of the English Church to the continent: the chapters on Ecgbert and his pupils, and above all on Willibrord,[160] suggest that Bede himself thought that mission to the Frisians and Saxons was an integral part of the *Historia Ecclesiastica Gentis Anglorum*.

There is, of course, more to the *Ecclesiatical History* than Christianisation, but from the middle of Book One to the end of Book Three, it is the driving force of Bede's narrative. Perhaps more than any previous historian since Luke in the Acts of the Apostles, Bede set himself a task where the history that he wished to cover was, to a large extent, missionary history.

## 9. ECGBERT AND WILFRID

The idea that the English should work as missionaries on the continent was not Bede's invention. He himself relates that Ecgbert, an English ascetic resident in the monastery of Rathmelsigi in Ireland, wished to evangelise the continental *Germani*, whom he regarded as being relatives of the English[161] – thus the idea that the Anglo-Saxons should be responsible for the evangelisation of their continental cousins was already in existence in the 680s. It was to this idea that Ecgbert's pupils, Willibrord, Wihtbert,

Swithbert and the Hewalds, responded.[162] Behind both Ecgbert and Willibrord, however, there was a slightly older figure: Wilfrid. He had been the first Anglo-Saxon to work on the continent, by accident as it seems, when he landed in Frisia.[163] Moreover, he retained an interest in Frisia, visiting Willibrord on at least one occasion.[164] It is perhaps relevant to Willibrord's own work in Frisia that he had initially been a pupil of Wilfrid at Ripon.[165]

It would be dangerous to argue that Wilfrid was alone responsible for the interest of the English in evangelising their continental relatives. Ecgbert may have been influenced by him on this issue, but there is nothing to show that this was the case. Further, although Wilfrid did have contacts with Wessex, there is no evidence to link Boniface's subsequent espousal of the idea[166] to Wilfridian influence. One can get no further than saying that a notion of evangelising on the continent was current in England in the late seventh and early eighth centuries – exactly where it originated is unclear. Further, of those who set the idea down in writing, Bede was the most influential.

Of course, Stephanus in his *Life of Wilfrid* had already described his saint's activities in Frisia,[167] before Bede began the *Ecclesiastical History*. But the *Vita Wilfridi* is like earlier hagiography in that mission is treated in an occasional chapter in what is essentially the *Life* of a bishop. What Bede's *Ecclesiastical History* does is alter the balance: because the history of the English Church in the seventh century had indeed been a history of evangelisation, Christianisation was almost inevitably a major feature in Bede's narrative. By spending so long on Ecgbert and his pupils, however, Bede seems deliberately to have been emphasising the missionary aspect of his work, and indeed to have been opening up the notion that the continent was the next port of call for would-be missionaries.

## 10. THE IMPACT OF THE *HISTORIA ECCLESIASTICA*

Richard Fletcher has noted that 'Bede's *Ecclesiastical History* provided a model for the missionary work of the Carolingian Age.'[168] Bede certainly directed the interest of Englishmen to the continent. This point can, however, be pushed a little further in a slightly different direction. Bede showed that mission could become a dominant strand in a narrative. It may well be that in so doing he created a standard way of interpreting mission. In order to describe the Christianisation of the English kingdoms as a coherent whole, Bede turned the history of mission into a political narrative: missionaries go to kings, convert them, and they then Christianise their subjects: moreover, if they are powerful kings, they use Christianity to spread their hegemony, and force subordinate kings to convert.[169] The model of Christianisation is from the top downwards. Bede did not have the will – and scarcely had the space – to include in his picture a history of the influence of British Christian groups who survived the English conquest.[170] He therefore omits any indication of a less direct pattern of Christianisation than that involving kings, caused by constant contact between pagan and Christian communities – and thus he ignores any indications of Christianisation which was anything other than top-down. His is one reading of the material, and only one, although it has become the dominant one in modern historiography.

In his narrative Bede does, however, find room to pause to depict the early Christian missionary and ascetic communities of England. He shows Augustine and his followers at Canterbury living like the apostles of the Early Church.[171] He makes a similar point in the *Life of Cuthbert*, where he comments that 'in accordance with the example of the Fathers, he considered it more fitting to live by the labour of his own hands'.[172] It is an image that we have already met in the *Vita Amandi*,[173] and it was one that Bede borrowed from the earlier, anonymous *Life of Cuthbert*, which related that the saint 'laboured daily and gained his food by the work of his hands, knowing that it is said: "He that will not work, neither shall he eat"' (II Thessalonians, 3, 10).[174] In Bede's formulation, the idea became a *topos* for missionary communities.

The *Ecclesiastical History* did not lead immediately to the development of mission-dominated historical or hagiographical writing. In the next generation, Bede's work was apparently unknown to Willibald, the author of the earliest *Life of Boniface*,[175] who certainly does not appear to have been interested in the missionary message of the *Historia Ecclesiastica* – and one might note that Bede's *History* was not among the works sought from England by Boniface.[176] As we shall see, it seems to have been Alcuin – versifier of the *Historia Ecclesiastica*[177] – who was the first to respond to that message. Before considering Alcuin, however, it is necessary to consider the earliest traditions relating to the career of Boniface, even though this means delaying any treatment of Boniface's older contemporary, Willibrord.

## Notes

1. Price, 'The holy man and Christianisation from the apocryphal apostles to St. Stephen of Perm', p. 234.
2. Fletcher, *The Conversion of Europe: from Paganism to Christianity 371–1386 AD*, p. 234.
3. L. Bieler, *The Patrician Texts in the Book of Armagh* (Dublin, 1979), pp. 1–2.
4. I follow the unravelling of the text by Howlett, *The Book of Letters of Saint Patrick the Bishop*, pp. 116–21.
5. D. N. Dumville, 'The death date of St Patrick', in Dumville (ed.), *Saint Patrick, A.D. 493–1993*. Like Dumville, I prefer the later date.

6. Patrick, *Confessio* 1; also Patrick, *Epistola ad milites Corotici* 10.
7. Patrick, *Confessio* 9–12.
8. Patrick, *Confessio* 1–2.
9. Patrick, *Confessio* 16, 23. The identification of both the sea – which could be western from the British rather than the Irish point of view – and the forest is uncertain.
10. Patrick, *Confessio* 17–18.
11. Patrick, *Confessio* 19–20.
12. Patrick, *Confessio* 23.
13. See Howlett, *The Book of Letters of Saint Patrick the Bishop*, pp. 117–8.
14. Patrick, *Confessio* 48: Howlett, *The Book of Letters of Saint Patrick the Bishop*, p. 119 suggests a return when he was about thirty.
15. Patrick, *Epistola* 3.
16. Patrick, *Confessio* 21–2.
17. Patrick, Confessio 27.
18. Patrick, *Confessio* 32.
19. Patrick, *Epistola* 6; Howlett, *The Book of Letters of Saint Patrick the Bishop*, p. 118.
20. Patrick, *Confessio* 38–43, 47–52; *Epistola* 6, 12.
21. Patrick, *Confessio* 32.
22. Patrick, *Confessio* 27.
23. Patrick, *Confessio* 10.
24. Patrick, *Confessio* 37.
25. Patrick, *Confessio* 10.
26. On the revival of autobiography in the eleventh century, C. Morris, *The Discovery of the Individual 1050–1200*, reprinted (Toronto, 1987), pp. 79–86.
27. M. Herbert, *Iona, Kells and Derry* (Oxford, 1988), pp. 53–4, 193.
28. Compare Tírechán, ed. Bieler, *The Patrician Texts in the Book of Armagh*, pp. 122–67, with the *Conversio Bagoariorum et Carantanorum*. See below, Chapter 8.
29. Charles-Edwards, 'Palladius, Prosper and Leo the Great: mission and primatial authority', pp. 1–12.
30. Sulpicius Severus, *Vita Martini* 12–15, ed. J. Fontaine, *Sulpice Sévère, Vie de Saint Martin*, Sources Chrétiennes 133–5 (Paris, 1967–9).
31. C. Stancliffe, 'From town to country: the Christianisation of the Touraine 370–600', *Studies in Church History* 16 (1979), pp. 43–59.
32. For the concerns of Sulpicius Severus, C. Stancliffe, *Saint Martin and his Hagiographer: History and Miracle in Sulpicius Severus* (Oxford, 1983).
33. See the comments in Price, 'The holy man and Christianisation from the apocryphal apostles to St. Stephen of Perm', pp. 219–21, 223–4, 237.
34. Sulpicius Severus, *Vita Martini* 12.
35. Sulpicius Severus, *Vita Martini* 13.
36. Sulpicius Severus, *Vita Martini* 14.
37. Sulpicius Severus, *Vita Martini* 15.
38. Alcuin, *Vita Willibrordi* 14. On Alcuin's and Willibald's indebtedness to Sulpicius Severus see the comments in Price, 'The holy man and Christianisation from the apocryphal apostles to St. Stephen of Perm', p. 221.
39. There is a useful survey of the relevant legends in E. Griffe, *La Gaule chrétienne à l'époque romaine*, vol. 1, 2nd edn., (Paris, 1964), pp. 104–15.
40. The text is edited in J. van der Straeten, 'Les actes des martyrs d'Aurélian en Bourgogne: le texte de Farfa', *Analecta Bollandiana* 79 (1961), pp. 447–68: there is a lengthy introduction in *id.*, 'Les actes des martyrs d'Aurélian en Bourgogne: étude littéraire',

*Analecta Bollandiana* 79 (1961), pp. 115–44. See also I. N. Wood, 'Cults, churches and conversion histories in the Auvergne and Burgundy 400–1000' (forthcoming).

41. van der Straeten, 'Les actes des martyrs d'Aurélian en Bourgogne: étude littéraire', pp. 135–43.

42. Gregory of Tours, *Liber in Gloria Martyrum* 50, ed. B. Krusch, MGH, SRM 1, 2 (Hanover, 1885); van der Straeten, 'Les actes des martyrs d'Aurélian en Bourgogne: étude littéraire', p. 128.

43. Gregory, *Decem Libri Historiarum* I 30; on this see Griffe, *La Gaule chrétienne à l'époque romaine*, vol. 1, pp. 111–5.

44. Gregory, *Decem Libri Historiarum* II 29–31.

45. Gregory, *Decem Libri Historiarum* VIII 15.

46. *Vita Aredii* 4, 45, ed. B. Krusch, MGH, SRM 3 (Hanover, 1896); on Aredius and paganism see Y. Hen, *Culture and Religion in Merovingian Gaul, AD 481–751* (Leiden, 1995), pp. 191–2.

47. Hen, *Culture and Religion in Merovingian Gaul, AD 481–751*, pp. 173–4.

48. Gregory, *Liber Vitae Patrum* VI 2, ed. B. Krusch, MGH, SRM 1, 2 (Hanover, 1885).

49. See the sceptical assessment by Hen, *Culture and Religion in Merovingian Gaul, AD 481–751*, pp. 154–206.

50. Columbanus, ep. 4, 5, ed. G S M Walker, *Sancti Columbani Opera* (Dublin, 1970). I have left out the name, which Walker reconstructed on very uncertain grounds.

51. Following Jonas, *Vita Columbani* I 4, he left Ireland in his 20th (or perhaps 30th) year [*vicensimum* is usually amended to *tricensimum*]; for the date of his arrival in Gaul, I. N. Wood, 'Jonas, the Merovingians, and Pope Honorius: *Diplomata* and the *Vita Columbani*', in A. C. Murray (ed.), *After Rome's Fall: Narrators and Sources of Early Medieval History* (Toronto, 1998), pp. 105–6. His stated age may be no more than a *topos*.

52. Jonas, *Vita Columbani* I 3, 4.

53. On the foundation of Luxeuil, Wood, 'Jonas, the Merovingians, and Pope Honorius: *Diplomata* and the *Vita Columbani*', pp. 102–10.

54. Jonas, *Vita Columbani* I 18–19.

55. Jonas, *Vita Columbani* I 27.

56. Jonas, *Vita Columbani* I 30.

57. C. Rohr, 'Hagiographie als historische Quelle: Ereignisgeschichte und Wunderberichte in der *Vita Columbani* des Ionas von Bobbio', *Mitteilungen des Instituts für Österreichische Geschichtsforschung* 103 (1995), p. 233.

58. I. N Wood, 'The *Vita Columbani* and Merovingian hagiography', *Peritia* 1 (1982), pp. 63–80.

59. Columbanus, epp. 1, 2, 5.

60. I. Müller, 'Die älteste Gallus-vita', *Zeitschrift für schweizerische Kirchengeschichte* 66 (1972), p. 249.

61. Wood, 'The *Vita Columbani* and Merovingian hagiography'; that Columbanus himself changed his ideas is, of course, possible.

62. Wood, 'Jonas, the Merovingians, and Pope Honorius: *Diplomata* and the *Vita Columbani*', p. 110; I. N. Wood, *The Merovingian Kingdoms 450–751* (London, 1994), pp. 194–7.

63. Jonas, *Vita Columbani* I 27: *Pollicitusque est Theudebertus se repperire intra suos terminos loca venusta et famuli Dei ad omni oportunitate congrua proximasque ad predicandum nationes undique haberi. Ad haec: 'Si', inquit vir Dei, 'pollicitationis tuae adminiculum preberis, et vademonio falsitatis noxa non opponeretur, quantisper se moraturum ac*

*probaturum, si in cordibus gentium vicinarum fidem serere valeat'. Dedit ergo rex optionem, quacumque in partem voluisset, experimento quereret locum, qui sibi et suis placuisset; inquisitumque locum, quem favor omnium reddebat laudabilem, intra Germaniae terminos, Reno tamen vicina, oppidum olim dirutum quem Bricantias nuncupabant.* For a commentary on this passage, Wood, 'Jonas, the Merovingians, and Pope Honorius: *Diplomata and the Vita Columbani'*, pp. 104–5.

64. Columbanus, ep. 4, 5.
65. Wood, 'The mission of Augustine of Canterbury to the English', pp. 6–8.
66. See especially *Vita Amandi*, ed. B. Krusch, MGH, SRM 5 (Hanover, 1910); also Wood, *The Merovingian Kingdoms, 450–751*, pp. 313–4; also Wolfram, *Die Geburt Mitteleuropas*, pp. 115–6; Wolfram, *Grenzen und Räume*, pp. 102–3. A further indication of mission in Dagobert's time may be found in the *Vita Richarii* 7, ed. B. Krusch, MGH, SRM 7 (Hanover, 1920).
67. Jonas, *Vita Columbani* I 27.
68. B. Krusch, *Ionae Vitae Sanctorum Columbani, Vedastis, Iohannis*, MGH, SRG (Hanover, 1905), pp. 295–6.
69. Jonas, *Vita Vedastis* 7.
70. Jonas, *Vita Columbani* I 27.
71. Wood, *The Merovingian Kingdoms, 450–751*, pp. 133–4.
72. Paul the Deacon, *Historia Langobardorum* IV 37, ed. G. Waitz, MGH, SRG (Hanover, 1878).
73. W. Fritze, *Untersuchungen zur frühslawischen und frühfränkischen Geschichte bis ins 7. Jahrhundert* (Frankfurt am Main, 1994), p. 82; W. Pohl, *Die Awaren. Ein Steppenvolk in Mitteleuropa* (Munich, 1988), pp. 238–40.
74. See A. Angenendt, *Monachi peregrini: Studien zu Pirmin und den monastischen Vorstellungen des frühen Mittelalters* (Munich, 1972).
75. *Passio Kiliani* 8–9; Arbeo, *Vita Corbiniani* 24. Compare the material listed in Wood, *The Merovingian Kingdoms, 450–751*, p. 73.
76. I. Müller, 'Die älteste Gallus-vita', pp. 209–49.
77. Jonas, *Vita Columbani* II 5
78. Jonas, *Vita Columbani* II 9.
79. Jonas, *Vita Columbani* II 23.
80. Jonas, *Vita Columbani*, ep. to Waldebert and Bobolenus.
81. Rohr, 'Hagiographie als historische Quelle: Ereignisgeschichte und Wunderberichte in der *Vita Columbani* des Ionas von Bobbio', pp. 229–64.
82. Jonas, *Vita Columbani* II 16 for a quotation from the Antiphonary of Bangor. For the relationship between Jonas' writing and monastic rules, see Wood, 'The *Vita Columbani* and Merovingian hagiography', pp. 67, 72–3.
83. Jonas, *Vita Columbani*, II 23; Wood, 'Jonas, the Merovingians, and Pope Honorius: *Diplomata and the Vita Columbani'*.
84. Jonas, *Vita Columbani* I 11.
85. Jonas, *Vita Columbani* I 17.
86. Jonas, *Vita Columbani* II 12.
87. Rohr, 'Hagiographie als historische Quelle: Ereignisgeschichte und Wunderberichte in der *Vita Columbani* des Ionas von Bobbio', p. 233.
88. Rohr, 'Hagiographie als historische Quelle: Ereignisgeschichte und Wunderberichte in der *Vita Columbani* des Ionas von Bobbio', pp. 243–4.
89. Jonas, *Vita Columbani* II 8.
90. Jonas, *Vita Columbani* II 9.

91. Jonas, *Vita Columbani* II 9–10.
92. Columbanus, ep. 5.
93. On changes, Wood, 'The *Vita Columbani* and Merovingian Hagiography', pp. 65–6.
94. On Rebais having a more accurate version of the foundation of Luxeuil, in *Vita Agili* I, 2–3 and II, 11, ed. J. Stilting, AASS, August 30th, vol. 6 (Paris, 1868); see also Wood, 'Jonas, the Merovingians, and Pope Honorius: *Diplomata* and the *Vita Columbani*', p. 106.
95. Rohr, 'Hagiographie als historische Quelle: Ereignisgeschichte und Wunderberichte in der *Vita Columbani* des Ionas von Bobbio', p. 253.
96. *Vita Agili*, III, 12–18.
97. Apart from numerous unacknowledged borrowings, see *Vita Agili*, II, 7, for a direct reference to Jonas' work.
98. Jonas, *Vita Columbani* II 8.
99. Jonas, *Vita Columbani*, *ep.*
100. Jonas, *Vita Columbani*, ep., II 7, 11, 21.
101. Bobolenus, *Vita Germani Grandivallensis* 6–9, ed. B. Krusch, MGH, SRM 5 (Hanover, 1910).
102. *Vita Balthildis* 7, ed. B. Krusch, MGH, SRM 2 (Hanover, 1888).
103. *Acta Aunemundi* 4–5, ed. P. F. Chifflet, AASS, Sept 28th, vol. 7 (Paris, 1867).
104. *Passio Leudegarii I*, 6, 12–14, ed. B. Krusch, MGH, SRM 5 (Hanover, 1910).
105. Wetti, *Vita Galli* 28.
106. On Gallus as a pupil of Columbanus, see Müller, 'Die älteste Gallus-vita'.
107. Wetti, *Vita Galli* 12; unfortunately the relevant passages of the *Vita Galli Vestustissima* have not survived, but it is fairly clear that Walahfrid – but not Wetti – was heavily dependent on the text: Müller, 'Die älteste Gallus-vita', p. 209.
108. *Vita Galli Vetustissima* 1.
109. Bede, *Historia Ecclesiastica* III 7; Fletcher, *The Conversion of Europe*, p. 161.
110. *Vita Eligii*, ed. B. Krusch, MGH, SRM 4 (Hanover, 1902). On the evidence of this text for Frankish paganism see Hen, *Culture and Religion in Merovingian Gaul, AD 451–751*, pp. 196–7.
111. W. H. Fritze, 'Universalis gentium confessio. Formeln, Träger und Wege universalmissionarischen Denkens im 7. Jahrhundert', *Frühmittelalterliche Studien* 3 (1969), pp. 78–130.
112. *Vita Amandi* 1.
113. *Vita Amandi* 4–6.
114. *Vita Amandi* 7–8. The best account remains E. de Moreau, *Saint Amand: apôtre de la Belgique et du Nord de la France* (Louvain, 1927): see p. 109.
115. *Vita Amandi* 18–19; Moreau, *Saint Amand*, pp. 113–5.
116. *Vita Amandi* 9.
117. *Vita Amandi* 10–12.
118. *Vita Amandi* 13.
119. *Vita Amandi* 14.
120. *Vita Amandi* 15.
121. *Vita Amandi* 16.
122. *Vita Amandi* 17.
123. *Vita Amandi* 18. Moreau, *Saint Amand*, p. 168, places this after Dagobert's death, although the hagiographer gives no hint as to which king was involved.
124. *Vita Amandi* 21.
125. *Vita Amandi* 22–3.

126. *Vita Amandi* 24.
127. Altfrid, *Vita Liudgeri* I 25.
128. On the use of Willibald's *Vita Bonifatii* 5 in *Vita Amandi* 7, see Krusch, MGH, SRM 5, p. 403.
129. Fletcher, *The Conversion of Europe*, p. 147; J. N. Hillgarth, *Christianity and Paganism, 350–750: the Conversion of Western Europe* (Philadelphia, 1986), p. 138; I. N. Wood, 'Forgery in Merovingian hagiography', in MGH Schriften 33, *Fälschungen im Mittelalter* 5 (Hanover, 1988), p. 369, n. 4.
130. J. Riedmann, 'Unbekannte frühkarolingische Handschriftenfragmente in der Bibliothek des Tiroler Landesmuseums Ferdinandeum', *Mitteilungen des Instituts für Österreichische Geschichtsforschung* 84 (1976), pp. 262–89; *id.*, 'Die ältesten Handschriftenfragmente in der Bibliothek des Museum Ferdinandeum', *Veröffentlichungen des Tiroler Landes-museums Ferdinandeum* 56 (1976), pp. 129–39. See also A. Verhulst and G. Declercq, 'L'action et le souvenir de saint Amand en Europe centrale. À propos de la découverte d'une *Vita Amandi antiqua*', in M. Van Uytfanghe and R. Demeulenaere, *Aevum inter Utrumque, Mélanges offerts à Gabriel Sanders* (Den Haag, 1991), pp. 503–26.
131. On the authorship, B. de Gaiffier, 'L'auteur de la Vie de S. Amand *BHL* 335', *Analecta Bollandiana* 97 (1979), p. 308. For the text of the *Vita Amandi* in the *Speculum Sanctorale*, see *Sancti Amandi episcopi vita ab auctore anonymo*, PL 87, cols. 1267–72.
132. Riedmann, 'Unbekannte frühkarolingische Handschriftenfragmente in der Bibliothek des Tiroler Landesmuseums Ferdinandeum', pp. 288–9.
133. *Vita Amandi* 13.
134. See below, Ch. 4.
135. Boniface, ep. 109.
136. W. Berschin, *Biographie und Epochenstil im lateinischen Mittelalter* II, *Merowingische Biographie Italien, Spanien und die Inseln im frühen Mittelalter*, Quellen und Unter-suchungen zur lateinischen Philologie des Mittelalters Band IX (Stuttgart, 1988), p. 50; though one should also note the significance of *monachi peregrini* in the eighth century, Angenendt, *Monachi peregrini*.
137. *Vita Amandi* 6–7, 12; Berschin, *Biographie und Epochenstil im lateinischen Mittelalter* II, *Merowingische Biographie Italien, Spanien und die Inseln im frühen Mittelalter*, p. 51.
138. Milo, *Vita Amandi* 1–2, ed. B. Krusch, MGH, SRM 5 (Hanover, 1910); Berschin, *Bio-graphie und Epochenstil im lateinischen Mittelalter* II, *Merowingische Biographie Italien, Spanien und die Inseln im frühen Mittelalter*, p. 51, citing the new edition of the letter by R. Riedinger, *Acta Conciliorum Oecumenicorum*, II 1, Concilium Lateranense a.649 celebratum (Berlin, 1984); Wood, *The Merovingian Kingdoms, 450–751*, pp. 245–6.
139. The anonymous *Vita Amandi* printed in PL 87, cols. 1267–72, does not entirely solve this problem. Although much of the text is concerned with mission, the saint seems to be interpreted (6, 13, 16) as a would-be martyr.
140. See n. 127 above.
141. T. Klüppel, 'Die Germania (750–950)', in G. Philippart ed., *Hagiographies*, 2, Corpus Christianorum (Turnhout, 1996), pp. 175, 177–8. If one accepts that the *Vita Prima* was influenced by Willibald, and that it in turn influenced Arbeo, this would provide a very precise and short period in which it was written (763/68–769/72). This may indicate a case for seeing Arbeo as being influenced by the earliest *Life* of Amandus, which is only represented by the Innsbruck fragments. Such a case might be sup-ported by the fishing incident in the PL 87 *Vita Amandi* (5) and in the survival of the hanged criminal (7), both of which can be paralleled in Arbeo's *Vita Corbiniani*. See Chapter 7 below.

142. Bede, *Historia Ecclesiastica* I 4.
143. Bede, *Historia Ecclesiastica* I 6–7.
144. Bede, *Historia Ecclesiastica* I 12.
145. Bede, *Historia Ecclesiastica* I 17–21.
146. Bede, *Historia Ecclesiastica* I 23–II 3.
147. For the parallels, I. N. Wood, 'Augustine and Aidan: bureaucrat and charismatic?', in C. de Dreuille (ed.), *L'Église et la mission au VIe siècle* (Paris, 2000), pp. 148–79.
148. Bede, *Historia Ecclesiastica* II 3–8.
149. Bede, *Historia Ecclesiastica* II 9–20.
150. Bede, *Historia Ecclesiastica* III 1–6.
151. Bede, *Historia Ecclesiastica* III 7.
152. Bede, *Historia Ecclesiastica* II 15.
153. Bede, *Historia Ecclesiastica* III 18.
154. Bede, *Historia Ecclesiastica* III 21.
155. Bede, *Historia Ecclesiastica* III 22.
156. Bede, *Historia Ecclesiastica* III 24.
157. Bede, *Historia Ecclesiastica* III 30.
158. Bede, *Historia Ecclesiastica* IV 13.
159. Bede, *Historia Ecclesiastica* IV 14 (16).
160. Bede, *Historia Ecclesiastica* V 9–11.
161. Bede, *Historia Ecclesiastica* V 9.
162. Bede, *Historia Ecclesiastica* V 9–11.
163. Stephanus, *Vita Wilfridi* 26, ed. B. Colgrave, *The Life of Bishop Wilfrid by Eddius Stephanus* (Cambridge, 1927); Bede, *Historia Ecclesiastica* V 19.
164. Bede, *Historia Ecclesiastica* III 13.
165. Stephanus, *Vita Wilfridi* 26.
166. Boniface, ep. 46.
167. Stephanus, *Vita Wilfridi* 26.
168. Fletcher, *The Conversion of Europe*, p. 234. See also M. B. Parkes, *The Scriptorium of Wearmouth-Jarrow*, Jarrow Lecture 1982, pp. 15–16.
169. See, for example, Angenendt, 'The conversion of the Anglo-Saxons considered against the background of the early medieval mission'; also Higham, *The Convert Kings*.
170. See, for example, Sims-Williams, *Religion and Literature in Western England, 600–800*, pp. 79–83.
171. Bede, *Historia Ecclesiastica* I 26.
172. Bede, *Vita Cuthberti* 19, ed. B. Colgrave, *Two Lives of Saint Cuthbert* (Cambridge, 1940).
173. *Vita Amandi* 13.
174. Anon., *Vita Cuthberti* III 5, ed. B. Colgrave, *Two Lives of Saint Cuthbert* (Cambridge, 1940).
175. Levison, ed., *Vitae sancti Bonifatii*, p. xi, does not list Bede among Willibald's sources, although he does cite Bedan parallels on p. 5, n.1 and p. 16, n.1. Hygeburg, also, seems not to have known the *Ecclesiastical History*, but may have read other of Bede's works: Hygeburg, *Vitae Willibaldi et Wynnebaldi*, ed. O. Holder-Egger, MGH, SS 15, 1 (Hanover, 1887), p. 97, nn. 4–5.
176. Boniface, epp. 75, 76, 91.
177. Alcuin's *Versus de patribus, regibus et sanctis Euboricensis Ecclesiae* is largely a poetic version of Bede's work: P. Godman (ed.), *Alcuin, The Bishops, Kings and Saints of York* (Oxford, 1982).

## 'MISSIONARY' *VITAE* OF THE EIGHTH AND NINTH CENTURIES

| Saint | Author | Date | Place |
|---|---|---|---|
| Boniface | Willibald | 763–68 | Mainz |
| | 'Radbod' | pre 849? | Utrecht? |
| Wynnebald | Hygeburg | post 763–8 | Heidenheim |
| Willibald | Hygeburg | pre 786 | Heidenheim |
| Hrobert | – | mid/late c. 8 | Salzburg |
| Corbinian | Arbeo | circa 769 | Freising |
| Emmeram | Arbeo | 772 | Freising |
| Kilian | – | post 772 | Würzburg |
| Burghard | – | | Würzburg |
| Sturm | Eigil | 794–800 | Fulda |
| Willibrord | Alcuin | 796 | Tours for Echternach |
| Richarius | Alcuin | 800(–4) | Tours for Saint-Riquier |
| Vedast | Alcuin | 800–4 | Tours for Saint-Vaast |
| Gregory | Liudger | 786/800–804 | Utrecht? |
| Wulfram | Harduin? | 796–807? | Saint-Wandrille |
| Leoba | Rudolf | 836 | Fulda |
| Wigbert | Lupus | 836 | Fulda? for Hersfeld |
| Sualo | Ermenrich | 839–42 | Ellwangen for Fulda |
| Liudger | Altfrid | 825–49 | Münster |
| Lebuin | – | post 825–49 | Münster/Werden? |
| | revised Hucbald | 918–36 | Saint-Amand |
| Willehad | – | 840–55 | Echternach |
| miracula | Anskar | 860–5 | Bremen |
| Anskar | Rimbert | 865–76 | Bremen for Corbie |
| Rimbert | – | post 888 | Nienheerse? |

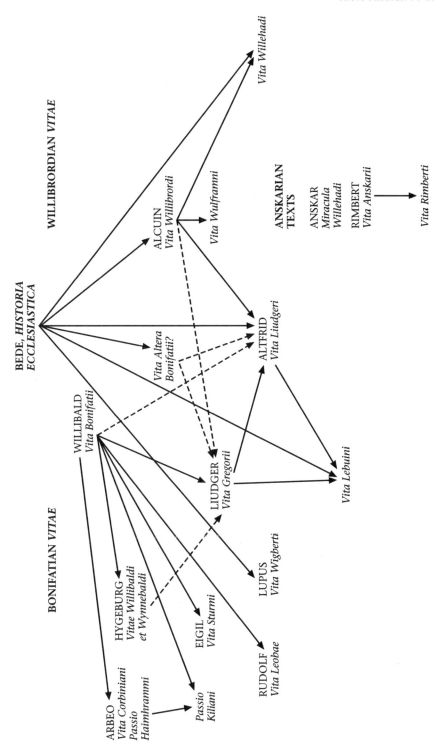

THE HAGIOGRAPHY OF MISSION IN THE EIGHTH AND NINTH CENTURIES

**BEDE, *HISTORIA ECCLESIASTICA***

**WILLIBRORDIAN VITAE**

**BONIFATIAN VITAE**

**ANSKARIAN TEXTS**

*Vita Willehadi*

ALCUIN
*Vita Willibrordi*

*Vita Wulframni*

ANSKAR
*Miracula Willehadi*

RIMBERT
*Vita Anskarii*

*Vita Rimberti*

*Vita Altera Bonifatii?*

ALTFRID
*Vita Liudgeri*

WILLIBALD
*Vita Bonifatii*

LIUDGER
*Vita Gregorii*

*Vita Lebuini*

ARBEO
*Vita Corbiniani*
*Passio Haimhrammi*

HYGEBURG
*Vitae Willibaldi et Wynnebaldi*

EIGIL
*Vita Sturmi*

LUPUS
*Vita Wigberti*

RUDOLF
*Vita Leobae*

*Passio Kiliani*

# PART 2

# THE ANGLO-SAXONS AND THEIR LEGACY

# Chapter 3

# BONIFACE, MAINZ AND FULDA

## 1. POLITICS AND CHRISTIANISATION IN THE EIGHTH CENTURY

The history of Christianisation east of the Rhine in the late seventh and eighth centuries is intimately tied up with the rise to power of the Pippinid (later to be the Carolingian) family.[1] Already in the Merovingian period the major peripheral duchies of Thuringia and Bavaria had been Christianised, even if the standards of the Church in those regions were not high. Eustasius of Luxeuil had sent missions to Bavaria, and the reign of Dagobert I (623–39) in particular had seen missionary activity, east of the Rhine. The king had even founded a mission station at Utrecht. Nevertheless, Frisia and Saxony had remained stubbornly pagan.

From the middle of the seventh century missionary activity seems to have fallen into abeyance, that is until *c*. 690, when a number of Anglo-Saxons, most notably Willibrord, established themselves as missionaries in the region of the lower Rhine. The successes and failures of Willibrord's Frisian mission were largely tied up with the relations of the Pippinids with Radbod, the pagan ruler of Frisia. From around 695, when he was defeated by Pippin II, until Pippin's death in 714, Radbod seems to have collaborated with the Austrasian Franks. Indeed, he married his daughter to Pippin's son.[2] The collaboration extended to the acceptance of missionaries, including Willibrord. Pippin's death, however, led to a political crisis, and the rejection of the missionaries, who were seen as agents of Radbod's new opponent, Charles Martel. The missionaries were not able to return until after Radbod himself had died, in 719. Thereafter, the Christianisation of Frisia went hand in hand with the expansion of Frankish power over the region, although the nature of the landscape – much of it islands in the tidal delta of the Rhine – made the work slow, and pockets of paganism remained. Boniface was to be martyred by Frisian pagans at Dokkum as late as 754, and even the next generation of missionaries – Lebuin, Willehad, Liudger – met with difficulties in the far north and east of Frisia.

In these regions it is difficult to draw a dividing line between Frisia and Saxony, and the Saxons continued to be both pagan and independent of the Franks. Indeed, their paganism seems to have bolstered their independence, and vice versa. Relations between Saxons and Franks had long been delicate: whenever possible the Franks had tried to reduce their warlike neighbours to tributary status, and the Saxons, for their part, tried to maintain their independence.[3] The presence of the Saxons on the borders of Francia, and the threats they posed, eventually drove Charlemagne to attempt all-out conquest – something which proved very much harder to achieve than he anticipated, and which took from 772 to 804 – although the main phase of the war ended with the submission and conversion of the Westfalian leader, Widukind, in 785. Hand in hand with conquest went mission, not least because Charlemagne thought that Christianity would help to break the independence of the Saxons. The very first campaign, in 772, witnessed the destruction of the great pagan sanctuary of the Irminsul.[4] On the whole, official missions in Saxony followed in the aftermath of Frankish victory, with the result that much of the missionary process was tied up, not with attempts to convert individual members of the aristocracy, but rather with the establishment of ecclesiastical organisation, from such centres as Bremen and Münster.

Although the chronology of the subjection of Frisia and Saxony is largely to be found in chronicles, the narratives of the careers of individual missionaries are provided by a whole host of saint's *Lives*. These *Lives*, however, were not written as works of history, but rather for a number of reasons, jurisdictional as well as ideological and spiritual. Thus, although we can glean evidence on which to reconstruct the career of a missionary from the hagiography, we have to come to terms first with the purposes of the texts themselves. In so doing we may also construct a history of changing views of mission and missionaries, which is every bit as important as a straightforward narrative – and which, indeed, can be set alongside that narrative, enhancing our understanding of the history of mission.

There is, however, a complicating factor: the earliest saint's *Life* of importance for an understanding of the development of missionary history in the eighth and ninth centuries is not concerned with the earliest missionary saint. It is necessary to begin not with Willibrord, but rather with Boniface, since Willibald's *Vita Bonifatii* lies at the head of a whole chain of saints' *Lives* which have become central to an understanding of mission: the history and interpretation of Willibrord will concern us in the next chapter.

## 2. BONIFACE

Boniface, the so-called 'apostle of Germany', towers across the history of mission as it is often represented. To him has been attributed the evangelisation of much of the land to the east of the Rhine: Hesse, Thuringia, even parts of Bavaria. This, indeed, was what he wished to achieve. Yet the image is deceptive, for he was less a missionary to the pagans than he himself had expected. Certainly, he went to the continent in 716 to be a missionary, and at the start and end of his continental career he worked among the pagans of Frisia. He also wished to evangelise the Saxons, because they were related to the English[5] – a point which had already been made by Willibrord's teacher, Ecgbert.[6] For a brief moment in 737 it looked as if the victories of Charles Martel would open up Saxony as a mission field, and Boniface lobbied his Anglo-Saxon contacts for support in the expected enterprise.[7] But in the event this came to nothing. As matters worked out, far more of Boniface's life was spent as a teacher, organiser and reformer of the Church, than in the mission field. He was, if we keep in mind the distinction between Christianisation and mission, always a Christianiser, but only occasionally a missionary. His career is well evidenced by his letters, and is plausibly, if partially, described by a group of saints' *Lives* written by and about his disciples. A rather different account, however, is also provided by other texts almost equally early in date, some of which come somewhat closer to presenting Boniface as the missionary of the popular imagination. For the moment we shall concentrate on those accounts which belong to the former group.

The picture to be gained from Boniface's letters, the canons of the Church councils with which he was involved, and the earliest *Life*, can be briefly sketched.[8] The man who was to be known as Boniface was born in Wessex, and was given the name Winfrith.[9] He became a monk at Exeter, and then moved to Nursling, where he was appointed *magister*, and had an apparently high reputation as a teacher: among his surviving works is a treatise on grammar.[10] In 716 he made his first, abortive, missionary trip to Frisia.[11] He returned to England, but in 718 set out for Rome to get permission from Pope Gregory II to preach in *Germania*. While in Rome in 719 he was given the name Bonifatius, and then, with papal backing, he went to Thuringia, before returning to Frisia, having heard of the death of the pagan ruler, Radbod. There he worked under the direction of Willibrord.[12] In 721, however, when Willibrord tried to appoint him as his successor in the see of Utrecht, he remembered his papal commission and moved back to *Germania*, and worked in Hesse. In 722 he returned to Rome, and was there consecrated missionary bishop, and was given letters of introduction to the leaders of the territories east of the Rhine, and especially to Charles Martel.[13]

On his return north he worked first in Hesse and then, further to the east, in Thuringia.[14] Within these areas he was, for the most part, organising a somewhat unstructured and sometimes heretical group of Christian churches, rather than preaching to the pagans, even though it was the pagans who were his avowed objective. He is, however, recorded as having one spectacular showdown with a backwoods pagan community, at Geismar, where he cut down a great oak tree associated with 'Jupiter'. Miraculously, the tree came down easily, dividing into four pieces as it fell.[15] This eye-catching story is not only unique in Willibald's account of Boniface's work in central Germany, it may also depend on an equivalent event in the *Vita Martini* of Sulpicius Severus.[16] It does not amount to representative evidence for Boniface's career east of the Rhine. Willibald's account is otherwise concerned rather with heresy and lapsed Christianity. A similar picture holds true for the saint's work in Bavaria, where, in 736, he embarked on reforming the Church at the behest of *dux* Odilo.[17] Meanwhile, Charles Martel was preparing for an invasion of Saxony, which opened up the prospects of a mission to the pagan Saxons – something which was dear to Boniface's heart: the most significant of his letters seeking English support for mission belong to this precise period.[18] In the event the opportunity passed, and Boniface set out for Rome again, being appointed papal legate by Pope Gregory III. He then returned to work in Bavaria, in 739.[19] The reactions to this period of his life will concern us when we turn to the hagiography produced in Salzburg and Freising.

Following the death of Charles Martel in 741, and the establishment of his sons, Pippin III and Carloman, in his place, Boniface turned his mind to reforming the Frankish Church – notably in a series of synods held between 742 and 744.[20] In the course of the reform a number of established clerics came under scrutiny, among them Bishop Gewilib of Mainz, who was removed from office in 745.[21] A year later, Boniface himself was appointed in his place: although he had held the position of missionary bishop since 722, he had not hitherto been the incumbent of a fixed diocese. Meanwhile, in 744 he had founded the monastery of Fulda, almost on the border of Thuringia and Hesse, appointing the Bavarian Sturm as abbot, and subsequently putting it under papal jurisdiction.[22] Fulda would be his most significant monastic foundation, not least because it came to be the burial place of Boniface himself. It was also to be a missionary centre, as we shall see, and a number of manuscripts associated with mission have been attributed to its scriptorium.[23] More important, in the long run, would be its intellectual achievements in the ninth century. Ultimately, having installed Lull as his successor at Mainz in 753, Boniface returned to Frisia to evangelise. He was martyred by armed pagans at or near Dokkum on 5 June 754, while preparing to confirm a group of recently baptised converts.[24] It is not clear whether the killers were pagan reactionaries or merely thieves. His body was subsequently taken to be buried, as he had wished, in the monastery of Fulda.[25]

## 3. WILLIBALD'S *VITA BONIFATII*

The picture just given is, to a large extent, a version of that provided by Boniface's first hagiographer, Willibald. About the author we know nothing other than what can be inferred from his *Life of Boniface*. To judge by his name he was an Anglo-Saxon: to judge by his Latin, which echoes the style of Aldhelm of Malmesbury,[26] he came, like Boniface, from Wessex. He appears, however, not to have been personally acquainted with Boniface. Given the number of disciples of Boniface still living in the 760s, his choice as biographer is curious. He was, nevertheless, commissioned to write the *Life* by Lull, Boniface's successor at Mainz from 754 to 785, and by Megingoz, Boniface's disciple who was bishop of Würzburg between 763 and 769.[27] It is Megingoz's episcopate which provides our best chronological indication for the composition of the *Vita Bonifatii*.

Lull is otherwise a more significant person for our purpose, since he provides us with some handle on Willibald's approach. As archbishop of Mainz, he was necessarily concerned with ecclesiastical organisation. While Mainz itself features rarely in the *vita*,[28] the organisation of the Church east of the Rhine, in Bavaria[29] and on its borders, at Eichstätt and Würzburg,[30] attracts attention. Willibald's interest in Church organisation may reflect the interests of Lull as well as the work of Boniface himself. Nevertheless, while mission to the pagans is not a dominant feature of the *Life*, there can be no doubt that it was an issue that interested Lull, since Charlemagne gave his monastic foundation of Hersfeld responsibility for part of the mission to Saxony.[31] The slightness of emphasis on mission in the *Vita Bonifatii* cannot, therefore, reflect a lack of interest in the subject on the part of the work's senior dedicatee.

Lull may have been influential in another way as well. On a number of occasions Willibald refers to letters of Boniface. Indeed, one might go so far as to say that, although he claims to have taken his information from Boniface's disciples, Lull and Megingoz included, the most important source for Willibald's *Vita Bonifatii* is Boniface's letters.[32] While it is impossible to talk of a single collection of these letters, since the manuscripts vary in their contents,[33] it is likely that the major repository for the letters themselves was Mainz, and that it was in the Mainz archive that Willibald was working.

Willibald's letter of dedication which fronts the *Vita Bonifatii* provides a fairly clear indication of his intentions.

> You have suggested that I write, following the model of those whose chaste lives and saintly manners have been turned into elegant words and put down on parchment by the holy fathers. Just so I will put down in writing an account of Boniface's life from the beginning through its midst up to its very end, as much as I know through investigation.[34]

He states that he follows Hegesippus, Eusebius of Caesarea and Gregory the Great. In addition he tells the reader, at the beginning of every chapter, what he is going to cover: saintly manners (*mores*); holy life-style (*conversatio*); pattern of contemplation (*forma contemplationis*); constancy, good deeds and religious routine (*religionis regimen*). These are for imitation.[35] The short scriptural epilogues appended to the end of each chapter are also indicative of the way Willibald wanted his work to be read. Significantly, these epilogues are taken exclusively from the Gospel according to St Matthew, the Gospel which more than any other emphasises mission, and from the Epistles of Paul, which might seem to indicate an apostolic interpretation of Boniface's life, even though the narrative itself scarcely supports any reading of the saint as being primarily a missionary.[36]

There are other tensions within Willibald's stated aims and also between his stated aims and his narrative. To begin with, for all the claim to follow earlier models, citations of previous hagiography are strikingly absent from Willibald's text. The hagiographer wants Boniface to appear as an apostle, directly comparable to Paul, rather than any saint of the Late Antique or early medieval Church. The miraculous, which is often thought of, albeit wrongly, as a *sine qua non* of early medieval hagiography, is almost, but not quite, absent. Despite the claims to have discussed Boniface's virtues, these virtues never really become a criterion for Willibald in organising his material. Further, for all the allusions to the apostle Paul, the hagiographer sticks closely enough to information in Boniface's letters to show that for the most part the martyr's career on the continent was devoted to improving standards and organising churches. The reference to the Church historians Hegesippus and Eusebius perhaps provides the best clue to the classification of Willibald's narrative,[37] which is closer to history than anything else. Ultimately, however, it seems necessary to conclude that the first *Vita Bonifatii* is a work of considerable originality, and that part of that originality stems from the fact that the author had done some real research, talking to Boniface's disciples and, more important, reading his letters. In this respect he is only a step away from the eighth-century author of the *Life of Desiderius of Cahors*,[38] who filled his *vita* with the saint's correspondence, and from the eleventh-century monk Otloh, who also transcribed whole letters in his version of the *Vita Bonifatii*.[39] Perhaps it was Willibald's abilities as a researcher which recommended him to Lull and Megingoz, over and above any disciple of Boniface.

Willibald's narrative is well based. That is not, of course, the same as saying that it is without bias. Boniface himself was an aligned participant in the affairs of his time. There is, not surprisingly, a pro-Carolingian bias in Willibald's work, visible in the dismissal, for instance, of the *duces* Theobald and Heden, who are held to be responsible for the lapse of Thuringia into semi-paganism:[40] a charge which can have nothing to do with the religious positions of the two individuals themselves, since Heden is a known early benefactor of Willibrord's foundation at Echternach.[41] Rather, the blame levelled at the *duces* of Thuringia reflects Carolingian hostility towards those rulers of the so-called peripheral duchies who did not support Charles Martel.[42] This policy of labelling opponents of the Carolingians as pagans or lukewarm Christians has been one of the major factors prompting modern historians to conclude that Boniface's work east of the Rhine was more concerned with evangelising pagans than was actually the case.

Bias of this sort cannot reasonably be blamed on Willibald – it is common in the early Carolingian world. Omission of material contained in Boniface's letters may, on the other hand, indicate choices made by his hagiographer. Willibald says nothing about Cologne,[43] which was where Boniface wished to be bishop, or about Boniface's conflict with Hildegar of Cologne over the Church in Frisia.[44] This was doubtless a battle which was no longer being fought in the 760s.[45] More puzzling, Willibald does not mention Popes Zacharias and Stephen,[46] both of whom had an infinitely higher profile in Carolingian politics than did Gregory II or III. Such omissions in the *Vita Bonifatii* may, however, be no more than a paring down of information to keep the narrative moving forward.

Willibald also has relatively little to say about Fulda.[47] In the light of his comparative silence over Mainz itself, or of Boniface's other monastic foundations of Amöneburg, Ohrdruf and Fritzlar,[48] one should beware of making too much of this: Willibald's account is not much interested in monasticism. On the other hand, the *Vita Bonifatii* was written at some point between 763 and 769, either during or immediately after the exile of Sturm, abbot of Fulda, which took place between 763 and 765.[49] As we shall see, the supposed conflict between Lull and Sturm, associated with this exile, may have been rather less significant than it was later thought to have been. Which is not to say that there is no relationship between Sturm's exile and the commissioning of the *Vita Bonifatii*. The date of composition must affect the work's meaning. If Willibald wrote before 765 he may have been concerned about the implications for Boniface's reputation of the supposed treason of Sturm, abbot of the martyr's beloved monastery. If he wrote after 765, Willibald may have been conscious of criticism of Lull's intervention at Fulda during Sturm's absence.[50] It may be significant here that Fulda was in the diocese of Würzburg, the diocese of the second dedicatee of the *Vita Bonifatii*, Megingoz – although, possessing a papal privilege,[51] it was not subject to the bishop. That the *Life* is in some ways a response to criticism may also be implied by the reference to Boniface's letters, which can reasonably be seen as a claim to authority. Nevertheless, Willibald's tone is relatively neutral, and indeed conciliatory. Even though Lull served as archdeacon of Mainz from 746,[52] and was his master's chosen successor,[53] Willibald makes little of his relationship to Boniface. If Willibald was in any way a propagandist for Lull, he was most discreet about the fact.

The first *Vita Bonifatii*, then, is a carefully researched work. Certainly, there are silences and biases, and the lack of any significant emphasis on Boniface as monastic founder can indeed be said to be unbalanced. The failure to make much of mission, however, does not seem to be a distortion of the reality of Boniface's career, however much the saint wished to be a missionary. Given Lull's own interest in mission, one might have expected Willibald to make more of Boniface's missionary activities. What little emphasis is placed on mission in the *Vita Bonifatii*, leaving aside the matter of the representation of the lukewarm Christianity of the leaders of Hesse and Thuringia, seems appropriate. Boniface had not been the great missionary figure of his dreams, nor was he represented as one by Willibald.

## 4. BONIFACE IN THE WORKS OF HYGEBURG OF HEIDENHEIM

Hygeburg of Heidenheim was an exact contemporary of Willibald. She was an Anglo-Saxon, and was related to the subjects of her hagiographical works,[54] two brothers, Willibald, bishop of Eichstätt, and not to be confused with the hagiographer, and Wynnebald, founder of the double monastery of Heidenheim. The latter died in 761, and his sister, Walburga, took over the running of the monastery, which Hygeburg joined. Sometime before the death of Willibald of Eichstätt in 786 she wrote his *vita*, otherwise known as the *Hodoeporicon*, which is largely an account of his travels, which included a visit to the Holy Land, and to this she appended her *Life of Wynnebald*. She seems to have had access to Willibald's *Vita Bonifatii*, despite the fact that it can only just have been written.[55]

The *Hodoeporicon* is a quite remarkable account, tracing the journeys of Willibald – which are presented as a prelude to his monastic formation at Montecassino and his episcopate at Eichstätt. Initially, he was accompanied by his brother, Wynnebald, and their unnamed father, but during the first journey to Rome the father died.[56] Wynnebald lacked the *Wanderlust* of his brother and returned to England, but later set out again, in the company of Willibald, for Rome, where he received a request from Boniface – whom Hygeburg here claims to have been a relative – to help, possibly in the proposed Saxon mission of 737/8.[57] On joining Boniface, however, he worked not in Saxony, but in Bavaria, with the support of *dux* Odilo.[58] He subsequently rejoined Boniface, and preached in the Mainz region,[59] until he decided that his vocation was to found the monastery of Heidenheim.[60] The site, in the Sualaveld, is described as being in the middle of forest, and the region was supposedly full of pagans, though this squares ill with the possibility that there was already a church there [61] – and it may be that the place-name (Heidenheim = the dwelling of pagans) is partly responsible for the picture. Even the detailed list of the evils of the area suggests not so much paganism, but a certain degree of syncretism, superstition and unorthodox practice, for Hygeburg talks of idolatory, omens, divination, fornication, together with marriage to the widow of one's brother and even clerical marriage.[62] This is not much different from the contents of a list of evils called the *Indiculus superstitionum et paganiarum* – a text closely associated with the Bonifatian reform council of 742 [63] – and it probably reflects the complex reality of many regions which are misleadingly labelled as pagan: it is, rather, a description of the normal, as opposed to ideal, state of Christianity, intermixed with some pockets of paganism. Wynnebald's missionary work was essentially the exercise of pastoral care in this context: *Non sicut mercenarius, sed sicut pastor perfectus acriis luporum mursibus circumeando obstabat*. He opposed the sharp bites of wolves, by travelling round, not like a mercenary, but like a perfect pastor.[64]

Willibald, who had set off for Montecassino when his brother went to join Boniface, was also summoned to work north of the Alps. He was appointed bishop of Eichstätt in 742.[65] Although Eichstätt and Heidenheim are not many miles apart, Hygeburg makes no mention of pagans when she describes Willibald's diocese, but she does say that the local landowners were initially troublesome.[66]

Boniface is, thus, a presence in the writings of Hygeburg, and he is responsible for calling both Wynnebald and Willibald to work in Bavaria. He is also depicted as being knowledgeable in the scriptures.[67] Yet, while being an *éminence grise*, he is scarcely depicted as the apostle of later tradition. Even his martyrdom is passed over discreetly: Hygeburg does report a three-week visit of Wynnebald to the tomb at Fulda[68] – a place which within weeks of the martyr's burial had become the focus for intense devotion, as can be seen from the monastery's charters.[69] Yet, overall, the position of Boniface in Hygeburg's writings is remarkably low-key when one considers that he was supposedly a relative of Wynnebald and Willibald, to whom the hagiographer was herself related. Moreover, while the *Hodoeporicon* was in part addressed to the clergy,[70] it was also intended for Willibald's sister, Walburga.[71] Although she went out of her way to present Wynnebald's work in the Heidenheim region as that of a missionary to pagans, Hygeburg did not depict Boniface as a great missionary figure, yet she had plenty of opportunity to do so had she wanted. In short, Hygeburg supports the impression given in Willibald's *Vita Bonifatii*, that Boniface was not thought of primarily as a missionary in the third quarter of the eighth century.

## 5. WIGBERT AND LUPUS OF FERRIÈRES

Before leaving the Anglo-Saxons who joined Boniface on the continent, it is useful to look forward to two texts of the ninth century, the *Life of Wigbert of Fritzlar*, written in 836 by Lupus of Ferrières,[72] and the *Life of Leoba*, written by Rudolf of Fulda at almost exactly the same time.[73] A third, nearly contemporary text also associated with Fulda, the *Vita Sualonis* of Ermenrich of Passau,[74] will concern us when we turn to the clergy who took offence at the work of the Byzantine missionary Methodius in Moravia.

Lupus of Ferrières, who was probably still a monk of Fulda at the time of writing,[75] set down an account of Wigbert of Fritzlar for the abbot and community of Hersfeld. Being a stylist, he compares his own work unfavourably to the writings of Sallust and Livy, and to those of Jerome and Ambrose. He also noted the infelicity of using Germanic names in a Latin work.[76] Lupus begins his work, like a number of other ninth-century hagiographers, with Bede. He recounts the coming of the Anglo-Saxons to Britain, before turning to Wigbert himself, whose nobility and education he emphasises.[77] He explains that Boniface came to hear of Wigbert and then goes out of his way to look forward to Boniface's martyrdom[78] – not surprising, in fact, since Lupus had been trained at Fulda, where the martyr had been buried.[79] Boniface summoned Wigbert, consecrating him priest and making him abbot of Fritzlar,[80] the foundation of which, in 732–3, gives some chronological indication of Wigbert's arrival.[81] Wigbert was not recruited for the Saxon mission, but rather to lead a monastic foundation: he may in any case have been of some age by the time of his arrival. His importance as a monastic figure was such that Boniface soon transferred him to the monastery of Ohrdruf.[82] Not long after, however, he fell ill, and wished to return to Fritzlar.[83] He died only a little while later,[84] and his death and its implications for Fritzlar are the subject of a letter written by Boniface, which has been dated to 746–7.[85]

Lupus follows up what he admits is a rather meagre account of Wigbert's career, based on limited evidence,[86] with an account of his relics and related miracles, a large number of which concern the removal of the saint's body for protection during a Saxon raid in 774,[87] and the subsequent translation of the saint, with the support of Lull, to Hersfeld.[88] Over half of Lupus' account, indeed, is concerned with events after Wigbert's death. This is scarcely surprising, given the audience of the *Life*: the community of Hersfeld – a community which was only founded after Wigbert's lifetime. Doubtless, the audience was happy to hear about the contacts between their saint and the martyr Boniface, and, doubtless, it was also happy in that Wigbert was a monastic figure of note. Although Hersfeld had been involved in mission in the late eighth century,[89] the community had no need of a missionary saint in the 830s – and, so far as we can see, Wigbert could not have fulfilled that need.[90]

## 6. RUDOLF OF FULDA'S *LIFE OF LEOBA*

The second of the *Lives* written in the mid-830s, Rudolf's *Life of Leoba*, was supposedly based on notes which were taken by a monk, Mago, who had been informed by four of Leoba's (female) disciples.[91] The literary influences in the text, however, are such as to make one treat it with considerable caution.[92]

Leoba, like the subjects of Hygeburg's writings, was a relative of Boniface – although this is a point which is set aside as insignificant by Rudolf.[93] The hagiographer's near-silence is the more noteworthy in that the familial tie is likely to have been a factor behind the depth of affection apparently shown by Boniface to Leoba, and in particular behind the martyr's concern that she should be buried next to him, within the precinct of the male monastery of Fulda.[94] Indeed, it is tempting to see in this concern a personal response to Leoba's plea, made before she even joined Boniface on the continent, that he should act as a brother to her since all her closer relatives were dead.[95] Rudolf wished to substitute affection for virtue for a recognition of the ties of kinship.

Like Wigbert, Wynnebald and Willibald, Leoba was one of the Anglo-Saxons deliberately sought out by Boniface. He specifically asked for her to become abbess of his foundation of Tauberbischofsheim, a request to which her own abbess, Tetta of Wimborne had to agree, although she was unhappy about it.[96] While Rudolf portrays Boniface's request as being geared towards providing support for his missionary work within Germany, it is clear from the *Life of Leoba* that what this actually meant was the establishment of an exemplary nunnery – and Tauberbischofsheim, lying as it does far to the south-east of Mainz, is scarcely on any pagan frontier. A nunnery could, of course, have supported mission, in terms of providing books for missionaries, and in praying for their success – but even if Tauberbischofsheim did this, there is no reason to think that the Christianisers in question were active in pagan territory. In any case, a nunnery was perfectly capable of adding to the in-depth Christianisation of a region, by providing a haven to which Christian families could send daughters. Leoba's role was to be like that of Wigbert at Fritzlar or Wynnebald and Walburga at Heidenheim – to strengthen monasticism in a world whose Christianity was relatively young and incompletely organised.

Rudolf, unlike Hygeburg, but like Lupus, does include a brief account of Boniface's martyrdom – not surprisingly, since the hagiographer was himself – again like Lupus – an inmate of Fulda.[97] More remarkable is the fact that he does so in the context of a description of the saint's last instructions to Lull, which included care for Leoba. Unlike Eigil, another albeit slightly earlier hagiographer from Fulda, who has nothing good to say of Boniface's successor in the see of Mainz, Rudolf is apparently well disposed to him.[98] Rudolf describes Leoba's visits to Boniface's tomb in some detail, perhaps because, as a woman having to enter the precincts of a male monastic community to perform her devotions, she presented very precise problems. Ruldolf gives greater prominence to Leoba's visits to Fulda than does Hygeburg to those of Wynnebald:[99] he may have thought the matter needed more careful treatment because the gender issue made the question more delicate. Gender is almost certain to have been a factor in the debates at Fulda over whether to bury Leoba in the same tomb as Boniface, although there may also have been genuine unease at opening the tomb of a martyr to add another body. Two years after the composition of the *Vita Leobae*, in other words in 838, the monks of Fulda were even to translate Leoba from the monastery to the church on the nearby Petersberg.[100]

Boniface has an unquestionably higher profile in Rudolf's work than he does in those of Hygeburg and Lupus. That Rudolf was, in certain respects, responding to new orthodoxies of the ninth century, particularly with regard to monasticism and gender, is more than likely,[101] though in many repects the overall impression of his portrait of Boniface is not dissimilar to that given by Hygeburg and Lupus. The saint was an *éminence grise* who encouraged monasticism as a force in the Christianisation of Germany, and he was a martyr. He was not, in this tradition, a major missionary figure himself. The same general impression may be derived from Eigil's *Life of Sturm*, written in the closing years of the eighth century – although some of Eigil's emphases are different, not least his interest in the saint's burial.

## 7. EIGIL, BONIFACE AND STURM

Sturm was born in Bavaria. There, to follow Eigil's narrative, he was discovered by Boniface, into whose hands his parents committed him. Boniface brought him back to Fritzlar, placing him in Wigbert's hands.[102] He has been identified, probably wrongly, with one of the recipients of the letter Boniface wrote after Wigbert's death:[103] if the letter is rightly dated to 746/7, he had left Fritzlar some time before, and was already abbot of Fulda. He initially left Fritzlar to become a hermit, with the permission of Boniface, living in a cell at the site of what was to become the monastery of Hersfeld.[104] Boniface, however, had doubts about the safety of the site, and sent Sturm off to find a better.[105] Ultimately, he chanced on the site of Fulda, higher up the same valley, which Boniface, being convinced that it was the right place, then secured from Carloman, who arranged that local landowners should also hand over their property for the foundation.[106] One may doubt whether they were as happy to do so as Eigil suggests. The monastery was established in 744. To ensure that its standards were of the highest, Sturm was sent to Italy and especially Montecassino, to observe and learn the best monastic practices.[107]

At this point Eigil inserts into his narrative an excursus which deals briefly with the death of Boniface and, at greater length, with what was clearly a major issue for Fulda, the martyr's burial – emphasising attempts by the people of Utrecht and Mainz, and especially Bishop Lull, to secure the body, despite the fact that the martyr himself had instructed that he should be buried at Fulda.[108] Whether Lull really did attempt to prevent the body leaving Mainz is an open question, to which we shall return. Eigil, however, presented Lull as a regular opponent of Sturm, being involved in the saint's exile, between 763 and 765 – an exile which probably had more to do with Pippin's suspicions of Sturm's Bavarian connections than with any plot to which Lull was party.[109] During Sturm's exile, Lull, according to Eigil, attempted to subordinate Fulda to the jurisdiction of Mainz.[110] Again, as we shall see, the picture is questionable. In all probability Lull intervened in Fulda simply because the monastery was temporarily without an abbot. As a result, he appointed Marcus in Sturm's place: but as an outsider Marcus was unpopular, and soon had to be replaced by the Fulda monk Prezzold, who led his community in prayers for Sturm's return.[111] Thereafter Pippin made peace with the abbot, reappointing him, and restoring the privileges of Pope Zacharias for Fulda.[112]

Sturm, according to Eigil, was now able to see to the wellbeing of his monastery,[113] but he also remained at the heart of Carolingian politics. After Charlemagne's succession in 768 he acted as an envoy to Bavaria, and he was also given a role to play in the Christianisation and establishment of an ecclesiastical structure for Saxony.[114] Charlemagne, however, was overoptimistic, and the missionary work of the 790s would soon be destroyed. Indeed, a Saxon band set out to attack Fulda itself, and Boniface's body had to be moved to safety – although, in the event, the invading troops were defeated.[115] Charlemagne was, nevertheless, determined to Christianise the Saxons, and resorted to the use of arms to do so. He summoned Sturm, but the abbot was already ill. He died in 779.[116]

Eigil wrote his *Life of Sturm* between 794 and 800.[117] He describes his work as being concerned with the childhood (*initia*) and life (*vita*) of Sturm and about the foundation (*primordia*) and legal difficulties (*causas*) of Fulda.[118] It is worth pausing over Eigil's words: this is to be the life of a monk and an abbot, as well as the early history of a monastery and its *causas*. The *causas* may reasonably be seen as including the attempt by the people of the Graffeld to prevent the foundation of Fulda,[119] but, even more obviously, they must relate to the banishment of Sturm, following accusations of treason, and the subsequent difficulties experienced in the monastery.[120] The legal aspects of the *Life* may be seen as mirrored in the literary strategy adopted by the author. Just as Willibald cited the letters of Boniface, Eigil referred to Pippinid charters.[121] The different source material reflects a different purpose in writing. The concern for land and possession may also explain the very careful naming of places thoughout the *Life*, but above all in those sections concerned with the discovery of the site in the forest of *Bochonia* where the monastery was to be founded.[122] The identification of Sturm's route is precise, not to say legalistic, and the description of the countryside apparently exact. The geographical precision of Eigil is very vivid, and thus adds an air of verisimilitude to his account. Yet its depiction of an unoccupied landscape – which, it should be said, has something in common with Hygeburg's comments on both Heidenheim and Eichstätt – is plainly fraudulent.[123] It may be too kind to see this as merely the depiction of a spiritual desert, although it is certainly that:[124] rather, by depicting the land as empty, Eigil could undermine the claims of those men and their descendents whose property rights were removed in the course of the foundation of Fulda.[125] Just as Willibald's literary strategy amounts to a claim to authority, so too does Eigil's geographical precision.

Within Eigil's narrative Boniface, who comes close to dominating the first half of the text, plays a number of very specific roles: he is the backer of Sturm, the founder of Fulda, and finally its greatest relic.[126] He first appears not in Frisia but in Noricum – in other words, Bavaria.[127] This is symbolic, since Bavaria was the homeland of Sturm – and indeed of Eigil[128] – and the place where the future abbot was offered to Boniface as a child oblate. On the whole, Eigil devotes little time to Boniface outside the strict confines of his own narrative. We meet him at Fritzlar, but largely because that is where Sturm goes to find his bishop.[129] After the foundation of Fulda we see him as a regular visitor to and benefactor of the monastery.[130] Eigil's Boniface is therefore Fulda's Boniface, and, as such, a useful addition to the portraits created in Mainz and – as we shall see – Utrecht. More precisely, perhaps, one should see the Boniface of the *Vita Sturmi* as a reply to Willibald's creation.

For Willibald Boniface was not really a monastic figure after he left England, despite his foundations of Amöneburg, Ohrdruf, Fritzlar, and Fulda, among others. Eigil plausibly presents a figure still committed to the monastic life. His emphasis on Boniface's love for Fulda can also be justified from the martyr's letters.[131] But for Eigil, Boniface's involvement in Fulda went further than mere affection. In the *Vita Sturmi* the bishop insisted that the site was foreordained.[132] Eigil was not the first Carolingian hagiographer to write of a monastic site as foreordained: Hygeburg had already said as much of Heidenheim.[133] In Eigil's narrative, however, the point has a subtext. The site of Fulda must be seen in direct contrast with that of Hersfeld, where Sturm originally settled, but which, following Eigil, Boniface did not regard as a divinely chosen site.[134] Hersfeld was subsequently the site of a monastery founded by Lull.[135] Hersfeld and Fulda were rival centres in the Saxon mission.

One might go further. The site of Hersfeld is the object not just of criticism, but more specifically of criticism made by Boniface in conversations.[136] Conversations between Boniface and Sturm are one of the structuring mechanisms of the first half of the *Vita Sturmi*.[137] While Willibald had appealed to Boniface's letters, Sturm was appealing to the spoken word of Boniface, and what he had to say against the suitability of Hersfeld was, by implication, critical of Lull.

Lull is the *bête noire* of the *Vita Sturmi*. Eigil reports a rumour that he was responsible for Sturm's exile.[138] During the period of exile he is said to have bribed Pippin to put Fulda under his jurisdiction, and his appointee as abbot, Marcus, was a disaster.[139] After his return to favour, Sturm had Fulda removed from Lull's *dominium*.[140] A final mark of Sturm's sanctity was his ability to forgive Lull on his deathbed.[141] At the very least this picture is a distortion of the facts. As even Eigil admitted, the accusations made against Sturm were made by three monks of Fulda.[142] In all probability they relate to the crisis in relations between the Carolingians and Bavaria in 763, and one should remember that Sturm, like Eigil, was a Bavarian.[143] Writing in the 790s, just after the fall of Tassilo of Bavaria, Eigil might have had good reason not to draw to attention any Bavarian dimension to Sturm's exile.[144] Whatever the cause of the exile, in the absence of an abbot, Lull as metropolitan of Mainz doubtless felt that he had to act. In so doing he apparently flouted Pope Zacharias' privilege for Fulda,[145] yet one should be careful about seeing Lull's action as a simple enfringement of the monastery's rights, since it was he who negotiated its papal privilege on Boniface's behalf.[146] Interestingly, Boniface stated his intention to be buried at Fulda in the very letter which Lull took to Zacharias.

Eigil describes the martyrdom of Boniface in very few words.[147] Instead, he concentrates on the return of the martyr's body to Fulda. Following his account, the monks of Utrecht went up to Dokkum and stole (*rapuerunt*) the bodies of Boniface and some of his companions. The companions they buried on their return, Boniface they placed in the small church of Utrecht, hoping for divine approval for their plan to keep the relics. They realised this was not forthcoming when they could not move the body, and so they sent it to Mainz. There a royal messenger announced it should stay, if it so wished. Sturm objected, on the grounds that the martyr had always wanted to be buried at Fulda. Lull's wishes to keep the body were overridden when a deacon had a vision of the irate Boniface asking why he had not been moved.[148]

Eigil's account needs to be compared with earlier narrations of Boniface's martyrdom and burial. According to Willibald, after the martyrdom of

71

Boniface, his body and those of the other martyrs were brought to Utrecht. It was there that the local prefect announced that, following the king's decree, the bodies should not be moved. Then follows one of the few miracles in Willibald's account: the bells of Utrecht rang out, and everyone realised that Boniface's body should not remain. It was therefore transferred to Mainz, where it arrived, by pure chance, at the same moment that Lull returned from Pippin's court. The body was then carried to Fulda.[149]

From this account Eigil seems to have borrowed the detail of a public announcement made by a secular official. Eigil is, thus, subverting Willibald's narrative[150] – and one of his intentions in so doing was to present Lull as a man who intended to flout Boniface's will by keeping his relics at Mainz. We cannot, however, conclude from the fact that Eigil distorts one of his sources, that Willibald provides an entirely accurate account of the return of Boniface's body from Dokkum to Mainz. The need for a miracle at Utrecht and the chance return of Lull to Mainz both invite suspicion. Perhaps adding to the suspicion, although certainly intended to allay it, is Willibald's very careful mention of the presence of Hadda, who was in the party sent to collect the martyr's body.[151] The reader is clearly meant to identify Hadda as providing Willibald with an eyewitness account. Nevertheless, in assessing the stance of the bishop of Mainz in all of this, the modern interpreter of these events must take into account the fact that Lull, as bearer of Boniface's letter to Zacharias in 751, knew very well where Boniface wished to be buried. All in all, one may reasonably question Eigil's account, even if one is suspicious of that of Willibald as well.[152] Precisely why Eigil was so determined to portray Lull as a villain, however, remains elusive. The solution is likely to relate as much to the 790s as to 754.[153] As we have seen, Rudolf of Fulda did not see Lull as Eigil had, even though he had opportunity to comment on Lull's involvement in the arrangements for Boniface's burial, had he wished to do so. Yet, whatever the differences between Eigil and Rudolf, the former's account of the martyrdom of Boniface was clearly popular enough at Fulda for the hagiographer to be elected abbot in place of the highly unpopular Ratgar – whose policies must have impinged in some way on Eigil's construction of the *Vita Sturmi*.

## 8. THE 'HEIRS' OF BONIFACE

The texts we have considered show the heirs of Boniface not as a group of like-minded individuals walking in the steps of the master, but as clerics and religious women taking very different stances for one reason or another. Clearly, there was rivalry over who should have Boniface's relics. Even if Lull made no move to keep the corpse in Mainz, there is unavoidable evidence of rivalry between Utrecht and Fulda over possession of the body – a subject to which we shall return. More generally, Fulda and Mainz were competing as heirs to the Bonifatian tradition – and we shall also see that Utrecht was involved in the same competition.

Nor was there a single Bonifatian tradition, but rather a varied inheritance that encompassed episcopal organisation, Church reform, monasticism and mission. Mainz was most concerned with Boniface as bishop: Fulda with the saint as monastic founder. In one sense the parties competing as heirs of Boniface were not competing for the same legacy. Not that that stopped the rivalry between Mainz and Fulda. Curiously, neither made extravagant claims about Boniface as missionary, although Fulda, in particular, had an interest in mission: it was to play an important part in mission to the Saxons, and seems to have been the place of origin of manuscripts containing vernacular conversion material.[154] Interest in different parts of the Bonifatian inheritance did, however, lead the hagiographers to use widely differing literary strategies: Willibald making a stance on genuine research, and Eigil appealing to legal documentation and to the private conversations of Boniface and Sturm.

In short, this corpus of texts points to different ways of exploiting the past, and all within a relatively confined tradition. As such, it is a reminder of the vast complexity of what is simply categorised as hagiography. It cannot be said that this transforms our impression of Boniface, although it may highlight the multifaceted nature of his career. Rather it sheds light on and raises questions about the next generation. For Boniface we are lucky because the documentation is full enough for it to be possible to be relatively sure about his career and character. Nevertheless, the conflicts within the Bonifatian tradition are a warning of the dangers inherent in reconstructing a career where there is only one source, and that hagiographical. As ever, a source tells us at least as much about its author and audience as about its subject matter.

What is clear, however, is that Boniface was not regarded by his immediate disciples as being primarily a missionary to the pagans – and their view does appear to be consistent with what is known of the saint's career. The transformation of Boniface from bishop, monastic founder and martyr, into apostle would take place a little later. Before considering when and why – and what it tells us about the development of mission – it is necessary to turn to Alcuin, and at the same time to look back to the career of another Anglo-Saxon, Boniface's older contemporary, Willibrord.

## Notes

1. For an account of the Merovingian period missions, Wood, *The Merovingian Kingdoms, 450–751*, pp. 304–21.
2. Wood, *The Merovingian Kingdoms, 450–751*, pp. 296–7.

3. Wood, *The Merovingian Kingdoms, 450–751*, pp. 160–4. R. Collins, *Charlemagne* (London, 1998), pp. 43–57.

4. *Annales Regni Francorum*, s.a. 772.

5. Boniface, ep. 46.

6. Bede, *Historica Ecclesiastica* V 9.

7. Boniface, epp. 46, 47; Hygeburg, *Vita Wynnebaldi* 4 probably refers to this same period; Hygeburg, *Vita Willibaldi* 5, refers to events a few years later.

8. The best account of Boniface is still that of T. Schieffer, *Winfrid-Bonifatius und die christliche Grunlegung Europas* (Freiburg, 1954) – although it will be clear that my own emphases are different from those of Schieffer. More recent, and finely judged, accounts can be found in T. Reuter, 'Saint Boniface and Europe', in T. Reuter (ed.), *The Greatest Englishman: Essays on St Boniface and the Church at Credition* (Exeter, 1980), pp. 71–94, and J. M. Wallace-Hadrill, *The Frankish Church* (Oxford, 1983), pp. 150–61. There is an extremely detailed chronological table in R. Buchner, *Briefe des Bonifatius: Willibalds Leben des Bonifatius* (Darmstadt, 1968), pp. 3–9.

9. Willibald, *Vita Bonifatii* 1.

10. Willibald, *Vita Bonifatii* 1–3; W. Levison, *England and the Continent in the Eighth Century* (Oxford, 1946), p. 71; Boniface, *Ars Grammatica*, ed. B. Löfstedt and G. J. Gebauer, Corpus Christianorum, Series Latinorum 133B (Turnhout, 1980).

11. Willibald, *Vita Bonifatii* 4.

12. Willibald, *Vita Bonifatii* 5: for the name change compare Boniface epp. 11–12; see Levison, *England and the Continent in the Eighth Century*, p. 72.

13. Willibald, *Vita Bonifatii* 6; Boniface, epp. 16–19, 21; ep. 20 to Charles Martel is a forgery, but see also ep. 22.

14. Willibald, *Vita Bonifatii* 6.

15. Willibald, *Vita Bonifatii* 6.

16. Sulpicius Severus, *Vita Martini* 13; Price, 'The Holy Man and Christianisation from the apocryphal apostles to St Stephen of Perm', pp. 221–4.

17. Willibald, *Vita Bonifatii* 7.

18. Boniface, epp. 46–7.

19. Boniface, ep. 45.

20. *Concilia Aevi Karolini*, ed. A. Weminghoff, MGH, Concilia 2 (Hanover, 1906–8).

21. Boniface, epp. 60, 87; Willibald, *Vita Bonifatii* 8.

22. Boniface, epp. 86, 89; Willibald, *Vita Bonifatii* 8; Eigil, *Vita Sturmi* 12–13, ed. P. Engelbert, *Die Vita Sturmi des Eigil von Fulda, literarkritisch-historische Untersuchung und Edition* (Marburg, 1968).

23. e.g. Cod. Vat. Pal. 577, which contains the *Indiculus Superstitionum et Paganiarum*.

24. Willibald, *Vita Bonifatii* 8; Boniface, ep. 111.

25. Willibald, *Vita Bonifatii* 8; Eigil, *Vita Sturmi* 15.

26. W. Berschin, *Karolingische Biographie 750–920 n. Chr.*, pp. 8–9.

27. Willibald, *Vita Bonifatii*, praef., ed. W. Levison, *Vitae sancti Bonifatii*.

28. Willibald, *Vita Bonifatii* 8.

29. Willibald, *Vita Bonifatii* 7.

30. Willibald, *Vita Bonifatii* 8.

31. H. Büttner, 'Mission und Kirchenorganisation des Frankenreiches bis zum Tode Karls des Großen', in W. Braunfels (ed.), *Karl der Große: Lebenswerk und Nachleben*, 1, *Persönlichkeit und Geschichte*, ed. H. Beumann, 3rd edn. (Düsseldorf, 1967), p. 474; P. Johanek, 'Der Ausbau der sächsischen Kirchenorganisation', in C. Stiegemann and M. Wemhoff (eds), *Kunst und Kultur der Karolingerzeit* (Mainz, 1999), Bd. 2, p. 497.

32. Willibald, *Vita Bonifatii* 5, 6.
33. See the introduction to Tangl's edition of the letters, *MGH, Epistolae Selectae* 1.
34. Willibald, *Vita Bonifatii*, praef, trans. T. Head, in T. F. X. Noble and T. Head, *Soldiers of Christ: Saints and Saint's Lives from Late Antiquity and the Early Middle Ages* (Philadelphia, 1995), p. 109.
35. Willibald, *Vita Bonifatii, praef*, 5.
36. Berschin, *Karolingische Biographie 750–920 n. Chr.*, p. 12.
37. Berschin, *Karolingische Biographie 750–920 n. Chr.*, p. 10.
38. *Vita Desiderii Cadurcensis*, ed. B. Krusch, MGH, SRM 4 (Hanover, 1902).
39. Otloh, *Vita Bonifatii*, ed. W. Levison, *Vitae sancti Bonifatii archiepiscopi Moguntini*, MGH, SRG 57 (Hanover, 1905).
40. Willibald, *Vita Bonifatii* 6.
41. *Liber Aureus Epternachensis*, 8, 26. The association of Theobald with a church inscription from Aschaffenburg is dismissed by Mordek, 'Die Hedenen als politische Kraft im austrasischen Frankenreich', p. 350.
42. Compare *Passio Kiliani* 14: the passage is discussed by Mordek, 'Die Hedenen als politische Kraft im austrasischen Frankenreich', pp. 346–8.
43. Berschin, *Karolingische Biographie 750–920 n. Chr.*, p. 13.
44. Boniface ep. 109.
45. For the relations of Cologne and Frisia in the 770s see Altfrid, *Vita Liudgeri* I 17.
46. Berschin, *Karolingische Biographie 750–920 n. Chr.*, p. 13.
47. Berschin, *Karolingische Biographie 750–920 n. Chr.*, p. 13.
48. Not to mention Kitzingen, Ochsenfurt and Tauberbischofsheim.
49. Eigil, *Vita Sturmi* 17/18, ed. P. Engelbert, *Die Vita Sturmi des Eigil von Fulda*.
50. Eigil, *Vita Sturmi* 18/17–19/18.
51. Boniface, ep. 89.
52. c.f. Boniface, ep. 85.
53. c.f. Boniface, ep. 93.
54. Hygeburg, *Vita Willibaldi*, prol.
55. For Hygeburg as a writer, Berschin, *Karolingische Biographie 750–920 n. Chr.*, pp. 18–27; for her dependence on Willibald's *Vita Bonifatii*, pp. 27, 61. See also Hygeburg, ed. O. Holder-Egger, p. 82, and idem p. 91, n. 4 for parallels between Hygeburg, *Vita Willibaldi* 3 and Willibald, *Vita Bonifatii* 4; p. 107, nn. 3, 4, for parallels between Hygeburg, *Vita Wynnebaldi* 2 and Willibald, *Vita Bonifatii* 3, 5; p. 11, n. 3 for parallels between Hygeburg, *Vita Wynnebaldi* 7 and Willibald, *Vita Bonifatii* 8.
56. Hygeburg, *Vita Willibaldi* 3; id., *Vita Wynnebaldi* 2.
57. Hygeburg, *Vita Wynnebaldi* 4; the date and the purpose are, however, only assumptions.
58. Hygeburg, *Vita Wynnebaldi* 5.
59. Hygeburg, *Vita Wynnebaldi* 6.
60. Hygeburg, *Vita Wynnebaldi* 7.
61. D. Parsons, 'Some churches of the Anglo-Saxon missionaries in southern Germany: a review of the evidence', *Early Medieval Europe* 8 (1999), pp. 40–1.
62. Hygeburg, *Vita Wynnebaldi* 7.
63. *Indiculus superstitionum et paganiarum*, ed. A. Dierkens, 'Superstitions, Christianisme et paganisme à la fin de l'époque mérovingienne', in H. Hasquin (ed.), *Magie, sorcellerie, parapsychologie* (Brussels, 1985), pp. 9–26.
64. Hygeburg, *Vita Wynnebaldi* 7.
65. Hygeburg, *Vita Willibaldi* 5; Parsons, 'Some churches of the Anglo-Saxon missionaries in southern Germany: a review of the evidence', pp. 39–40.

66. Hygeburg, *Vita Willibaldi* 6.
67. Hygeburg, *Vita Wynnebaldi* 4.
68. Hygeburg, *Vita Wynnebaldi* 8.
69. Already by 22 July 754 gifts to Fulda describe the monastery as *ubi ipse sanctus martyr sacro requiescit corpore*: *Urkundenbuch des Klosters Fulda* 1, ed. E. E. Stengel (Marburg, 1958), 24.
70. Hygeburg, *Vita Willibaldi*, prol.; S. Hollis, *Anglo-Saxon Women and the Church* (Woodbridge, 1992), p. 274.
71. Hygeburg, *Vita Willibaldi* 6.
72. ed. O. Holder-Egger, MGH SS 15, 1. On Lupus, Wallace-Hadrill, *The Frankish Church*, pp. 304–14; also T. F. X. Noble, 'Lupus of Ferrières in his Carolingian context', in A. C. Murray (ed.), *After Rome's Fall: Narrators and Sources of Early Medieval History* (Toronto, 1998), pp. 232–50.
73. ed. G. Waitz, MGH SS 15, 1, p. 118.
74. Ermenrich of Passau, *Sermo de vita Sualonis dicti Salo*, ed. O. Holder-Egger, MGH, SS 15, 1 (Hanover, 1887).
75. Klüppel, 'Die Germania (750–950)', pp. 173–4, 196.
76. Lupus, *Vita Wigberti*, pref. For Lupus' style, Berschin, *Karolingische Biographie 750–920 n. Chr.*, pp. 182–6.
77. Lupus, *Vita Wigberti* 1–2.
78. Lupus, *Vita Wigberti* 3.
79. Wallace-Hadrill, *The Frankish Church*, pp. 306–7.
80. Lupus, *Vita Wigberti* 5.
81. Schieffer, *Winfrid-Bonifatius*, p. 165. D. Parsons, 'Sites and monuments of the Anglo-Saxon mission in central Germany', *Archaeological Journal* 140 (1983), pp. 281–2, 285–6.
82. Lupus, *Vita Wigberti* 6.
83. Lupus, *Vita Wigberti* 7.
84. Lupus, *Vita Wigberti* 10.
85. Boniface, ep. 40. For the date, R. Buchner (ed.), *Briefe des Bonifatius: Willibalds Leben des Bonifatius* (Darmstadt, 1968), p. 120, n. 4.
86. Lupus, *Vita Wigberti*, pref.; Wallace-Hadrill, *The Frankish Church*, p. 312.
87. Lupus, *Vita Wigberti* 13–22.
88. Lupus, *Vita Wigberti* 24–5.
89. Büttner, 'Mission und Kirchenorganisation des Frankenreiches bis zum Tode Karls des Großen', p. 474.
90. Despite the comments of Wallace-Hadrill, *The Frankish Church*, p. 312.
91. Rudolf, *Vita Leobae*, prol.. See also Berschin, *Karolingische Biographie 750–920 n. Chr.*, pp. 260–2.
92. W. Levison, *England and the Continent in the Eighth Century*, p. 76, n. 2.
93. Rudolf, *Vita Leobae* 10; Hollis, *Anglo-Saxon Women and the Church*, p. 277, sees this as deliberately transcending kinship attachment – and that may well be what Rudolf himself intended to convey. See also Boniface, ep. 29.
94. Rudolf, *Vita Leobae* 17, 21; see the discussion of Hollis, *Anglo-Saxon Women and the Church*, pp. 283–8.
95. Boniface, ep. 29.
96. Rudolf, *Vita Leobae* 9–10.
97. Rudolf, *Vita Leobae* 17.
98. See also Rudolf, *Vita Leobae* 19.

99. Hygeburg, *Vita Wynnebaldi* 8.
100. Berschin, *Karolingische Biographie 750–920 n. Chr.*, p. 262.
101. Hollis, *Anglo-Saxon Women and the Church*, pp. 278–80, 285–6.
102. Eigil, *Vita Sturmi* 2.
103. Boniface, ep. 40.
104. Eigil, *Vita Sturmi* 4.
105. Eigil, *Vita Sturmi* 5.
106. Eigil, *Vita Sturmi* 5–12.
107. Eigil, *Vita Sturmi* 14.
108. Eigil, *Vita Sturmi* 15.
109. Eigil, *Vita Sturmi* 16.
110. Eigil, *Vita Sturmi* 17.
111. Eigil, *Vita Sturmi* 17.
112. Eigil, *Vita Sturmi* 18–19.
113. Eigil, *Vita Sturmi* 20.
114. Eigil, *Vita Sturmi* 22.
115. Eigil, *Vita Sturmi* 23.
116. Eigil, *Vita Sturmi* 24–5.
117. Berschin, *Karolingische Biographie 750–920 n. Chr.*, pp. 27, 62; for a discussion of the text, *ibid.*, pp. 33–41.
118. Eigil, *Vita Sturmi* prol.
119. Eigil, *Vita Sturmi* 11.
120. Eigil, *Vita Sturmi* 17–20.
121. Eigil, *Vita Sturmi* 12, 22; see also the language used in 13. It should be noted, however, that the impression of Fulda's landed base as given by Eigil is radically different from that to be had from the authentic early charters, which imply that the monastery was supported largely by donations from Mainz and Worms, with comparatively few grants being made by Carloman and Pippin. Land in the Graffeld itself is also notably absent.
122. Eigil, *Vita Sturmi* 4, 8, 9, 12.
123. P. Englebrecht, *Die Vita Sturmi des Eigil von Fulda*, pp. 85–6.
124. C. Wickham, 'European forests in the Early Middle Ages: landscape, and land clearance', *L'ambiente vegetale nell'alto medioevo*, Settimane di studio sull'alto medioevo 37 (Spoleto, 1990), pp. 483–4.
125. The first recorded charter conveying land in the Graffeld is dated 28 July 758, *Urkundenbuch des Klosters Fulda*, ed. Stengel, n. 32.
126. On Boniface as icon in the *Vita Sturmi*, Engelbrecht, *Die Vita Sturmi des Eigil von Fulda*, p. 33.
127. Eigil, *Vita Sturmi* 1.
128. Candidus, *Vita Eigilis* 1, ed. G. Waitz, MGH, SS 15, 1 (Hanover, 1887).
129. Eigil, *Vita Sturmi* 2, 6.
130. Eigil, *Vita Sturmi* 11–13.
131. Boniface, epp. 86, 87.
132. Eigil, *Vita Sturmi* 6, 9.
133. Hygeburg, *Vita Wynnebaldi* 7.
134. Eigil, *Vita Sturmi* 5.
135. Büttner, 'Mission und Kirchenorganisation des Frankenreiches bis zum Tode Karls des Großen', p. 474.
136. Eigil, *Vita Sturmi* 5, 6.

137. Engelbrecht, *Die Vita Sturmi des Eigil von Fulda*, p. 27.

138. Eigil, *Vita Sturmi* 17.

139. Eigil, *Vita Sturmi* 18.

140. Eigil, *Vita Sturmi* 20.

141. Eigil, *Vita Sturmi* 25.

142. Eigil, *Vita Sturmi* 17. It should be noted that conflict within the community of Fulda was almost endemic for the first century of the monastery's existence.

143. For the implications of the removal of Bavarian troops from Aquitaine by Tassilo, see Engelbrecht, *Die Vita Sturmi des Eigil von Fulda*, p. 102.

144. See now M. Becher, *Eid und Herrschaft. Untersuchungen zum Herrscherethos Karls des Großen* (Sigmaringen, 1993); also S. Airlie, 'Narratives of triumph and rituals of Submission: Charlemagne's mastering of Bavaria', *Transactions of the Royal Historical Society*, 6th series, 9 (1999), pp. 93–119.

145. Boniface, ep. 89: also *Urkundenbuch des Klosters Fulda*, 1, ed. Stengel, 15, pp. 25–32.

146. Boniface, ep. 86. Engelbrecht, *Die Vita Sturmi des Eigil von Fulda*, pp. 100–1 points out that the status of Fulda after Boniface's death was probably unclear. For a discussion of events see more generally Engelbrecht, *Die Vita Sturmi des Eigil von Fulda*, pp. 100–5. Lull's concern for Fulda during the years 763–5 may be seen in the purchases made on the monastery's behalf by the bishop in those years: *Urkundenbuch des Klosters Fulda*, 1, ed. Stengel, 40, 41, though it should be noted that these were purchases, not grants, made with Fulda's money, which may not have pleased the community.

147. Eigil, *Vita Sturmi* 15.

148. Eigil, *Vita Sturmi* 16.

149. Willibald, *Vita Bonifatii* 8.

150. For Eigil's dependence on Willibald, see Berschin, *Karolingische Biographie 750–920 n. Chr.*, p. 61.

151. Willibald, *Vita Bonifatii* 8.

152. Engelbrecht, *Die Vita Sturmi des Eigil von Fulda*, p. 98 points out that the *Vita IV Bonifatii*, a Mainz product, states that Lull wanted the body.

153. On the problems of following Eigil's own career in this period, Engelbrecht, *Die Vita Sturmi des Eigil von Fulda*, pp. 6–9. One can only lament the loss of the *Lives* of Baugulf and Ratgar.

154. Wallace-Hadrill, *The Frankish Church*, p. 379.

# Chapter 4

# ALCUIN AND ECHTERNACH

## 1. WILLIBRORD

Willibrord, of course, was Boniface's predecessor in the Frisian mission – though he received no *vita*, or rather none that survives,[1] until a generation after Willibald wrote the *Vita Bonifatii*. He did, however, attract the attention of Bede, who supplies us with the best account of the early years of the saint's career. Important details can be added from an entry, sometimes thought to have been written by Willibrord himself, in an ecclesiastical Calendar,[2] from the Echternach cartulary, which sheds light on the saint's own landholdings, particularly in Brabant,[3] and, in all probability, from a penitential recently ascribed to Willibrord. This remarkable text would certainly have been appropriate for work on either side of the Frisian frontier, dealing as it does with practices which are unquestionably non-Christian in origin, such as infanticide.[4] Assuming the attribution to be correct, the penitential implies that Willibrord had a very different view of the Christianising process from that to be found in the writings of Boniface – looking back as it does to the insular tradition of penance, and adopting a conciliatory attitude akin to that shown in Gregory the Great's revised instructions to Augustine.[5] Yet also, in its remarkably lenient attitude towards certain types of infanticide,[6] it prompts comparison with the stance taken at the Althing when the Icelanders accepted Christianity, but allowed the practice of child exposure to continue.[7]

Willibrord was born in Northumbria, the son of Wilgils, who had estates on Spurn Point.[8] The date of his birth, 657 or 658 can be inferred from later chronological indications. His mother gave him the name Willibrord,[9] and his father subsequently offered him to the monastery of Ripon,[10] but the saint left at the age of twenty to study under the Anglo-Saxon monk Ecgbert, who had established himself in Ireland, and he remained with him for twelve years.[11] In his thirty-third year he set off to work as a missionary in Frisia. His arrival can be dated to 690.[12] He went first to the Frankish *maior palatii*, Pippin II, who had recently annexed the southern part of Frisia, *Frisia citerior*,[13] but then travelled on to Rome to get permission to preach from Pope Sergius.[14] He returned to work in Frisia, but was sent to Rome once again in 795, and this time was consecrated bishop, and given the name of Clemens.[15] Pippin subsequently installed him in the diocese of Utrecht – a city which already had a missionary tradition in the second quarter of the seventh century, albeit one that had lapsed.[16] Not long after his return from Rome, in 698, Willibrord was given the estate of Echternach, near Trier, by Irmina, Pippin's mother-in-law.[17] There he established a monastery, which Pippin and his wife, Plectrudis, took into their protection some years later.[18] It was to be one of the great monasteries of the eighth century, not least because of its manuscript production, which illustrates graphically the fusion of Anglo-Saxon, Irish and Frankish culture associated with Willibrord's circle.[19] More prosaically, it provided a potential retreat for the bishop of a frontier diocese, with responsibility for mission among the pagans. From Utrecht Willibrord was able to work within the Frisian kingdom, with the acquiescence of the pagan king, Radbod,[20] not least because the king was related to Pippin by marriage, since his daughter, Theudesinda, married the *maior*'s son, Grimoald.[21]

This cosy setup changed dramatically in 714, when Grimoald was murdered, and Pippin died. The result was that Charles Martel, a son of Pippin by Alpaida and not Plectrudis, seized power, excluding Grimoald's young son, Theudoald.[22] Further, Willibrord, who had been very much a protégé of Plectrudis, decided to throw in his lot with Charles Martel.[23] Not surprisingly, Radbod instantly drove out the mission, since Willibrord had become the ally of the man who had effectively deprived his grandson of power among the Franks. This then was the situation at the time of Boniface's first coming to Frisia.[24] It was only the subsequent victories of Charles Martel over the Frisians and the death of Radbod which allowed the return of both Willibrord and Boniface.[25] Willibrord was by this time a good age, and he therefore asked Boniface to take over from him, but this request led Boniface to reconsider his own papal commission, and to leave for *Germania*. Willibrord himself was to survive until he was 81, dying in 739.

## 2. ALCUIN

It may have been a long time before the first surviving *Vita Willibrordi* was composed, but its author could not have had better credentials. He was a relative of Willibrord, and had indeed inherited Wilgils' chapel on Spurn Point.[26] He was also one of the leading intellectuals of the day. He had been master at the School of York,[27] before being induced to join Charlemagne's court in 781/2, where he remained, apart from two visits to Northumbria, for most of the next fourteen years. Although he clearly continued to have an input into royal policy, he left court to become abbot of St Martin's at Tours in 796,[28] and it was there, within months, that he wrote the *Vita*

*Willibrordi*, a twin work in prose and verse: the prose version to be read publicly, the verse to be contemplated in private.[29] The work's dedicatee was Beornrad, bishop from 785 and then archbishop of Sens from *c.* 792, and also abbot of Echternach from *c.* 775.[30] It is his death in 797 which provides the *terminus ante quem* for the *Vita Willibrordi*. Like Alcuin, and indeed like his own predecessor as abbot of Echternach, Aldbert, Beornrad was a relative of Willibrord.[31] Alcuin himself died in 804.

## 3. THE *VITA WILLIBRORDI* AND ITS AUDIENCE

Alcuin's *Vita Willibrordi* is a notoriously unsatisfactory text for the historian.[32] Despite the unquestionable importance of Willibrord himself, there is an extraordinary absence of detail in his *vita*: even the saint's episcopal seat, Utrecht, is mentioned by name only twice in the prose version of the *Life*,[33] and the same is true of his monastic foundation, Echternach.[34] Yet Alcuin could undoubtedly have written a better-informed account of Willibrord had he wanted to. He had, in his poem on the saints of the Church of York (*Versus de sanctis Euboricensis ecclesiae*), effectively versified Bede's *Historia Ecclesiastica*,[35] and had therefore not merely read, but even rewritten, the major narrative source for the first half of Willibrord's life available to modern historians.[36] He was also, as we have seen, a relative of his subject. Further, since Echternach was the inheritance of Willibrord's family, and since it was to the abbot of the monastery that Alcuin addressed the *Life* of his relative, he could surely have had access to family traditions and, indeed, to any traditions preserved at Echternach. The fact that he wrote a *Life* so lacking in historical detail must, therefore, be the result of a deliberate choice.

In order to understand what he was doing, it is as well to begin with the preface to the *Vita Willibrordi*, addressed to Beornrad.[37] Here Alcuin announces that Beornrad has commissioned him to write about the life (*vita*), habits (*mores*), and miracles (*miracula*) of Willibrord. In response to this he has written two volumes: a prose *Life* for the *fratres* – presumably the monks of Echternach – and a verse *Life*, for private contemplation by scholars in their cells (*cubicula*). He explains that he has added to the prose *Life* a homily for public preaching, and to the verse an elegy on Wilgils. The scheme is elaborate and deliberate, but the complete text, as envisaged by Alcuin, is unfortunately only to be found in Poncelet's edition for the *Acta Sanctorum*.[38]

Clearly, the *Vita Willibrordi* is, to some extent, a family work. It is about a relative, and it is addressed to a relative. Moreover, the family connection is made clear in the opening and closing chapters of the prose *Life*, the contents of which are resumed in the elegy which closes the verse *Life*. Wilgils, father of Willibrord, and relative of Beornrad and Alcuin, provides the outer borders and one of the hinges of this diptych. Yet, having acknowledged a family interest, at least for those who knew the relationships involved, Alcuin does not make much of that interest in the main body of his text. Indeed, despite the dedication to Beornrad, the envisaged audience of the *Vita Willibrordi* is the monks of Echternach, the *fratres*, who are to hear the prose *Life* in church, and Beornrad's *scolastici* who are to contemplate the verse text in their *cubicula*. The homily, which Beornrad might want to read to the general public, the *populus*, may seem to be intended for a different audience. The text itself, however, makes it clear that it is to be read at the tomb of Willibrord: the *populus* is no more than the people who could get access to the shrine of the saint on the anniversary of his death.[39] The initial audience of the *Vita Willibrordi* is, therefore, the community at Echternach – and one should remember that because Echternach was a family monastery, the founder's family were of considerable interest to the community. Whether this was the entire intended audience is a question to which we shall have to return.

The community were to hear the prose *Life* read out in church. What they would hear was not a historical narrative so much as a theological rendering of moments in Willibrord's history. This theological rendering, moreover, is not controlled primarily by the pattern of *vita, mores, miracula*, announced in the preface. Instead the text revolves around the statement which lies in the very centre of the work, and which opens Chapter 14:

> Although the ministry of evangelical preaching is to be preferred to all working of miracles and showing of signs, yet I think that the deeds which are told should not be kept silent, for the glory of God the giver, but rather should be written down, so that what is known to have happened in earlier times should not be lost to later centuries.[40]

This idea was central to Alcuin's thinking not only in the *Vita Willibrordi*, but also in his revision of the Merovingian *Vita Richarii*: there too, at a central moment in the text Alcuin announced that

> the office of preaching is doubtless greater than any showing of signs, but the perpetration of signs which divine clemency worked through him (Richarius) was not lacking on account of the opportunity of the times or the convenience of objects.[41]

In the prose *Vita Willibrordi* even more than the *Vita Richarii* the elevation of preaching over the miraculous comes in the physical centre of the text, and it is this theological statement which determines the structure of the first part of Alcuin's work. Preaching is, therefore, superior to wonder-working, although wonder-working is worth recording for the benefit of coming generations.

According to Alcuin's preface to the *Vita Willibrordi*, however, if we want to understand the full import of the work we should read not the prose, but the verse *Life*, which the scholars were meant to contemplate in private. Unfortunately, this text is at first sight even less useful than the prose *Life* to the modern historian. It has distinctly fewer details: Willibrord's career in Britain and Ireland is covered in a very few lines. Radbod and Ongendus are unnamed, and since Alcuin does name Pippin and Charles this cannot be because of a desire to avoid Germanic names in verse.[42] There are fewer miracles; indeed, the reader is cross-referred to the prose *Life* if he wants to learn about them.[43] Oddly, though, the verse *Life* does add Willibrord's age at the time of his death.[44]

There are other, more interesting, differences. The exclusion of any account of Wilgils at the start of the verse text, and the gathering of all the material on him into a final elegy, alters the balance of the work – Wilgils could be considered separately, within the context of the elegy, by the *scolastici*, but his history provided the opening and closing sections of the prose *vita* which was to be read to the brothers in church. More important, in both the prose and verse *Lives* Alcuin addresses the audience directly at specific moments, but the points of address are different. Alcuin uses the history of the deacon who stole from the church of Echternach to warn his audience of *fratres* against committing theft.[45] The *scolastici* apparently needed no such warning: instead, the verse *Life* includes an address in the context of a description of the sweet smell of the saint's tomb.[46] In general, however, it is not through new material, but through greater selectivity that Alcuin highlights his concerns in the verse *Life*. Despite Alcuin's injunction that we should read the *vita metrica* to understand his intentions in full, the major concerns of both texts are, not surprisingly, the same.

## 4. PREACHING AND MIRACLES

Both versions of the *Vita Willibrordi* are concerned to present Willibrord as a preacher, a *praedicator*, sponsored by Pippin II and subsequently by Charles Martel.[47] So too is the homily appended to the prose *Life*.[48] This concept of the preacher is, in fact, central to Alcuin's work. It can be seen in his other hagiographical writings. His version of the *Vita Vedasti* begins with a disquisition on preaching which has no counterpart in the original version of the *Life*, written a hundred and fifty years earlier by Jonas of Bobbio.[49] Later, Alcuin is at pains to show that Vedast explained the faith before administering baptism.[50] Vedast, like Willibord, was to be portrayed as a model preacher. The same holds for Richarius. While the original Merovingian version of his *Life* does portray Richarius as a preacher, time and again Alcuin strengthens or adds to the portrayal.[51]

Alcuin's letters frequently deal with the importance of preaching. In particular, in a group of letters addressed to Charlemagne,[52] the treasurer,

Megenfrid,[53] and Archbishop Arno of Salzburg,[54] Alcuin explained the need to begin with the simplest of ideas, milk to the young, and only gradually to introduce ideas of greater complexity. Writing to Charlemagne, he supports his point by citing Augustine's *De catechizandis rudibus*. Baptism had to be preceded by extensive education: the need for preaching to precede baptism is set out in the *Vita Vedasti*[55] and the letter to Arno[56] in very similar terms.[57] Although the idea is a commonplace – preaching and baptism are juxta-posed, for instance, in Eigil's *Vita Sturmi*[58] – it is clear that Alcuin was concerned that the Christian message should be understood before anyone accepted baptism. By implication he denied the validity of the clause in the *Capitulatio de partibus Saxoniae* of 782 which required everyone to undergo baptism, apparently with no consideration of their faith.[59]

Alcuin's concern about adequate instruction is part of a larger vision of pastoral care. Even in his letters he cites Gregory the Great's manual on a number of occasions.[60] He was bothered about episcopal negligence.[61] Of more regular concern was the fact that preachers could become predators.[62] Yet more specifically he was concerned about the way in which the levying of tithes became an impediment to faith.[63] Again he is not the only writer at the time to express such ideas. We have already seen Hygeburg describe Wynnebald as a perfect pastor and not a mercenary.[64] The problem would long continue.[65]

Although preaching is clearly Alcuin's prime concern in the *Vita Willibrordi*, he does devote the second half of each version of the *Life* to the miraculous. The first miracle describes how the guardian of a pagan shrine on the island of Walcheren tried to kill him, but was unable to.[66] The remainder of the anecdotes are concerned with the effect of the miraculous within the Chris-tian community, both at large and within a community of nuns[67] – the stories themselves are not difficult to parallel from the stock of Biblical and hagiographical wonders. Nevertheless, it is clear from his division of the work that Alcuin thought the miraculous to be an issue of significance. Alcuin's discussion of miracles certainly points to divine intervention supporting the activities of the holy man. On Walcheren, for instance, Willibrord refused to allow his companions to lynch the custodian of the shrine who had attacked him. He had no need because God killed the sinner three days later.[68] The saint's intervention preventing bloodshed is not present in what may have been Alcuin's source for the miracle, Sulpicius Severus' *Vita Martini*.[69] The author's intended moral is made with absolute clarity in the verse *Life*:

*Sic suos sanctos Christus ulciscitur ultro.*
[Thus too Christ avenges his saints.]

The miraculous thus illustrates the Biblical epigram, 'Vengeance is mine; I will repay, saith the Lord' (Romans 12, 19) – a passage that Alcuin himself quotes.[70] In the course of mission the Christian should not resort to violence: that should be left to God.

## 5. 796

Many of the ideas set out in the *Vita Willibrordi* recur regularly, as we have seen, in his writings, but they have particular resonance in the year 796 – in other words, at almost exactly the time at which the *Life of Willibrord* was written. That was the year in which the Avar kingdom, centred on the plains of Hungary, collapsed, and the ruler of the Avars gave himself up and was converted.[71] Suddenly, a completely new mission field had opened up. The possibilities were discussed at a synod held on the Danube.[72] Alcuin had already written to Paulinus, patriarch of Aquileia, about his hopes for evangelisation,[73] and now he wrote to Charlemagne,[74] his chamberlain, Meginfrid,[75] and three times to Arno, archbishop of Salzburg.[76] He wanted to ensure a sensible policy of mission once the Avars had been truly subjected,[77] and he effectively provided Arno with a missionary handbook for the purpose.[78]

Alcuin did not, however, criticise the use of force in the initial subjection of a people. He understood that, after Willibrord's initial failures at the courts of Radbod and Ongendus, the subjection of the whole of Frisia to the saint's ecclesiastical jurisdiction was dependent on Charles Martel's conquest of the region. Indeed, he rather oversimplified the process in remarking

*et gens tota simul Fresonum subditur illi.*
[And the whole people of the Frisians was subjected to him at the same time.][79]

Even in 796 he did not question the association of soldiers and missionaries, when he wrote to Arno about the Avar mission.[80] Alcuin accepted the premise of the military subjugation of the Saxons and the Avars, but saw that as something to be built on peacefully, and not by force.[81] However wicked the Saxons might be, and Alcuin was every bit as aggravated by recalcitrant Saxons[82] as was Eigil,[83] Christianisation could only be effected by a full process of preaching. If any physical violence was needed it should be left to God, who could be relied on – following the *Vita Willibrordi* – to protect his saints. Nevertheless, it should be noted that he did not consistently criticise the use of threats: although he suggested that Charlemagne might back-pedal on their use against the Saxons in 799,[84] he had offered no criticism of the king's method of Christianising the Frisians and Saxons, *alios praemiis et alios minis* – [some by rewards and some by threats], when he wrote to Colcus in 790.[85]

Consideration of a possible Avar mission led Alcuin to think historically. He was only too aware of missions that had gone wrong, not least missions to the Saxons. Back in 775 it had been assumed that, with the submission of the East and Westfalians and the Angrarians, Christianisation would result shortly thereafter.[86] Despite a rebellion, renewed submission and mass baptism in the following year[87] prompted the composition of an epic poem *De conversione Saxonum*, which depicted Charlemagne as enforcing Christianity on the Saxons.[88] Nevertheless, there was a further uprising in 778, which provoked Frankish retaliation in the two following years.[89] Carolingian success was such in 780 that mass baptisms,[90] church building,[91] and church organisation[92] were all recorded. Subsequently, perhaps in 782, Charlemagne issued his first Saxon capitulary, the *Capitulatio de partibus Saxoniae*, which supported the enforcement of Christianity with considerable legal brutality. Among the requirements of a good Christian was regular payment of the tithe.[93] This legislation seems to have led almost immediately to the rebellion of the Westfalian leader, Widukind,[94] but in 785 he was forced to capitulate and accept baptism,[95] and the Christianisation of Saxony recommenced in earnest, as Alcuin himself recorded in letters of 789 and 790.[96] Even this, however, was not to go unchallenged. Yet another Saxon rebellion took place in either 792 or 793,[97] and Charlemagne had to direct armies to the region every year between 794 and 799, and thereafter in 802 and 804.[98] It is no wonder that Alcuin, as he considered the possibilities of mission among the Avars, stopped to think about the mistakes that had been made in Saxony.

One of the mistakes he singled out for particular comment: writing to Arno he stated plainly that tithes had actually been a stumbling block in the Christianisation of Saxony,[99] and he repeated the point in letters to Charlemagne, both in 796 and 799.[100] It was necessary first to preach, then to baptise, and only once a man was of firm faith to submit him to the imposition of the tithe. Alcuin's 796 letter to Charlemagne reads like a remarkably public statement, intended perhaps for the ears of the whole court.[101] It is possible that Alcuin had some effect. Charlemagne's second Saxon capitulary, the *Capitulare Saxonicum* of 797,[102] is markedly milder than the first, although it is not clear that it rescinded it. Alcuin himself seems to have seen the new policy as an improvement, for his letters of 799 denounce Saxon obstinacy rather than Frankish missionary policy.[103]

## 6. ALCUIN AND BONIFACE

While Alcuin contemplated previous missions, it is almost inconceivable that he did not stop to think about Boniface. It might be argued that he knew nothing of the hagiography written in the second half of the eighth century. Certainly, there are few if any verbal parallels of significance between the *Vita Willibrordi* and Willibald's *Vita Bonifatii*.[104] On the other hand, as someone who visited Fulda at least once, and who was to be concerned with the relation between Abbot Baugulf and his monks in the years 801–2,[105] it is unlikely that he knew nothing of the Bonifatian traditions of that monastery. Moreover, there are hints in the *Vita Willibrordi* that Alcuin was concerned to deny the importance of certain types of mission associated with Boniface himself. Thus in the homily appended to the prose *Life of Willibrord* he described the Northumbrian saint as one *quem Deus ob multorum servavit salutem, quatenus majori praedicationis gloria honoraretur, quam si solus martyrio coronaretur* [whom God preserved for the salvation of others, so that he might be honoured by the greater glory of preaching, than if he had been crowned by martyrdom alone].[106] Just as miracles were less important than preaching, so too was martyrdom. It is difficult not to see this as a comment on overemphasis on Boniface as martyr. Indeed, Alcuin's rejection of martyrdom as a serious aspect of evangelisation is made apparent in the narrative of the *Vita Willibrordi*, in which, after the desecration of the shrine at Helgoland, Willibrord and his companions are taken before Radbod, and lots are cast to see if they should be executed, and as a result one of the group is martyred. Astonishingly, Alcuin deals with the martyrdom in a single phrase: *nisi unus tantum ex sociis sorte monstratus et martyrio coronatus est* [only one of his companions was picked out by lot and crowned with martyrdom].[107] No name is given, and no attention is paid to the event. Admittedly, it could be seen as a failure of divine protection – but so could any martyrdom. Essentially, Alcuin denies the value of martyrdom and thus of a portion of the Bonifatian tradition.

Nor is this the only way in which Alcuin's *Vita Willibrordi* excludes Boniface. No mention is made of him in the narrative, despite his three-year sojourn with Willibrord – a sojourn which was to become singularly important in Utrecht tradition through the account by Liudger[108] and that in the second *Life of Boniface*.[109] Moreover, the curt assertion that the whole of Frisia was subjected to Willibrord implicitly denies the need for subsequent missions by outsiders, and thus effectively challenges the necessity of the mission to Dokkum, the scene of Boniface's murder in 754.[110] Of course Alcuin still revered Boniface: he sent a missal to his shrine, and he told the monks of Fulda to unite round the saint's relics.[111] He also wrote a poem on the church built by Liudger at the site of the saint's martyrdom.[112] To revere a saint, however, did not necessitate enthusiasm for all aspects of his career, and it certainly did not necessitate acceptance of all current traditions, hagiographical or otherwise, which presented him as a model.

Denial of the necessity of martyrdom, silence on Boniface's own work in Frisia, and an assertion of Willibrord's authority in the region, might, of course, be no more than a way of promoting the cult of the archbishop of Utrecht. Boniface's reputation was so much greater than that of Willibrord, that to have allowed him to appear in the *Vita Willibrordi* would have put the protagonist of the *Life* himself in the shade. This is a possible reason for various of Alcuin's assertions and silences – although it was not a strategy used by other hagiographers in comparable circumstances, as we shall see in the case of the *Vita Vulframni*. It is necessary, therefore, to look further at some of the ideas present in other hagiographical works, to see if the differences between Alcuin and contemporary hagiographers were anything other than a defensive action, designed to preserve Willibrord from unfavourable comparisons.

There are, in fact, some indications that both Sturm and Lull may have favoured Charlemagne's early policy of Christianisation as represented in the *Capitulatio de partibus Saxoniae*. In the *Vita Sturmi* Eigil records that after Carloman had granted the territory of Fulda to Boniface he sent messengers to the aristocracy of the region. The messengers said that '"The king ordered all of you to be greeted by him,[113] and asked and demanded that everyone who is known to have property in the place which is called Einloha, should hand it over completely to the monks, so they can live there." When they heard this they gave everything they could possess there to Sturm, the man of God, instantly, with God's approval.'[114] This required transfer of property to the community being established at Fulda might reasonably be compared with a clause of the *Capitulatio de partibus Saxoniae*, insisting that *pagenses* give a *curtis* and two *mansi* of land to the Church.[115] Whether this parallel between the *Vita Sturmi* and the *Capitulatio* is enough to suggest that Fulda provided some input into the legislation is open to question. Similarly, the fact that Pippin III's letter to Lull on the enforcement of tithes was preserved among the letters of Boniface and Lull[116] does not necessarily prove that the tithe legislation in the *Capitulatio de partibus Saxoniae* would have been supported by the clergy of Mainz.[117] Such evidence may constitute straws in the wind, and may help identify the origins of the *Capitulatio*, but it does no more than indicate the existence of groups which would not have agreed completely with Alcuin's views on mission. On the other hand, it would not be surprising if Fulda and Mainz had had a considerable input into the missionary policy of Charlemagne's early years. Lull's foundation of Hersfeld had been responsible for mission in part of Saxony, as revealed by a charter of Charlemagne for 780.[118] And since Lull himself died in 786, he was certainly in a position to influence the contents of the first Saxon cartulary. Although Sturm died in 779, and thus was dead by the time the cartulary was issued, he too had been put in charge of mission in part of Saxony, and had been involved in the ecclesiastical organisation of the region.[119]

# 7. ECHTERNACH AND THE SAXON MISSION

Even if there is no implied criticism of the missionary ideology of Lull and Sturm in the *Vita Willibrordi*, there can be no question that Alcuin's work should be set alongside his missionary letters of 796. Moreover, there is further evidence to indicate that the *Life* was connected with mission to the Saxons. The immediate audience of the *Vita Willibrordi* was certainly the community of Echternach. There is good evidence that Echternach itself was involved in missionary work in Saxony.

The clearest evidence suggests an indirect involvement. Although Echternach may have ceased to be a missionary centre after Willibrord's death in 739, it was there that Willehad's clergy would subsequently regroup after they were driven out of Wigmodia in the course of Widukind's uprising between 782 and 785.[120] Willehad himself rejoined them there after a visit to Rome. It may be significant that Alcuin followed the subsequent restoration of Willehad's mission with considerable interest.[121]

There is, however, one further point. The second *Life of Liudger* refers to missionary work in Münsterland conducted by a certain abbot called Bernrad, who died soon after taking up his commission, in which he was followed by Liudger.[122] No more detail is given on the identity of Bernrad, but he is best identified with Abbot Beornrad of Echternach.[123] Following this identification, Alcuin addressed his *Vita Willibrordi* to Beornrad at exactly the moment that the latter was preparing for his mission to Münsterland. It would, therefore, have been a blueprint for a particular mission – and it may well be the model intentions of the text which caused Alcuin to leave out so much detail and to write in a way that has caused such distress to modern hunters after facts. Assuming that Beornrad would have been accompanied by his own monks, they would indeed have had to contemplate Alcuin's writings with care. Of course, Alcuin's hagiographical work may have had a broader audience as well, and it might have joined his letters of 796 in influencing court attitudes towards mission.

The Avar and Saxon missions of the late 790s and the debates that surrounded them unquestionably form a background to the *Vita Willibrordi*, while Beornrad's intended mission seems to have provided the stimulus for writing the work. Alcuin may have been prompted to set his ideas on mission in the form of a *vita* because of his knowledge of Bede's *Ecclesiastical History*, with its missionary message – even though the *Vita Willibrordi* itself reduces history to a minimum. Thus, although the *Life* has proved disappointing as evidence for the career of Willibrord, which has to be reconstructed largely from fragmentary evidence, it takes us to the heart of the debate about missionary strategy – it is, indeed, a central text for understanding the developing ideologies of mission in the late eighth century.

Moreover, in writing a blueprint for a Saxon mission in 796/7, Alcuin effectively created a hagiography which was specifically concerned with mission.

## 8. THE *VITA WILLEHADI*

There is one further indication of the interest of Echternach in mission: the composition of the *Life of Willehad*.[124] Although Adam of Bremen attributed this text to Archbishop Anskar,[125] it is clear that the latter neither wrote nor even knew the work.[126] In fact the *Life* seems to have been written at Echternach, certainly after the death of Bishop Willerich of Bremen (838), who is described as being *bonae memoriae*,[127] and probably during the reign of the emperor Lothar (840–55).[128]

According to his *vita*, Willehad received permission to work as a missionary in Frisia from a Northumbrian Church council, called by King Alhred. He stopped first at Dokkum, and then moved further south, to Humsterland, where the pagans are said to have cast lots to see if he should be killed for sacrilege – divine intervention, however, ensured that the lots did not condemn him.[129] In the province of Drenthe a further attempt was made on his life, but he was protected by the box of relics which he wore round his neck.[130] If the *vita* is accurate, it is remarkable that the saint was able to work for so long without Carolingian authorisation. Nevertheless, Charlemagne did ultimately get to hear of him, and sent him to work in north-eastern Frisia, in Wigmodia. This work was interrupted by Widukind's uprising in 782, and Willehad had to flee the region. He was fortunate to escape, for a number of his followers were killed: strangely, the author of the *Life* makes no attempt to suggest that a martyr cult developed.[131] The setback caused by Widukind prompted Willehad to go on pilgrimage to Rome, on his return from which he joined up with those of his followers who had escaped from Wigmodia and regrouped at Echternach. While at Echternach Willehad copied the Epistles of St Paul: the manuscript still survived in the author's day.[132] Thereafter Willehad returned to Wigmodia, although he was given a bolt hole by Charlemagne at Mont-Justin. Then, following the submission and conversion of Widukind, he was appointed to the new see of Bremen (787).[133] He died two years later. Miracles were supposedly worked at his tomb, but the author of the *vita* provided no details.[134] He was rather more concerned to emphasise the saint's asceticism, which may have been a point of significance in Echternach, where the appointment of Adalbard as lay abbot in 849 led to conflict between secular clergy and the monks.[135]

The likelihood that the *Vita Willehadi* was written in the reign of Lothar and during a period of internal crisis within the monastery raises interesting questions about the author's interest in mission. Echternach was probably not a missionary centre in the years after the division of Louis the Pious' kingdom in 843: it had no obvious access to mission fields. Yet the *Vita Willehadi* emphasises mission, even if it has little that might be called reliable detail. Indeed, much of the detail that there is seems to derive from Alcuin's *Vita Willibrordi*. There too divine intervention prevents lots from condemning the saint to death.[136] So too an attempt on the saint's life failed.[137] As for martyrs, just as Alcuin has little to say about the one follower of Willibrord who was killed as a result of the casting of lots,[138] so too the *Vita Willehadi* has practically nothing to say about the followers of Willehad martyred in Wigmodia.[139] One might also note the apparent failure to develop a major cult of Boniface's companions, who were martyred with him at Dokkum and were subsequently buried at Utrecht. Further, the issue of preaching is as significant in the *Life of Willehad* as it is in the *Vita Willibrordi*.

In view of the context in which the *Vita Willehadi* was written, it seems likely that a clue to the work's purpose is to be found in its dependence on Alcuin. As we have seen, Echternach was initially a family monastery. Interestingly, Thiotfrid, who wrote a new version of the *Life of Willibrord* around the year 1100, reported that Willehad was a relative of Beornrad.[140] Moreover, Willehad seems to have been regarded as a 'house-saint' in the twelfth century.[141] If Willehad really was a relative of Beornrad, he was by definition a relative of Alcuin and Willibrord. That he was close to Alcuin is clear from the latter's letters.[142] A family association with Echternach would easily explain why Willehad rejoined his disciples there, and why the community remembered him. In might also be that to write a *Life* of a relative of the founder, in the style of the *Life of Willibrord* written by another relative, was one way in which the monastic party in Echternach could claim to represent traditional values in the course of the monastery's internal struggles. Certainly, the author of the *Life* was concerned to make the *Vita Willehadi* the vehicle for the restatement of Alcuin's ideas.

## 9. ANGLO-SAXON MISSIONARIES ON THE CONTINENT

The fact that Willehad was a relative of Beornrad, Alcuin and Willibrord, raises an important issue relating to the so-called Anglo-Saxon missionaries on the continent. The English men and women who went abroad belonged largely, although not entirely, to two very compact groups. Boniface's family and connections have been well established;[143] Willibrord tends to be regarded as a rather more lonely figure, but his family was to pursue his ideals for over a century. When we talk of the English mission on the continent, we are, therefore, talking to some extent about two families with their close associates. At the same time, these families did not often have the missionary opportunities that they had expected. There is a danger in putting much stress on the Anglo-Saxon commitment to missionary work on the continent – just as there is a danger is overemphasising the role of the Irish *peregrini* in mission as opposed to subsequent Christianisation. Although a number of English did work on the continent, and although a good proportion of those did expect to act as missionaries, the missionary work they actually undertook within pagan areas was relatively slight: far more had been achieved by the Frankish clergy than Boniface and his compatriots realised when they set out.[144] It was only really in Frisia and Saxony that the English could act as missionaries to the pagans. The picture that we are usually given of the Christianisation of Germany depends on a rather optimistic, not to say misleading, reading (in several instances by nineteenth- and twentieth-century enthusiasts for mission) of what is a very tight group of literary sources.

## 10. WULFRAM OF SENS

Alcuin's missionary ideology seems to have triumphed in 797, but his history was challenged almost immediately. *The Life of Wulfram of Sens* was certainly written between 796/7 and 807 in the monastery of Saint-Wandrille, probably by Harduin.[145] It provides an account of a supposed contemporary of Willibrord, who, it claims, came near to converting King Radbod. The work can, however, be shown to be a forgery, since the author, who names himself as Jonas and addresses his work to Abbot Bainus, who died in 709,[146] provides two chronologies: he claims that Wulfram was a contemporary of Bishop Ansbert of Rouen, who died in 691,[147] but the central narrative in this missionary history culminates in Radbod's death, in other words in 718.[148] The first of these chronologies for Wulfram's career can be defended:[149] the second cannot, for although the *Vita Vulframni* puts the saint's death in 720, he is known to have been dead by 704.[150] Yet, while chronologically the narrative is clearly impossible, and while the preface is simply fraudulent, the text is not valueless: the issues put forward by Radbod in his debate with Wulfram, particularly the king's concern about a post-humous separation from his pagan ancestors,[151] were certainly raised by others in the Early Middle Ages,[152] while the description of Frisian paganism, dominated by the tides,[153] is quite compatible with what is known from other sources – not least the *Vita Liudgeri* of Altfrid.[154] Further, despite the clear errors in the text, it is highly likely that Wulfram did work in Frisia.[155] So, probably, did another of Saint-Wandrille's saints, Abbot Wando, who is said to have accompanied Wulfram on his mission,[156] and who certainly spent a period of exile after 719 in Maastricht, and perhaps also in Utrecht, where he would have met Willibrord.[157] In addition, there were Frisians within the community of Saint-Wandrille.[158] Why then did the author perpetrate what was in effect a forgery, when he could have written a genuine account of a missionary bishop?

It may, of course, be that what were actually a number of links between Saint-Wandrille and Frisia in the late seventh and early eighth centuries had become confused and amalgamated in the monastic memory by 800. Yet part of the answer must lie in the fact that the *Vita Vulframni* responds directly to the *Vita Willibrordi*. Alcuin's description of Radbod with his heart of stone, *saxum eius cor*,[159] is taken over verbatim.[160] The fact that the author knew of Alcuin's work within at most a decade of its composition is in itself an important indication that the *Vita Willibrordi* had from the start been circulated outside Echternach. Clearly, the Saint-Wandrille forger thought his response would be more effective if he included Willibrord in his narrative, where he plays a minor role,[161] than if he ignored him altogether. Apparently, Willibrord's history was well enough known for an author to have had to acknowledge it, even if he were writing the *Life* of a missionary who was active before the Anglo-Saxon's arrival. By contrast, Wulfram's mission seems to have been largely forgotten by the late eighth century.

Despite his decision to redate Wulfram's missionary career to the time of Willibrord, the author of the *Vita Vulframni* was, nevertheless, intent on establishing the precedence of his saint in the missionary field of Frisia. Yet that does not seem to have been the sole reason for his writing a *Life of Wulfram*. His emphases were also different from those of Alcuin. In addition to describing the discussion of Wulfram and Radbod beside the font,[162] the hagiographer also relates a number of incidents concerning victims rescued from sacrifice, baptised and sent to Saint-Wandrille for education in the monastery.[163] In each case the miraculous rescue leads to conversion and baptism. It is scarcely a scenario recognised by the *Vita Willibrordi*, since it downplays the process of preaching which, in Alcuin's view, should precede baptism, and at the same time it emphasises the miraculous.

For all its invention the *Vita Vulframni* may include a record of genuine events, and its depiction of Frisian paganism may not be wide of the mark. Certainly, it is memorable in its vibrant detail, which is absolutely alien to the considered argument of Alcuin. Perhaps it was thought that vividness was enough to establish the importance of the community of Saint-Wandrille in the mission field. Alcuin, however, does not seem to have been concerned with claims of precedence, but with the process of mission itself. In using hagiography to set out a model for evangelisation he had linked the genre of the saint's *Life* to mission in a new way. In so doing he established a precedent which would be followed almost immediately by Liudger. The latter was a pupil of both Alcuin and of Gregory of Utrecht, who was himself a disciple of Boniface. Liudger was also a missionary in his own right. As a result he would combine the lessons of the *Vita Willibrordi* with personal experience in the mission field – and at the same time, quite unlike Alcuin, he made room for Boniface. To understand the result it is necessary to turn to the third Bonifatian tradition, which lies alongside those of Mainz and Fulda: that of Utrecht.

## Notes

1. C. Plummer, *Baedae Opera Historica*, II, p. 287, quotes the evidence of Thio(t)frid, *Vita Willibrordi* 25, ed. A. Poncelet, AASS, Nov. 7th, vol. 3, that Alcuin used an earlier work by an Irishman.
2. *Calendar of St Willibrord*, ed. H. W. Wilson, Henry Bradshaw Society 55 (London, 1918), under November.
3. *Liber Aureus Epternacensis*.
4. R. Meens, 'Willibrords boeteboek?', *Tijdschrift voor Geschiedenis* 106 (1993), pp. 163–78; R. Meens, 'Christentum und Heidentum aus der Sicht Willibrords? Überlegungen zum *Paenitentiale Oxoniense II*', in M. Polfer, *Die Christianisierung der Region zwischen Maas und Mosel und die Gründung der Abtei Echternach (5.–9. Jahrhundert)* (forthcoming).
5. Bede, *Historia Ecclesiastica* 1 30.
6. Meens, 'Willibrords boeteboek?', p. 168, n. 21.
7. Jochens, 'Late and peaceful: Iceland's conversion through arbitration in 1000', p. 650.
8. Alcuin, *Vita Willibrordi* 1, 2; there are reasonable editions of the prose *Life* by W. Levison, MGH, SRM 7 (Hanover, 1920) and by H.-J. Reischmann, *Willibrord – Apostel der Friesen* (Sigmaringendorf, 1989). Alcuin's actual composition, however, involved a united prose and verse *Life*: the latter was edited by Dümmler, MGH, Poetae Latini aevi Carolini 1 (Berlin, 1881), but the only edition which properly combines the two parts is that by A. Poncelet in AASS, November vol. 3. Levison's account of Willibrord's career, in *England and the Continent in the Eighth Century* (Oxford, 1946), pp. 53–69, remains a classic. In the following footnotes reference simply to the *Vita Willibrordi* automatically refers to the prose *Life*, although I have occasionally also used the words *Vita Willibrordi prosa* to avoid confusion. I have always used the phrase *Vita Willibrordi metrica* to refer to the verse *Life*.
9. Alcuin, *Vita Willibrordi* 3; astonishingly Levison (and after him Reischmann) emended *mater* to *pater*: D. Townsend, 'Alcuin's Willibrord, Wilhelm Levison, and the MGH', in R. Frank (ed.), *The Politics of Editing Medieval Texts* (New York, 1993), p. 127.
10. Alcuin, *Vita Willibrordi* 3; Stephanus, *Vita Wilfridi* 26.
11. Alcuin, *Vita Willibrordi* 4.
12. The date is given in the *Calendar of St Willibrord*; on the chronology, Plummer, *Baedae Opera Historica*, 2, pp. 291–2.
13. Bede, *Historia Ecclesiastica* V 10.
14. Bede, *Historia Ecclesiastica* V 11.
15. Alcuin, *Vita Willibrordi* 6–7; Bede, *Historia Ecclesiastica* V 11; Levison, *England and the Continent in the Eighth Century*, pp. 59–60.
16. Boniface, ep. 109.
17. Wampach, *Geschichte der Grundherrschaft Echternach im Frühmittelalter*, 1, 2, no. 3 (Luxemberg, 1930).

18. Wampach, *Geschichte der Grundherrschaft Echternach im Frühmittelalter*, 1, 2, no. 15.
19. N. Netzer, *Cultural Interplay in the Eighth Century: the Trier Gospels and the Making of a Scriptorium at Echternach* (Cambridge, 1994).
20. This is essentially the picture provided by Alcuin, *Vita Willibrordi* 9–11.
21. *Liber Historiae Francorum* 50, ed. B. Krusch, MGH, SRM 2 (Hanover, 1885).
22. R. Gerberding, *The Rise of the Carolingians and the Liber Historiae Francorum* (Oxford, 1987), p. 115.
23. Gerberding, *The Rise of the Carolingians and the Liber Historiae Francorum*, pp. 134–7.
24. Willibald, *Vita Bonifatii* 4.
25. Willibald, *Vita Bonifatii* 5.
26. Alcuin, *Vita Willibrordi* 1.
27. Godman (ed.), *Alcuin, The Bishops, Kings and Saints of York* (Oxford, 1982), p. xxxvi.
28. Godman (ed.), *Alcuin, The Bishops, Kings and Saints of York*, pp. xxxvii–viii.
29. Alcuin, *Vita Willibrordi*, praef. On the notion of *opus geminatum* see Godman (ed.), *Alcuin, The Bishops, Kings and Saints of York*, pp. lxxviii–lxxxviii.
30. The dates are provided by the Echternach charters: Wampach, *Geschichte der Grundherrschaft Echternach im Frühmittelalter*, 1, 2, nos. 79–113.
31. Alcuin, *Vita Willibrordi* 1, reveals Echternach to have been a family monastery.
32. See the comments of Plummer, *Baedae Opera Historica*, 2, pp. 287–8; Levison, *England and the Continent in the Eighth Century*, p. 54. Also Townsend, 'Alcuin's Willibrord, Wilhelm Levison and the MGH', pp. 114, 118.
33. Alcuin, *Vita Willibrordi* 5, 13.
34. Alcuin, *Vita Willibrordi* 21, 24.
35. Godman (ed.), *Alcuin, The Bishops, Kings and Saints of York*.
36. See in particular Alcuin, *Versus de sanctis Euboricensis ecclesiae*, ll. pp. 1008–43.
37. See also the discussion in Berschin, *Karolingische Biographie 750–920 n. Chr.*, pp. 115–39; Reischmann, *Willibrord – Apostel der Friesen*, pp. 11–41.
38. See Townsend, 'Alcuin's Willibrord, Wilhelm Levison and the MGH', pp. 111–4 for the problems of categorising the work and pp. 114–6 for the problems caused by the MGH's division of the work into separately edited prose and verse works.
39. Alcuin, *Vita Willibrordi prosa* 32, ed. Poncelet.
40. *Licet omni miraculorum operatione et signorum ostentione ministerium evangelicae praedicationis praeferendum sit, tamen quod gesta narrantur, ad gloriam donantis Dei non tacenda esse censeo, sed magis stilo alliganda, ne pereant posteris saeculis, quae priscis temporibus acta esse noscuntur.*
41. Alcuin, *Vita Richarii* 9, ed. B. Krusch, MGH SRM 4 (Hanover, 1902).
42. Alcuin, *Vita Willibrordi metrica* 23.
43. Alcuin, *Vita Willibrordi metrica* 13.
44. Alcuin, *Vita Willibrordi metrica* 24. Berschin, *Karolingische Biographie 750–920 n. Chr.*, p. 131.
45. Alcuin, *Vita Willibrordi prosa* 30.
46. Alcuin, *Vita Willibrordi metrica* 29.
47. Alcuin, *Vita Willibrordi prosa* 6–8, 12–13; *Vita Willibrordi metrica* 2, 6–8, 10–12, 16; see also I. Deug-Su, *L'Opera agiografica di Alcuino* (Spoleto, 1983), pp. 43–56.
48. Alcuin, *Vita Willibrordi prosa* 32 (2).
49. Alcuin, *Vita Vedasti* 1, ed. B. Krusch, MGH, SRM 7 (Hanover, 1920).
50. Alcuin, *Vita Vedasti* 2.
51. Alcuin, *Vita Richarii* 1–2, 4–6, 8–11.
52. Alcuin, ep. 110, ed. E. Dümmler, MGH, Epistolae IV, Karolini Aevi 2 (Berlin, 1895).

53. Alcuin, ep. 111.
54. Alcuin, ep. 113. On the Arno letters see also F. Unterkircher, *Alkuin-Briefe und andere Traktate*, Codices Selecti Phototypice Impressi 20 (Graz, 1969).
55. Alcuin, *Vita Vedasti* 2.
56. Alcuin, ep. 113.
57. For Alcuin's views of baptism, ep. 134.
58. Eigil, *Vita Sturmi* 23.
59. *Capitulatio de partibus Saxoniae*, 8, ed. A. Boretius, Capitularia Regum Francorum 1, MGH, Leges, sectio 2 (Hanover, 1883).
60. Alcuin, epp. 39, 113, 116, 124, 209.
61. Alcuin, ep. 184.
62. Alcuin, ep. 111; compare ep. 254.
63. Alcuin, epp. 107, 110, 111, 174.
64. Hygeburg, *Vita Wynnebaldi* 7.
65. E.g. Adam of Bremen, *Gesta Hammaburgensis Ecclesiae Pontificum* III 23; see also Vlasto, *The Entry of the Slavs into Christendom*, p. 150, with p. 365, n. 237.
66. Alcuin, *Vita Willibrordi* 14.
67. Alcuin, *Vita Willibrordi* 21.
68. Alcuin, *Vita Willibrordi prosa* 14; *Vita Willibrordi metrica* 14.
69. Sulpicius Severus, *Vita Martini* 15.
70. Alcuin, *Vita Willibrordi* 14.
71. *Annales Regni Francorum*, s.a. 796.
72. *Conventus episcoporum ad ripas Danubii, Concilia Aevi Karolini* 20, ed. A. Weminghoff, MGH, Leges 3, Concilia 2 (Hanover, 1906–8).
73. Alcuin, ep. 99.
74. Alcuin, ep. 110.
75. Alcuin, ep. 111.
76. Alcuin, epp. 107, 112, 113.
77. R. E. Sullivan, 'Carolingian missionary theories', *Catholic Historical Review* 42 (1956), pp. 276–8, repr. in *id., Christian Missionary Activity in the Early Middle Ages* (Aldershot, 1994).
78. Unterkircher, *Alkuin-Briefe und andere Traktate*.
79. Alcuin, *Vita Willibrordi* 13; *Vita Willibrordi metrica* 8–11.
80. Alcuin, ep. 107.
81. Alcuin, epp. 7, 110.
82. Alcuin, epp. 110, 184.
83. Eigil, *Vita Sturmi* 23.
84. Alcuin, ep. 174.
85. Alcuin, ep. 7; R. E. Sullivan, 'The Carolingian missionary and the pagan', *Speculum* 28 (1953), p. 723.
86. *Annales Regni Francorum*, s.a. 775.
87. *Annales Regni Francorum*, s.a. 776.
88. Ed. and commentary in S. A. Rabe, *Faith, Art and Politics at Saint-Riquier: the Symbolic Vision of Angilbert* (Philadelphia, 1995), pp. 54–74.
89. *Annales Regni Francorum*, s.a. 778–80.
90. *Annales Regni Francorum*, s.a. 780.
91. *Annales Petaviani*, s.a. 780, ed. G. H. Pertz, MGH, SS 1 (Hanover, 1826).
92. *Annales Mosellani*, s.a. 780, ed. Pertz, MGH, SS 1.
93. *Capitulatio de partibus Saxoniae*, 17.

94. *Annales Regni Francorum*, s.a. 782.
95. *Annales Regni Francorum*, s.a. 785.
96. Alcuin, epp. 6, 7.
97. *Annales Laureshamenses*, s.a. 792, ed. Pertz, MGH, SS 1 (Hanover, 1826); *Annales Regni Francorum*, s.a. 793.
98. *Annales Regni Francorum*, s.a. 794–9, 802, 804.
99. Alcuin, ep. 107.
100. Alcuin, epp. 110, 174.
101. I am indebted to Donald Bullough for this observation.
102. *Capitulare Saxonicum*, 27, ed. A. Boretius, *Capitularia Regum Francorum* 1, MGH, Leges, sectio 2 (Hanover, 1883).
103. Alcuin, epp. 174, 177, 184.
104. It may be significant that Alcuin, *Homilia de natale sancti Willibrordi* 3 (= Alcuin, *Vita Willlibrordi* 32) and Eigil, *Vita Sturmi* 2, both quote Psalm 1, 2, but it is not clear which of the two texts is earlier. Compare Alcuin, *Homilia* 3: *Meditatio tua fuit in lege Domini die ac nocte; ideo sicut palma floruisti in domu Domini;* Eigil, *Vita Sturmi*, 2: *Erat quippe, ut scriptum est, meditatio eius in lege Domini die ac nocte.*
105. Alcuin, ep. 250.
106. Alcuin, *Vita Willibrordi* 32.
107. Alcuin, *Vita Willibrordi* 11.
108. Liudger, *Vita Gregorii* 2, ed. O. Holder-Egger, MGH SS 15, 1 (Hanover, 1887).
109. *Vita Altera Bonifatii* 9, 10, ed. W. Levison, *Vitae sancti Bonifatii*, MGH, SRG 57 (Hanover, 1905).
110. Alcuin, *Vita Willibrordi metrica* 11.
111. Alcuin, ep. 250.
112. Altfrid, *Vita Liudgeri*, I 20.
113. The Latin is ungrammatical, but it cannot be translated as it is by Talbot: '"All of you have come here in obedience to the king's command . . ."': Noble and Head, *Soldiers of Christ*, p. 175.
114. Eigil, *Vita Sturmi* 12.
115. *Capitulatio de partibus Saxoniae* 15. Compare Liudger, *Vita Gregorii* 3.
116. Boniface, ep. 118.
117. Also on tithes, Boniface, epp. 78, 83. One might also note the inclusion of tithes in the forged version of Zacharias' charter for Fulda (Boniface, ep. 89), dated 809–12 by Tangl and 822–3 by Stengel, *Urkundenbuch des Klosters Fulda* 1.
118. On Hersfeld, Büttner, 'Mission und Kirchenorganisation des Frankenreiches bis zum Tode Karls des Großen', p. 474; Johanek, 'Der Ausbau der sächsischen Kirchenorganisation', p. 497.
119. Eigil, *Vita Sturmi*, 23(22)–24(23). For this early period of Saxon mission see P. D. King, *Charlemagne: Translated Sources* (Lancaster, 1987), pp. 44–5; Büttner, 'Mission und Kirchenorganisation des Frankenreiches bis zum Tode Karls des Großen', p. 473; Johanek, 'Der Ausbau der sächsischen Kirchenorganisation', p. 496.
120. *Vita Willehadi*, 7.
121. Alcuin, ep. 6.
122. *Vita Secunda Liudgeri*, I, 17, ed. W. Diekamp, *Die Vitae Sancti Liudgeri* (Münster, 1881): *Ea quoque tempestate devicto sive converso Widukindo, abbas quidam religiosus Bernradh nomine occidentalibus Saxonibus a rege missus fuerat doctor. Qui non multo post migrante ad Deum. . . .*
123. B. Senger, *Liudger, Leben und Werk* (Münster, 1984), p. 52.

124. G. Niemeyer, 'Die Herkunft der *Vita Willehadi*', *Deutsches Archiv* 12 (1956), pp. 17–35. This article is unaccountably overlooked by Berschin, *Karolingische Biographie 750–920 n. Chr.*, p. 341.

125. Adam of Bremen, *Gesta Hammaburgensis Ecclesiae Pontificum* I 13 (14).

126. Niemeyer, 'Die Herkunft der *Vita Willehadi*', p. 18. The importance of Niemeyer's work seems to have escaped both Berschin and Klüppel: the latter, 'Die Germania (750–950)', p. 198 continues to assert Poncelet's view that the text was written in Bremen.

127. *Vita Willehadi* 11.

128. Niemeyer, 'Die Herkunft der *Vita Willehadi*', p. 35.

129. *Vita Willehadi* 1–3.

130. *Vita Willehadi* 4.

131. *Vita Willehadi* 5–6.

132. *Vita Willehadi* 7.

133. *Vita Willehadi* 8.

134. *Vita Willehadi* 10–11.

135. *Vita Willehadi* 9: Niemeyer, 'Die Herkunft der *Vita Willehadi*', p. 32.

136. Compare Alcuin, *Vita Willibrordi* 11 with *Vita Willehadi* 3.

137. Compare Alcuin, *Vita Willibrordi* 14 with *Vita Willehadi* 4.

138. Alcuin, *Vita Willibrordi* 11.

139. *Vita Willehadi* 6.

140. Thio(t)frid, *Vita Willibrordi* 29. Niemeyer, 'Die Herkunft der *Vita Willehadi*', p. 29.

141. Niemeyer, 'Die Herkunft der *Vita Willehadi*', p. 30.

142. Alcuin, ep. 6.

143. L. von Padberg, *Heilige und Familie: Studien zur Bedeutung familiengebundener Aspekte in den Viten des Verwandten- und Schülerkreises um Willibrord, Bonifatius und Liudger* (Münster, 1981). See also R. McKitterick, *Anglo-Saxon Missionaries in Germany*, Eighth Brixworth Lecture, Vaughan Paper 36 (Leicester, 1991).

144. Green, *Language and History in the Early Germanic World*, pp. 325–56.

145. I. N. Wood, 'Saint-Wandrille and its hagiography', in I. N. Wood and G. A. Loud (eds), *Church and Chronicle in the Middle Ages* (London, 1991), pp. 3, 13–14.

146. *Vita Vulframni*, pref., ed. W. Levison, MGH, SRM 5 (Hanover, 1910).

147. *Vita Vulframni*, pref., 3.

148. *Vita Vulframni*, 10; the date is given in *Annales Xantenses*, ed. B. von Simson, MGH, SRG (Hanover, 1909).

149. S. Lebecq, 'Le baptême manqué du roi Radbod', in O. Redon and B. Rosenberger, (eds), *Les assises du pouvoir: temps médiévaux, territorires africains* (St-Denis, 1994), pp. 141–50.

150. *Vita Vulframni* 14.

151. *Vita Vulframni* 9.

152. See Fletcher, *The Conversion of Europe*, p. 406.

153. *Vita Vulframni* 8.

154. Altfrid, *Vita Liudgeri* I 6–7.

155. S. Lebecq, 'Le baptême manqué du roi Radbod'; Levison, *England and the Continent in the Eighth Century*, p. 56, n. 2.

156. *Vita Vulframni* 5.

157. *Gesta sanctorum patrum Fontenallensis coenobii* III 1, VIII 1, IX 1, ed. F. Lohier and J. Laporte (Rouen and Paris, 1931); Wood, 'Saint-Wandrille and its hagiography', pp. 13–14.

158. *Vita Vulframni*, pref., 6, 7; Levison, *England and the Continent in the Eighth Century*, p. 56, n. 2.
159. Alcuin, *Vita Willibrordi* 9.
160. *Vita Vulframni* 8.
161. *Vita Vulframni* 9.
162. *Vita Vulframni* 9; compare also Alcuin, *Vita Willibrordi* 11.
163. *Vita Vulframni* 6–8.

# Chapter 5

# UTRECHT AND MÜNSTER

## 1. LIUDGER AND BONIFACE

In the late eighth and early ninth centuries three centres laid particular claim to Boniface's inheritance: Mainz, where he had been archbishop, Fulda, where he had been buried, and Utrecht, the base from which he attempted to evangelise Frisia, and to which his body was initially brought after his martyrdom. The Mainz tradition was set out by Willibald, that of Fulda in Eigil's *Life of Sturm*. Liudger wrote a *Life of Gregory of Utrecht*, whose first half is in fact a joint *Life* of Boniface and Gregory, as the author himself admits.[1] Indeed, the text was described as a *Commemoratio de sancto Bonifatio atque Gregorio* in a lost manuscript from Fulda.[2] Although it can scarcely be called historical,[3] it is necessary to come to grips with Liudger's view of Boniface if we are to understand the development of the missionary tradition. We shall return to Liudger's account of Gregory of Utrecht, in the same text, in due course.

Liudger announces the arrival of Boniface *sicut lucifer*[4] – the noun being used in its positive sense to mean 'light-bringing'. The author emphasises his subject's sanctity and preaching, under Charles Martel, Carloman, and Pippin III, but also makes much of the fact that he had numerous disciples.[5] It is scarcely surprising that a work concerned with Gregory of Utrecht should emphasise the number of Boniface's followers, but the stress placed on the point is considerable, and even extends to listing Lull at Mainz, Megingoz at Würzburg, Willibald at Eichstätt, Wynnebald, Sturm at Fulda,[6] as well as Wigbert of Fritzlar and Burghard of Würzburg, who predeceased their master.[7]

Returning to the narrative of Boniface's career, Liudger relates that the saint spent thirteen years working in Frisia: seven at Woerden, three at Achtienhoven and three at Velsen.[8] The statement is clearly false, for the period referred to is the three years spent with Willibrord between 719 and 721. The geography is, however, interesting, for the area designated as being Boniface's early mission field lies around Utrecht, and it was there too that the main estates of Liudger's own family lay.[9] After this stint in Frisia, Boniface set off for Hesse and Thuringia, stopping at Trier, where he met the young Gregory.[10]

Liudger turns next to Boniface's work in Thuringia, which was threatened by a pagan uprising[11] – which may be a yet more exaggerated account of the rule of Heden than that in Willibald's *Vita Bonifatii*.[12] It may also reflect Liudger's own experience of setbacks caused by the Saxon uprisings of the 780s and 790s.[13] Despite all this, Boniface and Gregory soldiered on as pastors, living in the style of the Early Church, by the work of their own hands. It is not easy to see to what extent this fits into the realities of Boniface's career. Liudger, however, uses the image to draw a contrast with present laxity, commenting that nowadays we do not help our flocks, but rather enrich ourselves.[14] The point brings to mind Hygeburg's contrast between pastors and mercenaries,[15] and Alcuin's fear of preachers becoming predators.[16]

Meanwhile, criticism at court prompted King Charles, in other words the *maior palatii* Charles Martel – but the possibility of confusion with Charlemagne might be intentional – to summon Boniface. The result was that the saint was held in even higher regard by right-thinkers.[17] Returning to Thuringia and Hesse, Boniface established churches at Erfurt and Fritzlar. The origins of Fritzlar probably date to *c.* 732,[18] while the establishment of a see at Erfurt is dated to 742 by Boniface's own letters.[19]

At this point Liudger announces the succession of Carloman and Pippin III, an event which can be dated to 741. Although Boniface and his disciples often preached at the palace, and although there was general agreement that he should become a bishop, his critics reasserted themselves. They are identified as bishops, though Liudger states oddly that their names are not known: *nescitur qui fuerint isti adversarii*.[20] It is not difficult to see here a memory of the conflict between Boniface and such established Frankish bishops as Gewilib of Mainz and Milo of Trier.[21] Indeed, Liudger goes on to talk of Boniface's appointment to the archdiocese of Mainz, which he gained in 745. He then explains that he is not going to discuss the reform synods, that is the synods of 742–4.[22] Chronological confusion returns with the announcement that Boniface was subsequently sent to Rome for consecration by Gregory III, who gave him the name Bonifatius in place of Winfrith,[23] something which had in fact happened in 722 at the hands of Gregory II.[24] It may be that Liudger here made the logical deduction that Boniface went to Rome after being appointed to Mainz, not realising that he had been bishop without a see for twenty-three years.

At this point Liudger turns his attention to Gregory, though he does briefly mention Boniface's death in the context of discussing Gregory's work at Utrecht. He explains that after the martyrdom Pippin appointed Gregory to preach in Frisia, where Willibrord had been the first to preach – this being the first time that Willibrord appears in the work.[25] Liudger goes on to state that after Willibrord's death Boniface succeeded to the see of

Utrecht – a point which is clearly contradicted by Boniface's own correspondence, where he sets out his long-standing conflict with Bishop Hildegar
over control of the church.[26] According to Liudger, Gregory was Boniface's
heir in Utrecht[27] – though no other source suggests that he ever became
bishop.

Liudger's account of Boniface is so confused that it demands some explanation. Individual points of misunderstanding can, of course, be explained
away – as over the misplacing of Boniface's consecration at the hands of
Gregory (II). But the overall picture is so much at odds with what can be
reconstructed of Boniface's career that there must be more at stake than
a series of misunderstandings. Further, Liudger states clearly that he had
read an account of Boniface's martyrdom: he remarks that Boniface glowed
like the sun in his preaching, as is clearly shown in the book written about
his passion: *ista omnia in libello de passione ipsius scripto plane et lucide
manifestantur.*[28] This might be a reference to Willibald's *Vita Bonifatii*, but if
so it stretches the language of the original.[29] There are, however, some other
possible indications that Liudger did know Willibald's *Life*.[30] Both writers
emphasise the apostolic life-style of their subjects, and do so specifically in
the context of the problems they faced in Thuringia,[31] though Willibald
also returns to the point in describing Boniface's final days of preaching in
Frisia.[32] If such points of comparison are accepted as indicating that Liudger
knew Willibald's work, his chronological errors are all the more in need of
explanation.

## 2. THE *VITA ALTERA BONIFATII*

There is, though, the additional possibility that Liudger knew another
account of Boniface either as well as or instead of Willibald's work. In the
*Vita Liudgeri*, Altfrid attributes a *Life* of Boniface to Liudger himself.[33] This
could well be a reference to the first part of the *Vita Gregorii* – and in any
case it does not help us in our search for a source for Liudger's own knowledge. More important, Altfrid cites a *Life* of Boniface, where the place
of the saint's martyrdom is named as Dokkum.[34] Willibald provides no such
information, nor indeed does Liudger, but an anonymous text known as
the *Vita Altera Bonifatii* does exactly that.[35] It is worth asking whether this
text, or an earlier version of it than now survives, may either have been
available to Liudger or might at least help explain some of the errors of the
*Vita Gregorii*.

This text is, at first sight, promising. The author claims to have met an old
woman who witnessed the death of Boniface.[36] If true, this could scarcely
place the work any later than the beginning of the ninth century. On the
other hand, this claim might be no more than an attempt to gain credibility

for a forgery: one manuscript, admittedly of the fourteenth century, attributes the work to Radbod, bishop of Utrecht between 899 and 917.[37] There are, however, good reasons not to attribute the work – or at least the majority of its narrative – to Radbod,[38] who left a number of other hagiographical works, with which comparison may be made. First, although Radbod, like the author of the *Vita Altera*, enjoyed classical references, those in the *Life* of Boniface are somewhat wild, while those in Radbod's work are carefully integrated into the argument. Thus the *Vita Altera* populates *Frisia Ulterior* with *larvae* (demons), *lemures* (ghosts), fauns, satyrs, dryads and *napeae* (dell-nymphs):[39] Radbod makes comparison with Cicero and Plato,[40] and with Alexander, Xerxes and Augustus.[41] Further, although Radbod does appeal to oral witness elsewhere in his writings,[42] bogus claims are not obviously a part of his use of the past. In dealing with Swithbert, for instance, he quotes Bede verbatim, and then, when he runs out of sources, admits as much openly and goes on to explain what, nevertheless, can be assumed about the saint.[43] Perhaps more important, Radbod and the author of the *Vita Altera* treat the Vikings very differently: in the *Vita Altera* they are simply *pyratae* from the North, who arrive in England and are driven out;[44] in the *Libellus de miraculo sancti Martini* Radbod gives their history from 841 to 903.[45] Here further comparison can be made with Altfrid's *Life of Liudger*, written between 839 and 849,[46] where the threat of major devastation caused by the Vikings in Frisia is the subject of one of the saint's prophecies.[47] The author of the *Vita Altera* seems to have written at a time when the Vikings were still a relatively minor threat to the Frisian Church – though this implies no more than a date before the 830s. With regard to establishing a *terminus post quem* for the text, there are, as we shall see, distinct problems in pushing it earlier than the beginning of the ninth century.

All in all, we can accept that Radbod was not the original author of the *Vita Altera Bonifatii* – although it is possible, indeed likely, that he revised the work in some way.[48] So too the *Vita Altera* cannot be the *Life* of Boniface ascribed to Liudger by Altfrid,[49] which, as we have seen is almost certainly the *Vita Gregorii* itself, although an earlier recension could be the source for Altfrid's reference to Dokkum. The differences in approach between the *Vita Gregorii* and the *Vita Altera Bonifatii* are dramatic: as we shall see, Liudger's notion of paganism was radically different from that of the anonymous author. The best that can be said is that the *Vita Altera* is a Carolingian composition, perhaps originally written before Altfrid's *Vita Liudgeri*.[50] The surviving recension could be a reworked version of the text known by Altfrid. If there had indeed been an earlier version of the work, that may well have been one of Liudger's own sources for the *Vita Gregorii*, although that is uncertain. Perhaps more important – and more easily answered – is the question of whether, along with the works of Liudger and Radbod, it represents a Frisian hagiographical tradition centred on Utrecht,[51] where it seems to have been written, by a monk of the community of Saint Martin.[52]

The *Vita Altera* differs radically from Willibald's *Life of Boniface*, and indeed from the *Vita Gregorii*. Its coverage is different: the space spent on Boniface's early life in England is minimal[53] and the mission to Frisia in 716 is sketched in,[54] as is the 718 visit to Rome.[55] With Boniface's work among the pagans of *Germania* the author becomes more expansive,[56] and naturally he covers Boniface's collaboration with Willibrord in some detail.[57] This is followed by an account of Boniface's 722 journey to Rome, by more work among the *Germani*,[58] and then, in rather rapid succession, by Boniface's third (737) visit to the papacy and his appointment to the see of Mainz in 746.[59] On learning of Willibrord's death (which actually occured in 739),[60] Boniface set off for Frisia and his martyrdom.[61] Thus far the chronological confusion must indicate that the author had not read the *Vita Bonifatii* of Willibald. This impression is not contradicted by what the two authors have to say about the spring at Dokkum. According to the anonymous author it had been found by Boniface,[62] while Willibald, who omits any place name, attributes the miraculous discovery of the spring to the horse of a servant of the local governor.[63] It is best to see these details in the *Vita Altera* as a witness to traditions disseminated from *Frisia Ulterior*.

One other story in the *Vita Altera* can usefully be seen in this light. It is here that one finds, for the first time, and attributed to a very old lady who was present, mention of Boniface defending himself with a Gospel book at the time of his death.[64] Significantly, the story does not originate in Fulda, and when Fulda did produce the supposed manuscript with which the saint defended himself it was not a Gospel book, but a manuscript containing works of Jerome, Augustine and Gregory, together with Isidore's *Synonyma*.[65] One is forced to the conclusion that the relic was invented: and that when it came to hacking up a manuscript with a sword, even the monks of Fulda would not attack a Bible.

Not only is the coverage of Willibald's *Vita Bonifatii* different from that of the *Vita Altera*, the approaches of the two authors to their subject matter are dissimilar. Whereas Willibald largely limits his Biblical citations to Matthew and the Epistles, the anonymous writer is promiscuous with Biblical quotations and although the *Vita Altera* draws comparisons between Paul and Boniface it is in a somewhat uncontrolled way. Paul's reception at Miletus is compared with that of Boniface by the Frisians. More curious, Paul being bitten by a viper is compared to Boniface being decapitated.[66] Unlike Willibald, the author of the *Vita Altera* revels in comparisons with other saints.[67] More important, in place of Willibald's cautious depiction of the heretical Christianity of *Germania*, the *Vita Altera* fills its Germanic land-scape with spirits from classical tradition.[68]

Paganism counts for much more in the *Vita Altera* than it does in the work of Willibald. This, of course, may reflect the position of Utrecht, much closer to the front line of missionary work than was Mainz. Yet it is worth noting that the paganism described by the author is a literary construct. And not only does it differ from that referred to by Willibald, it is also radically different from that in Liudger's *Life of Gregory*, where the pagans are essentially rebels, who present a military threat to the work of Boniface:[69] a description which may well reflect Liudger's own experience as well as that of Boniface.[70] Nor do the *Vita Altera*'s comments compare with the rich account of Frisian paganism in Altfrid's *Vita Liudgeri*.[71] In short, the pagans of the *Vita Altera* are not real beings, but a device for identifying a frontier: the people of *Germania* and also of *Frisia Ulterior* are 'Other'. The Frisians are indeed described as people 'who almost dwell in water, by which they are surrounded on all sides, so that they rarely have access to the outside world, unless they travel by ship', and as 'remote from other nations and thus brutish and barbarous'.[72] The author, apparently writing in Utrecht,[73] scarcely identified himself with such marginal beings.

The *Vita Altera*, therefore, faces us with the curious paradox of the *Life* of a saint who is presented as being a missionary, written in what had been a missionary centre in the eighth century, in which the objects of mission are no more than a literary construct. With regard to the question of the date of the text already raised, this must carry the implication that the *Life* as we have it was written when Frisian paganism had ceased to be a matter of concern at Utrecht – and that would suggest a date no earlier than the very end of the eighth century, and perhaps later, or with significant later revision.

There is one other puzzle which needs discussion. The *Vita Altera* makes little of the return of Boniface's body to Utrecht after his martyrdom. Yet Willibald recounts how the *comes* of the region had announced that the body was to remain in Utrecht, and it was only the miraculous tolling of the church bell which led to the people allowing the corpse to be moved on to Mainz.[74] In Eigil's *Life of Sturm* the people of Utrecht bury the bodies of the martyr's companions, and hope to be able to keep that of Boniface, but again a miracle made plain his desire to be moved.[75] In Mainz, however, an official decreed that that body could remain there, which is, we are told, what Lull wanted, but Boniface himself appeared to prevent this happening.[76] Whether Lull really did make such an attempt is, as we have seen, open to question. What is clear, though, is that in Fulda tradition Utrecht and Mainz wanted to keep the body, and in Mainz tradition Utrecht wished to do so. In Utrecht tradition, however, keeping Boniface's body is presented as no more than a pious hope – nor, indeed, did Utrecht make much of the other numerous bodies of Boniface's companions, particularly that of Bishop Eoban, which they certainly did keep. This failure to promote what could have been a major cult of the companions of Boniface is extraordinary – although we have already noted other failures to create martyr cults in Alcuin's *Vita Willibrordi*[77] and in the *Vita Willehadi*.[78]

The fact that the *Vita Altera* makes nothing of the genuine relics preserved in Utrecht suggests that whatever the author, or at least the author of the surviving recension, was doing, he was not concerned to promote a cult – in fact, he furiously denounces the need to add an account of miracles to the end of his text.[79] What we are looking at is a *Life* explicitly written at and for a monastic community, apparently that of St Martin's.[80] Not surprisingly, what concerns the author is not pagans or their conversion, but the conversion of the inner man.[81]

The *Vita Altera* indeed begins with a discussion of *timor Dei*, and the need for spiritual cures.[82] The author also compares the lavish ornamentation of the buildings dedicated to Martin in Mainz and Utrecht unfavourably with the spiritual ornamentation of Boniface.[83] In what is clearly an addition to the work, the author, having dealt with the career of Boniface, states that the previous portion of the text was read out at the request of the monks, *fratres*, but that some of them then complained that the *vita* had failed to deal with the miraculous.[84] Recognising that some people could not do without signs, the author offers his excuses for omitting miracles, which he recognises as having an edificatory function,[85] but he returns to the importance of Boniface as the doctor of the inner man, of the incredulous, the ignorant, the hard of heart, those not knowing the law, the avaricious, the detractors, the jealous, the lustful, gluttons, drunkards and those sick with mental disorders.[86] For the author of the *Vita Altera* such people needed spiritual guidance, but they would not respond to the miraculous. 'Signs do not inflame, but they edify'. The miraculous was useful to those already converted: the merciful, the sympathetic, the poor in Christ.[87] In arguing in this way he was directly denying the position of Gregory the Great, that the miraculous was appropriate to periods of Christianisation.[88] At the same time one is driven to conclude that the conversion of the inner man did not really apply to the pagans of northern Frisia, but rather that it was a matter for the inmates of St Martin's.

The *Vita Altera* in its current form is unlikely to have been the source of Liudger's confusions over Boniface – it is difficult, though not impossible, to see it as the earlier of the two works. The two texts between them, however, show clearly that there was a developing tradition of depicting Boniface in Utrecht, which was independent of those in Fulda and Mainz. It was, moreover, a tradition in which Boniface was seen largely in missionary guise. Although the Utrecht tradition is marginally later than those produced by the other two Bonifatian centres, and although it is apparently more fanciful, its image of a predominantly missionary Boniface may well have influenced much later writing. Whilst Alcuin seems to have created a model for writing missionary hagiography, Liudger and the author of the *Vita Altera Bonifatii* created the image of Boniface as missionary.

The *Vita Altera* itself is a strange text, and one may conclude that the author was stretching his material in unconventional ways. Yet, if we place the *Vita Altera* later than Liudger's *Vita Gregorii*, it was not the earliest unconventional work of hagiography associated with Utrecht. Pride of place may go to Liudger, to whose account of Gregory we should return.

## 3. LIUDGER AND GREGORY

Liudger tells us that Gregory was his abbot and his guide.[89] The saint makes his first appearance in the narrative when Boniface stops at the abbey of Pfalzel near Trier. The abbess, Addula, appointed her grandson, Gregory, although he was only a child aged fourteen or fifteen, to read at dinner. After he had read a little, Boniface asked him if he understood what he was reading. The boy simply reread the passage, and when told to paraphrase it, was unable to do so. Boniface then offered an exegesis that so dazzled the boy that the child decided instantly to follow the preacher. Thereafter, says Liudger, Gregory worked with Boniface until the latter's martyrdom.[90] This statement, and the constant depiction of Gregory as Boniface's closest disciple fit ill with the fact that Gregory only appears once in the collection of letters associated with Boniface, and then only in a letter of thanks from Lull written between 747 and 752[91] – although one might conclude that Gregory never received a letter from Boniface because he never left his side.

Apart from referring to Gregory as a disciple and companion of Boniface, Liudger provides little additional detail until he describes Boniface's consecration by Pope Gregory, an event which he places (wrongly) near the end of the martyr's career. At that point Liudger reveals that Gregory, who was apparently with Boniface in Rome, acquired a large number of books, especially for the Anglian brothers, Marchelm and Marcwin.[92] Marchelm was to be a source of information for Liudger[93] – and he also makes several appearances in the *Vita Liudgeri*.[94]

Having described Boniface's visit to Rome, Liudger finally turns his attention properly to Gregory. His first substantial anecdote deals with the killing of two of Gregory's half-brothers by thieves, whom the saint saved from execution and freed, rejecting vengeance and following the counsel of perfection[95]. However, Liudger later explains that those who did not show Gregory appropriate deference were struck by divine vengeance and forced to show him his due, albeit under compulsion: *quod pene omnes hi qui tanto*

107

*viro honorem debitum impendere noluerunt ultione divina percussi sunt et ad cognitionem sui, licet coacti et inviti, reducti sunt* [that almost all those who did not want to show due reverence to such a man were struck with divine vengeance, and were reduced to recognising him, albeit under compulsion and unwillingly][96] – a passage which might call to mind Alcuin's emphasis on vengeance as a divine prerogative.[97] After recounting the story of the murder of Gregory's brothers, Liudger turns to the setting up of the see of Utrecht by Willibrord, and the subsequent succession, first of Boniface (!) and then of Gregory. Thereafter he talks of the latter's disciples,[98] creating a nice parallel to his earlier emphasis on Boniface's disciples. That Gregory did create a significant school at Utrecht, and that he played a major role in organising missions to the further parts of Frisia and the frontiers of Saxony is not in question.[99]

The list of Gregory's virtues which follows, and which includes the information on divine vengeance, is to a large extent predictable, though much is made of the saint's lack of interest in wealth, and in his almsgiving, as well as his preaching.[100] The account of his death, however, has more individual touches. Liudger describes how Gregory, at the age of seventy, was paralysed, but could still move and teach. He then tells how the saint divided his books between his disciples, giving Liudger himself a copy of Augustine's *Enchiridion*.[101] Even in his last days Gregory had books by him. As for the timing of his death, miraculously he survived until his appointed successor, Alberic, had returned from Italy, which he was visiting on royal business.[102]

Such details give an impression of Liudger's own proximity to Gregory – and there can be no doubt that he was genuinely attached to his master. They fit awkwardly with the inaccurate history that we have seen in other parts of the work, and with its recurrent ideological aspects. To get further in understanding the *Vita Gregorii*, it is necessary to turn to Liudger himself, and to the account of his career given by his nephew, Altfrid.

## 4. LIUDGER

Liudger, according to Altfrid, was the son of Theodgrim and Liafburg.[103] His paternal grandfather, Wrssing, had been a Frisian opponent of Radbod, and had gone into exile, where he was well received by Grimoald, who also happened to be Radbod's son-in-law. It was through his influence that Wrssing was baptised.[104] Liudger's maternal grandmother, Adelburga, had the distinction of handing her brothers over to Willibrord to be brought up: they were, says Altfrid, to become the first native Frisian clerics.[105] Liudger was, thus, the offspring of a notable Christian Frisian family, and one which, we are told, had estates to the north of Utrecht, at Loenen and Muiderberg[106] and, more surprisingly, at Werden in Westfalia.[107]

Liudger himself was born in 742.[108] His first actions, as recorded by Altfrid, were to play with skins and bark, which he claimed were books which he had written. When asked who had taught him to write, he replied, 'God'.[109] The anecdote, which is clearly intended to emphasise Liudger's precocious spirituality and bookishness, might be set alongside the saint's own careful description of Gregory of Utrecht's reading.[110] This bookishness is picked up again by Altfrid, when giving a final description of Liudger, before narrating his death.[111] There he talks of his education, his writings on Gregory, Alberic and Boniface. Liudger's concern to follow the teachings to be found in books, as described by Altfrid, seems to link up with Liudger's own descrip-tion of Gregory's book collection, and with his reference to the copy of Augustine's *Enchiridion*, which he received from his old master.[112] It should also be set alongside the fact that Liudger's later foundations had notable early *scriptoria*, and that some manuscripts were once ascribed to his own hand.[113]

Although Willibrord had died before Liudger was born, the boy was of an age to have seen Boniface, as the martyr-to-be passed through Utrecht to Dokkum in 754, and he remembered him as an old, white-haired man.[114] About a year later, he was sent to the monastery at Utrecht, to be educated under the guidance of Gregory.[115]

The next major change in Liudger's career came in 767. Gregory, whom Altfrid admits to being a priest and not a bishop, was keen that the Anglo-Saxon Alubert should become *corepiscopus* – there is no mention of secular involvement here. Alubert, however, wished to be consecrated by his own archbishop, Ælberht of York. Gregory agreed, and sent Liudger and Sigbod to accompany him. When Ælberht consecrated Alubert, he also ordained Liudger and Sigbod as priests. While in York Liudger attached himself to Alcuin, who was then master of the school.[116] The Northumbrian connec-tion would be an important one, and not just for Liudger. At about this time the Anglian Willehad approached King Alhred of Northumbria for permission to work as a missionary in Frisia. The king summoned a council, as a result of which he agreed to Willehad's request.[117] Archbishop Ælberht must have been involved in the council, and it may be that Willehad's inspiration to work in Frisia came from Alubreht's visit to York – although, as we have seen, being related to Beornrad and thus to Willibrord, he had other reasons to go to the Frisian mission field. One visit to York, however, was not enough for Liudger. Having returned home, he sought permission to go back to York in order to study longer under Alcuin, which he did for three years, until a Frisian merchant killed a local official, making life in the

Northumbrian city unsafe for foreigners. Liudger therefore returned to Gregory, armed, as we are told, with books.[118]

The next stage of Liudger's career, as described by Altfrid, involved yet another Anglo-Saxon working on the continent. Lebuin, or, more properly, Liafwin, as his name appears in its Old English form, had gone to Gregory for permission to evangelise, and was sent, together with Marchelm, to the valley of the Yssel south of Deventer. This work was to be interrupted by a Saxon uprising, although Lebuin was able to return to the region, preaching until his death in c. 773, when he was buried in Deventer.[119] The church there was, however, destroyed soon after by yet another Saxon incursion. Meanwhile, Gregory himself died (775), his place being filled by his nephew, Alberic, who sent Liudger to rebuild the church at Deventer, which he did, at the same time rediscovering the tomb of Lebuin.[120] Thereafter, Alberic appointed Liudger to evangelise among the Frisians, with instructions to destroy their pagan shrines and idols: *fana deorum et varias culturas idolorum*. In the course of doing so, the saint discovered considerable quantities of treasure, two-thirds of which were sent to Charlemagne and one-third to Alberic.[121]

At this moment Alberic was appointed to the diocese of Cologne. In order not to abandon the Utrecht mission-base, he organised a rota in which he, Liudger, Adalgar and Thiadbraht were each to spend three months there. At the same time he ordained Liudger priest and set him over the Ostracha, or Ostergau, centred on Dokkum.[122] While in Utrecht Liudger had a vision which was interpreted to indicate that he would be put in charge of three different groups of people:[123] the vision may, of course, be an invention by Altfrid to justify subsequent events – it may also have had a Biblical model, in that the extension of the Church in the Acts of the Apostles is prefaced by a vision seen by Peter at Joppa.[124] Certainly, visions play a recurrent role in inspiring missionaries in accounts from the ninth and tenth century – just as they are central to the *Confessio* of Patrick.

Liudger's work in the Dokkum region, which included the building of a church on the supposed site of Boniface's martyrdom, for which Alcuin wrote a poem, ended after seven years, with the pagan uprising of Widukind in Westfalia, which led to the expulsion of Christian missionaries and the resurgence of paganism in Frisia. Driven out of the Ostergau, Liudger embarked on a pilgrimage to Montecassino, in the company of his brother, Hildigrim, among others, to learn the Rule of St Benedict at source.[125]

On his return in 787, Liudger came to the attention of Charlemagne, who in the aftermath of Widukind's submission and baptism, was intent on the Christianisation of Saxony and of northern Frisia – indeed, the boundary between Frisia and Saxony is not easy to draw.[126] He set Liudger over five *pagi* to the east of the River Lauwers.[127] From there Liudger also worked in the border region between Frisians and Danes, in particular crossing to the island of Fosite, destroying the shrine there, and using the sacred spring to baptise the locals. Altfrid admits that Willibrord had previously baptised three people there, and the whole passage is indeed modelled on Alcuin's description of that episode in the *Vita Willibrordi*.[128] The episode might have been invented by Altfrid, using Alcuin's work as a model, but it is just as likely that Liudger himself was deliberately echoing Willibrord's actions. He had, after all, already taken to fruition the work of Boniface at Dokkum and Lebuin at Deventer.

Success in Frisia led Charlemagne to increase Liudger's commission, setting him up as a pastor in Westfalia, with his base at Münster, where he founded a monastery, while at the same time evangelising the region, founding churches and exercising pastoral care.[129] Shortly afterwards, Liudger also founded a monastery at Werden, further to the south, but still in Saxony, and also, as it happens, on his own ancestral property.[130] Full recognition of Liudger's success came in 805,[131] with his appointment as bishop of Münster, and the creation of a diocese which included the five Frisian *pagi* east of the Lauwers as well as territory in Westfalia. Charlemagne also gave him *Lotusa* (Leuze) in Brabant[132] – the idea of a retreat far from the missionary zone can be paralleled by Willehad's Mont-Justin,[133] and may have been inspired by Willibrord's possession of Echternach. It was to be repeated in the endowments of other missionary bishops.[134] Presumably, it was at this late stage in his career that Liudger broached the possibility of a Danish mission, but Charlemagne forbade it.[135] In any case Liudger died in 809, after only four years as a bishop.

## 5. THE PURPOSE OF THE *VITA GREGORII*

With Liudger's career sketched in, it may now be possible to come closer to an understanding of the *Vita Gregorii*. First, it is a book which is about Boniface and Gregory, much as Eigil's *Vita Sturmi* is about Boniface and Sturm. As such, it takes a very different attitude towards Boniface than that apparent in Alcuin's *Vita Willibrordi*, despite the close contacts between Liudger and Alcuin. This is not surprising in that Liudger was a pupil of Gregory, who was himself a disciple of Boniface: he had also been given ecclesiatical jurisdiction at Dokkum, where he was responsible for building a church to Boniface. This does, on the other hand, call to mind, once again, the oddity of Alcuin's silence on Boniface in the *Vita Willibrordi*, for he actually wrote a poem about the church.[136]

In the *Vita Gregorii* Liudger has little to say about Willibrord, but he does not entirely ignore him. Whether he already knew the *Vita Willibrordi* is a more complicated question, which depends on the date at which one thinks

Liudger wrote the *Vita Gregorii*. There is, fortunately, a telling phrase in the *Life* of Gregory, where Liudger says of Boniface that he cast light just as *lucifer* lights the east in the morning, *sicut lucifer mane oriens illuminavit,*[137] which seems to be lifted directly from Alcuin's *Vita Richarii*.[138] which can be dated to 800 and 801.[139] If the *Vita Gregorii* is to be dated later than the turn of the century, it is almost inconceivable that the author had not read the *Vita Willibrordi*.

What Liudger learnt from Alcuin, however, was not a respect for Willibrord – that he had surely received from his own family[140] – but rather the importance of preaching.[141] The enormous emphasis on preaching in the *Vita Gregorii*, which is apparent from Boniface's first appearance,[142] and underlies the famous story about Gregory not being able to understand what he had read,[143] surely derives from, or was reinforced by, Liudger's own education at Alcuin's hand. The *Vita Gregorii* is, therefore, a work imbued with Alcuin's notion of what constituted mission, and at the same time with a respect for Boniface.[144]

It is rather more than that, though. It is an intensely personal work. Boniface's (invented or exaggerated) Frisian mission is located in an area that Liudger knew well and the depiction of it therefore has a sense of immediacy, of here-and-nowness. Gregory's learning seems to reflect Liudger's own learning. Both of them are said to have had a great fondness for books – perhaps Liudger here was influenced by Gregory, or perhaps he transferred to his master his own passion, which is apparent both in his own mention of the copy of Augustine's *Enchiridion* which was given to him, and in what is known of the *scriptoria* of his foundations. Finally, Liudger's own experience of mission, even under the threat of Saxon uprisings, seems to have informed his interpretation of the experience of Boniface and Gregory in Thuringia. It is as if Liudger has used his *Vita Gregorii* to express his own experiences. Indeed, the *Vita Gregorii* is almost a displaced autobiography: the careers of Boniface and Gregory have become pegs upon which Liudger could hang his own experiences.

Liudger's *Vita Gregorii* is more than a critique of churchmen in his own day, although it is that too.[145] It is work which is intent on exploring mission, and to do so it presents Boniface, inaccurately, as being primarily a missionary to the pagans, and it may even be responsible for creating that image. It is, however, something other than an academic blueprint for mission, which is what we have seen the *Vita Willibrordi* to be. It clearly shares Alcuin's appreciation of preaching, but it infuses that appreciation with a knowledge of what mission in a pagan area was actually like. In addition it is an act of homage to his own master, Gregory. To judge by Altfrid's account, Liudger was equally appreciative of Alcuin, but he was still living, and the *Vita Gregorii* was scarcely the place to express that appreciation.

## 6. ALTFRID'S *VITA LIUDGERI*

It has been possible to unravel some of the complexity of Liudger's *Life of Gregory* – and hence of the development of missionary ideology following Alcuin's *Life of Willibrord* – because of the points of comparison it affords with earlier works, and above all because of the existence of a *Life* of Liudger himself, written by his nephew, Altfrid, who was also to become bishop of Münster and rector of the family monastery of Werden in 839. Of course it would be wrong to assume that Altfrid's account is purely historical, and that the author and his own concerns have not in any way affected the work – though the overlap in attitude between the *Vita Gregorii* and the *Vita Liudgeri* is reason enough to think that Altfrid does accurately represent some of his uncle's interests.

To some extent Altfrid had it easy: Liudger was his uncle; he was writing family hagiography, about a man who was genuinely responsible for the foundation of the monastery and the establishment of the see with which he was charged. Further, so far as anyone can tell, the family had played a considerable role in the Christianisation of Frisia. The opening chapters of the *Vita Liudgeri*, which concern Liudger's and hence Altfrid's own forebears, provide perhaps the most convincing account to be found of a family's role in the process of Christianisation. First, there was Liudger's paternal grandfather, Wrssing, who fell foul of Radbod, while still a pagan, and fled to Francia, where he was received by Grimoald, and where he and his family were subsequently baptised. Radbod's attempt to patch up the breach, when he fell ill, led to negotiations with Wrssing, the return of the younger son, and the restoration of the family's land. Wrssing and the rest of the family only followed after Radbod's death, and thereafter they gave considerable support to Willibrord.[146]

Next there were the matriarchs on Liudger's mother's side. There was the black sheep of the family, Liudger's pagan great-grandmother, who was so angry when her daughter-in-law kept on producing female offspring that she ordered the death of a new-born child. The story affords extraordinary insight into prechristian practices in Frisia: it was permissible to kill children who had not eaten earthly food – a practice which is reflected in the different levels of penance imposed by the penitential now ascribed to Willibrord, where the killing of neonates is treated more harshly if they have tasted milk.[147] In the case described by Altfrid the method of execution was drowning – in this instance in a tub. Fortunately, the child clung onto the side of the receptacle into which it was thrown, and was then saved by neighbours who gave it honey, thus rendering it immune from such exposure: the child was Liafburg, Liudger's mother.[148] But Liafburg's own mother is worthy of note, for she was a Christian who was in a position to hand her brothers over to Willibrord, for a Christian upbringing.[149] Secular women, both rich and poor, are regular and notable presences in hagiography relating to Frisia and Saxony – and this must suggest something of their position in society.

Altfrid seems to have had good access to family tradition. He also seems to have understood very clearly the new hagiographical models of Liudger's day, although the extent to which he did is obscured by what is still the best edition of the *Vita Liudgeri*: that of Diekamp from 1881. The problem here is the addition of book and chapter numbers, which are Diekamp's own. In dividing the work into two books and taking the break at Liudger's death, the editor simply destroyed the structure of the work. If one ignores the imposed divisions, and turns instead to the exact halfway point[150] one finds the following statement: 'although the ministry of evangelical preaching should take precedence and [so too there is] the illumination of many hearts by the operations of miracles and the showing of signs, which we hear were done by that holy man, which, however, we attribute in writing to the honour of God the giver' [*quamvis praeponendum sit ministerium evangelicae predicationis et multorum inluminatio cordium operationibus miraculorum ostensionibusque signorum, ad honorem tamen largientis Domini stilo alligari fecimus, quae ob eodem santo viro facta recolimus*].[151] This is nothing other than a slight restatement of the central point of Alcuin's *Vita Willibrordi*,[152] although the slightly altered phraseology suggests more interest in the miraculous than evinced by Alcuin. For all the difference in tone between the *Vita Liudgeri* and the *Vita Willibrordi* – the former is one of the texts most abounding in detail, the latter one of the texts which remains most firmly theoretical – Altfrid wrote a work whose structure was modelled exactly on Alcuin's.

The miracles as recounted by Altfrid begin with an extensive account of a blind pagan, Bernlef, who was notable for being able to sing of the deeds of the old kings. Liudger cured him, by having him confess and do penance, then by making the sign of the cross. Thereafter, during one of the periods in which he had to withdraw from the region because of pagan resurgence, Liudger sent Bernlef among the women of Frisia to encourage them to have their infants baptised. Later Liudger taught him the psalms.[153] The anecdote seems to reflect the missionary world of Liudger.

In other respects the miraculous brings us closer to concerns which are more obviously those of Altfrid rather than of Liudger. The majority of miracles take place after the saint's death, and it seems reasonable to link this interest with the probability that Altfrid was responsible for building a crypt to which Liudger's body was translated.[154] So too, the saint's vision of dark clouds chasing the sun, which he saw while staying at his estate of Muiderberg, where he had built a church, and which is interpreted as foreshadowing the coming of the Vikings, suggests a rather more direct concern of Altfrid than of Liudger.[155] One might also wonder whether the saint's desire to evangelise the Northmen[156] did not have a particular resonance for Altfrid, not just because of the Viking attacks, but also because of missions to Denmark and Sweden which were under way at precisely the time of Altfrid's writing. The *Vita Liudgeri* may take us very close to the interests of the work's subject, and it may well contain a more factually accurate narrative than other hagiographical works which preceded it. At the same time it illustrates the development of a tradition of missionary hagiography derived from Alcuin and developed by Liudger. On the other hand, it should not be entirely separated from its time of composition.

## 7. *VITA LEBUINI ANTIQUA*

There is another, well-known, but problematic, text associated with this group, which requires consideration. In the course of his narrative Altfrid dealt at some length with the career of Lebuin, and in so doing he provided the author of the *Vita Lebuini Antiqua* with a considerable amount of his information. According to Altfrid, Lebuin, or Liafwin as he calls him, following Old English and Saxon orthography, arrived in Frisia from England: he went to Gregory of Utrecht, and was sent to work in the valley of the Yssel, on the border between the Frisians and the Saxons. There he received support from the matron Avaerhilda and others, who built him an oratory at Huilpa (Wilp) and subsequently a church at nearby Deventer itself. The Saxons, however, drove him from the region, destroying the church. Lebuin retreated to Utrecht, but later returned to preach and to restore the church at Deventer, where he was buried. A subsequent Saxon incursion led to further destruction, particularly of the church, which Liudger was sent to make good.[157]

The first *Life of Lebuin* takes the story of the saint's work at Wilp, but prefaces it with a short discussion on the holy men of England, derived in part from Bede's *Ecclesiastical History*,[158] and then with a description of Gregory of Utrecht, derived from Altfrid's *Vita Liudgeri* and Liudger's *Vita Gregorii*.[159] More important, he follows up the story of the foundation of the church at Wilp with an account of Lebuin's missionary escapades in Saxony. He relates how the saint converted many, including one Folcbraht in the Südergau – the region round Münster.[160] Although the pagans destroyed his church (it is not clear whether this is a reference to a church in Saxony or to that at Deventer) and attempted to throw him out, he resolved to appeal directly to the Saxons at their annual meeting at Marklo. Despite the protests of Folcbraht, he did exactly that, announcing to the assembly that, if the Saxons did not accept Christianity, they would soon be enslaved by a neighbouring king: an obvious reference to Charlemagne. This speech inflamed a number of those present, but Lebuin escaped, and thereafter wiser counsel prevailed, allowing him to preach wherever he wanted.[161] The final chapter of the *Vita Lebuini*, recounting his death, burial, and the restoration of his church at Deventer by Liudger, is taken directly from Altfrid.[162]

The *Vita Lebuini Antiqua* attracts attention not just because of its account of Lebuin's work, but also because of what it has to say about the political structure of Saxony. The author explains how the Saxons were ruled not by kings, but by satraps set over each *pagus*. Every year these satraps gathered at Marklo on the Weser to renew laws, discuss lawsuits and decide whether there should be war or not. Each satrap was accompanied to the assembly by twelve nobles, twelve free men and twelve *laeti*.[163] Exactly what is meant by this description is unclear, but what is certain is that we should be careful of thinking that the author had in mind a remarkably early example of democracy. Those accompanying the satraps are more likely to have been chosen by them, than by a free election.[164]

The value of the description is, in any case, doubtful. Apart from his account of Marklo, the author is totally dependent on written sources. Even the description of the rule of satraps begins with words from Bede.[165] Admittedly, Bede was not the only Anglo-Saxon writer of the eighth century to use the term 'satrap': it is used by the West Saxon king, Cynewulf, to describe his own nobles, in addressing Lull.[166] Writing on the continent, Hygeburg employs it to describe the local aristocrats – Bavarians, not Saxons – who attended the translation of Wynnebald at Heidenheim.[167] So too Arbeo of Freising uses the word to describe Bavarian nobles,[168] and it appears in a charter which he signed in 763.[169] It is even used to denote the Lombard aristocracy in the *Liber Pontificalis*.[170] One might also note that the term is used to refer to Attila and his followers in the *Waltarius* of Gaeraldus[171] Later, in tenth-century Scotland it even appears as a synonym for 'mormaer', 'great steward'.[172]

What was in Bede's mind, however, is relatively clear: it was the Book of Samuel, where the leaders of the Philistines are called satraps,[173] in passages which Bede himself had commented on.[174] Whether the rest of the description of Saxon political organisation and the meeting at Marklo depends on reliable evidence, and whether the picture refers to the whole of Saxony or just to Westfalia, one can only speculate. It is, however, likely that the *Vita Lebuini Antiqua* is a dangerous text on which to build an account of Saxon political structures in the eighth century, especially as they can hardly have survived the conquest by Charlemagne, or the Stellinga revolts of the mid-ninth century.[175]

It is crucial to remember that the *Vita Lebuini Antiqua* was written after Altfrid's *Vita Liudgeri* – that is, in the 840s at the earliest. The *terminus ante quem* for its composition is the early tenth-century rewrite by Hucbald of Saint-Amand (d. *c.* 930).[176] As for the place of composition, the only indicators are that it must have been written somewhere where the *Vita Gregorii* and the *Vita Liudgeri* were available[177] – although the substitution of the name form 'Lebuin' for 'Liafwin' suggests a Romance rather than a Frisian, Saxon or Anglo-Saxon author – and may indicate a place of composition associated with Saint-Amand, thus helping to explain the later interest of Hucbald. It is just possible, though, that a clue to the context in which the work was written is to be found in the attention paid to Lebuin's chief supporters, particularly Folcbraht, a namesake of whom appears as a benefactor of Werden in 799.[178] Perhaps the text was in part meant to extol the family of Folcbraht, just as the *Translatio sancti Alexandri* extolled the descendents of the Westfalian leader, Widukind,[179] and the *Vita Liutbirgae* those of the Ostfalian Hessi.[180] If, however, this were the case, the use of the name-form 'Lebuin' is particularly curious.

The *Vita Lebuini Antiqua* is an interesting postlude to the writings of Liudger and Altfrid, but as a text on the history of mission it is a very uncertain witness, even of missionary attitudes. And while Lebuin's sermon, in its warning to the Saxons that they should accept Christianity or run the risk of being enslaved by a neighbouring king, seems entirely appropriate to the period before 772, one might note that a ninth-century Byzantine missionary is said to have made exactly the same threat a hundred years later,[181] in other words at roughly the time at which the *Vita Lebuini Antiqua* was written.

The narratives of missions to eastern Frisia and northern Saxony are best studied, not in the *Life of Lebuin*, but in Altfrid's *Life of Liudger* and, perhaps, the anonymous *Life of Willehad*. But the ideology which came to dominate those missions, and the changes within that ideology, are best studied in Alcuin's *Life of Willibrord* and Liudger's *Life of Gregory*. These last texts may be of little importance for reconstructing the narrative of events, but they are crucial for understanding the development of a missionary ideology, which was largely expressed through an exploration of a less than accurate view of the past. Alcuin's notion of mission as preaching, devoid of the use of force, had effectively triumphed, and Liudger and Altfrid had taken what is essentially the work of an armchair theoretician and added to it a sense of the reality of action in the missionary field.

## Notes

1. Liudger, *Vita Gregorii* 9. See the comments in Berschin, *Karolingische Biographie 750–920 n. Chr.*, pp. 41–50.
2. Berschin, *Karolingische Biographie 750–920 n. Chr.*, p. 49.

3. Berschin, *Karolingische Biographie 750–920 n. Chr.*, pp. 46–7 argues that it is neither historical nor hagiographical, but rather a Pauline *sermo*.

4. Liudger, *Vita Gregorii* 1.

5. Liudger, *Vita Gregorii* 1.

6. Liudger, *Vita Gregorii* 5. See Berschin, *Karolingische Biographie 750–920 n. Chr.*, p. 44.

7. Liudger, *Vita Gregorii* 6.

8. Liudger, *Vita Gregorii* 2.

9. Altfrid, *Vita Liudgeri* I 4, 27. Senger, *Liudger, Leben und Werk*, pp. 100–103.

10. Liudger, *Vita Gregorii* 2.

11. Liudger, *Vita Gregorii* 2.

12. Willibald, *Vita Bonifatii* 4.

13. Altfrid, *Vita Liudgeri* I 14, 15, 21.

14. H. Löwe, 'Liudger als Zeitkritiker', *Historisches Jahrbuch* 74 (1955), pp. 79–91, reprinted in Löwe, *Von Cassiodor zu Dante: Ausgewählte Aufsätze zur Geschichtschreibung und politischen Ideenwelt des Mittelalters* (Berlin, 1973), pp. 111–22.

15. Hygeburg, *Vita Wynnebaldi* 7.

16. Alcuin, ep. 111; compare ep. 254.

17. Liudger, *Vita Gregorii* 3.

18. T. Schieffer, *Winfrid-Bonifatius*, p. 165. Parsons, 'Sites and monuments of the Anglo-Saxon mission in central Germany', pp. 281–2.

19. Boniface, epp. 50, 51.

20. Liudger, *Vita Gregorii* 4.

21. Schieffer, *Winfrid-Bonifatius*, pp. 226–8; Wallace-Hadrill, *The Frankish Church*, p. 137.

22. Liudger, *Vita Gregorii* 4.

23. Liudger, *Vita Gregorii* 7.

24. Boniface, epp. 16–18.

25. Liudger, *Vita Gregorii* 10.

26. Boniface, ep. 109.

27. Liudger, *Vita Gregorii* 10.

28. Liudger, *Vita Gregorii* 4.

29. c.f. Willibald, *Vita Bonifatii* 8: *per Fresiam inluxerat splendor*.

30. Berschin, *Karolingische Biographie 750–920 n. Chr.*, p. 49 argues that Liudger knew Willibald's work.

31. Liudger, *Vita Gregorii* 2; Willibald, *Vita Bonifatii* 6.

32. Willibald, *Vita Bonifatii* 8, citing Acts 4, 32.

33. Altfrid, *Vita Liudgeri* I 30.

34. Altfrid, *Vita Liudgeri* I 5.

35. *Vita Altera Bonifatii* 16.

36. *Vita Altera Bonifatii* 16. The dating of the *vita* is discussed by Levison, *Vitae sancti Bonifatii*, pp. xlviii–liv: his conclusions are repeated by Berschin, *Karolingische Biographie 750–920 n. Chr.*, p. 14.

37. Levison, *Vitae sancti Bonifatii*, p. xlix.

38. Klüppel, 'Die Germania (750–950)', p. 167, states, 'Die *Vita II S. Bonifatii* eines Verfassers aus Utrecht (*BHL* 1401) ist nicht erst die Amtzeit Bischof Radbods (899–917) zuzuordnen, sondern gehört in die erste Hälfte des IX. Jahrhunderts . . .'

39. *Vita Altera Bonifatii* 8.

40. Radbod, *Libellus de miraculo sancti Martini*, prol., ed. O. Holder-Egger, MGH, SS 15 2 (Hanover, 1888); *Homilia de sancto Lebuino*, PL 132, col. 556.

41. Radbod, *Libellus de miraculo sancti Martini* 3.

42. Radbod, *Libellus de miraculo sancti Martini* 7.

43. Radbod, *Sermo de Swithberto* 3, PL 132.

44. *Vita Altera Bonifatii* 6; see the discussion of Levison, *Vitae sancti Bonifatii*, p. lii.

45. Radbod, *Libellus de miraculo sancti Martini* 4–6.

46. The dates are determined by Altfrid's episcopate, since he names himself as bishop in the prologue to the work; for those dates I have followed K. Hauck, *Apostolischer Geist im Genus sacerdotale des Liudgeriden* (Essen, 1986).

47. Altfrid, *Vita Liudgeri* I 27.

48. The argument for Radbod as reviser is set out in M. Carasso-Kok, 'Le diocèse d'Utrecht, 900–1200', in G. Philippart, *Hagiographies*, 2, Corpus Christianorum (Turnhout, 1996), pp. 385–6.

49. Altfrid, *Vita Liudgeri* I 30.

50. Berschin, *Karolingische Biographie 750–920 n. Chr.*, p. 16 opts for a date *c.* 825, placing the text in the context of the Carolingian rationalism of Claudius of Turin and Agobard of Lyons, and identifying as a possible author Friedrich of Utrecht. He does, however, allow for the possibility of a revision by Radbod.

51. Compare Liudger, *Vita Gregorii* 7 with Radbod, *Homilia de sancto Lebwino*, col. 556.

52. c.f. the use of the word *fratres* in *Vita Altera Bonifatii* 18. For the link with St Martin's see also the emphasis on the cult of Martin at Tours, Mainz and Utrecht, in *Vita Altera Bonifatii* 1–3, 22–3.

53. *Vita Altera Bonifatii* 6.

54. *Vita Altera Bonifatii* 6.

55. *Vita Altera Bonifatii* 7.

56. *Vita Altera Bonifatii* 8–9.

57. *Vita Altera Bonifatii* 9–10.

58. *Vita Altera Bonifatii* 10.

59. *Vita Altera Bonifatii* 11.

60. *Vita Altera Bonifatii* 13.

61. *Vita Altera Bonifatii* 14–16.

62. *Vita Altera Bonifatii* 16.

63. Willibald, *Vita Bonifatii* 9.

64. *Vita Altera Bonifatii* 16.

65. Fulda, Domschatz, Cod. Bonifatii 2.

66. *Vita Altera Bonifatii* 14. A general comparison of Paul and Boniface, implicit in Willibald's *Vita Bonifatii*, is also present in Alcuin's poem on the church built by Liudger at Dokkum: Altfrid, *Vita Liudgeri* I 20.

67. *Vita Altera Bonifatii* 2, 19.

68. *Vita Altera Bonifatii* 8.

69. Liudger, *Vita Gregorii* 2, 3.

70. Altfrid, *Vita Liudgeri* I 14, 15–16, 21.

71. Altfrid, *Vita Liudgeri* I 6–7, 14, 16, 22, 25.

72. *Vita Altera Bonifatii* 9.

73. See above n. 51.

74. Willibald, *Vita Bonifatii* 8.

75. Eigil, *Vita Sturmi* 15a.

76. Eigil, *Vita Sturmi* 51b.

77. Alcuin, *Vita Willibrordi* 11.

78. *Vita Willehadi* 6.

79. *Vita Altera Bonifatii* 18.

80. C.f. the emphasis on the cult of Martin at Tours, Mainz and Utrecht, in *Vita Altera Bonifatii* 1–3, 22–3.
81. This is a point that Levison seems crucially to have missed, *Vitae sancti Bonifatii*, p. liii.
82. *Vita Altera Bonifatii* 1.
83. *Vita Altera Bonifatii* 3–4.
84. *Vita Altera Bonifatii* 18.
85. *Vita Altera Bonifatii* 19.
86. *Vita Altera Bonifatii* 20.
87. *Vita Altera Bonifatii* 19.
88. Wood, 'The mission of Augustine of Canterbury to the English', pp. 13–15.
89. Liudger, *Vita Gregorii*, pref., 8, 9, 14.
90. Liudger, *Vita Gregorii* 2.
91. Boniface, ep. 92.
92. Liudger, *Vita Gregorii* 8.
93. Liudger, *Vita Gregorii* 10.
94. Altfrid, *Vita Liudgeri* I 13, 18, 24.
95. Liudger, *Vita Gregorii* 9.
96. Liudger, *Vita Gregorii* 12.
97. Alcuin, *Vita Willibrordi* 14.
98. Liudger, *Vita Gregorii* 11.
99. Altfrid, *Vita Liudgeri* I 9, 13.
100. Liudger, *Vita Gregorii* 11–12.
101. Liudger, *Vita Gregorii* 14.
102. Liudger, *Vita Gregorii* 15.
103. Altfrid, *Vita Liudgeri* I 5, 8. The history of Liudger is usefully discussed in Senger, *Liudger, Leben und Werk*.
104. Altfrid, *Vita Liudgeri* I 1–3.
105. Altfrid, *Vita Liudgeri* I 5.
106. Altfrid, *Vita Liudgeri* I 4, 27. See the discussion in Senger, *Liudger, Leben und Werk*, pp. 100–3.
107. Altfrid, *Vita Liudgeri* I 27.
108. The date is Senger's, *Liudger, Leben und Werk*, p. 16.
109. Altfrid, *Vita Liudgeri* I 8.
110. Liudger, *Vita Gregorii* 2.
111. Altfrid, *Vita Liudgeri* I 30.
112. Liudger, *Vita Gregorii* 2, 8, 14, 15.
113. e.g. the manuscript of the Pauline epistles, Berlin, Staatsbibliothek zu Berlin – Preußischer Kulturbesitz, Ms. lat. fol. 366. See *799 Kunst und Kultur der Karolingerzeit, Karl der Große und Papst Leo III. in Paderborn*, ed. C. Stiegemann and M. Wemhoff, 2, pp. 483–5. See also pp. 469–71 and 479–91 in the same catalogue.
114. Liudger, *Vita Gregorii* 10.
115. Altfrid, *Vita Liudgeri* I 9.
116. Altfrid, *Vita Liudgeri* I 10.
117. *Vita Willehadi* 1.
118. Altfrid, *Vita Liudgeri* I 11–12.
119. Altfrid, *Vita Liudgeri* I 13–14. For the *Vita Lebuini Antiquissima*, which is dependent on Altfrid's work, see below. The date of Lebuin's death is that given by Senger, *Liudger, Leben und Werk*, p. 30.

120. Altfrid, *Vita Liudgeri* I 15.
121. Altfrid, *Vita Liudgeri* I 16.
122. Altfrid, *Vita Liudgeri* I 17.
123. Altfrid, *Vita Liudgeri* I 18.
124. Acts 10, 10–17.
125. Altfrid, *Vita Liudgeri* I 22.
126. See, for example, Rudolf of Fulda/Meginhart of Fulda, *Translatio sancti Alexandri* 4, ed. B. Krusch, 'Die Übertragung des H. Alexander von Rom nach Wildeshausen durch den Enkel Widukings 851: Das älteste niedersächsische Geschichtsdenkmal', *Nachrichten von der Gesellschaft der Wissenschaften zu Göttingen* aus dem Jahre 1933, Philologisch-Historische Klasse (Berlin, Weidmann, 1933).
127. Altfrid, *Vita Liudgeri* I 22.
128. Altfrid, *Vita Liudgeri* I 22; Alcuin, *Vita Willibrordi* 10.
129. Altfrid, *Vita Liudgeri* I 23.
130. Altfrid, *Vita Liudgeri* I 32.
131. The date is that of A. Schröer, 'Das Datum der Bischofsweihe Liudgers von Münster', *Historisches Jahrbuch* 76 (1957), pp. 106–17.
132. Altfrid, *Vita Liudgeri* I 24.
133. *Vita Willehadi* 8.
134. Rimbert, *Vita Anskarii* 12.
135. Altfrid, *Vita Liudgeri* I 10. Alcuin had already mentioned the possibility of a Danish mission in his letter to Willehad, ep. 6.
136. Altfrid, *Vita Liudgeri* I 20.
137. Liudger, *Vita Gregorii* 5.
138. Alcuin, *Vita Richarii* 1, *velut lucifer inter umbras oriens emicuit.*
139. For 800, Berschin, *Karolingische Biographie 750–920 n. Chr.*, p. 141; for 801, Deug-Su, *L'Opera agiographica di Alcuino*, pp. 115, 190.
140. Altfrid, *Vita Liudgeri* I 5.
141. Berschin, *Karolingische Biographie 750–920 n. Chr.*, p. 47, sees *sermo* as the crucial word.
142. Liudger, *Vita Gregorii* 1.
143. Liudger, *Vita Gregorii* 2.
144. Klüppel, 'Die Germania (750–950)', pp. 171–2: 'In Wirklichkeit stellt die Gregorvita sowohl Lebensbeschreibung wie Predigt dar, sie intendiert keine Heiligenverehrung, sie will das große Programm des Bonifatius weitergeben, die Mission fortsetzen, also verkündigen.'
145. Löwe, 'Liudger als Zeitkritiker'.
146. Altfrid, *Vita Liudgeri* I 1–4.
147. See also Meens, 'Willibrords boeteboek?', pp. 168–9.
148. Altfrid, *Vita Liudgeri* I 6–7.
149. Altfrid, *Vita Liudgeri* I 5.
150. Paying attention to Diekamp's own note, *Die Vitae sancti Liudgeri*, p. 30, a: 'Die Ausgaben beginnen hier den liber secundus mit neuer Capitelzählung'.
151. Altfrid, *Vita Liudgeri* I 25.
152. Alcuin, *Vita Willibrordi* 14.
153. Altfrid, *Vita Liudgeri* I 25–6.
154. Hauck, *Apostolischer Geist im Genus sacerdotale der Liudgeriden*, pp. 20–22.
155. Altfrid, *Vita Liudgeri* I 27.
156. Altfrid, *Vita Liudgeri* I 30.

157. Altfrid, *Vita Liudgeri* I 13–15.

158. *Vita Lebuini Antiqua* 1, ed. O. Hofmeister, MGH, SS 30 (Leipzig, 1934).

159. *Vita Lebuini Antiqua* 2; Altfrid, *Vita Liudgeri* I 13; Liudger, *Vita Gregorii* 1.

160. *Vita Lebuini Antiqua* 3.

161. *Vita Lebuini Antiqua* 4–6.

162. *Vita Lebuini Antiqua* 7; Altfrid, *Vita Liudgeri* I 15.

163. *Vita Lebuini Antiqua* 4.

164. M. Springer, 'Was Lebuins Lebensbeschreibung über die Verfassung Sachsens wirklich sagt oder warum man sich mit einselnen Wörter beschäftigen muß', *Studien zur Sachsenforschung* 12 (Oldenburg, 1999), pp. 223–39.

165. Bede, *Historia Ecclesiastica* V 10; M. Becher, '*Non habent regem idem Antiqui Saxones* . . . Verfassung und Ethnogenese in Sachsen während des 8. Jahrhunderts', *Studien zur Sachsenforschung* 12 (Oldenburg, 1999), pp. 1–32.

166. Boniface, ep. 139.

167. Hygeburg, *Vita Wynnebaldi* 13.

168. Arbeo, *Vita Haimhrammi* 10, 34; *id.*, *Vita Corbiniani* 15, 42.

169. *Die Traditionen des Hochstifts Freising*, ed. T. Bitterauf, 1 (Munich, 1905), n. 19.

170. *Liber Pontificalis*, 93, 7, ed. L. Duchesne, *Le Liber Pontificalis* (Paris, 1886–92).

171. Gaeraldus, *Waltarius*, ll. 43, 136, ed. A. K. Bate (Reading, 1978).

172. A. Grant, 'The construction of the early Scottish state', in J. R. Maddicott and D. M. Palliser, *The Medieval State* (London, 2000), p. 65.

173. Samuel I 5, 11; 6, 16.

174. Bede, *In primam partem Samuelis Libri IIII*, ed. D. Hurst, Corpus Christianorum Series Latina 119 (Turnhout, 1962). Bede also commented on satraps in his commentary on Ezrah and Nehemiah, but it is unlikely to have been these passages he had in mind in discussing Saxony: see I. N. Wood, 'Beyond satraps and ostriches: political and social structures of the Saxons in the early Carolingian period' (forthcoming).

175. E. J. Goldberg, 'Popular revolt, dynastic politics and aristocratic factionalism in the Early Middle Ages: the Saxon Stellinga reconsidered', *Speculum* 70 (1995), pp. 467–501.

176. J. M. H. Smith, 'The hagiography of Hucbald of Saint-Amand', *Studi Medievali* 35 (1994), pp. 517–42. See also the comments of Price, 'The holy man and Christianisation from the apocryphal apostles to St Stephen of Perm', p. 222.

177. Thus Klüppel, 'Die Germania (750–950)', p. 173, opts for Werden, Utrecht or Deventer.

178. Hofmeister, ed. *Vita Lebuini Antiqua*, MGH, SS 30, 2, p. 792, n.12.

179. ed. B. Krusch, 'Die Übertragung des H. Alexander von Rom nach Wildeshausen durch den Enkel Widukinds 851: Das älteste niedersächsische Geschichtsdenkmal', pp. 405–36.

180. ed. O. Menzel, *Das Leben des Liutbirg*, Deutsches Mittelalter, Kritische Studientexte des Reichsinstituts für ältere deutsche Geschichtskunde, MGH 3 (Leipzig, 1937).

181. *Vita Methodii* 11, ed. A. Vaillant, *Textes vieux-slaves*, 2 vols (Paris, 1968).

# Chapter 6

# HAMBURG AND BREMEN

## 1. ANSKAR

The first phase of the Christianisation of Saxony was achieved under Char- (*died 814 AD*) lemagne with establishment of such dioceses as Bremen and Münster. Other diocesan centres would be established under Charlemagne's son and successor, Louis the Pious.[1] But there were still thought to be pagans around in the middle of the century, according to the *Life of Liutbirga*.[2] The relics of St Alexander were deliberately brought from Rome to Saxony in 840 by Widukind's grandson, Waltbraht, who thought that this would aid in the process of Christianisation.[3] Yet Saxony was no longer the chief field for missionary activity after the death of Liudger. Instead, eyes turned to Denmark.

There is little evidence for the mission of Archbishop Ebo of Rheims in 823, although he had received legatine authority in the North from Pope Paschal the previous year,[4] and he was successful enough to induce King Harald Klak to convert and then accept baptism under the aegis of Louis the Pious, at Mainz, three years later.[5] There it was decided to send a clerical party back to Denmark with the Danish king: among those sent was a monk of Corvey called Anskar, whose career was to be described at length by his pupil, Rimbert. His *Vita Anskarii* is, inevitably, the backbone of any narrative of the saint.

Anskar himself was born in west Francia in *c.* 801. At the age of five he was sent for schooling to the monastery of Corbie, where he subsequently became a monk, though it was the death of Charlemagne in 814 which prompted his commitment to a truly ascetic life.[6] Shortly thereafter he became master of the school.[7] In 815, however, Louis the Pious founded a monastery on the Weser as a daughter house of Corbie, *Nova Corbeia* or Corvey, and Anskar was among those transferred to the new foundation.[8] It was from Corvey that Anskar was taken, with the permission of his abbot, to join Harald on his return to Denmark.[9] Although Harald was not the best of company, he did provide the environment for two years of missionary work, which included the purchase and education of young boys.[10] At the end of that time Anskar returned to Corvey – possibly because Harald himself had been driven out of his kingdom.[11]

In a sense this was fortuitous, because in 829 a Swedish legation arrived at the court of Louis the Pious, and Anskar was once again chosen to take part.[12] Despite the loss of all their books and liturgical vessels at the hands of pirates, Anskar and his companion, Witmar, his fellow master from Corbie days,[13] reached Birka on Lake Mäleren. According to Rimbert, when they arrived, the king of the region, Bern, asked why they had come – a strange question, since they had supposedly come in response to a Swedish request made to Louis – and they were then given permission to preach, which they did for six months, before reporting back to Louis the Pious.[14] Shortly after his return, Anskar was appointed to the new bishopric of Hamburg (831), and was provided with Torhout in Flanders as a possible place of retreat, away from the front line of mission – a property he was to lose in the division of Louis the Pious' empire after 840.[15] Having been appointed to Hamburg, Anskar was then sent to Rome to collect the *pallium*, thus gaining archepiscopal status, and while there, he was put in charge of mission to the Danes, Swedes and Slavs, along with Ebo.[16] Thereafter, he continued his work in Denmark and among the Slavs, once again pursuing his policy of purchasing young boys for future missionary work.[17] Ebo, meanwhile, put forward his nephew, Gauzbert, to take over the Swedish mission.[18]

Ebo's own position in the ensuing years was to change dramatically. Like Wala, Anskar's abbot at Corbie, he was a supporter of Louis the Pious' son, Lothar, who was the figurehead of opposition to his father. As a result, Ebo was involved in the deposition of Louis in 833.[19] For this he was deprived of his bishopric two years later.[20] Subsequently, in 846, after the death of Louis the Pious, he was appointed to the see of Hildesheim. Despite these ups and down – which Rimbert tactfully ignores – he continued to advise Anskar: Rimbert records conversations between the two men which Anskar seems to have found particularly supportive.[21] As for Gauzbert, although he was thrown out by the Swedes in 845, and returned to east Francia to become bishop of Osnabrück, he continued to exercise legatine authority until his death in 859. Nor was he the only member of Ebo's family to become involved in the northern mission. When the Swedes turned on him in 845, his nephew, Nithard, who was with him, was killed,[22] and later, when Gauzbert decided not to return to the Swedes, another of his nephews, Erembert, was sent in his place.[23] Gauzbert himself sent the priest, Ansfrid, who had been trained by Ebo, to the Swedes, on a subsequent occasion.[24] Although Rimbert provides relatively little detail on Ebo and his family, he makes it clear that they played a crucial role in the Swedish mission.

Despite the changing political scene in the Empire, the 830s and early 840s were a period of apparent success for Anskar. This suddenly came to an end with the expulsion of Gauzbert's mission from Sweden,[25] and, more dramatic still, the unexpected sack of Hamburg by Vikings in 845.[26] The destruction of Anskar's church and of his treasures and books was devastating. In fact, the devastation was such that the diocese of Hamburg was deemed to be beyond restoration, and Anskar was instead appointed to the diocese of Bremen in 847.[27] This arrangement, however, was thought to be inappropriate, since Hamburg had been an archdiocese: the result was that Hamburg and Bremen were amalgamated, giving rise to long-standing hostility from the archbishops of Cologne, to whom Bremen had been subject. The argument was not to be ended until Pope Nicolas I judged in Anskar's favour in 864.[28]

Despite the setbacks of 845, Anskar continued missionary work in Denmark, managing to strike up a remarkable working relationship with King Horic I[29] – the man who may have been responsible for the attack on Hamburg.[30] He also revived the Swedish mission in the early 850s,[31] although its position was never particularly secure.[32] But in 854 disaster struck again, when Horic was killed. In the ensuing civil war the Danish mission was badly disrupted. In the end, the next ruler to emerge, Horic II, opted to collaborate with Anskar, who came to establish as good relations with the new king as with his older namesake.[33] It was Horic II who allowed the foundation of a church at Ribe.[34] Anskar, however, died in 865,[35] and Horic cannot have long survived him. Rimbert, the saint's hagiographer, succeeded his master as archbishop of Hamburg-Bremen, and continued his missionary work, albeit in increasingly unpropitious circumstances.

## 2. RIMBERT'S *VITA ANSKARII*: SOURCES AND AUDIENCE

Anskar died in 865. Rimbert apparently wrote his *vita* of the saint shortly thereafter: he makes it plain that he and his community are still grief-stricken at the time of writing.[36] On the other hand he apparently wrote the *Life* while at Bremen (or perhaps Hamburg),[37] and, since he spent the months immediately after his own appointment to the episcopate in Corvey,[38] this would imply a composition date several months after Anskar's death, at the earliest.

The text that he wrote is made up of a variety of elements: it is entitled 'the life, deeds and death' [*vita vel gesta seu obitum*], but Rimbert himself says three-quarters of the way through that he has said much about the matter of the saint's legation and the care with which he desired to save others [*de causa legationis eius et cura qua alios salvare cupiebat*]. He then goes on to talk about Anskar's lifestyle.[39] The word *causa* implies that Rimbert is concerned to provide more than a narrative account of Anskar's missions, since he is also concerned with its legal basis, while the word *cura* indicates his intention to discuss the more pastoral aspects of the saint's work. But the first three-quarters of the *vita* are not simply a discussion of Anskar's missionary work and its legal basis. In particular, there is considerable discussion of the saint as a visionary. Rimbert himself explains that the visionary material was added (*interserere*) to the work (*opus*) after Anskar's death.[40] This implies that there was an early draft in existence while Anskar was still alive. This can scarcely have included the account of Anskar's early life, which is dominated by visionary material, nor the final discussion of his sanctity, which would have been vainglorious – and pride was a particular fear of the saint and his biographer.[41]

Anskar had an account of the history of his legation compiled before his death, and circulated to Louis the German, his son and his bishops.[42] In all probability, this account of the *legatio* was basically a legal text intended to restate the case for the amalgamation of Hamburg/Bremen, which had only just been confirmed by Nicolas I in 864,[43] though in dealing with the *causa legationis* it may well have also contained a chronological narrative of Anskar's visits to Denmark and Sweden. It is certainly likely that this document provided the essential framework to which Rimbert added the visionary material. Such a source would explain the presence of material on Ebo, Gauzbert and others, who feature in the *Vita Anskarii*, even if never to the extent of overshadowing the protagonist: at times indeed the *Vita Anskarii* is more like a history of the whole northern mission than a simple *Life* of one saint. The implication of this is that the factual basis of Rimbert's account of Anskar's legation is likely to be largely accurate, even though the material is not always arranged chronologically, and despite the fact that there are certain crucial events, like the expulsion of Harald Klak from Denmark, and the deposition of Louis the Pious and the removal of Ebo of Rheims from his see, which are left unmentioned. It is one thing to deploy material in a non-chronological way, and another actually to state a falsehood. In a document intended to demonstrate a legal right in the face of considerable opposition one does not usually make unnecessary errors. That Rimbert may also have sent the earliest surviving copy of the *Vita Anskarii* to Solomon of Konstanz, who negotiated the papal ruling in 864, would further suggest that in its coverage of the more formal/legalistic side of Anskar's *legatio* the text is accurate, albeit biased.[44]

Bias can unquestionably be seen in the structure of the *Vita Anskarii*, which is such that the ruling of Pope Nicolas falls exactly midway through the text,[45] although chronologically it is one of the most recent events recorded by Rimbert. The ruling is thus given pride of place. Its position is achieved by a sleight of hand: Rimbert treats the whole issue of the amalgamation of Hamburg/Bremen as a single topic, effectively as an excursus,[46] thus not actually misdating the events, but taking them outside chronology. The importance of the halfway mark is further strengthened by the fact that the foundation of the see of Hamburg falls a quarter of the way through the text,[47] and that the final quarter of the work is concerned not with narrative, but with Anskar's Christian lifestyle.[48]

The legal basis for the amalgamation of Hamburg/Bremen was clearly something that concerned Rimbert himself, which is not surprising in that he was Anskar's successor. His personal concern that matters should be legally correct is also apparent in the legalism of his behaviour at his own consecration, as described in the *Vita Rimberti*.[49] The king and bishops of Louis the German's kingdom, with their interest in the rights of individual dioceses, were not the only audience of the *Vita Anskarii*. Even though the structure of the text, indeed what holds all the elements in the work together, is determined by the legal history of Hamburg/Bremen, the work itself is addressed to the fathers and monks of Corbie.[50] It was at Corbie that Anskar had originally been a monk,[51] and had been master,[52] and from Corbie that he was moved to the daughter-house of Corvey.[53] Since Corvey was initially under the charge of the same abbot, it was by the abbot of Corbie, Wala, that he was put forward for the Danish mission in 826,[54] and again for the Swedish mission in 829.[55] Anskar's attachment to his erstwhile abbots is apparent in the role Adalhard, Wala's brother and predecessor, plays in one of the saint's visions.[56]

There was yet more, however, to the Corbie connection. When Anskar went on his first mission to Sweden his companion, Witmar, was a monk of Corbie, selected by Wala.[57] Monks from Corbie continued to be involved in the Scandinavian mission until the division of the Carolingian kingdom following Louis the Pious' death in 840.[58] Even afterwards the monastery may have continued to send books to Anskar.[59] Certainly, Rimbert regarded Ratramnus of Corbie as a man who could be turned to for advice.[60] It may be that we should see in Rimbert's treatment of Anskar's foreknowledge a pale reflection of the predestinarian debate surrounding Gottschalk, a some-time monk at Corbie, who had some limited support from Ratramnus.[61] Not surprisingly, the Corbie audience is a significant one: it is appealed to in the *Vita Anskarii* on more than one occasion.[62] It may account for Rimbert's emphasis on Anskar as monk,[63] though the author had his own monastic sympathies, most apparent in his decision to become a monk immediately before taking up his episcopal office.[64]

## 3. VISIONS

There are at least two other elements in Rimbert's narrative which demand consideration: the visions and the long excursus on proto-Christianity in Denmark and Sweden. They take us beyond the monastic and episcopal audiences of the *Vita Anskarii*. Visions are not a new feature in missionary

texts – we have met them in Patrick's *Confessio*, and in missionary hagiography of the ninth century: they are a feature of *Lives* concerned with
saints active in Saxony.[65] Liudger, in particular, is said to have had a number
of visionary experiences.[66] Their prominence in the *Vita Anskarii* is, however, unusual,[67] and Rimbert himself stresses their being a distinctive feature
of his work.[68] According to his own hagiographer, Rimbert was personally
influenced by Anskar's visions.[69] Like the material relating to Hamburg/
Bremen, they provide another structural feature in the *vita*. They also serve,
for Rimbert, to place his subject between earth and heaven.[70]

   That Anskar really did have the visions recorded by Rimbert is implied by
the simple point that the saint was misled by one of his experiences into
expecting martyrdom.[71] The fact that he was not martyred caused him
considerable distress, and left Rimbert with the problem of explaining away
the non-martyrdom – a problem that he deals with partly theologically[72]
and partly by shifting the normal definitions of martyrdom. Thus, rather
surprisingly, the boy Fulbert, killed when thumped on the head by a fellow pupil with a writing-tablet, enters the house of martyrs,[73] while
Nithard's death at the hands of Swedes is seen as martyrdom, but passed
over rapidly,[74] and Ragenbert's murder at the hands of pirates is seen as
no more than a cause for grief.[75] These are, as we have seen, not the first
martyrdoms of missionaries to be passed over almost without comment by
eighth- and ninth-century hagiographers.

   Anskar's visions perform a number of very clear functions: first the saint
is prompted to adopt a truly religious lifestyle by a vision in which he
wanted to join his mother in the entourage of the Virgin Mary;[76] then a
series of visions reassured him that his sins had been forgiven.[77] These had
to be balanced by another in which he saw all mankind as created out of
mud in a vale of tears, which effectively stifled his growing pride.[78] More
immediately important, as Rimbert explained, Anskar did nothing until he
understood what to do through a visionary experience: thus it took a vision
to prompt him to remonstrate with Saxon nobles for capturing Christians
who had escaped from slavery among the Danes, and then either selling
them back or keeping them as slaves themselves.[79] Occasionally, he acted
on a vision which he had experienced long before, but which he had
previously interpreted in a different light.[80] Sometimes this is construed as
foreknowledge,[81] though foreknowledge at the time of the debate over
predestination might have been a rather dangerous concept. More generally, visions could be treated as a type of consolation. This is stated most
specifically in the case of the death of Fulbert, killed by a blow from his
fellow's writing tablet: Anskar came to understand the death as martyrdom,
because, following a vision, he realised that Fulbert had prayed for his
assailant: the realisation consoled him.[82] In short, following Rimbert, Anskar's

visions had a psychological function, guiding him to action and to understanding, as well as consoling him.

## 4. MIRACLES

Rimbert includes a number of lengthy chapters on Christians in Scandinavia. These sections on early Christianity among the Danes and Swedes have an overlapping function in the text: they are concerned with God's protection of those that believe in him, and his vengeance against those who do not show appropriate reverence. The stories are also potentially crucial for our understanding of religious and social beliefs among those two peoples, and it is worth resuming in some detail the stories of God's vengeance against the family of the Viking who stole a missionary's book,[83] of Herigar,[84] Frideburg and Catla,[85] and the attack of the Swedes on the *Cori*.[86]

Three of these stories are situated in the period after the rejection of Gauzbert's Swedish mission in *c*. 845. The first relates specifically to the aftermath of the attack on Gauzbert, and to God's subsequent vengeance.[87] Among those involved in the conspiracy against the missionaries, which Rimbert is at pains to explain was popular and not prompted by the king,[88] was a man who looted a book. This he took home, with the effect that he, his wife, son and daughter all died, leaving only his father and a small boy. The thief's father decided to consult a diviner to see what was causing the disaster, and was told that although all the other gods were happy with him, Christ was not, because of a consecrated book which he had in his house. Since there was no priest around he had no idea what to do with the book, so he hung it publicly on a post. In time a Christian found it and took it away. Later, although unlettered, the Christian learnt to say the psalms: an almost inconsequential point for Rimbert, which was presumably intended to show how even illiterate Christians revered books. The hagiographer's chief concern was that Christ's vengeance was made plain.

Immediately after this Rimbert relates the story of the prefect of Birka, Herigar.[89] He had been converted and baptised at the beginning of the Swedish mission, and had even built a church on his property.[90] Despite the setback of the expulsion of Gauzbert, he continued in his faith. On one occasion, having been taunted by his religious opponents at a public gathering (*placitum*), he challenged them to see who could avoid being drenched by a rainstorm: in a version of the confrontation of Elijah and the prophets of Baal he and his servant remained dry, while the pagans were soaked and their wooden shelter destroyed. In addition, when Herigar became lame, he was told to turn to the protection of the gods: instead, he had himself carried to his church, where he was cured.

At the end of this excursus Rimbert describes the public benefits of Herigar's Christianity. An exiled king of the Swedes, Anound, had gathered together a group of Danes to help him return to his throne: as payment he offered to let them plunder Birka. Anound arrived with a fleet of thirty-two ships and besieged the emporium. The people of Birka, having offered sacrifices to demons, much to Herigar's fury, then offered to buy off Anound, and paid 100lbs of silver. The attacker's Danish supporters, however, were furious at this and determined to continue the siege, as a result of which Herigar pointed out the uselessness of applying to pagan gods, and persuaded the besieged to turn to his God. Meanwhile, Anound, who cast lots to see if Birka would fall, discovered that the Christian God would not allow it. Instead, the lots instructed his followers to attack the Slavs. Anound himself stayed behind, repaying the 100lbs of silver.

The third of the stories also relates to this same period after the rejection of Gauzbert's mission.[91] An elderly Christian woman, Frideburg, despairing of the absence of a priest in the community, set aside wine, instructing her daughter, Catla, to give it to her in place of the viaticum when she died. As it so happened, Anskar had already sent a hermit, Ardgar, to minister to the Christians in Birka.[92] After his arrival she regularly attended mass. When she was about to die, he was able to give her the viaticum. After Frideburg's death, Catla, on her mother's instructions, set out to distribute her wealth to the poor, but as there were none in Birka, she went to Dorestad, where she went round the shrines of the saints distributing alms. She discovered that what she gave in alms was replenished miraculously by God, while what she spent on herself was not. Apart from this stock miracle, what this story illustrates above all, like that of Herigar, is the constancy of Christians, and God's concern for them.

The final story is somewhat closer to the Anound episode in the Herigar tales. It is placed rather later by Rimbert, in the aftermath of Anskar's re-establishment of the Swedish mission.[93] The Danes had failed disastrously to plunder the *Cori*, a Slavic people who had previously been subject to the Swedes. Incited by this failure, the Swedish king, Olaf, decided to attack the *Cori*, and initially, at Grobin, he had some success. Marching on to Seeburg, however, he met his match. Having failed to take the town, he wondered how he might withdraw in safety. He cast lots, only to discover that no pagan god would help. Following the suggestion of a merchant, he discovered, also through the casting of lots, that the Christian God would help. Inspired by this, he made a final assault on the town, which promptly paid him off with the gold and arms taken the previous year from the Danes, together with half a pound of silver for each man as ransom, and a promise to return to subjection to the Swedes. As a result, Olaf set off home, where his followers showed their appreciation to the Christian God in fasting and almsgiving, although not, apparently, through conversion. As at Birka, the Christian God had shown his willingness to help even pagans, if they were prepared to call on his help. Both stories are remarkable, not just because they show pagan exploitation of the Christian God, but also because Rimbert was prepared to present them in that way.

All of these stories are remarkable for the picture they paint of Swedish society in the time of Anskar. There is a vivid picture of the public processes of the Swedes, meeting in *placita*, and casting lots to determine action. A similar process is described on the occasion of the reintroduction of Christianity among the Swedes in the time of Olaf, where lots are cast at least once and three meetings are held to discuss the re-establishment of Christianity.[94] The meetings themselves seem to have been envisaged as having an exact counterpart in a meeting of the gods, *conventus deorum*, which offered to elect the dead King Eric as a god, while opposing the introduction of Christianity.[95] Equally important are the more intimate pictures of Herigar and Frideburg. These stories may, of course, be figments of Rimbert's imagination, and there is certainly a problem in his suggestion that there were no poor in Birka in Frideburg's time, whereas there were plenty in the aftermath of Olaf's campaign.[96] Even more suspect is the picture of Dorestad, with its numerous shrines, and its crowd of holy women accompanying Catla as she distributed her alms – this is not what the archaeology of wharves and warehouses at the site suggests.[97] This picture of Dorestad certainly seems to be more conventional than that of Birka, which is strange, given the fact that Rimbert's audience is far more likely to have known the Frisian city than the Swedish emporium.[98] Whether or not the stories are accurate, they at least show how Rimbert chose to depict Birka.

Description of the setting was not Rimbert's prime concern, however. What interested him most was the religious lesson to be learnt from the narrative he had to tell. Nevertheless, although these stories of the Christian community in Birka show divine consolation, they differ from the stories of consolation relating to Anskar himself in certain significant ways. First, the miraculous is more obviously present in the consolation of Herigar and Frideburg than elsewhere in the *Vita Anskarii*, even though Rimbert implies the intervention of God in the casting of lots, both when Anskar is present and when he is absent.[99] Herigar performs a rerun of the miracle of Elijah and the prophets of Baal,[100] while Catla, in traditional fashion, finds that her supply of alms is not diminished by distribution.[101] By contrast, Anskar's miracles, like those of other missionaries in eighth- and ninth-century hagiography, including the *Life of Rimbert*,[102] take up little space: there is a general statement to say that Anskar performed wonders, and an example is given in terms of the destruction of crops of those who worked, against the saint's commands, on a feast day.[103] The absence of miracles

131

worked by Anskar is recognised by Rimbert, and is explained in the standard terms of the saint's humility.[104] One might, though, compare the miracles associated with Herigar and Catla with the comment on the miraculous in the *Vita Altera Bonifatii*,[105] that miracles primarily have a edificatory and consolatory function.

## 5. ANSKAR'S *MIRACULA WILLEHADI*

That this was a view shared, at least in part, by Anskar himself is shown by his own hagiographical work: the *Miracula Willehadi* – the *Miracles of Willehad*, the first bishop of Bremen – the see to which he was appointed in 847, after the sack of Hamburg. When Anskar was given the see of Bremen, and subsequently when Hamburg and Bremen were amalgamated, the arrangement prompted considerable hostility.[106] It is not surprising, therefore, that Anskar should have made some attempt to associate himself with the founding bishop of the diocese – although it is odd that he seems neither to have attempted to write or commission a *Life of Willehad*, nor to have known of the one that was written in the years 843–55.[107] What he did do, however, was to write an account of an outbreak of miracles which took place at Willehad's tomb in *c.* 860.

The date is probably not without significance. In 858 Bremen was attacked by Vikings.[108] Such a disaster must have looked only too like an echo of 845. Anskar and his flock needed divine reassurance, and they received it in a profusion of miracles. Anskar is explicit that he wrote the *Miracula Willehadi* as evidence that God was not forgetful of his people, even in the midst of the disasters inflicted by the pagans.[109] It is a work in which the weakest in society, in particular, are shown to be the recipients of divine grace: even compared with other accounts of the miraculous from Frisia and Saxony, which regularly pay remarkable attention to women, the *Miracula Willehadi* is extraordinary for its concentration on poor or servile females. Anskar's own hagiographical work is not about mission, but crucially it is about the need for divine reassurance in the face of pagan hostility. It speaks volumes for the atmosphere in new Christian communities which were at risk from aggressive pagan neighbours.

## 6. RIMBERT AND ANSKAR

To come to any closer understanding of the *Vita Anskarii* it is necessary to turn to the history of Rimbert himself. He was a pupil of Anskar, who was discovered by him in the region of Torhout, subsequently educated there, and then became his inseparable companion.[110] According to his biographer, as Anskar's successor at Hamburg/Bremen he modelled himself entirely on his mentor,[111] and one might compare the two saints' actions in ransoming captives,[112] in helping the poor and giving alms.[113] Perhaps the *Vita Anskarii* should be read as much as a model for Rimbert's own episcopate as an account of Anskar's. As bishop of a Church which was responsible not only for the region of the Empire north of the Elbe, but also for the Danes, Swedes and Slavs,[114] Rimbert had particularly good reason to represent each of those peoples in the text. Nor is it surprising that he should also pay considerable attention to what being a missionary bishop entailed. He thus spells out the need for discussing missionary strategy at home, for instance with Ebo.[115] He puts a high premium on negotiations with kings.[116] Perhaps more interesting because less apparent in other sources, he specifies the need to travel with merchants,[117] and he is very sensitive to the interests of merchants in having a religion which they could practise at home and abroad.[118] He also notes the importance of a body of well-disposed magnates among both the Swedes and the Danes.[119] In the follow-up to obtaining the right to preach in a region he was concerned to emphasise the role of priests,[120] and he stressed Anskar's concern about their personal behaviour:[121] it was a concern that was also noted by Rimbert's own biographer.[122] With priests went the provision of cult, which features crucially in Rimbert's narrative,[123] and with cult went a need for books and liturgical vessels.[124] Rimbert's own commitment to books is also recorded in his *vita*,[125] although it should be noted that he is said there to have put a higher value on ransoming captives than on preserving liturgical vessels.[126] The provision of churches, especially of a church with bells, also attracted his attention.[127]

Rimbert thus provides detail relating to the organisation and mission and institution of Christian cult, subjects which are often, though not always, absent from hagiography. It is reasonable to see in this his own interests in setting out Anskar's episcopate as a model to be followed. Yet Rimbert's concern with mission is psychological as much as it is organisational. His interest in psychology is apparent in his other surviving work, which is transcribed in the *Vita Rimberli*, a letter on virginity, where, combining Biblical citations, Gregory the Great and Augustine, he traces the relationship between pride and lust – arguing that humility and chastity go hand in hand.[128]

The Christianisation of Scandinavia took the Church into relatively unknown areas. Willibrord had made a brief attempt to work in Denmark,[129] but Charlemagne had prevented Liudger from going to the Northmen.[130] Saxony, for all its dangers, was a well-known entity. By contrast, Scandinavia was the edge of the world. According to Rimbert, Anskar's friends tried to persuade him not to go to preach to unknown barbarians,[131] and in one of Anskar's own visions Sweden is identified as being the end of the world, *extremum terrae*.[132] Such a description must have had apocalyptic overtones, for Christ had said 'And the gospel of the kingdom shall be preached in all the world for a witness unto all nations; and then shall the end come' (Matthew, 24, 14). According to Rimbert, Ebo saw Anskar's work as being *ad fines orbis terrae*.[133]

That Rimbert himself saw the region as beyond the normal is clear from a letter of Ratramnus of Corbie responding to a question about the nature of *cynocephali*, dog-headed men. Rimbert had clearly expected to meet such creatures in his work among the Danes, and wished to know whether they should be converted or not.[134] Ratramnus used information provided by Rimbert – on their clothes and their agriculture – to conclude that *cynocephali* had human souls. There could be no clearer indication of Rimbert's sense of moving into a marginal world, beyond the normal limits of human expectation, than his desire to know how to treat these monsters.[135] Not surprisingly, he was troubled by the whole question of the frontiers of missionary experience. The theme of divine consolation which runs throughout the *Vita Anskarii* is thus at least as significant as an insight into Rimbert's experience as into his master's. The image of Job, which recurs on a number of occasions in the *Life of Anskar*, would have been as important for Rimbert as for his predecessor.[136]

## 7. THE *VITA RIMBERTI*

That there was a strong psychological bond between Rimbert and Anskar is made very apparent by the *Vita Rimberti*, the first half of which is – like Eigil's *Life of Sturm* and Liudger's *Life of Gregory* – as concerned with the master as with his pupil. The two saints are depicted as being kindred spirits[137] and inseparable.[138] They were to be in heaven together.[139] They shared the same heart, soul, spirit and faith.[140] As we have seen, Rimbert himself is said to have acted on the inspiration of Anskar's visions,[141] a point which can be supported by the numerous visions recorded in the *Vita Anskarii* and by the presence of Anskar's visions[142] as well as Rimbert's in the *Vita Rimberti*.[143] One might also compare their joint capacity for tears.[144]

Of course the author of the *Vita Rimberti* could have created the image of Rimbert's attachment to Anskar from a reading of the latter's *vita*, which was certainly at hand.[145] This raises the problem of the date and authorship of the *Life of Rimbert*. It claims to be a contemporary work,[146] though the text as it now survives is certainly interpolated.[147] There are, however, indications that the earliest version of the work was written soon after the subject's death, and it may be possible to identify the author.[148] The likelihood is that the text was written within a monastery for a monastic audience: although interpolations may have altered the structure of the text, the *vita* as it now stands has as its central moment Rimbert's entry into the monastery of Corvey directly after his consecration as archbishop.[149] Further, even if this were not the central moment in the original text, monasticism is a matter of considerable significance in the *Life*,[150] and Rimbert's own work on virginity, addressed to a nun of Nienheerse, near Paderborn, takes up a notable portion of the whole text.[151] So too a nun is the subject of the longest miracle story, in which Rimbert frees a captive *sanctimonialis* in Schleswig.[152]

The author of the *Life* makes much of the fact that Rimbert, like the disciple whom Jesus loved, did not identify himself as the author of the *Vita Anskari*.[153] Perhaps parallel to this, the name of the addressee of Rimbert's work on virginity is deliberately removed in the *Vita Rimberti*,[154] even though the nun in question, who is identified as being the niece of Bishop Liuthard of Paderborn, is said to have been very specially commended to Rimbert.[155] Could this be an indication that the recipient of the letter was also the author of the *Life*? Moreover, the author of the *Vita Rimberti* does seem to have shared certain of the saint's intellectual concerns: he or she has a good knowledge of the works of Gregory the Great, especially the *Homeliae in Evangelium*, which the hagiographer assumes the reader will have close at hand:[156] in its enthusiasm for Gregory the *vita* claims to be following Rimbert, and indeed at two significant moments the *Vita Anskarii* cites the *Homeliae*.[157] In addition, the work's exploration of allegory[158] suggests that it was written in a world where spiritual contemplation was encouraged.

If the recipient of Rimbert's work on virginity did write the *Vita Rimberti* she would have once been in close contact with her subject and also with his successor, Adalgar, who is referred to on a number of occasions in the text, not least as having been involved in communications between the nuns of Nienheerse and Rimbert.[159] Adalgar is also recorded as still being alive at the time of composition.[160] As a correspondent of Rimbert, the nun of Nienheerse would have been well aware of his ideas, and being in contact with Adalgar, who succeeded Rimbert as archbishop,[161] she would have been well placed to cover the saint's last days.

The *Vita Rimberti* is not a rich quarry for missionary history: there are only two chapters which concentrate on it, and even they are as concerned with pastoral care for captives taken by the Vikings as with the process of mission itself.[162] It is much more concerned with monasticism and a monastic lifestyle, and, more generally, with issues of piety and pastoral care. Nevertheless, its psychological portrait of Rimbert is important for an understanding of the history of mission. It tends to confirm that the saint really did share Anskar's ideas, and thus strengthens the case that the *Vita Anskarii*, like the *Life* of Gregory of Utrecht, is as much a text in which the author dealt with his own concerns as with those of his subject.

## 8. THE END OF A TRADITION

The *Lives* of Anskar and Rimbert come at the end of a tradition. While it is possible to trace an uninterrupted line of hagiography from the eighth to the late ninth century relating to Frisia, Saxony and southern Scandinavia, that line peters out with the *Vita Rimberti*. When Adam of Bremen came to write up the *History of the Bishops of the Church of Hamburg* in the second half of the eleventh century he had access to the *Lives* of Willehad, Anskar and Rimbert, but thereafter hagiography failed him. There were no *Lives* of the episcopal successors of Rimbert, not even of Bishop Unni (918–36), who revived the Danish mission,[163] or of Adaldag who consecrated the first bishops of Denmark.[164] The missionary Poppo, whose miraculous wearing of a hot iron glove was responsible for the conversion of Harald Bluetooth, may have been the subject of a saint's *Life*, to judge from the iconography of the altar from Tamdrup in Denmark, but if so, it has not survived, and there is no indication that Adam knew of it. His original text did not even include the story of Poppo's miracle,[165] which is best known from Widukind of Corvey[166] and Thietmar of Merseburg.[167]

The tenth-century missions to Denmark, in any case, belong to a phase of mission backed by the Ottonians, which was directed as much at the Slavs as the Scandinavians.[168] After Rimbert there had been a break, marked effectively by Adam's comment that he had been unable to find out anything more about Danish history after Adalgar became bishop of Hamburg/Bremen (889–909).[169] That the mission had already hit difficulties before then, however, is clear from the tone of Rimbert's writing. And here, although his account of Anskar's early missionary work may be factually accurate, it may be misleading. Ermoldus Nigellus' description of Harald Klak's baptism and return to Denmark is a good deal more joyous[170] than the equivalent passage in Rimbert's *Vita Anskarii*.[171] In all probability Anskar shared in the untrammelled optimism of 826, while the more tempered picture in the *Vita Anskarii* reflects the viewpoint of the saint and his biographer after twenty years of near-continuous crisis.

This should make us wary of accepting Rimbert's account as giving a consistently accurate sense of events. On the other hand, it reinforces the impression of a growing sensitivity among the hagiographers of mission to the realities of missionary work. For Willibald and Eigil, mission had been a relatively minor issue – indeed, in the hagiography of Mainz and Fulda Boniface had scarcely been portrayed as a missionary. The hagiographers' concerns lay elsewhere, and, in any case, for the majority of his career Boniface had not worked among pagans. Alcuin, influenced by Bede's *Ecclesiastical History*, and concerned with the increasingly important missionary policies of Charlemagne, had, on the other hand, put mission at the heart of hagiography,[172] but his observation was that of a theorist, little concerned with the reality of work among the pagans – even though Willibrord ought to have provided him with material for a more flesh-and-blood rendering of a missionary's life. Unlike Alcuin, Liudger had indeed worked in the field, and seems to have put some of his concerns and experience into the *Vita Gregorii*, although to square those concerns with the careers of Boniface and Gregory meant considerable adjustment of events. Boniface, in particular, was radically reinterpreted, making him the model missionary which he had wished to be, but which had eluded him except during two short periods when he worked in Frisia. The image would, nevertheless, stick. With Rimbert, the narrative and observations presented by the author and the career and experiences of the subject seem to have come nearest to overlapping. While Liudger had turned hagiography into a vehicle for exploring personal concerns, regardless of the actual events of his subject's life, with Rimbert his concerns could be fitted neatly onto the career and concerns of Anskar – or so a reconstruction of events suggests. In the early eleventh century the interests of the hagiographer and those of the saint being described would, it seems, fuse at least as well in the writings and career of Bruno of Querfurt. For the time being, however, missionary concerns and missionary hagiography were on hold in the North – broken by the Viking Age. Meanwhile, another tradition of missionary hagiography had evolved in Bavaria. Again it took its starting point from the career of Boniface, but in a radically different way from the more northerly tradition – and it developed differently as well.

## Notes

1. See Johanek, 'Der Ausbau der sächsischen Kirchenorganisation', pp. 502–3. For Halberstadt, which was closely associated with Liudger's family, see Hauck, *Apostolischer Geist im Genus sacerdotale der Liudgeriden*, pp. 14–20.
2. *Vita Liutbirgue* 12.
3. Rudolf/Meginhart, *Translatio sancti Alexandri* 4.
4. Rimbert, *Vita Anskarii* 13.
5. Ermoldus Nigellus, *In honorem Hludovici Pii* ll. 1882–2513; *Annales Regni Francorum*, s.a. 826; *Annales Xantenses*, s.a. 826, ed. B. von Simson, MGH, SRG (Hanover, 1909); Astronomer, *Vita Hludowici* 40, ed. R. Rau, *Quellen zur karolingischen Reichsgeschichte* 1 (Darmstadt, 1968); Thegan, *Vita Hludowici* 33, ed. R. Rau, *Quellen zur karolingischen Reichsgeschichte* 1 (Darmstadt, 1968).
6. Rimbert, *Vita Anskarii* 2–3.
7. Rimbert, *Vita Anskarii* 4.
8. Rimbert, *Vita Anskarii* 6.
9. Rimbert, *Vita Anskarii* 7.
10. Rimbert, *Vita Anskarii* 8.
11. *Annales Regnum Francorum*, s.a. 827.

12. Rimbert, *Vita Anskarii* 9.

13. Rimbert, *Vita Anskarii* 9–10.

14. Rimbert, *Vita Anskarii* 11–12.

15. Rimbert, *Vita Anskarii* 12.

16. Rimbert, *Vita Anskarii* 13.

17. Rimbert, *Vita Anskarii* 15; see also *Vita Anskarii* 8, 35, 37, 38.

18. Rimbert, *Vita Anskarii* 14.

19. *Annales Bertiniani*, s.a. 833, ed. G. Waitz, MGH, SRG (Hanover, 1883); trans. J. L. Nelson, *The Annals of St-Bertin* (Manchester, 1991).

20. *Annales Bertiniani*, s.a. 835.

21. Rimbert, *Vita Anskarii* 34.

22. Rimbert, *Vita Anskarii* 17.

23. Rimbert, *Vita Anskarii* 28, 30.

24. Rimbert, *Vita Anskarii* 33.

25. Rimbert, *Vita Anskarii* 18.

26. Rimbert, *Vita Anskarii* 16–17.

27. Niemeyer, 'Die Herkunft der *Vita Willehadi*', pp. 19–20.

28. Rimbert, *Vita Anskarii* 23.

29. Rimbert, *Vita Anskarii* 24.

30. *Annales Bertiniani*, s.a. 845.

31. Rimbert, *Vita Anskarii* 25–6.

32. Rimbert, *Vita Anskarii* 33.

33. Rimbert, *Vita Anskarii* 32. See also Wood, 'Christians and pagans in ninth-century Scandinavia', pp. 44–5, 48–9, 52.

34. Rimbert, *Vita Anskarii* 33.

35. Rimbert, *Vita Anskarii* 41.

36. Rimbert, *Vita Anskarii* 1, 42. Klüppel, 'Die Germania (750–950)', p. 200, notes also that Rimbert speaks in c. 22 of Louis the German being still alive, thus providing a fixed *terminus ante quem* of 876.

37. c.f. the word *hinc*, Rimbert, *Vita Anskarii* 24; c.f. also 35.

38. *Vita Rimberti* 12, ed. G. Waitz, MGH, SRG 55 (Hanover, 1884).

39. Rimbert, *Vita Anskarii* 35.

40. Rimbert, *Vita Anskarii* 2.

41. Rimbert, *Vita Anskarii* 35; see also *Vita Rimberti* 6, 8, 10, 15, 24.

42. Rimbert, *Vita Anskarii* 41.

43. Rimbert, *Vita Anskarii* 23.

44. That the manuscript Stuttgart, Württembergische Landesbibliothek, HB XIV 7, was written for Solomon, albeit unprovable, is a very attractive, and plausible, idea. See the entry in *799. Kunst und Kultur der Karolingerzeit, Karl der Große und Papst Leo III. in Paderborn*, ed. Stiegemann and Wemhoff, 2, pp. 526–7. See also Klüppel, 'Die Germania (750–950)', pp. 200–1.

45. Rimbert, *Vita Anskarii* 23.

46. Rimbert, *Vita Anskarii* 24.

47. Rimbert, *Vita Anskarii* 12.

48. Rimbert, *Vita Anskarii* 35–42.

49. *Vita Rimberti* 11; see also 2.

50. Rimbert, *Vita Anskarii* 1.

51. Rimbert, *Vita Anskarii* 2, 35.

52. Rimbert, *Vita Anskarii* 4–6.

53. Rimbert, *Vita Anskarii* 6.
54. Rimbert, *Vita Anskarii* 7.
55. Rimbert, *Vita Anskarii* 9.
56. Rimbert, *Vita Anskarii* 25.
57. Rimbert, *Vita Anskarii* 10; on Witmar see also *Vita Anskarii* 8.
58. Rimbert, *Vita Anskarii* 15, 21.
59. Rimbert, *Vita Anskarii* 35.
60. Ratramnus of Corbie, epp. 12, 13, ed. E. Dümmler, *Epistolae Variorum*, in MGH, Epistolae 6 (Karolini Aevi 4) (Berlin, 1925).
61. Rimbert, *Vita Anskarii* 46; Ratramnus, epp. 8, 9. On the Gottschalk affair see D. Ganz, 'The debate on predestination', in M. Gibson and J. L. Nelson (eds), *Charles the Bald, Court and Kingdom*, 2nd edn. (London, 1990), pp. 283–302.
62. Rimbert, *Vita Anskarii* 1, 2, 3, 15.
63. Rimbert, *Vita Anskarii* 2–6, 35, 42; see also the strong liturgical aspect of the saint's death, *Vita Anskarii* 41–2.
64. *Vita Rimberti* 12; see also the general monastic tone of the *Vita Rimberti* 12, 13, 15, 18, 23.
65. Niemeyer, 'Die Herkunft der *Vita Willehadi*', p. 24.
66. Altfrid, *Vita Liudgeri* I 18, 24.
67. W. Lammers, 'Ansgar, visionäre Erlebnisformen und Missionsauftrag', in C. Bauer, L. Böhm and M. Müller (eds), *Speculum Historiale* (Munich, 1965), pp. 541–58. See also P. E. Dutton, *The Politics of Dreaming in the Carolingian Empire* (Lincoln, Nebraska, 1994), pp. 51–4.
68. Rimbert, *Vita Anskarii* 2, 6.
69. *Vita Rimberti* 19; see also Anskar's visions in *Vita Rimberti* 5, 6, 11 and Rimbert's in *Vita Rimberti* 7, 8, 11, 22, 24.
70. Rimbert, *Vita Anskarii* 42.
71. Rimbert, *Vita Anskarii* 3.
72. Rimbert, *Vita Anskarii* 25, 40, 42.
73. Rimbert, *Vita Anskarii* 5.
74. Rimbert, *Vita Anskarii* 18.
75. Rimbert, *Vita Anskarii* 33.
76. Rimbert, *Vita Anskarii* 2.
77. Rimbert, *Vita Anskarii* 3, 4, 9.
78. Rimbert, *Vita Anskarii* 35.
79. Rimbert, *Vita Anskarii* 38.
80. Rimbert, *Vita Anskarii* 29, 36.
81. Rimbert, *Vita Anskarii* 25, 27, 36.
82. Rimbert, *Vita Anskarii* 5; on consolation in general, *Vita Anskarii* 3, 5, 7, 27, 34, 39, 40. Compare the consolation of Herigar, *Vita Anskarii* 19, and Frideburg, *Vita Anskarii* 20.
83. Rimbert, *Vita Anskarii* 18.
84. Rimbert, *Vita Anskarii* 19.
85. Rimbert, *Vita Anskarii* 20.
86. Rimbert, *Vita Anskarii* 30.
87. Rimbert, *Vita Anskarii* 18.
88. Rimbert, *Vita Anskarii* 17, 26.
89. Rimbert, *Vita Anskarii* 19.
90. Rimbert, *Vita Anskarii* 11.

91. Rimbert, *Vita Anskarii* 20.
92. Rimbert, *Vita Anskarii* 19.
93. Rimbert, *Vita Anskarii* 30.
94. Rimbert, *Vita Anskarii* 26–8.
95. Rimbert, *Vita Anskarii* 26.
96. Compare Rimbert, *Vita Anskarii* 20 and 30.
97. W. J. H. Verwers, 'Wijk bij Duurstede-Dorestad', in W. A. Van Es and W. A. M. Hessing, *Romeinen, Friezen en Franken* (Den Haag, 1994), pp. 234–8.
98. On the problems of squaring the current archaeology at Birka with Rimbert's narrative see B. Ambrosiani and H. Clarke (eds), *Investigations in the Black Earth*, Birka Studies 1 (Stockholm, 1992).
99. Rimbert, *Vita Anskarii* 18, 19, 27, 33.
100. Rimbert, *Vita Anskarii* 19.
101. Rimbert, *Vita Anskarii* 20.
102. *Vita Rimberti* 18, 20, 25.
103. Rimbert, *Vita Anskarii* 37, 39.
104. Rimbert, *Vita Anskarii* 39.
105. *Vita Altera Bonifatii* 19.
106. Niemeyer, 'Die Herkunft der *Vita Willehadi*', p. 20.
107. Niemeyer, 'Die Herkunft der *Vita Willehadi*', p. 18.
108. Niemeyer, 'Die Herkunft der *Vita Willehadi*', p. 20, citing O. H. May, *Regesten der Erzbischöfe von Bremen* 1 (1937), 12, no. 28. That there had been a disaster before the miracles began is implied by Anskar, *Miracula Willehadi*, prol, ed. A. Poncelet, AASS, 8 Nov., vol. 3, pp. 847–51.
109. Anskar, *Miracula Willehadi*, prol.
110. *Vita Rimberti* 3, 5, 9.
111. *Vita Rimberti* 5, 7, 10, 11, 14, 19, 22, 24.
112. Rimbert, *Vita Anskarii* 35; *Vita Rimberti* 16–18.
113. Rimbert, *Vita Anskarii* 28, 35; *Vita Rimberti* 14.
114. Rimbert, *Vita Anskarii* 12, 13, 23.
115. Rimbert, *Vita Anskarii* 14, 34.
116. Rimbert, *Vita Anskarii* 7–9, 11–12, 14, 24–8, 30, 32, 33.
117. Rimbert, *Vita Anskarii* 10, 33.
118. Rimbert, *Vita Anskarii* 19, 24; see also 33 on a merchant who knows about Christianity.
119. Rimbert, *Vita Anskarii* 11, 19, 20, 26, 32.
120. Rimbert, *Vita Anskarii* 9, 12, 18, 19, 20, 24, 25, 28, 31, 32, 33.
121. Rimbert, *Vita Anskarii* 33.
122. *Vita Rimberti* 16.
123. Rimbert, *Vita Anskarii* 11, 20, 27, 28, 33, 35, 41.
124. Rimbert, *Vita Anskarii* 7, 10, 14, 16, 18, 35.
125. *Vita Rimberti* 15.
126. *Vita Rimberti* 17.
127. Rimbert, *Vita Anskarii* 11, 14, 19, 24, 28, 31, 32; on the symbolism of bells, compare *Vita Rimberti* 7.
128. *Vita Rimberti* 15.
129. Alcuin, *Vita Willibrordi* 9.
130. Altfrid, *Vita Liudgeri* I 30.
131. Rimbert, *Vita Anskarii* 7; on the North as barbarous, *Vita Anskarii* 12.

132. Rimbert, *Vita Anskarii* 25.
133. Rimbert, *Vita Anskarii* 34.
134. Ratramnus, ep. 12.
135. Wood, 'Christians and pagans in ninth-century Scandinavia', pp. 64–6.
136. Rimbert, *Vita Anskarii* 16, 35, 40.
137. *Vita Rimberti* 3.
138. *Vita Rimberti* 5.
139. *Vita Rimberti* 6, 22, 24.
140. *Vita Rimberti* 9.
141. *Vita Rimberti* 19.
142. *Vita Rimberti* 5, 6, 8, 11.
143. *Vita Rimberti* 7, 8, 22, 24.
144. Rimbert, *Vita Anskarii* 35; *Vita Rimberti* 18.
145. *Vita Rimberti* 5, 6, 9.
146. *Vita Rimberti* 12. The early date is accepted by Klüppel, 'Die Germania (750–950)', p. 201.
147. See *Vita Rimberti* 1.
148. Klüppel, 'Die Germania (750–950)', p. 201, argues for composition in Corvey on the grounds of *Vita Rimberti* 12; there is, however, nothing in the references to Corvey or its abbots to prove that the author came from there.
149. *Vita Rimberti* 12.
150. *Vita Rimberti* 10, 121, 13, 15, 18, 23.
151. *Vita Rimberti* 15.
152. *Vita Rimberti* 18; see also the role of Helawih in *Vita Rimberti* 9.
153. *Vita Rimberti* 9.
154. *Vita Rimberti* 15.
155. *Vita Rimberti* 15.
156. *Vita Rimberti* 20; compare 6, 8, 15.
157. Rimbert, *Vita Anskarii* 37, 42.
158. *Vita Rimberti* 7, 15, 16, 22, 24.
159. *Vita Rimberti* 15.
160. *Vita Rimberti* 12.
161. On Adalgar, see Adam, *Gesta Hammaburgensis Ecclesiae Pontificum* I 45(47)–50(52).
162. *Vita Rimberti* 16, 17.
163. Adam of Bremen, *Gesta Hammaburgensis Ecclesiae Pontificum* I 54(56)–63(65). See Klüppel, 'Die Germania (750–950)', p. 202.
164. Adam of Bremen, *Gesta Hammaburgensis Ecclesiae Pontificum* II 4.
165. It is only recorded as a scholion to Adam of Bremen, *Gesta Hammaburgensis Ecclesiae Pontificum* II 25(22).
166. Widukind, *Res Gestae Saxonicae* III 65.
167. Thietmar, *Chronicon* II 14.
168. Vlasto, *The Entry of the Slavs into Christendom*, p. 147.
169. Adam of Bremen, *Gesta Hammaburgensis Ecclesiae Pontificum* I 47(49).
170. Ermoldus Nigellus, *In honorem Ludovici Pii*, ll. 1882–2513.
171. Rimbert, *Vita Anskarii* 7, 8.
172. On Alcuin's 'reinterpretation' of Remigius as an evangelical figure, see A. Thacker, 'Peculiaris patronus noster: the saint as patron of the state in the Early Middle Ages', in Maddicott and Palliser, *The Medieval State*, p. 8.

141

## PART 3

---

# BAVARIANS, SLAVS AND SAXONS

# Chapter 7

# SALZBURG AND FREISING IN THE EIGHTH CENTURY

## 1. VIRGIL OF SALZBURG

Boniface and his reputation dominate the history of the eighth-century Church. That reputation, however, meant different things to different groups of his successors. At the same time, there were plenty who were less impressed by the saint both during his lifetime and after his death. He had enemies among the established clergy in Francia.[1] In Bavaria too he had his opponents, notably the Irishman Virgil, who was to become bishop of Salzburg. To be opposed to a saint or his memory, however, did not exclude knowledge of the hagiography associated with him.

The hagiographers we have considered so far were almost entirely favourable to Boniface, even though their representations of him differed. In Bavaria some eighth-century writers were rather less positive – by implication at least. A number of texts seem to constitute an attack either on the work of Boniface himself, or on the representation of him provided by Willibald. Despite the influence of Willibald's work, however, Bavarian hagiography does not present us with a chain of interlinked *Lives* comparable to those concerned with Frisia and Saxony – there is just one small group of *vitae*. As for the cluster of texts associated with Salzburg, which will concern us in the next chapter, they are not works of hagiography.

To follow the Bavarian hagiographical tradition of the eighth century, connected as it was with that of Boniface, we must, initially, turn away from missionaries to other holy men, who were rather closer to *peregrini pro Christo*. The non-hagiographical sources to which we will subsequently turn will bring us back more directly to the history of mission with what is, in many respects, the most single-minded account of Christianisation to have been written in the Early Middle Ages: the *Conversio Bagoariorum et Carantanorum*. For the moment, however, it is a genuine Irish *peregrinus*, albeit one deeply involved in organising missions, Virgil of Salzburg, who requires consideration.

Virgil turned up at the court of Pippin III at Quierzy in 743/4.[2] The Frankish *dux* sent him on to Bavaria, perhaps to strengthen his influence in the region, since he had recently been at war with its ruler, Odilo.[3]

145

Nevertheless, in 746, Virgil came into conflict with Boniface, who had been given papal authority two years previously to preach in Gallia and Bavaria, and to reform the Churches in both areas.[4] A precise disagreement between them emerged over the case of a Bavarian cleric who had baptised *In nomine Patria, Filia et Spiritus Sancti*, 'in the name [of] the Fatherland, the Daughter and the Holy Spirit': this Boniface thought was heretical and ordered rebaptism; Virgil and a fellow priest, Sidonius, saw the error merely as a matter of grammar, and took it to be of little significance; Pope Zacharias accepted their point of view.[5] This was not the end of the conflict between Boniface and Virgil, though. Two years later, in 748, Boniface again wrote to Zacharias, accusing Virgil of stirring up trouble between himself and Odilo, and stating that he, Virgil, was claiming that the pope had promised him one of the four sees to which Boniface had consecrated bishops in 739.[6] At the same time the Englishman accused the Irishman of heresy, more precisely of believing that there was another world under this one, a charge which Zacharias summoned Virgil to answer. What happened at the Rome meeting is unknown, but Virgil became abbot of St Peter's Salzburg, probably in 747/8,[7] and in 749 he was raised to the episcopate as bishop of Salzburg,[8] thus gaining one of the sees created by Boniface. Virgil was to outlive his rival by a considerable length of time, not dying until 784. In the course of his long pontificate he was to achieve much – he has been called 'Salzburg's Boniface'[9] – although in terms of the history of mission one might argue that the impact of his successor, Arno (785–821), was as important.[10]

## 2. THE REPRESENTATION OF RUPERT OF SALZBURG

The contributions of Virgil and Arno to the Christianisation of Carinthia will concern us in the next chapter, but first it is worth looking to the past, and to the foundation of the diocese of Salzburg, since that is a story which links once again with the question of the representation of Boniface in our sources, as well as providing the starting point for the Carantanian mission.

The cornerstone for the Christian history of Bavaria in Carolingian sources is the career of Rupert of Salzburg.[11] In so far as it can be reconstructed, Rupert, a member of the anti-Pippinid opposition, moved to Salzburg – perhaps as a result of political conflict – at the latest by 696. He worked as a reformer and Christianiser in the region until *c.* 712. Thereafter he may have returned to Worms to die.[12] Certainly, he was no longer alive in Salzburg in 716.[13]

The story of Rupert of Salzburg is told in four major sources from the eighth and ninth centuries, the *Gesta Hrodberti*,[14] the *Notitia Arnonis*,[15] the

*Breves Notitiae,*[16] and the *Conversio Carantanorum et Bagoariorum.* The differences between these four texts imply that there was a version of the *Life* of Rupert earlier than the surviving *Gesta Hrodberti.* This may seem a rather technical matter, but it is of some importance, because the identification of the initial composition of a *Life* of Rupert sheds light on Bavarian reactions to Boniface, while the development of the portrayal of the saint reveals a reinterpretation of the history of the Christianisation of Bavaria itself, as well as a growing sense of missionary history.

The *Gesta Hrodberti* tells of a bishop of Worms, of royal blood, Hrodbert (to stick to the name used by the hagiographer, in order to clarify the various different traditions about the saint), in the second year of Childebert, which was 695/6.[17] The saint's virtues are described, in words taken from the *Acta Sebastiani.* These virtues reached the ears of Theoto, *dux* of Bavaria, who begged him to come to his province to preach.[18] Having sent some messengers on ahead, Hrodbert himself followed. The *dux* was delighted, going out to meet him, before receiving him in Regensburg.[19] There he preached, converting many nobles to the true faith and strengthening them in religion. Subsequently, the *dux* allowed Hrodbert to travel where he wanted, restoring churches. He went first by boat to Lorch, and then to the Wallersee.[20] Later he heard of the site of Salzburg, once a Roman centre, now dilapidated. He asked Theoto for land there, so that he could purify it and establish an ecclesiastical centre.[21] Theoto obliged with a massive grant. As a result, Hrodbert built a church on the site, and also a monastery. Thereafter he asked Theoto for an estate called Piding, which he bought for the enormous sum of 1000 *solidi.*[22] Further gifts followed. Meanwhile, Hrodbert decided to bring in some more helpers, so he returned to Worms, and gathered twelve disciples together with the nun Erintrude, all of whom followed him back to Salzburg, where, in the upper *castrum,* he founded a nunnery.[23] His death-day, however, was approaching: some holy men saw boys ready for mass, and heard mysterious singing. Hrodbert died on Easter Day. Miracles took place at his tomb.[24]

As it stands, the *Gesta* cannot be earlier than the 790s, since the work includes a quotation from a charter of *c.* 790.[25] It is usually dated to 793.[26] There are, however, indications that the text is based on a *Life* of Rupert written somewhat earlier. The majority of the text, indeed, seems to have been written before 793, since it omits a number of significant events of the mid-to late eighth century. It makes no mention of the translation in 774 of Rupert's body to a new church, which had been built by Virgil,[27] and it also ignores Rupert's involvement in the foundation of the Maximilianszelle, a community which, probably in 746/7 and definitely before 748, was at the centre of an argument between *dux* Odilo and Virgil.[28] Since Virgil himself almost certainly compiled a dossier on Rupert's involvement with the

147

Maximilianszelle,[29] the absence of an account of the foundation suggests that the postulated first, lost, *Life* of Rupert, on which the *Gesta Hrodberti* was based, was composed before that date. On the other hand, the absence of any mention of the Piding transaction in the account of Rupert given in the *Conversio Bagoariorum et Carantanorum* may imply that it did not feature in the original *Life* of Rupert and is an addition incorporated into the *Gesta*.

Although it is impossible to be certain that a postulated first *Life* of Rupert was commissioned or written by Virgil, there is at least a case for putting an original composition of such a work immediately after Virgil's arrival in Bavaria. Assuming that Virgil was involved in the work's composition, it would have had a context shortly after Boniface's foundation of the see of Salzburg in 739, and even more shortly after he had been given authority to reform the Bavarian Church in 744. In the light of the conflict with Virgil in 746, it is not impossible to see in the *Life* of Rupert an attempt to emphasise the existence of an ecclesiastical tradition in the Salzburg region prior to Boniface's arrival. Interestingly, there was no attempt to look back to the work of Eustasius of Luxeuil – rather, stress was laid on the importance of Rupert, an opponent of the Pippinid ancestors of the Carolingians. Although Virgil himself was effectively a representative of Pippin III,[30] he may have had an eye on ingratiating himself on his arrival in Bavaria with the Agilolfing ruler, Odilo, who had only recently been at war with Pippin.[31]

The changes made to the representation of Rupert in the course of the late eighth and ninth centuries are of some importance in understanding Salzburg's developing attitude towards the past and towards mission. The earliest surviving source, the *Notitia Arnonis*, apparently dates from 788–90,[32] and thus antedates the recension of the *Gesta Hrodberti* which survives. The *Notitia Arnonis* is essentially a register of land grants drawn up by the deacon Benedict for Virgil's successor, Arno. It describes the church of St Peter at Salzburg, which was the foundation and burial place of Hrodbert, and it notes the nunnery built by the saint for Erintrude.[33] It then mentions Theodo's (sic) other gifts to Hrodbert, including Piding.[34] Subsequently it tells the tale of Hrodbert's construction, consecration and acquisition of Maximilianszelle.[35] Interestingly, the text refers to Hrodbert as *domnus*, *episcopus* and *confessor*, but never *sanctus*.

Approximately ten years after the compilation of the *Notitia Arnonis* a further account of the estates acquired by Salzburg was drawn up for Bishop Arno, the *Breves Notitiae*.[36] This begins with an account of Rudbert (sic), who is called bishop, but without any diocese being mentioned, preaching at the court of Theodo, whom he supposedly baptised, along with his nobles. Thereafter Theodo gave him permission to go round his duchy to find a site for his cathedral (*sedes episcopii*), to build churches and to teach the people. As a result Rudbert went to the Wallersee, where he built a church to

St Peter, and was then given the surrounding land by Theodo.[37] Rudbert, however, decided that the site was not suitable to be a cathedral centre, and with the permission of the *dux* he went on to Salzburg, which Theodo also gave him. The selection of the site may call to mind Sturm's discovery of Fulda, after the rejection of Hersfeld.[38] The *Breves Notitiae* then lists numerous other grants from the *dux*.[39] Thereafter it tells the tale of the foundation of the Maximilianszelle, and the grant of the estate by Theodo, together with subsequent grants by Theodo's son, Theodbert, in the region.[40] Among other grants, Theodebert also gave Rudbert the upper *castrum* at Salzburg, for Erindrude's (i.e. Erintrude's) nunnery.[41]

The three important differences between this account and those of the *Gesta* and the *Breves Notitiae* are, first, that Theodo/Theoto and his court are seen not as a Christians in need of reform, but as pagans. This would not have been a welcome portrayal while the Agilolfings still held power in Bavaria, but after their fall such a misrepresentation was possible. Second, since mission was very much on Arno's mind following the Avar capitulation in 796, it enhanced the missionary status of Rupert. Third, Rupert is now seen as the founder of the diocese of Salzburg, something which even Virgil did not claim.

The final version of Rupert's career, that given by the *Conversio Bagoariorum et Carantanorum*, essentially provides a text very close to that of the *Gesta Hrodberti*,[42] though with some slight, but notable changes. Thus, at Theoto's court, Roudbert (sic), named once again as bishop of Worms, is explicitly said to have baptised many.[43] The *Conversio* spends time on the saint's preaching after the foundation of the nunnery in Salzburg, and it announces that Roudbert consecrated clergy, including his unnamed successor. This emphasis on foundation and ordination is, as we shall see, a regular concern of the *Conversio* for very particular reasons, and marks a specific approach to missionary history.

Like that of Boniface himself, the interpretation of Rupert's career changed in the course of the eighth and ninth centuries. It is worth summing up the changes in the representation of the saint in Salzburg sources of this period: in the *Gesta*, he is a bishop of Worms called in to reform the Christianity of Bavaria; there is no explicit mention of his baptising Theodo and his nobles. He does, however, convert men to true faith; he strengthens religion, and he founds a number of churches, notably that of St Peter in Salzburg, as well as two monastic communities in the same centre. St Peter's is not depicted as his cathedral church, nor is Rupert presented as bishop of Salzburg. This picture, however, is altered in the *Breves Notitiae*, where Theodo is pagan on Rudbert's arrival, and where Salzburg is explicitly presented as Rudbert's *sedes*.[44] This new picture of Rupert as a saint active in a pagan area is subsequently modified in the *Conversio Bagoariorum et*

*Carantanorum*, which presents an account closer to that of the *Gesta Hrodberti*, despite incorporating the notion that Hrodbert did baptise Theoto and many of his followers.

The surviving *Gesta Hrodberti*, with the exception of its sentences on Piding, seems to provide a reasonably accurate indication of the first written traditions relating to Rupert. If those traditions can rightly be seen as being set down in *c.*746, they present a picture of a long-established Church in Bavaria which had been reformed a mere generation before Boniface received his appointment to reform the Bavarian Church in 744. Other accounts of Rupert, by contrast, make him into a missionary saint working among pagans – thus portraying the Bavarian Church as a more recent creation, but at the same time enhancing Rupert's achievement. It is also worth noting that the *Gesta Hrodberti* depicts the nunnery at Salzburg as being set up according to a *canonicus ordo*, already in Rupert's day.[45] Although it makes less of Rupert's achievement than do other sources, in making the saint a reformer whose interests stretched to include regular monasticism, the *Gesta Hroberti*, and presumably the postulated *Life* of Rupert which preceded it, can be seen as questioning the importance of Boniface's work in Bavaria: there was little need for reform, for the Bavarian Church had been thoroughly reformed half a century earlier.[46]

One particular aspect of the Bonifatian position, however, was not challenged initially: Hrodbert is only described as bishop of Worms, and while Salzburg is the focus of his Bavarian operations, the *Gesta Hrodberti*, unlike other accounts of Rupert's career, does not use the word *sedes* to describe Salzburg; Boniface could still be seen as creating a diocese there, and appointing its first bishop. In considering the relatively unadventurous claims of the *Gesta Hrodberti*, it is worth remembering that in 746 Virgil was a new arrival, perhaps not yet abbot of St Peter's. In writing or commissioning a *Life of Rupert* he could have been doing his homework on his new homeland. Nevertheless, that homework still had its value in cutting the work of Boniface down to size.

## 3. ARBEO OF FREISING'S *LIVES* OF EMMERAM AND CORBINIAN

Assuming that the postulated *Life* of Rupert was indeed written in the 740s, it would be one of three major *Lives* of Bavarian saints written in the mid-eighth century. The other two, the *Lives* of Emmeram of Regensburg and of Corbinian of Freising, were both written by Arbeo, bishop of Freising from 764 to 783.[47] According to Arbeo, Emmeram was a native of Poitiers, where he became bishop.[48] Hearing of Avar idolatory, he resolved to preach in

Pannonia.[49] Whether he was elevated to the episcopate in Poitiers one might doubt. And why he should have determined to evangelise the Avars is a matter for speculation, although one might wonder whether this was a last flickering of the ideals of Eustasius and Amandus. In any case, Arbeo tells us, he was stopped by the Bavarian *dux* – once again Rupert's patron, Theoto – who was at the time at war with the Avars. Instead, the *dux* asked him to work in Bavaria, whose population was still young in its Christianity.[50] He agreed, being struck by the beauty of the region, but already foreseeing his martyrdom, asked to be allowed to go to Rome.[51] At the same time Theoto's daughter, Ota, had been made pregnant by the son of a local *iudex*. Not knowing what to do, the girl and her lover approached Emmeram for advice. He told them to do penance, and also to accuse him in his absence of being the father.[52] He then set off, supposedly for Rome, but really in search of a place to await martyrdom, for which he chose a particularly beautiful spot. Meanwhile, Ota made her accusation.[53] As soon as she had done so her brother, Landperht, set off in pursuit of the bishop, finding Emmeram at Helfendorf. There he had him bound and then ordered the amputation of his arms and legs, and had his eyes pulled out and his ears, nose, testicles and tongue cut off.[54] Afterwards Landperht departed, leaving the still living Emmeram to ask for water. When his interpreter, Vitalis, opined that it would be better for him to die, he imposed a penance of intermittent madness on him.[55] According to Arbeo the amputated limbs, which had been placed in a tree, miraculously vanished, and the saint's living torso was taken by cart in the direction of Aschheim, but after nine miles the martyr died.[56] The site of the martyrdom thereafter remained springlike throughout the year.[57] Meanwhile, three of the martyr's killers were seized by demons (the other two, having acted under duress, suffered no such problem), and Landperht went into exile.[58] Miracles followed: since the martyr had wanted to be buried in Regensburg it rained for forty days until his body was taken there.[59] After his initial burial, it was decided that his body should be translated.[60] Thereafter there were yet more miracles: the longest, and least miraculous of them, concerned a man who wished to go to the shrine, but was kidnapped on the way, sold into slavery, forced to marry, despite the fact that he already had a wife at home, but was able to escape before having intercourse, and to make his way to Regensburg.[61]

This final miracle might seem to be the most plausible section in the whole text, but it was apparently drawn from Jerome's *Vita Malchi*.[62] Indeed much of the *Life* seems to have been drawn from literary models, which is not to say that there is no kernel of truth in it.[63] Although there is no direct evidence to support any aspect of Arbeo's portrayal of Emmeram, a clause of *Lex Baiuwariorum* about the murder of bishops does suggest that a particularly brutal episcopal killing did take place,[64] while a pilgrimage to Rome undertaken by Theoto in 716 has plausibly been seen as penance following the martyrdom of Emmeram.[65]

The *Life of Corbinian*, which Arbeo dedicated to Virgil, lacks the extremes of the *Vita Haimhrammi*, although there is much in its narrative which is factually questionable.[66] Corbinian is said to have come from Melun, near Paris; his father died before he was born, and his mother, Corbiniana, gave her only child her name. Unfortunately, Arbeo later forgets that he had described Corbinian as *unigenitus*, and gives him a brother.[67] The saint opted for a life of asceticism at *Castrus*, where he performed miracles, not least when a thief tried to steal his mule, but found himself back at the holy man's cell, where Corbinian imposed a penance on him.[68] As a result of such deeds the saint became famous. Hearing of him, Pippin sent him the jewelled garment he wore annually on the Campus Martius.[69] Such fame, however, drove Corbinian to embark on a pilgrimage to Rome, to see Gregory II.[70] He asked to be allowed to remain quietly under papal jurisdiction, living a regular life, by the work of his hands. Gregory told him not to hide his light under a bushel and elevated him first to the priesthood, and then to the episcopate.[71] Endowed with the *pallium*, he returned to Gaul, where he was summoned to see Pippin.[72] On the way he tried to save a criminal from execution, but although the tribune refused to stay the hanging until Corbinian had asked Pippin for a pardon, the man survived on the gibbet until he was taken down; thereafter he lived under the saint's spiritual direction.[73] After preaching for a further seven years, Corbinian decided to return to Rome for advice,[74] and on the way passed through Bavaria. There Theoto – once again – was *dux*, although he had divided his province into four with his sons. Theoto wanted Corbinian to stay, but he refused, moving on to the court of his son, Grimoald, who also tried to persuade him to remain.[75] The saint insisted on travelling on to Pavia, although one of his horses was stolen on the way: a theft which would be miraculously remedied in time. A second horse was stolen between Pavia and Rome, again with miraculous results.[76] Equally miraculous was the feeding of Corbinian and his companions, not least on the coast, where his companion, Ansaric, caught a huge fish, after a considerable fight at sea, both against the fish and against local fishermen. Corbinian had the fishermen beaten, but then paid, so that they should not return home penniless after a day's work.[77] When he reached Rome the pope listened to his wish for a quiet ascetic life, but refused to countenance it. Corbinian therefore set off back to Bavaria.[78] *En route* the miraculous results of the various thefts of his southward journey became known.[79] On reaching the frontier near Mais, he was detained by Grimoald's men, who had been told not to let him pass without agreeing to go to court. While waiting, he visited the shrine of Valentinus at Mais.[80] He then went to Grimoald's court, where he insisted on the *dux* giving up his wife, Pilitrude, who was the widow of his brother, Theodoald. Grimoald agreed and accepted penance. Pilitrude was not so happy, and tried to exploit every opportunity to get her own back.[81] Finally, the saint beat an old woman whom he had accused of witchcraft after she had cured Pilitrude's son. This prompted an attempt on Corbinian's life by Pilitrude's henchman, while he was staying at his villa of Freising.[82] As a result he left for Mais.[83] Subsequently, Grimoald's family all came to a bad end.[84] Hucpert, however, who succeeded to the duchy, recalled the saint, asking him to become godfather of his child.[85] Thereafter Corbinian died,[86] but his body was translated to Mais, as he had instructed.[87] Miracles followed, including one which involved the young Arbeo.[88] Later the body of Valentinus was moved from Mais, first, by the Lombards to Trent, and then by Tassilo to Passau.[89] In *c.* 768 Arbeo, by now bishop of Freising, and worried that he could not show appropriate reverence to Corbinian's body, decided to translate it to his episcopal seat.[90] The text of the earliest recension of the *Vita Corbiniani* breaks off during the description of the transfer of the saint's body. The *Life*, which at this point can be reconstructed with the help of the second recension, probably concluded with Corbinian's burial at Freising.

## 4. POLITICS AND ARBEO'S *LIVES*

One striking element of the *Lives* of Emmeram and Corbinian is the criticism of the ducal family of Bavaria. Among those criticised by Arbeo, leaving aside the wretched Ota, there is her brother, Landperht, who was responsible for the martyrdom of Emmeram,[91] whilst Grimoald is depicted as adulterous, on account of his marriage to his sister-in-law, Pilitrude.[92] Arbeo does not appear to lament the fact that Grimoald's family received its comeuppance.[93] This comeuppance, however, did not prevent the marriage of Pilitrude's daughter, Sunnichild, to Charles Martel, or the birth of his son, Gripho, who was to cause considerable problems for Carlomann and Pippin III.[94] Further, in squeezing Gripho out of Bavaria, Pippin established a grandson of Sunnichild, Tassilo III, as *dux* in Bavaria in 748.[95]

Arbeo cannot have been unaware that the ruler of Bavaria, at the time that he was writing, was indeed a descendent of the family he had written off in the *Vita Corbiniani*. One aspect of the bishop of Freising's hagiography must, therefore, be criticism of the Agilolfing family. Yet the criticism has its limits, and some *duces* are actually praised.[96] Further, although there is a striking absence of donations by Tassilo to Freising in Arbeo's time, it would be wrong to see this as an indication of extreme hostility between the bishop and the Agilolfings: there are ducal grants to daughter-houses of

Freising from this period.[97] Politics may be a factor in Arbeo's hagiography, but it does not seem to be the driving force.

## 5. RELIGIOUS PURPOSES IN ARBEO'S *LIVES*

Religious issues were more important. Arbeo was clearly intent on developing a major saint cult at Freising, and perhaps also at the various sites, two of which lay within his diocese, associated with the martyr Emmeram. He was also setting out, as do almost all hagiographers, a model of the Christian life. His heroes have a standard range of Christian virtues.[98] They are preachers.[99] They live ascetic lives, even if Corbinian's asceticism, and his desire to withdraw from the world, came into conflict with his success as a holy man.[100] Corbinian was keen to live according to a rule.[101] Arbeo seems to envisage this rule as being the Rule of St Benedict, a text on which he drew frequently.[102] Indeed, the hagiographer seems to have presented Corbinian as a Benedictine, even though the Rule was apparently not followed among the community of Freising or among other monasteries associated with the bishop, with the single exception of Schliersee.[103]

Equally important in the *Lives* of Emmeram and Corbinian is the emphasis on penance. Most obviously there is the penance imposed by Corbinian on Grimoald, for his adulterous marriage,[104] and on Ota for having intercourse with Sigibald.[105] There is also the intermittent madness imposed on Vitalis for questioning the mutilated Emmeram's desire for water.[106] Corbinian confessed the criminal condemned to be hanged,[107] and received Grimoald back into his grace after the *dux* had repented of throwing food blessed by the saint to his dogs.[108] Sinners are regularly driven by supernatural forces to confess: thus it was with the thief who took Corbinian's mule,[109] and with the men who stole his horses, one of whom instructed his wife to pay the saint 200 *solidi*,[110] while the other lived to make the payment himself.[111] Magata, the girl who gossiped about Corbinian sleeping with her, was struck with deformity, and spent the rest of her days confessing that she had fabricated the story.[112] The two killers of Emmeram who prayed for pardon before committing the deed escaped without divine retribution.[113] More mundanely, the man who was kidnapped *en route* to the shrine of Emmeram was on his way to confess his sins.[114]

This emphasis on confession and penance certainly reflects Arbeo's own interests: he sets out at length the story of a woman on whom he had imposed penance for adultery, and who was unable to approach the shrine of Emmeram, because she had not obeyed the bishop.[115] This concern with penance and confession Arbeo may have derived from Irish tradition, passed on by Virgil of Salzburg.[116] On the other hand, there may have been a penitential tradition in Bavaria since the early eighth century: Gregory II, in letter apparently addressed to the Bavarian Church in 716, emphasised the need for penance.[117]

## 6. THE LITERARY FORM OF ARBEO'S *LIVES*

Arbeo set these ideas in two narratives which drew heavily from earlier hagiographical sources. Arbeo's indebtedness to the *Dialogues* of Gregory the Great, Jerome's hagiography, Rufinus' translation of Eusebius and the first *Passio* of Leodegar is well known.[118] In the case of Jerome, it is even possible to point to the manuscript of his saint's *Lives* to which Arbeo had access.[119] Whether or not the extent of hagiographical borrowing in Arbeo's *vitae* renders them valueless as historical records for Emmeram and Corbinian is a problem that cannot be solved, because of the absence of any material to support or disprove the hagiographer's narrative.[120] We can work on Arbeo's representations of the saints, but scarcely on the saints themselves.

The representation is, however, not entirely derived from previous authors. There is indeed much that is individual about Arbeo's hagiography. Certainly, the general image of the *peregrinus* is something that Arbeo could have taken from numerous sources, not least the *Gesta Hrodberti*. The delight in the picaresque, which is most apparent in the tale of the man kidnapped on his way to Regensburg, but apparent in the general theme of travel which pervades the *Life* of Corbinian and is present in that of Emmeram, could well derive from Jerome's *Life of Malchus*. It is also possible to set Arbeo's delight in the bizarre alongside an equally bizarre text, the Aethicus Ister. Regardless of whether or not Virgil of Salzburg was the author of this strange cosmology, it is likely that it was copied in Salzburg at this time,[121] and it is probable that Arbeo's own copy of the text survives.[122] There are even traces of verbal influences of the cosmography in *Lives* of Corbinian and Emmeram.[123]

## 7. THE ODDITIES OF ARBEO'S *LIVES*

None of this explains all the oddities of Arbeo's texts. Arbeo's personal voice is clear from his delight in natural description.[124] It is also clear from his admiration of physical strength, notably that of Ansaric, when he swims out to catch an enormous fish.[125] It may be that one can see in this the reflection of aristocratic attitudes, but there is no need to invoke the notion of the *Adelsheiliger*, or to see Arbeo simply as a proponent of a certain type of aristocratic – or perhaps one should say muscular – sanctity.[126] Besides, there are certain aspects of Arbeo's writing which go beyond anything that might be seen as belonging to aristocratic values. Perhaps an aristocratic Christian would have enjoyed the brutality involved in the killing of

Emmeram,[127] or in the story of how Ansaric, having caught his fish, beat up the fishermen who tried to take his prize from him.[128] Certainly, this incident was represented in a relief on Corbinian's tomb.[129] Another story, which was also represented on the tomb, caused offence, however. On the saint's second journey to Rome two of his horses were stolen. The thief who took the first was a Lombard official, Husing, who was based in Trent.[130] On Corbinian's return from his visit to the pope, he saw his stallion emaciated, and with his pizzle, too large for any vagina, hanging down to his hooves. The earliest surviving recension of the *Vita Corbiniani* comments that the description of the stallion is shameful, and goes on to say that the representation of the scene has been removed from the silver relief on the saint's tomb.[131] Since Arbeo was responsible for the saint's tomb, Brunhölzl quite reasonably concluded that the squeamishness was an interpolation, but it must have been made soon after the original composition.[132] The second recension of the text omits the offending words altogether.

Arbeo's inclusion of the story and his commissioning of its representation on Corbinian's tomb perhaps raises the issue not so much of aristocratic sanctity, but of the author's attitude towards sex and pudenda, which appear with remarkable frequency. Equally important is Arbeo's sense of humour. This is apparent in the story of Corbinian leaping off his horse to beat up an old lady, whom he had accused of being a witch, and who had used diabolic means to cure the son of Grimoald. The saint beat the *anum* with his own hands.[133] Both Krusch and Brunhölzl failed to understand the passage, Brunhölzl amending the unfortunate *anum* into a *canem*, not realising that *anus* is a perfectly good word for an old woman, and one that allows a dirty joke: the saint beat the old woman on her buttocks. Nor was Arbeo the only hagiographer to enjoy this precise crack: the author of the *Vita Samsonis* found it to be equally funny.[134] Perhaps Virgil and the communities of Salzburg and Freising would have roared with laughter at this impropriety. If so there may have been more than a smirk at the various mentions of pudenda in the *Lives* of Emmeram and Corbinian.[135]

## 8. THE CONTEXT OF ARBEO'S *LIVES*: THE DATE

The oddities of Arbeo's work cry out for attention, but their function is quite opaque. The only way to procede further with an understanding of some part of the *Lives* of Corbinian and Emmeram is to place them in some sort of context. There is no clear way of determining which of the two *vitae* written by Arbeo is the earlier,[136] although it would seem to be more likely that the hagiographer wrote the *Life* of a saint who was buried in his own diocese before he wrote that of the martyr of a neighbouring see.[137] In all probability Arbeo completed his *Vita Corbiniani* shortly after the translation of the saint's body into the new cathedral church of Freising in 769.[138] The *Life of Emmeram* could have been written in the context of a visit to Regensburg, the burial place of the martyr, by Arbeo, in 772,[139] and of the acquisition of the site of martyrdom at Helfendorf by the church of Freising on 7 October 772.[140] Both *Lives* can reasonably be placed in the three years between 769 and 772. Equally important, this evidence shows that Arbeo had connections with both saints. He himself spent time in Mais, where Corbinian had long been buried, and he organised the saint's *translatio* to his own cathedral church: in addition, as just mentioned, the church of Freising acquired the site at which Emmeram had been martyred. In terms of the pressures leading Arbeo to put pen to parchment, as significant may have been Virgil's request that he should write the *Life of Corbinian*.[141] Arbeo therefore wrote one of his hagiographical works at the instigation of Virgil, who had apparently already been involved in challenging the Bonifatian view of the Bavarian Church. Further, he wrote almost immediately after the composition of the *Vita Bonifatii*. Even more significantly, there are indications that he had read Willibald's work before writing himself.

## 9. WILLIBALD AND ARBEO

The shadow of Boniface did not fade for the Bavarians with the saint's martyrdom in 754. The seminal position of the martyr for the Bavarian Church was spelt out only too clearly in Willibald's *Life of Boniface*. A whole chapter of the *Vita Bonifatii*, which is a mere nine chapters long, is dedicated to the expulsion of heretics from Bavaria and the subsequent division of the region into four dioceses.[142] Three of the four dioceses are named: there is Salzburg, with John as bishop, Freising with Erembert and Regensburg with Garibald. Willibald could not name the fourth, Passau, with its bishop, Vivilo, because he had actually been appointed by Gregory III prior to Boniface's division of the region into four sees.[143] Willibald set out this claim at some point during the episcopate of Megingoz of Würzburg, 763–9. In the *Gesta Hrodberti* the prior history of Salzburg had already been explored. Between *c.* 769 and 772 the earlier histories of Freising and Regensburg would be written up by Arbeo. It can scarcely have been chance that three out of four of the dioceses created by Boniface had their pre-Bonifatian histories explored in such a short space of time, and that the only diocese left without an earlier history was Passau, whose bishop had in any case been appointed not by Boniface but by the pope. Even Passau attracted Arbeo's attention indirectly, when he dealt with the translation there of the body of Saint Valentinus.[144]

The clearest indications of borrowing from Willibald's *Vita Bonifatii* come in Arbeo's accounts of Corbinian's journeys to Rome. In telling of the

157

saint's first visit to Rome, notably in his reception by Gregory and his elevation to the episcopate, Arbeo seems to have been intent on emulating Willibald's account.[145] So too the second visit of Corbinian to Rome seems to have been derived from the *Vita Bonifatii*.[146] There is no other evidence that Corbinian ever visited Rome, and the second visit in particular may be total invention.[147] Moreover, Arbeo's account of the first visit is chronologically impossible, since Gregory II became pope after Pippin II's death.[148] It must be concluded, therefore, that, in some way, Arbeo was replying to Willibald's account of Boniface's relations with the papacy.

In talking of the division of Bavaria by Theoto into four, with each section under one of his sons and their clergy,[149] by making Corbinian into a bishop[150] and giving him a *sedes* at Freising, and by elevating Emmeram to the episcopate in Poitiers,[151] and settling him in Regensburg, Arbeo provided an episcopal history for two of Boniface's new sees. With Rupert, bishop of Worms, active in Salzburg, and with Vivilo, a papal appointee in Passau, the case for Boniface as the founder of the Bavarian Church had effectively been destroyed – though it should be noted that initially Rupert is not called bishop of Salzburg, nor Emmeram bishop of Regensburg, while Corbinian is supposedly elevated to the episcopate long before he gets a *sedes* at Freising. Further, by saying that Gregory had conferred on Corbinian the authority to preach *per universum orbem*,[152] Arbeo had also trumped the licence given by Gregory III to Boniface in 744 to preach in Bavaria and Gaul.[153]

If Arbeo's general portrayal of the Churches of Regensburg and Freising was intended as a reply to Willibald's account of the Bavarian Church, it is possible that certain of the details in Arbeo's text have a similar critical function. The implication that Corbinian lived a life inspired by the Rule of St Benedict might be seen as deliberately placing the saint within the monastic tradition which the English in general and Boniface in particular were popularising. One might even see in the extremes of Arbeo's writing a deliberate sense of subversion. If the Aethicus Ister, whether written by Virgil or anyone else in Bavaria, could indulge in satire, perhaps Arbeo too could use humour as a means of responding to the reputation of Boniface and the spirituality he represented.

## 10. THE BAVARIAN PAST

The fact that Arbeo's work is of dubious historical validity, and that it is in part a polemical reply to Willibald's generally well-founded narrative, does not negate the idea that the Bavarian Church had strong connections with the papacy before Boniface's arrival. For one reason or another Theoto had made a pilgrimage to Rome in 716,[154] and Gregory II is credited with drawing up a plan for the division of Bavaria into three or four dioceses in the same year.[155] The plan carried out by Boniface in 739 thus had a precedent, which had apparently not been implemented. Nor does the failure to implement the plan destroy the notion that the rule of Theoto was a vital period in the history of the Bavarian Church, however much one may reject the detail presented by the author of the *Gesta Hrodberti* and Arbeo. It is plausible to see Rupert as having a career in Bavaria between *c.* 696 and 712,[156] to date the martyrdom of Emmeram in 715, with Theoto's penitential pilgrimage a year later,[157] and to see Corbinian as a younger contemporary. Although the *Lives* of Rupert, Emmeram and Corbinian lack any direct corroboration from other sources, they do imply a period of active reform in the Bavarian Church in the generation before Boniface's arrival.

What is more problematic is the state of Christianity in Bavaria before the arrival of Rupert. Theoto and his family are first portrayed as pagans in the *Breves Notitiae* – from what we can reconstruct of earlier tradition, they had previously been portrayed as Christians, and there is every reason to think that the Agilolfings had been Christian since the sixth century. It is reasonable, therefore, to assume that the region had already been Christianised. For some parts of Bavaria it is possible to argue for a continuity of Christianity from the Late Roman period.[158] It is also clear that monks were sent from Luxeuil in the days of Abbot Eustasius,[159] and that Amandus worked in the region.[160] To this earlier conversion history, however, neither the author of the *Gesta Hrodberti* nor Arbeo makes direct reference.[161] The absence of any reference to Eustasius, at least, has the negative effect of implying that Arbeo was not educated at Bobbio, although such has been claimed for him.[162] It is, nevertheless, likely that he had read the *Vita Columbani*.[163] When all is said and done, however, a reasonably secure picture of Christianity in Bavaria can only be drawn from Theoto's day onwards.

## 11. MISSION

The picture of Rupert, Emmeram and Corbinian is, for the most part, a picture of reformers, though there are indications that they could also be thought of as missionaries. The *Breves Notitiae* expressly has Rudbert baptise Theodo,[164] despite the fact that the earlier sources do not see the saint as a missionary. Emmeram was depicted from the start as having missionary intentions: he left Gaul to convert the Avars in Pannonia, and was only prevented from doing so by the fact that the Bavarians were at war with the Avars at the time of his planned mission.[165] Corbinian, although nowhere depicted as a missionary, is said to have received authority from Gregory II to preach *per universum orbem*.[166] Regardless of whether or not there is some truth in this commission,[167] it is probable that Arbeo recorded it as a counter to Boniface's commission of 744.

There was, however, another reason for dealing with the issue of mission within the context of Bavarian hagiography of the eighth century. Certainly, it is possible that missions to the Avars and Slavs had been considered in the course of the seventh century.[168] More importantly, missions to the *Carantani* were being directed from Salzburg in the course of the later eighth century, and notably by Virgil himself.[169] Further, he had been granted Carantania as a missionary province by a series of popes, Zacharias (741–52), the very pope who gave Boniface authority in Bavaria,[170] by Stephen (752–7) and Paul II (757–67).[171] In other words, to speak about mission in the context of Rupert or Emmeram was not simply to parry some of the claims of Boniface or Mainz, it was also to explore issues which were relevant to the Bavarian Church of the mid-eighth century – and, indeed, later: Arno was, after all, to be involved in missions to the Avars, and for that reason received from Alcuin several major letters concerned with the subject of mission.[172] As we have seen, he may also have been responsible for bringing a text of the *Life* of the great missionary figure Amandus to Bavaria. In dealing with mission in the context of figures who were apparently reformers rather than missionaries, Arbeo may also be compared with Jonas. The latter's *Life of Columbanus* depicted a saint, apparently little concerned with mission, in such a way as to highlight what few missionary concerns he did have – perhaps because of his own interest and that of others of Columbanus' disciples who did work as missionaries.

## 12. THE *PASSIO KILIANI*: CONSENSUS IN WÜRZBURG?

One other text tackled the issue of mission in the south German region: the *Life* of Kilian of Würzburg. Kilian was supposedly an Irishman who left Ireland on hearing a divine voice which told him to take up the cross.[173] He travelled to Würzburg, which was ruled by a pagan *dux* called Gozbert.[174] Taking note of the beauty of the place and of the paganism there, Kilian and his followers resolved to get papal permission to preach. They set off, expecting to find Pope John (685–6), but when they arrived he had been succeeded by Conon (686–7).[175] Having received permission to preach, Kilian and his companions returned to Würzburg, where Kilian baptised Gozbert.[176] The *dux* had married his brother's widow, Geila, which was an old custom. Kilian persuaded him to set aside his wife, which Gozbert did.[177] Geila, however, objected, and sent a murderer to dispatch Kilian and his companions.[178] The bodies were buried, along with the saint's vestments and books.[179] Geila claimed to have no knowledge of the saint's whereabouts, though the killer went mad, biting himself to death.[180] God then took vengeance against

Geila, Gozbert and Gozbert's son, Hetan.[181] Following the occurrence of miracles at the site of the burial, a later bishop of Würzburg, Burghard, had Kilian's relics translated with the permission of Zacharias and Boniface.[182]

The *Passio Kiliani* can be dated to the second half of the eighth century.[183] It is, moreover, clear that the author had access to the work of Arbeo. This might be deduced from the general structure of the text, with its foreign ecclesiastic coming to Würzburg, visiting the papacy, returning, criticising the ruler's marriage, and as a result earning the enmity of the ruler's wife, with a coda on the later disasters which befell the ducal family. The story is almost an amalgamation of the *Lives* of Emmeram and Corbinian. Further, verbal parallels confirm the impression of Arbeo's influence on the author of the *Passio Kiliani*.[184] It is, therefore, possible that the descriptive passages in the *Life* of Emmeram inspired the reference to the beauty of Würzburg,[185] and that Arbeo's writings prompted the inclusion of a speech in which the need for penance is stressed.[186]

Yet if the *Passio Kiliani* was inspired by Arbeo's writings, it was also apparently written with the correspondence of Boniface at hand.[187] Moreover, the author also had access to Willibald's *Life of Boniface*[188] – and one might guess that the condemnation of Hetan/Heden was either inspired by the earlier work, or by the Carolingian propaganda which underlay it. Yet unlike Arbeo, who seems to have used Willibald's work in order to contradict it, the author of the *Passio Kiliani* was clearly intent on drawing together Bavarian and Mainz tradition. It would have been surprising if such had not been the case. Burghard, who translated the body of Kilian, was an appointee of Boniface,[189] and he carried out the translation of Kilian with the approval of Boniface and Zacharias.[190] In Würzburg, Boniface himself therefore acknowledged the achievements of a previous generation of saints. The *Passio Kiliani* went one stage further and, just as Liudger had brought the approaches of Willibald and Alcuin together, it combined those of Willibald and Arbeo.

Not everyone was as polarised over the history of the Bavarian Church as were Willibald on the one hand and Virgil and Arbeo on the other. Boniface himself had appointed Erembert – apparently Corbinian's brother –[191] to the see of Freising.[192] Boniface's appointee to the see of Regensburg, Garibald,[193] was responsible for the *translatio* of Emmeram.[194] Lull even appears in the *Liber Confraternitatum* of Salzburg.[195] One might also note, though, that the bishop of Mainz did not prevent the letters of Boniface accusing Virgil of heresy from being preserved and subsequently disseminated.[196] The evidence, therefore, suggests that the hostility between Virgil and Boniface and the critique of Willibald's writings implicit in the *Lives* of Corbinian and Emmeram, do not reflect a complete polarisation between Bavaria and Mainz. On the other hand, there was tension, and it clearly fed into the hagiography of eighth-century Bavaria. As for the missions directed from Salzburg during this period, they would be written up a century later in very different circumstances.

## Notes

1. Wallace-Hadrill, *The Frankish Church*, pp. 137, 160; E. Ewig, 'Milo et eiusmodi similes', *Sankt Bonifatius. Gedenkengabe zum zwölfhundertsten Todestag* (Fulda, 1953), pp. 412–40; reprinted in *id.*, *Spätantikes und fränkisches Gallien* 2 (Munich, 1979), pp. 189–219.
2. *Conversio Bagoariorum et Carantanorum* 2; for the chonology, H. Wolfram, *Salzburg, Bayern, Österreich. Die Conversio Bagoariorum et Carantanorum und die Quellen ihrer Zeit* (Vienna, 1995), pp. 253–60.
3. Fredegar, continuations 25–6, ed. J. M. Wallace-Hadrill, *The Fourth Book of the Chronicle of Fredegar* (London, 1960).
4. Boniface, ep. 58.
5. Boniface, ep. 68.
6. Boniface, ep. 80. On the 739 organisation see Willibald, *Vita Bonifatii* 7, and Boniface ep. 45.
7. Wolfram, *Salzburg, Bayern, Österreich*, p. 258.
8. Wolfram, *Salzburg, Bayern, Österreich*, p. 262.
9. H. Wolfram, 'Virgil of St Peter's at Salzburg', in P. Ní Chatháin and M. Richter, *Irland und die Christenheit* (Stuttgart, 1987), p. 420.
10. For Arno, Wolfram, *Die Geburt Mitteleuropas*, pp. 206–16.
11. See especially Wolfram, *Salzburg, Bayern, Österreich*, pp. 227–51. Also Wood, *The Merovingian Kingdoms, 450–751*, pp. 266, 269.
12. This remains an open question, despite Wolfram, *Salzburg, Bayern, Österreich*, pp. 241–2. He is said to have returned *ad propriam sedem* in *Conversio Bagoariorum et Carantanorum* 1, which should mean that he went to Worms. But the *Breves Notitiae* 2 (3, 4, 5, 6, 7, 9, 11), 3 (11, 12), 8 (3), ed. F. Losek, '*Notitia Arnonis* und *Breves Notitiae*', in *Mitteilungen der Gesellschaft für Salzburger Landeskunde* 130 (1990), already describe Salzburg as Rudbert's *sedes*.
13. Wolfram, *Salzburg, Bayern, Österreich*, p. 245; on the papal plans of 716, Wolfram, *Grenzen und Räume*, p. 83.
14. *Gesta Hrodberti*, ed. W. Levison, MGH, SRM 6 (Hanover, 1913).
15. *Notitia Arnonis*, ed. F. Losek, '*Notitia Arnonis* und *Breves Notitiae*'.
16. *Breves Notitiae*, ed. Losek.
17. *Gesta Hrodberti* 1.
18. *Gesta Hrodberti* 3.
19. *Gesta Hrodberti* 4.
20. *Gesta Hrodberti* 5.
21. *Gesta Hrodberti* 7.
22. *Gesta Hrodberti* 8.
23. *Gesta Hrodberti* 9.
24. *Gesta Hrodberti* 10.
25. *Gesta Hrodberti* 8; compare *Diplomata Karolinorum* 1, 168, ed. E. Mühlbacher, MGH, Diplomata (Hanover, 1906), where the date is given as Dec. 790.
26. See the date-chart in Wolfram, *Salzburg, Bayern, Österreich*, p. 228.

27. For the *translatio*, Wolfram, *Grenzen und Räume*, p. 119.
28. Wolfram, *Salzburg, Bayern, Österreich*, pp. 202–4.
29. This postulated work is termed the *Libellus Virgilii*: its contents have to be reconstructed from the *Breves Notitiae*, 3 (1–16), 8 (1–15) and 13 (1–7).
30. *Conversio Bagoariorum et Carantanorum* 2.
31. Fredegar, continuations 26.
32. *Notitia Arnonis*, ed. Losek, 'Notitia Arnonis und Breves Notitiae'; for the date of composition, pp. 31–4.
33. *Notitia Arnonis*, pref., ed. Losek, 'Notitia Arnonis und Breves Notitiae', pp. 80–96.
34. *Notitia Arnonis* 1.
35. *Notitia Arnonis* 8.
36. For the date, Losek, 'Notitia Arnonis und Breves Notitiae', pp. 34–42.
37. *Breves Notitiae* 1.
38. Eigil, *Vita Sturmi* 5, 10.
39. *Breves Notitiae* 2.
40. *Breves Notitiae* 3.
41. *Breves Notitae* 4.
42. Losek conveniently prints the text of the *Gesta Hrodberti* in the footnotes to his edition of the *Conversio Bagoariorum et Carantanorum*, pp. 91–8.
43. *Conversio Bagoariorum et Carantanorum* 1.
44. *Breves Notitiae* 2 (3, 4, 5, 6, 7, 9, 11), 3 (11, 12), 8 (3).
45. *Gesta Hrodberti* 9.
46. See Willibald, *Vita Bonifatii* 7. J. Jahn, 'Virgil, Arbeo und Cozroh: Verfassungsgeschichtliche Beobachtungen an bairischen Quellen des 8. Jahrhunderts', in *Mitteilungen der Gesellschaft für Salzburger Landeskunde* 130 (1990), pp. 220–1.
47. On Arbeo's episcopate H. Glaser, 'Bischof Arbeo von Freising als Gegenstand der neueren Forschung', in H. Glaser, F. Brunhölzl and S. Benker, *Vita Corbiniani: Bischof Arbeo von Freising und die Lebensgeschichte des hl. Korbinian* (Munich, 1983), p. 50.
48. Arbeo, *Vita Haimhrammi* 1.
49. Arbeo, *Vita Haimhrammi* 3.
50. Arbeo, *Vita Haimhrammi* 4–7.
51. Arbeo, *Vita Haimhrammi* 8.
52. Arbeo, *Vita Haimhrammi* 9.
53. Arbeo, *Vita Haimhrammi* 10–12.
54. Arbeo, *Vita Haimhrammi* 13–18.
55. Arbeo, *Vita Haimhrammi* 19–21.
56. Arbeo, *Vita Haimhrammi* 22–4.
57. Arbeo, *Vita Haimhrammi* 25.
58. Arbeo, *Vita Haimhrammi* 26–8.
59. Arbeo, *Vita Haimhrammi* 32–4.
60. Arbeo, *Vita Haimhrammi* 35.
61. Arbeo, *Vita Haimhrammi* 37–43.
62. Glaser, 'Bischof Arbeo von Freising als Gegenstand der neueren Forschung', p. 64.
63. For a very reasonable summary of the arguments for and against the evidential value of the *Life*, Glaser, 'Bischof Arbeo von Freising als Gegenstand der neueren Forschung', pp. 53–64.
64. *Leges Baiuwariorum* I 10, ed. E. von Schwind, MGH, Leges 5, 2 (Hanover, 1926).
65. Wolfram, *Salzburg, Bayern, Österreich*, p. 235; Paul the Deacon, *Historia Langobardorum*, VI 44; *Liber Pontificalis*, 91, 4.

66. For a survey of debates about the historical reliability of the *Vita Corbiniani*, see Glaser, 'Bischof Arbeo von Freising als Gegenstand der neueren Forschung', pp. 61–4.

67. Arbeo, *Vita Corbiniani* 1, 30, 33. The word, of course, makes him look more Christlike.

68. Arbeo, *Vita Corbiniani* 2–4.

69. Arbeo, *Vita Corbiniani* 5.

70. Arbeo, *Vita Corbiniani* 7. Chronologically, a visit to Gregory II during the lifetime of Pippin II is, of course, impossible.

71. Arbeo, *Vita Corbiniani* 8.

72. Arbeo, *Vita Corbiniani* 9–10.

73. Arbeo, *Vita Corbiniani* 11–13.

74. Arbeo, *Vita Corbiniani* 14.

75. Arbeo, *Vita Corbiniani* 15.

76. Arbeo, *Vita Corbiniani* 16, 21–2.

77. Arbeo, *Vita Corbiniani* 17–19.

78. Arbeo, *Vita Corbiniani* 20.

79. Arbeo, *Vita Corbiniani* 21–2.

80. Arbeo, *Vita Corbiniani* 23.

81. Arbeo, *Vita Corbiniani* 24.

82. Arbeo, *Vita Corbiniani* 29.

83. Arbeo, *Vita Corbiniani* 30.

84. Arbeo, *Vita Corbiniani* 31.

85. Arbeo, *Vita Corbiniani* 32.

86. Arbeo, *Vita Corbiniani* 33.

87. Arbeo, *Vita Corbiniani* 37–8.

88. Arbeo, *Vita Corbiniani* 40. As Glaser states, 'Bischof Arbeo von Freising als Gegenstand der neueren Forschung', p. 28, this does not prove that he was actually a native of Meran; on his connections with the west Bavarian aristocracy see *ibid.*, pp. 28–32.

89. Arbeo, *Vita Corbiniani* 41.

90. For the date, Glaser, 'Bischof Arbeo von Freising als Gegenstand der neueren Forschung', p. 53.

91. Arbeo, *Vita Haimhrammi* 13–18.

92. Arbeo, *Vita Corbiniani* 24.

93. Arbeo, *Vita Corbiniani* 31.

94. Wood, *The Merovingian Kingdoms, 450–751*, pp. 288–90.

95. J. Jahn, 'Hausmeier und Herzöge. Bemerkungen zur agilolfingisch-karolingischen Rivalität bis zum Tode Karl Martels', in J. Jarnut, U. Nonn and M. Richter, *Karl Martel in seiner Zeit* (Sigmaringen, 1994), pp. 332–5: Airlie, 'Narratives of triumph and rituals of submission: Charlemagne's mastering of Bavaria', *Transactions of the Royal Historical Society*, 6th series, 9 (1999), pp. 98, 105–6.

96. c.f. Theoto and Hucbert in Arbeo, *Vita Corbiniani* 15, 32.

97. Glaser, 'Bischof Arbeo von Freising als Gegenstand der neueren Forschung', p. 68; see more generally pp. 67–76.

98. Arbeo, *Vita Corbiniani* 1; *Vita Haimhrammi* 2.

99. Arbeo, *Vita Corbiniani* 2, 9, 14, 15; *Vita Haimhrammi* 2, 3, 4, 7, 8.

100. Arbeo, *Vita Corbiniani* 6–8, 15, 20.

101. Arbeo, *Vita Corbiniani* 7.

102. Arbeo, *Vita Corbiniani* 3, 7, 14; Glaser, 'Bischof Arbeo von Freising als Gegenstand der neueren Forschung', p. 49, n. 131.

103. Glaser, 'Bischof Arbeo von Freising als Gegenstand der neueren Forschung', pp. 47–50.

104. Arbeo, *Vita Corbiniani* 24.
105. Arbeo, *Vita Haimhrammi* 9.
106. Arbeo, *Vita Haimhrammi* 19–21.
107. Arbeo, *Vita Corbiniani* 10.
108. Arbeo, *Vita Corbiniani* 26.
109. Arbeo, *Vita Corbiniani* 4.
110. One should note the fact that there are two people who offer the same sum of money – such duplets are a feature of the *Vita Corbiniani*: Glaser, 'Bischof Arbeo von Freising als Gegenstand der neueren Forschung', p. 64.
111. Arbeo, *Vita Corbiniani* 21, 22.
112. Arbeo, *Vita Corbiniani* 36.
113. Arbeo, *Vita Haimhrammi* 17.
114. Arbeo, *Vita Haimhrammi* 37.
115. Arbeo, *Vita Haimhrammi* 36. On the penitential element in the *Vita Haimhrammi*, see F. Graus, *Volk, Herrsher und heilige im Reich der Merowinger* (Prague, 1965), pp. 120–1.
116. H. Löwe, 'Arbeo von Freising: eine Studie zu Religiosität und Bildung im 8. Jahrhundert', in *id.*, *Von Cassiodor zu Dante: Ausgewählte Aufsätze zur Geschichtschreibung und politischen Ideenwelt des Mittelalters* (Berlin, 1973), pp. 87, 92–4.
117. Gregory II, *Literae decretales* 12, ed. J. Merkel, MGH, Leges in folio 3 (Hanover, 1863), pp. 451–4; B. Krusch, *Arbeonis Episcopi Frisingensis Vitae Sanctorum Haimhrammi et Corbiniani*, MGH SRG 13 (Hanover, 1920). There may, however, be a question mark over the authenticity of Gregory's decretals.
118. Löwe, 'Arbeo von Freising: eine Studie zu Religiosität und Bildung im 8. Jahrhundert', p. 97; Glaser, 'Bischof Arbeo von Freising als Gegenstand der neueren Forschung', p. 64.
119. Löwe, 'Arbeo von Freising: eine Studie zu Religiosität und Bildung im 8. Jahrhundert', pp. 88–9.
120. Glaser, 'Bischof Arbeo von Freising als Gegenstand der neueren Forschung', p. 64.
121. W. Stelzer, 'Ein Alt-Salzburger Fragment der Kosmographie des Aethicus Ister', *Mitteilungen des Instituts für Österreichische Geschichtsforschung* 100 (1992), pp. 132–9.
122. Löwe, 'Arbeo von Freising: eine Studie zu Religiosität und Bildung im 8. Jahrhundert', p. 89.
123. Glaser, 'Bischof Arbeo von Freising als Gegenstand der neueren Forschung', pp. 25–6.
124. Arbeo, *Vita Corbiniani* 40; Arbeo, *Passio Haimhrammi* 12, 25, 30.
125. Arbeo, *Vita Corbiniani* 18–19.
126. Glaser, 'Bischof Arbeo von Freising als Gegenstand der neueren Forschung', pp. 55–61 provides a useful survey of the discussion of the *Adelsheilige* in relation to Arbeo's work.
127. Arbeo, *Vita Haimhrammi* 17–18.
128. Arbeo, *Vita Corbiniani* 18–19.
129. Arbeo, *Vita Corbiniani* 19.
130. Arbeo, *Vita Corbiniani* 16.
131. Arbeo, *Vita Corbiniani* 22.
132. Glaser, 'Bischof Arbeo von Freising als Gegenstand der neueren Forschung', p. 54; see also Brunhölzl's edition of the text in the same volume.
133. Arbeo, *Vita Corbiniani* 29.
134. *Vita Samsonis* 26, ed. P. Flobert, *La vie ancienne de saint Samson de Dol* (Paris, 1997); Wood, 'Forgery in Merovingian hagiography', p. 383.
135. See also the cutting off of Emmeram's testicles, Arbeo, *Vita Haimhrammi* 18. The references to sex in the *Lives* are less likely to have been smutty. The refusal of the

servant to have sex with his wife in Arbeo *Vita Haimhrammi* 38–40, like other references to adultery, makes a deadly serious point.

136. Glaser, 'Bischof Arbeo von Freising als Gegenstand der neueren Forschung', pp. 25–6 dismisses Heinz Löwe's attempt to use the Aethicus Ister as a means of establishing a relative chronology.

137. Glaser, 'Bischof Arbeo von Freising als Gegenstand der neueren Forschung', p. 54.

138. Glaser, 'Bischof Arbeo von Freising als Gegenstand der neueren Forschung', p. 54.

139. Krusch, *Arbeonis Vitae Sanctorum Haimhrammi et Corbiniani*, p. 134.

140. Glaser, 'Bischof Arbeo von Freising als Gegenstand der neueren Forschung', pp. 54–5, with n. 147; Jahn, 'Virgil, Arbeo und Cozroh, p. 228.

141. Arbeo, *Vita Corbiniani*, prol.

142. Willibald, *Vita Bonifatii* 7.

143. See Boniface, ep. 44; Wolfram, *Die Geburt Mitteleuropas*, p. 125: 'Auch der Passauer Bischof Vivilo war noch vor 739 von Gregor III. persönlich in Rom geweiht worden.'

144. *Vita Corbiniani* 41.

145. Compare Arbeo, *Vita Corbiniani* 7–9 with Willibald, *Vita Bonifatii* 6. Individually, the verbal parallels adduced by Krusch, *Arbeonis Vitae Sanctorum Haimhrammi et Corbiniani*, p. 139, are not very convincing, but when they are taken together the case seems unassailable.

146. Compare Arbeo, *Vita Corbiniani* 20, with Willibald, *Vita Bonifatii* 6: Krusch, *Arbeonis Vitae Sanctorum Haimhrammi et Corbiniani*, p. 140.

147. Krusch, *Arbeonis Vitae Sanctorum Haimhrammi et Corbiniani*, pp. 140–1.

148. Krusch, *Arbeonis Vitae Sanctorum Haimhrammi et Corbiniani*, p. 138.

149. Arbeo, *Vita Corbiniani* 15. The problem of a fourfold division with only three sons named may in itself be explained by Willibald's reference to a fourfold division with only three dioceses named: *Vita Bonifatii* 7.

150. Arbeo, *Vita Corbiniani* 8.

151. Arbeo, *Vita Haimhrammi*, 1.

152. Arbeo, *Vita Corbiniani* 9.

153. Boniface, ep. 58.

154. Wolfram, *Salzburg, Bayern, Österreich*, p. 235; Paul the Deacon, *Historia Langobardorum* VI 44; *Liber Pontificalis* 91, 4.

155. Gregory II, *Literae decretales*: again there is a question over the authenticity of the text.

156. Wolfram, *Salzburg, Bayern, Österreich*, pp. 244–5.

157. Wolfram, *Salzburg, Bayern, Österreich*, p. 235.

158. On Augsburg, Wolfram, *Die Geburt Mitteleuropas*, pp. 115–16; for Salzburg, Wolfram, *Salzburg, Bayern, Österreich*, pp. 247, 251.

159. Jonas, *Vita Columbani* II 8.

160. *Vita Amandi* 16. See also A. Verhulst and G. Declercq, 'L'action et le souvenir de saint Amand en Europe centrale. À propos de la découverte d'une *Vita Amandi antiqua*', in *M. Van Uytfanghe and R. Demeulenaere, Aevum inter Utrumque, Mélanges offerts à Gabrial Sanders*. One might note that there are considerable similarities between the narrative of the *Vita Amandi* and that of Arbeo's *Vita Corbiniani*, notably in the stories of journeys to Rome, of a miraculous catch of fish, of the saving of a hanged man and of the involvement of the saint in a royal/ducal baptism: *Vita Amandi* 6–7, 10 (Rome), 11 (fish), 14 (hanged man), 17 (royal baptism); Arbeo, *Vita Corbiniani* 6–9, 14–20 (Rome), 17–18 (fish), 10–11 (hanged man), 32 (baptism).

161. Although Klüppel, 'Die Germania (750–950)', p. 175, does list the *Vita Amandi* as a source for Arbeo's *Passio Haimhrammi*.

162. Löwe, 'Arbeo von Freising: eine Studie zu Religiosität und Bildung im 8. Jahrhundert', p. 83. See Glaser, 'Bischof Arbeo von Freising als Gegenstand der neueren Forschung', p. 23.

163. It has regularly been suggested that the figure of Pilitrude in Arbeo, *Vita Corbiniani* 30 is modelled on Brunhild in Jonas, *Vita Columbani* I 18. It might also be noted that the destruction of a complete branch of the ruling family is also referred to in both texts: Arbeo, *Vita Corbiniani* 31; Jonas, *Vita Columbani* I 29. See Glaser, 'Bischof Arbeo von Freising als Gegenstand der neueren Forschung', p. 21.

164. *Breves Notitiae* 1.

165. Arbeo, *Vita Haimhrammi* 4–6.

166. Arbeo, *Vita Corbiniani* 9.

167. Glaser, 'Bischof Arbeo von Freising als Gegenstand der neueren Forschung', p. 63.

168. *Vita Amandi* 16.

169. *Conversio Bagoariorum et Carantanorum* 5; Wolfram, *Salzburg, Bayern, Österreich*, pp. 280–5.

170. Boniface, ep. 58.

171. *Diplomata Karolinorum* 1, 211.

172. Alcuin, epp. 107, 112, 113. See also the documentation for the *Conventus episcoporum ad ripas Danubii* of 796, in which Arno and Paulinus of Aquileia were involved: ed. A. Weminghoff, MGH, Concilia 2, Aevi Karolini 1 (Hanover, 1906), pp. 172–6.

173. *Passio Kiliani* 1–2.

174. *Passio Kiliani* 3.

175. *Passio Kiliani* 4–5.

176. *Passio Kiliani* 6–7.

177. *Passio Kiliani* 8.

178. *Passio Kiliani* 9–10.

179. *Passio Kiliani* 11.

180. *Passio Kiliani* 12–13.

181. *Passio Kiliani* 14.

182. *Passio Kiliani* 15.

183. Levison, ed., *Passio Kiliani*, p. 713; Berschin, *Karolingische Biographie 750–920 n. Chr.*, p. 92, places it shortly before 800.

184. Levison, ed., *Passio Kiliani*, p. 716 if anything underestimates the strength of his case. Compare *Passio Kiliani* 9 and *Vita Corbiniani* 20; *Passio Kiliani* 14 and *Vita Corbiniani* 24. See Klüppel, 'Die Germania (750–950)', pp. 177–8 for the influence of Arbeo's *Vita Corbiniani* and the *Vita Amandi*.

185. *Passio Kiliani* 4.

186. *Passio Kiliani* 13.

187. Compare *Passio Kiliani* 6 with Boniface epp. 50–1.

188. Compare *Passio Kiliani* 9 and Willibald, *Vita Bonifatii* 8; *Passio Kiliani* 10 and Willibald, *Vita Bonifatii* 8; *Passio Kiliani* 15 and Willibald, *Vita Bonifatii* 8.

189. Willibald, *Vita Bonifatii* 8.

190. *Passio Kiliani* 15.

191. Arbeo, *Vita Corbiniani* 30, 33.

192. Willibald, *Vita Bonifatii* 7.

193. Willibald, *Vita Bonifatii* 7.

194. Arbeo, *Vita Haimhrammi* 35.

195. Jahn, 'Virgil, Arbeo und Cozroh', p. 209.

196. Boniface, epp. 68, 80.

# Chapter 8

# NINTH-CENTURY SALZBURG

## 1. THE NARRATIVE OF THE *CONVERSIO BAGOARIORUM ET CARANTANORUM*

In 870 or thereabouts the archbishop of Salzburg, Adalwin was responsible for – that is, he either wrote or commissioned – a remarkable account of the Christianisation of the Carantanian Slavs.[1] The work begins with the history of the Christianisation of Bavaria itself, and does so, as we have seen, by retelling the *Life* of Rupert of Salzburg.[2] There follows a catalogue of the bishops and abbots of Salzburg who succeeded Rupert, before the narrative opens up once more to provide an account of the arrival of the Irishman Virgil. He supposedly approached Pippin III at Quierzy, who detained him for two years, and then sent him to Odilo, *dux* of Bavaria, who may have offered him the bishopric of Salzburg as early as 747. Virgil put off consecration for two years, relying on his companion, the Irish bishop Dobdagrecus, to carry out episcopal functions. Finally, he did accept consecration as bishop, at the request of the people and bishops – the date given in the *Conversio* is 767, although modern commentators place the event in 749.[3] At this point the author announces that hitherto he has provided an account of the Christianisation of the Bavarians, and a list of the bishops and abbots of Salzburg.[4]

In fact, as we have seen, the Christian history of Bavaria was rather more complex – with the survival of a Christian cult from the Roman period in Augsburg,[5] the establishment of a Frankish Christian family, the Agilolfings, as *duces* of Bavaria in the sixth century,[6] and missionary work by such figures as Eustasius of Luxeuil in the seventh,[7] to say nothing of the histories of Emmeram and Corbinian, with all that they imply for the state of Christianity in Regensburg and Freising.[8] Nevertheless, for the purposes of the author of the *Conversio* it was enough to see the Christianisation of Bavaria in terms of the establishment of the diocese of Salzburg.

The arrival of Virgil marks the transition in the *Conversio* to a concern with the Christianisation of the Carantanian Slavs. The author begins this section with a potted history. He recounts that the Huns expelled the Romans, Goths and Gepids from *Pannonia inferior*, taking over the region, until they were defeated by Franks, Bavarians and Carantanians. The term

'Hun' covers a number of Hunnic groups, culminating in the Avars, and the defeat refers to those of the mid-790s.[9] After the defeat, the 'Huns' who accepted baptism became tributary, and remained so until the author's own day.[10] As for the Carantanians, their history is traced back to the days of Dagobert I and the rule of Samo, who is here identified as a Slav and not as a Frank, which is how he appears in Fredegar's seventh-century account.[11] According to the *Conversio*, Dagobert and his forces defeated Samo and forced him and the Carantanians into subjection.[12] According to Fredegar, Samo and his Slav followers defeated Dagobert's Austrasian troops, though they did suffer at the hands of his Alaman and Lombard allies.[13]

Having related the episode of Samo, the author leaps forward to the mid-eighth century to relate a 'Hunnic', in other words Avar, attack on the Carantanian Slavs, whose leader, Boruth, asked for help from the Bavarians. As a result, not only were the Avars defeated, but the *Carantani* were subjected to Frankish overlordship. Further, when Boruth sent his son, Cacatius, and his nephew, Chietmar, as hostages to Bavaria, he asked that they be brought up as Christians. Then, when Boruth died, first Cacatius and then Chietmar succeeded to the leadership of the Carantanians. Chietmar sent his nephew, Majorian, to be prepared for the priesthood. In the event, the boy entered the monastic community in Salzburg.[14]

With his account of Chietmar's rule the author embarks on a remarkable presentation of the process of Christianisation. Chietmar asked Virgil to pay a visit to the Carantanians. Unable to go in person, Virgil sent Bishop Modestus and a number of other clerics – each carefully named, to teach, consecrate priests and ordain clergy, according to the canons. Just as the clergy are named, so too are the churches they dedicated. When Modestus died, Chietmar asked Virgil to send another bishop, but he refused in view of unrest which caused difficulties until after Chietmar's death. Subsequently, however, Virgil did send more clergy – again each one carefully named, at the request of *dux* Waltunc. Mission in the *Conversio Bagoariorum et Carantanorum* is carefully delineated not so much in terms of converts as in terms of clergy supplied and churches dedicated.[15]

Having listed Virgil's achievements, the author now turns his attention to those of his successor, Arno. Again the account starts with some past history. In ancient times the part of *Pannonia inferior* south of the Danube was under Roman control. According to the author, the Romans even subdued the Goths and the Gepids – a statement which is clearly wrong. The erroneous reconstruction of events continues with the statement that Huns from north of the Danube crossed the river in 377, and expelled the Romans, Goths and Gepids. Subsequently, when the 'Huns' (Avars) were driven out, the Slavs settled in the region. In 796 Charlemagne sent *comes* Eric against the 'Huns', who surrendered. In the same year Charles's son, Pippin, also led an army

169

against them, and their leaders all submitted. Here the *Conversio* refers to events which prompted Alcuin's letters to Arno concerning the evangelisation of the Avars.[16] Charlemagne, according to the *Conversio*, then handed the region round Lake Balaton to Bishop Arno of Salzburg, a concession he reiterated in 803.[17]

The author goes on to explain that Arno busied himself with pastoral work as Virgil had done. This time, however, rather than listing all the priests sent, he concentrates on one called Ingo. This man was so popular that he was obeyed even when he simply sent out a sheet of parchment with no writing on it. One anecdote in particular is singled out. Ingo invited the Christian servants of pagan masters to supper, serving them on gold plates: their masters were fed outside like dogs, with bread, meat and wine in filthy jugs. Ingo told them that, not being baptised, they were not worthy to eat with Christians. As a result, many underwent baptism.[18] The story may not be true – it has Biblical echoes[19] – but it was plausible enough for other similar stories to circulate, most notably that concerning the conversion of Borivoj, the grandfather of Wenceslas of Bohemia, at the court of Svatopluk of Moravia.[20] Arbeo had also included a story relating to dogs and food in the *Vita Corbiniani*, where the saint stormed out of a meal with Grimoald, when the *dux* had unthinkingly thrown to his dogs some bread which Corbinian had blessed.[21]

The *Conversio* then returns to Arno, who went to Rome in 798 to receive the *pallium* from Pope Leo. In the course of his return journey he received a message from Charlemagne, ordering him to preach to the Slavs. Despite his objections, he was forced to do so. He also consecrated churches and ordained priests. Having seen the situation at first hand, Arno advised Charlemagne of the possibilities for mission, and proposed that Deoderic should undertake the task. Arno and *comes* Gerold then accompanied Deoderic to *Sclavinia*, and presented him as bishop to the leaders there. He was to preach, consecrate churches, and ordain priests subject to Salzburg.[22]

When Arno died in 821 he was succeeded by Adalram, who extended his work, as did his own successors: and so too with Deoderic's successors, who continued to be subject to Salzburg.[23] The *Conversio* goes on to list the secular officials of the region down to the time of Louis the Pious, when Mojmir, *dux* of the Moravians, exiled the Carantanian chieftain, Priwina (833). The latter fled to Ratbod, the official charged with the defence of the eastern frontier, who presented him to Louis. As a result he was given Christian instruction and was baptised at Traismauer. He was then made subordinate to Ratbod, but he soon fell out with his superior, and fled to Bulgaria.[24] Subsequently, however, he made his peace and as a result was given a benefice in *Pannonia inferior*. Already, before his exile from Moravia at the hands of Mojmir, he had built a church at Nitra, which Archbishop Adalram of Salzburg had consecrated in 827/8. He now built a second church, which Adalram's successor, Archbishop Liupram, consecrated in 850. The author gives a list of all those present, who witnessed the agreement between Liupram and Priwina. The latter handed his priest, Dominic, over to the archbishop, who gave him permission to say mass, commending the church and people to him. There follows an account of Liupram's journey through the region, consecrating priests and dedicating churches. More consecrations followed in subsequent years. Names and places of priests are carefully given. The author concludes the chapter by affirming that he has given a list of churches constructed in the days of Priwina and consecrated by the bishops of Salzburg.[25]

Priwina came to impress Louis the German more and more, to the extent that the king conceded to him as a *beneficium* all that he already held, except what belonged to the Church of Salzburg. In making the concession, the king defined what belonged to the bishop, and the whole was witnessed on 12 October 848. This was effectively the base line for Salzburg's power, and it continued to increase during the lifetime of Priwina. Subsequently, the arrangement between Priwina and the archbishops, which had started with the commendation of Dominic, continued under his successors, Swarnagal and then Rihpald. And so matters remained, claims the author, until the Greek Methodius began to celebrate masses in Slavonic, which prompted Rihpald to return to Salzburg.[26]

At some point in 860/1 Priwina was killed by the Moravians,[27] and his son, Chezilo, succeeded him. He continued his father's close association with the Church of Salzburg, entertaining Archbishop Adalwin on one of his estates for Christmas 864. This was followed in the New Year by the dedication of six churches, and the appointment of the necessary clergy. In 866 the archbishop returned, preaching in the churches he had already dedicated, dedicating yet more, and appointing more priests.[28]

The author of the *Conversio* then summed up his story: in the seventy-five years from Charlemagne's grant of eastern Pannonia to the bishops of Salzburg, there had been no ecclesiastical authority in the region other than that of the bishops themselves. No priest was allowed to act there for more than three months without submitting *epistola dimissoria* – a formal letter issued by the diocesan bishop of a cleric, providing information on his training, learning and status and permission for him to travel outside his diocese of ordination.[29] Thus it was – says the author of the *Conversio* – until the new teaching of the philosopher, Methodius, arrived.[30]

## 2. MISSIONARY HISTORY AS LEGAL HISTORY

The *Conversio Bagoariorum et Carantanorum* is justly recognised as a remarkable source, and is often plundered for information. Yet its extraordinary nature has perhaps been underemphasised by scholars.[31] First, as a history of Christianisation, it has no clear model. Bede comes closest to writing such a history in the *Historia Ecclesiastica Gentis Anglorum*, but his narrative is less tightly focused. The next Church to be subject to an equivalent account would be that of Hamburg-Bremen, in Adam's eleventh-century *Gesta Hammaburgensis Ecclesiae Pontificum*. Such focus is, however, to be found in earlier texts apparently from the Church of Armagh, notably in Tírechán's *Life of Patrick*, which uses the saint's perambulations to make claims about the jurisdiction of his supposed Church.[32] Although the parallel between this and the *Conversio* is by no means exact, one might ask whether Virgil of Salzburg had not brought with him from Ireland an awareness of such a way of expressing legal claims. Although he is usually linked with Iona, because of the insertion of a list of abbots of that monastery into the *Liber Confraternitatum* of St Peter's, the list is preceded by the name of Patrick.[33]

Second, the form of the *Conversio* is itself unusual. Whereas Bede had littered his missionary history with the accounts of saints, there is only one clearly hagiographical section in the *Conversio*, the opening chapter on Rupert – significantly, the chapter is alone in containing a large number of echoes of earlier hagiography.[34] Otherwise, the only cleric to be the subject of an anecdote of any length is Ingo.[35] Even Virgil and Arno, important though they are to the narrative of church foundation and dedication, and of the ordination of clergy, are presented essentially as church officials. In this they reflect the tone of the main body of the work, which is legalistic.

The legalistic nature of the *Confessio* is not confined to its lists of churches founded and priests ordained. Its very detail seems to have depended on charters. Thus the description of Louis the German's definition of the rights of Salzburg in 848 uses the phrase *ad sanctum Petrum principem apostolorum et beatissimum Hrodbertum, ubi ipse corpore requiescit*, which is a diplomatic formula. And the statement is provided with a witness list and a date.[36] So too the dedication of the church at Nitra during Adalram's visit of 850 is provided with a witness list, and the whole episode is defined as a *complicitatio*.[37] The *Conversio*, in other words, is suffused with the legal language of charters.

Clearly, the choice of language reflects the purpose of the document: the text is not concerned with mission as the work of holy men, or with saints as models, but with legal claims. It was not the first time that the Church of Salzburg had embued a narrative source with legal formulae. This had already been done in two documents of the eighth century, the *Notitia Arnonis* of 788–90 and the *Breves Notitiae* of 798–800.[38] The preface to the former even uses a charter formula similar to that employed by the *Conversio*: *ubi et domnus Hrodbertus episcopus atque confessor . . . corpore requiescit*[39] – both phrases are strongly reminiscent of that used to refer to Fulda, where of course the body is that of the martyr Boniface. This it follows with a list of donations to the Church of Salzburg made by the Agilolfing rulers of Bavaria, Theoto, Theodbert, Hucbert, Odilo and Tassilo.[40] Like that of the *Conversio*, the narrative of the *Notitia* is rarely expansive, but it does include one relatively long anecdote – on the discovery of the Maximilianszelle and its acquisition by Rupert.[41] The *Notitia* concludes with a statement that 'I Arno, with the consent and licence of the most pious king, the lord Charles, in the same year in which he received the region of Bavaria into his power, have sought out most diligently from truly old and honest men, from monks and laymen and I have had it written down so it should be remembered.' He then lists his witnesses.[42]

The *Breves Notitiae* adopt a similar format, although this time they open (as does the *Conversio*) with a lengthy account of Rupert in Bavaria.[43] This is followed by lists of ducal gifts, from Theodbert, Hucbert, Odilo and Tassilo,[44] as well as a series of anecdotes, split up to reflect the chronology, which add up to an account of the history of the Maximilianszelle.[45] The ducal gifts are followed by those of nobles and people of middling rank,[46] and once again the somewhat dry catalogue is enlivened by an anecdote, this time by one relating to Virgil of Salzburg's acquisition of Otting.[47]

The author of the *Conversio* thus had models in earlier Salzburg documents when he sat down to compile his text – and those models may themselves look back to the similar combination of legal claims and narrative history made for Armagh by Tírechán. These models provided examples of how one might integrate diplomatic information into what is essentially a narrative form. But while the Salzburg models had been essentially concerned with the acquisition of property, the *Conversio* was only interested in property in so far as it reflected the jurisdictional claims of the archbishops of Salzburg in what had once been Pannonia. These claims were best expressed through lists of churches dedicated and clergy ordained. As a result, Adalwin of Salzburg, or the author of the *Conversio*, effectively created a way of writing missionary history in terms of jurisdiction and the creation of a church organisation. Such an approach was made possible by the documents commissioned by Arno, but it was made necessary by the presence of Methodius.

## 3. CONSTANTINE AND METHODIUS

The *Conversio Bagoariorum et Carantanorum* concerns itself with the ecclesiastical jurisdiction over the Carantanian Slavs. There were, however, other Slavonic groups, not least the Moravians. Moravians and Bohemians are mentioned at the court of Louis the Pious in 822,[48] and a mass baptism of Moravians by Bishop Reginhar of Passau is recorded in the very skimpy *Notae de episcopis Pataviensibus* for 831.[49] It is possible that the conversion of the Moravian leader, Mojmir, who was to be responsible for Priwina's exile, had already taken place in the context of the Slav embassy to Louis' court.[50] Presumably, he had links with the Church of Passau, indeed, Passau seems to have been to Moravia what Salzburg was to Carinthia: alas, it produced no direct equivalent to the Salzburg *Conversio* which has survived.

On Mojmir's death in 846 his nephew, Rastislav, took over the rule of Moravia, with the support of Louis the German.[51] But this did not make the new ruler a reliable subordinate of the German king. By 855 he was already at war with Louis,[52] and in such a circumstance he must have been keen to break any dependence of the Moravian Church on that of Bavaria. In 860 he seems to have appealed to Pope Nicolas I, and two years later he sent a delegation to Constantinople, seeking an alternative source of senior clergy.[53] According to the *Life of Constantine*, when he wrote to the Byzantine Emperor, he asked for a man who could teach in Slavonic. It was supposedly after receiving this commission from the emperor that Constantine invented the Slavonic alphabet.[54]

Constantine and Methodius set out for Moravia in *c.* 862. There they were well received by Rastislav. Pupils were handed over to Constantine for instruction, and at the same time he translated liturgical offices into Slavonic. This, according to the *Life of Constantine*, caused a furious reaction from the Latins and Franks, who claimed that there were only three holy languages, Hebrew, Greek and Latin. The onslaught prompted Constantine to retaliate with the denunciation of Western errors. The list of errors supplied by the hagiographer is curious: supposedly, Westerners believed in the existence of men under the world with large heads, regarded reptiles as agents of the devil, thought that killing a snake gained forgiveness for nine sins, and ordered three months' drinking from a wooden mug for killing a man. Constantine is also said to have accused them of allowing sacrifice and polygamy.[55] Within this list one may discern a parodic retaliation to the use of penitentials and also, perhaps, a reference to a belief which Boniface ascribed to Virgil of Salzburg, that men lived under the earth.[56] After three years' work in Moravia Constantine was invited to Carinthia by Priwina's son, Kotsel, who, we are told, was impressed by the missionary's use of Slavonic.

The growing conflict over the use of Slavonic had, however. become too great for the pope to ignore, and at this point (867) Nicolas summoned Constantine and Methodius to Rome. By the time they arrived Nicolas was dead, and it was left to his successor, Hadrian II, to deal with the linguistic debate. This he did by blessing copies of the liturgical books which had been translated into Slavonic.[57] Not long after this Constantine died, but before doing so he charged his brother to continue his work.[58]

When Kotsel asked for Methodius' return, Hadrian elevated the Greek to the episcopate, with a broad area of jurisdiction, as archbishop of Sirmium, and he gave him a letter addressed to Rastislav, Svatopluk, his nephew, and Kotsel.[59] The letter contained approval for the use of Slavonic, but insisted that during the mass the Epistle and Gospel should first be read in Latin. Although Methodius was well received by Kotsel, matters were very different in the heart of Moravia. There Svatopluk had seized power from Rastislav, with German help.[60] When Methodius arrived, he was bundled off to Regensburg to face trial by the Bavarian episcopate, and possibly by Louis the German.[61] The accusation was one of infringement of ecclesiastical jurisdiction – presumably in Pannonia.[62] As far as can be ascertained, the *Conversio Bagoariorum et Carantanorum* is essentially Salzburg's contribution to the case for the prosecution. It is possible that the bishops of Passau, Regensburg and Freising had compiled their own dossiers.[63] Language was clearly an issue between the Bavarian Church and Methodius – the *Conversio* claims that 'the Greek Methodius, like a philosopher, overriding the Latin tongue, Roman doctrine and Latin letters with newly invented Slav letters, made vile for the whole people, in part, the mass, Gospels, and the offices of their ecclesiastics, who celebrated these in Latin'.[64] Doctrine was also an issue.[65] But the *Conversio* is almost entirely concerned with jurisdiction, and it implies that that is what was the real bone of contention.

The result of the trial for Methodius was imprisonment in Swabia.[66] When Pope John VIII discovered his fate – which was apparently not for some time[67] – he was furious,[68] and anathematised at least one of the German bishops, Ermenrich of Passau, who is said to have threatened to take a whip to the interloper.[69] Since four of the bishops involved died soon after, this was taken as a sign of divine vengeance. Methodius himself returned to Moravia, where he was accepted as archbishop, and at the same time the German clerics were forced out. The result, according to the *Vita Methodii*, was the expansion of the Church.[70] But there was a backlash to come: Methodius was accused of heresy by those who espoused the addition of the *filioque* clause to the Creed, and was, according to his *vita*, driven out of Moravia.[71] Papal evidence suggests rather that he was summoned to Rome over the question of the use of the Slav language.[72] Meanwhile, Svatopluk was looking to a rapprochement with the German Church, and asked that a Frank, Wiching, be consecrated as bishop of Nitra.[73] The pope, still John VIII, steered a middle course, both consecrating Wiching and upholding the orthodoxy of Methodius.[74] He may also have exploited a visit of Methodius to Constantinople in 881.[75] Methodius himself returned to the West in 882, and died three years later.[76] At this point Wiching seized

175

his opportunity to establish himself as the leading bishop in the region, and to persecute Methodius' clergy – however, he fled from Moravia in 892/3, while the arrival of the Magyars in 907 ensured that there would be no immediate revival of the Slavonic Church.[77]


## 4. ERMENRICH OF PASSAU AND THE ATTITUDE OF THE BAVARIAN CHURCH

Hagiography relating to Constantine and Methodius is not easy to assess. One Latin *Life* of Constantine, the so-called Italian legend, which is essentially an account of the transfer of the relics of pope Clement from Cherson in the Crimea to Rome, seems to be dependent on a translation of Slavonic texts made for Gauderic of Velletri by Anastasius Bibliotecarius in the period 869–82.[78] The more famous Slav *Lives* of Constantine and Methodius, however, only survive in late medieval versions of what appear to have been ninth-century works written in Slavonic in Moravia. The linguistic problems they present are such that they are the preserve of Slav experts, and what hagiographical context can be reconstructed for them appears to be Byzantine rather than Western – although there does appear to be an apologetic element to the *Life* of Methodius, suggesting some concern with the German reaction to his career.[79] Certainly, the *Vita Constantini-Cyrilli cum translatione s. Clementis* apart, which is in any case largely an account of the translation of Clement, the *Lives* of the Thessalonian brothers take us out of the field of Latin hagiography.

It is, nevertheless, easy to sympathise with the author of the *Life* of Methodius and to see the saint's treatment at the hand of the Bavarian Church as fully fledged persecution. Further, the linguistic achievements of Constantine and his brother meant that their contribution to the development of Christianity far exceeded that of any bishop of Salzburg. Nevertheless, it is important not to ignore what those bishops, and indeed their compatriots at Passau and Regensburg, had achieved. Even Ermenrich of Passau, who can easily appear as the villain of the piece, condemned as he was by Pope John VIII in 873,[80] seems to have been a figure genuinely committed to Christianisation. He spent time at Fulda, Reichenau and St Gallen, and he kept up contact with all three centres.[81] He was imbued enough with the traditions of Boniface, as represented at Fulda, to write the *Life* of a supposed associate of the martyr, an Anglo-Saxon hermit called Sualo. The *Vita Sualonis* he addressed to Rudolf of Fulda and to the court chaplain, Gundram.[82] In the *vita* he claimed that 'King' Pippin had committed Francia and Alamannia to Boniface.[83] Moreover, he described both Boniface and Sualo as apostles.

As important for Ermenrich's attitude to mission is his letter to Abbot Grimbold of St Gallen, written in *c.* 850–5. Here he treats a whole series of issues, but especially the history of Gallus;[84] indeed, the letter was partly written in response to a request for a metrical *vita* of the saint:[85] it has been called 'a complete introduction to a *Life* of Gallus'.[86] Ermenrich groups Columbanus, Gallus and Boniface together,[87] and he explicitly states that Columbanus and Gallus left Ireland 'to convert the unbelief of the barbarians to the faith of Christ' [*ut barbarorum incredulitatem ad fidem Christi usquequaque converterent*].[88] Before he ever became bishop of Passau he had, therefore, considered the question of evangelisation – albeit within an officially Christian area: Christianisation rather than mission to the pagans.[89] His own commitment to evangelisation is probably reflected in his being chosen by Louis the German to head a missionary embassy to Bulgaria in 867, only to find on arrival that the papacy had forestalled him.[90] By a strange coincidence he had considered the scansion of the name *Vulgáres* (Bulgars) in the extraordinary display of classical learning which dominates the opening sections of his letter to Grimbold.[91] Simply to pick up the accusation that Ermenrich threatened to take a horsewhip to Methodius[92] is to miss the depth of involvement in Christianisation shown by the Bavarian Church, and the genuine grievance caused by the Byzantine missionary and the papacy.

Ermenrich was, thus, not merely a figure concerned with jurisdiction – behind the jealous protection of the rights of Passau was a deep interest in the Christian past, which he construed in terms of such saints as Columbanus, Gallus and Boniface, whom he saw as missionaries. In dealing with the latter, however, he specifically notes his consecration of bishops and ordination of priests.[93] In so doing he shows an attitude similar to that of the whole line of Salzburg bishops treated in the *Conversio*, with its clear description of the establishment of an ecclesiatical structure of churches and clergy in Moravia and *Pannonia Inferior*. Yet, while the *Conversio* is essentially a legal document, it also spells out a full and committed strategy for the Christianisation of the Carantanian Slavs. One might also wish to see in the short and obscure *Descriptio civitatum et regionum ad septentrionalem plagam Danubii* – a simple list of places and districts north of the Danube – another document relating to Bavarian ecclesiastical strategies at the time of Methodius.[94]

The creation of an ecclesiastical structure belongs to a second phase of Christianisation, for it depended on the prior conversion of leaders, such as Cacatius and Chietmar, Mojmir and Priwina, all of whom were converted in the context of their relations with the German kingdom. Since an ecclesiastical structure seems already to have been in place in much of Moravia before the arrival of Constantine and Methodius, one has to conclude that the Thessalonian brothers were very much Johnnies-come-lately.[95] The Bavarian Churches had good reason to feel that their noses had been put out of joint.

Methodius' tribulations were in part the result of the fact that he was a pawn in the world of central European politics. The initial request for Greek clergy reflected Rastislav's wish for priests who were not dependent on the German Church. The subsequent removal of support for Methodius by Svatopluk reflects a changed political situation, and the need for a Moravian ruler to cooperate more with the kingdom of Germany. On the other hand, the Bavarian bishops saw their achievements, which were the product of generations of work, taken from them, to suit the wishes of a Moravian ruler, and also because of a new interest in mission shown by the papacy.

## 5. NICOLAS I AND THE PAPAL INVOLVEMENT IN MISSION

Nicolas I (858–67), the pope who summoned Constantine and Methodius to Rome in 867, but who did not live to see their arrival, involved himself in the organisation and furtherance of mission to a greater extent than any other early medieval pope, even Gregory the Great.[96] He had taken a considerable interest in the progress of the Scandinavian mission, perhaps because the question of the combination of the sees of Hamburg and Bremen had been brought to his notice. He even wrote to the Danish king, Horic II, thanking him for gifts, but criticising him for not actually converting to Christianity[97] – a rather less hard-line stance was taken by Anskar, who fully appreciated the amount of support he was given by Horic.[98] Meanwhile, Nicolas also became embroiled in the problem of the Christianisation of Bulgaria. In the course of negotiations with Louis the German held at Tulln, perhaps in 863, Khan Boris had indicated a willingness to accept Christianity.[99] His intention of attaching himself and his kingdom to the Latin Church, however, was thwarted when he was defeated by the Byzantines and had to accept baptism at the hands of the patriach of Constantinople in 864/5. This carried with it the danger of subordination to Byzantium, and Boris continued to be in contact with the West, asking advice from Pope Nicolas in 865. In return he received from the pope the longest and most sophisticated of early medieval discussions of the problems of Christianisation.[100] In the event, politics and the death of Nicolas meant that the Bulgarian Church remained within the Greek orbit.

Of more direct significance for the Frankish Church, Nicolas had also been concerned to keep new Christian communities under the eye of the papacy. He specifically intervened in Dalmatia, claiming in a letter to the Church of Nin that the papal see alone had the right to establish new basilicas (*basilicae*) as well as ecclesiastical units (*ecclesia*).[101] The implications of this for an expansionist Church like that of Salzburg were only too clear. Papal involvement in the case of Methodius, whether by Nicolas himself, or his like-minded successor, Hadrian II, marked the expansion of papal claims to a region in which the Bavarian Church had long been active.

## 6. THE LETTER OF THEOTMAR

The death of Methodius, and the persecution of the Slavonic Church in Moravia, which ensued under Wiching,[102] did not resolve the conflict between the Bavarian Church and the papacy. Wiching himself was a papal appointment – although the Bavarian bishops were later to let this fact pass, by pretending that his diocese had been in territory newly conquered by Svatopluk.[103] For a short while after 884 Wiching had his own way, but as an Alaman he must have found the growing hostility between King Arnulf and Svatopluk after 890 increasingly awkward.[104] In 893 he fled to Arnulf's court, becoming the king's chancellor.[105] His next move, however, was not supported by the Bavarian bishops. Although Arnulf had him consecrated bishop of Passau in 899, his appointment was instantly condemned as uncanonical, and he was removed by Archbishop Theotmar of Salzburg.[106]

A year later Theotmar was responsible for one more account of the Christianisation of Moravia, in a letter written to Pope John IX. The letter has not always been accepted as authentic – indeed, it has been seen as a forgery compiled by Bishop Pilgrim of Passau (971–91) in his attempt to remove his diocese from the jurisdiction of Salzburg, and to establish his own metropolitanate over Moravia and Pannonia. While it came to be included in dossiers created by Pilgrim, the letter does appear to be genuine.[107]

The letter was written on behalf of the Bavarian episcopate in response to Pope John's appointing an archbishop, John, and two bishops, Benedict and Daniel, to Moravia, at the request of Svatopluk, in 899.[108] Theotmar, who often lapses into sarcasm in the course of the letter, explains that the pope has created bishops for a region which was already subject to the bishop of Passau.[109] The bishop's rights were clear, because the part of Moravia in question, which had been subject to the secular control of Bavarian *comites*, had been evangelised from Passau, and the bishop indeed had the right to move round the diocese as he pleased.[110] This subjection to Bavaria had lasted until the devil had tempted the Moravians to rebel, rejecting Christianity, and closing clerical access to the region. The identification of this rebellion is not entirely clear, but the reference may well be to events in Moravia which followed the trial of Methodius in 870,[111] in which case the supposed pagan uprising must rather be a rejection of Bavarian clerics.

By appointing John, Benedict and Daniel, the pope had, according to Theotmar, made matters worse. Since they had been sent to territory which had been subject to Passau, the pope had divided a diocese without consultation, and since John had been given the status of archbishop there was a further canonical problem, because it was quite improper for there to be two archbishops within one archdiocese.[112] The author goes on to list the canons preventing such action. Wiching's appointment by Pope John VIII was, according to Theotmar, a different matter, since his diocese had been in territory which had never been under Passau.[113]

Theotmar, having challenged the claims of the new bishops, that there was division between Bavarians, Franks and Alamans,[114] then embarks on an essentially racist comparison of the Bavarians and Moravians, comparing the Christian ancestry of Louis IV with the pagan and ethnic forbears of Mojmir II's Slavs.[115] He notes that the former had protected the papacy and Christians, while the latter had attacked and persecuted them.[116]

As an instance of persecution he states that the Slavs colluded with the Hungarians, unleashing them on 'our Christians'.[117] To rub home the subversion which has taken place, Theotmar draws attention to the shaven heads of the pseudo-Christian Hungarians – *more eorum capita suorum pseudochristianorum penitus detonderunt*. This manner of hairstyle was a well-known feature of the Magyars, and is noted by Regino of Prüm.[118] The intention here is presumably to present the Hungarians as a parody of tonsured Christian clergy who would genuinely look after their flock. At the same time, says Theotmar, the Moravians themselves kill, imprison, exile and enslave Christians, nobles included.[119] The account is remarkably close to what is said in Slavonic sources of the persecution of the disciples of Methodius after his death[120] – it is effectively a mirror image of it, and suggests that brutality was not confined to the pro-German party alone. The destruction of churches is so great, claims Theotmar, that not one church survives in 'our' Pannonia, and he tells the pope to ask the three bishops he had sent to Moravia for verification.[121]

Theotmar then turns to Italy, claiming that when the Bavarians discovered that it had been invaded by the Hungarians – an event well recorded in the *Annals of Fulda*[122] – they tried to negotiate a peace with the Slavs, so they could come to the assistance of the Italians without fear of attack from the rear, but they were unable to do so.[123] Peace with Moravia was in fact only secured in 901.[124] The fact that the Slavs had prevented the Bavarians from protecting Italy allows Theotmar a final irony: he is unable to send the dues owed to the pope, because the pagan threat makes it impossible, but he will do so once Italy has been liberated.[125] Since John VIII had made a point of stressing prompt payment in the letter in which he conceded the *pallium* to Theotmar in 877,[126] this must have been a particularly sweet irony.

Many of the points in Theotmar's letter are picked up in a contemporary epistle addressed by Archbishop Hatto of Mainz to Pope John IX.[127] Like the letter of Theotmar, that of Hatto has been seen as a forgery associated with Pilgrim of Passau, but the case for accepting it as genuine seems to be strong.[128] Hatto writes shortly after the death of the emperor Arnulf, and the election of Louis the Child, in other words, at the very end of 899 or the start of 900 – but after a short interval, because communications had been interrupted by pagans[129] – a point reminiscent of Theotmar. He then states that the Bavarians have complained about a Moravian insurrection, linked to the papal concession of their own metropolitan.[130] Hatto praises the pastoral work of the Bavarian clergy, and asks the pope to end the arrogance of the Moravians, warning him that the conflict will lead to bloodshed.[131] Hatto may have been aware of the long-standing nature of the conflict between the Moravian and Bavarian Churches, and of interventions by the papacy which had harmed the interests of Passau. Like Ermenrich, he had contacts with the monastery of Ellwangen:[132] he may well have been aware of the treatment of the Bavarian bishops by John VIII.

Theotmar's letter provides yet another example of Salzburg's use of the history of mission in defence of its rights. More generally, whereas the northern tradition of missionary history had come to concentrate on the theory of mission and the experience of the missionary in the field, both issues explored through hagiography, the Bavarian emphasis had been concerned with the foundation of churches, the provision of a priesthood, and the jurisdictional questions that these actions raised. A logical conclusion to this approach would be the dossiers of texts, forged, and in the case of the letters of Theotmar and Hatto, apparently authentic, put together by Pilgrim of Passau.[133] The Latin documentation of the missionary period in Moravia thus follows a precise line of development, which is legalistic rather than hagiographical: as a result, what hagiography there is – leaving aside Ermenrich's exploration of the past – relates not to the Bavarian missionaries, but to their Byzantine rivals, and is written not in Latin, but in Slavonic.

The achievements of Constantine and Methodius in Moravia were undermined by Wiching, but were finally swept away by the Hungarian invasions, which were already a feature of the days of Theotmar as he wrote his letter to John IX. Just to the north, in Bohemia, however, a different Christian history was beginning.

## Notes

1. See above, Chapter 7. For the authorship, Losek, ed., *Die Conversio Bagoariorum et Carantanorum*, pp. 5–8. For a full historical commentary on the text there is Wolfram, ed., *Conversio Bagoariorum et Carantanorum: Das Weißbuch der Salzburger Kirche über*

*die erfolgreiche Mission in Karantanien und Pannonien,* or, more recently, Wolfram, *Salzburg, Bayern, Österreich.*

2. *Conversio Bagoariorum et Carantanorum* 1.
3. *Conversio Bagoariorum et Carantanorum* 2, with comments in the editions of Losek and Wolfram. It should be noted that the different chronologies have led to diverse interpretations of Virgil: according to the old interpretation, in which he remained as abbot for 21 years, without becoming bishop – indeed, with a bishop subordinate to him – he acted very like an abbot of Iona. In the more recent interpretation of Wolfram, *Salzburg, Bayern, Österreich,* pp. 258–63 (with full discussion of previous arguments), in which he only put off consecration for two years, this impression is considerably weakened.
4. *Conversio Bagoariorum et Carantanorum* 4.
5. Wolfram, *Die Geburt Mitteleuropas,* pp. 115–6.
6. Zöllner, 'Die Herrkunft der Agilolfinger'; Wolfram, *Die Geburt Mitteleuropas,* pp. 83–163.
7. Wolfram, *Die Geburt Mitteleuropas,* pp. 116–8.
8. Wolfram, *Die Geburt Mitteleuropas,* pp. 146–9.
9. Pohl, *Die Awaren. Ein Steppenvolk in Mitteleuropa 567–822 n. Chr.* (Munich, 1988), pp. 32, 215.
10. *Conversio Bagoariorum et Carantanorum* 3.
11. Fredegar IV 48, ed. J. M. Wallace-Hadrill, *The Fourth Book of the Chronicle of Fredegar.*
12. *Conversio Bagoariorum et Carantanorum* 4. The majority of our information on Samo comes from Fredegar, IV 48. See W. H. Fritze, *Untersuchungen zur frühslawischen und frühfränkischen Geschichte bis ins 7. Jahrhundert* (Frankfurt am Main, 1994), pp. 83–108.
13. Fredegar IV 48, 68.
14. *Conversio Bagoariorum et Carantanorum* 4.
15. *Conversio Bagoariorum et Carantanorum* 5.
16. Alcuin, epp. 107, 112, 113, 184, 207; see also epp. 7, 99, 118.
17. *Conversio Bagoariorum et Carantanorum* 6.
18. *Conversio Bagoariorum et Carantanorum* 7.
19. e.g. Matthew 15, 26–7.
20. Wolfram, ed., *Conversio Bagoariorum et Carantanorum,* p. 101; Vlasto, *The Entry of the Slavs into Christendom,* p. 87, with p. 345, n. 6.
21. Arbeo, *Vita Corbiniani* 26.
22. *Conversio Bagoariorum et Carantanorum* 8.
23. *Conversio Bagoariorum et Carantanorum* 9.
24. *Conversio Bagoariorum et Carantanorum* 10.
25. *Conversio Bagoariorum et Carantanorum* 11.
26. *Conversio Bagoariorum et Carantanorum* 12.
27. For the date, Wolfram, *Salzburg, Bayern, Österreich,* p. 315.
28. *Conversio Bagoariorum et Carantanorum* 13.
29. For an example, R. A. Fletcher, 'An *Epistola Formata* from Léon', *Bulletin of the Institute of Historical Research* 45 (1972), pp. 122–8.
30. *Conversio Bagoariorum et Carantanorum* 14.
31. The major exceptions are Herwig Wolfram and Fritz Losek. For Wolfram's work see both his edition of the *Conversio* and also *Salzburg, Bayern, Österreich;* for Losek's contribution, see his edition of the text.
32. ed. L. Bieler, *The Patrician Texts in the Book of Armagh* (Dublin, 1979), pp. 122–63.

182

33. Wolfram, 'Virgil of St Peter's at Salzburg', p. 415.
34. See the notes to Losek's edition, pp. 90–9.
35. *Conversio Bagoariorum et Carantanorum* 7.
36. *Conversio Bagoariorum et Carantanorum* 12; for the underlying *formulae* see the notes to Losek's edition, pp. 128–9.
37. *Conversio Bagoariorum et Carantanorum* 11: for the underlying *formulae* see the notes to Losek's edition, pp. 124–5.
38. See the editions by Losek, '*Notitia Arnonis* und *Breves Notitiae*'.
39. *Notitia Arnonis*, pref.. See Losek (ed.), *Conversio Bagoariorum et Carantanorum*, p. 128, n. 152.
40. *Notitia Arnonis* 1–7.
41. *Notitia Arnonis* 8.
42. *Notitia Arnonis* 8.
43. *Breves Notitiae* 1–4.
44. *Breves Notitiae* 5–7, 9–10.
45. *Breves Notitiae* 3, 8.
46. *Breves Notitiae* 12–24.
47. *Breves Notitiae* 13.
48. *Annales qui dicuntur Einhardi*, s.a. 822, ed., F. Kurze, MGH, SRG (Hanover, 1895).
49. *Notae de episcopis Pataviensibus*, ed. G. Waitz, MGH, SS 25 (Hanover, 1880), p. 623.
50. Vlasto, *The Entry of the Slavs into Christendom*, p. 24; *Annales Regni Francorum*, s.a. 822.
51. Vlasto, *The Entry of the Slavs into Christendom*, p. 25.
52. *Annales Fuldenses*, s.a. 855.
53. Vlasto, *The Entry of the Slavs into Christendom*, p. 26.
54. *Vita Constantini* 14, ed. A. Vaillant, *Textes Vieux-Slaves* (Paris, 1968).
55. *Vita Constantini* 15.
56. Boniface, ep. 80.
57. *Vita Constantini* 17; *Vita Methodii* 6.
58. *Vita Methodii* 7.
59. *Vita Methodii* 8.
60. *Annales Fuldenses*, s.a. 870.
61. Louis was in Bavaria in November: *Annales Fuldenses*, s.a. 870.
62. *Vita Methodii* 9.
63. On the bishop of Passau at the time see H. Löwe, 'Ermenrich von Passau, Gegner des Methodius. Versuch eines Persönlichkeitsbildes', *Mitteilungen der Gesellschaft für Salzburger Landeskunde* 126 (1986), pp. 221–41, reprinted in *id.*, *Religiosität und Bildung im frühen Mittelalter* (Stuttgart, 1994), pp. 327–47.
64. *Conversio Bagoariorum et Carantanorum* 12; see also the attached *Excerptum de Karentanis* 1.
65. *Conversio Bagoariorum et Carantanorum* 14: '*nova orta est doctrina Methodii philosophi.*'
66. *Vita Methodii* 9.
67. Vlasto, *The Entry of the Slavs into Christendom*, p. 69.
68. John VIII, *fragmenta registri*, 16, 20, 21–3, ed. E. Caspar, MGH, Epp. 7 = Karolini Aevi 5 (Berlin, 1928); Vlasto, *The Entry of the Slavs into Christendom*, pp. 69–70, with p. 339; n. 209; Löwe, 'Ermenrich von Passau, Gegner des Methodius. Versuch eines Persönlichkeitsbildes', pp. 337–45.
69. *Vita Methodii* 10; John VIII, frag. ep. 22. Löwe, 'Ermenrich von Passau, Gegner des Methodius. Versuch eines Persönlichkeitsbildes'.

70. *Vita Methodii* 10. On Methodius' archiepiscopal title, John VIII, epp. 200, 255, 276; Vlasto, *The Entry of the Slavs into Christendom*, p. 70.
71. *Vita Methodii* 12.
72. John VIII, ep. 201.
73. John VIII, ep. 255; Vlasto, *The Entry of the Slavs into Christendom*, pp. 73–4.
74. Vlasto, *The Entry of the Slavs into Christendom*, pp. 74–5.
75. *Vita Methodii* 13; Vlasto, *The Entry of the Slavs into Christendom*, pp. 75–6.
76. *Vita Methodii* 17; Vlasto, *The Entry of the Slavs into Christendom*, pp. 76–7.
77. Vlasto, *The Entry of the Slavs into Christendom*, pp. 80–5. For the arrival of the Magyars see also P. F. Sugar (ed.), *A History of Hungary* (Bloomington, 1990), pp. 12–14.
78. *Vita Constantini-Cyrilli cum translatione s. Clementis*, ed. D. Bartonkova, L. Havlik, J. Ludvikovsky, Z. Masarik and R. Vecerka, *Magnae Moraviae Fontes Historici* 2 (Brun, 1967), pp. 120–32. This may be associated with the work referred to in Anastasius Bibliothecarius, ep. 15, ed. E. Perels and G. Laehr, MGH, Epistolae 7, Karolini Aevi 5 (Munich, 1978), pp. 435–8. See L. Boyle, 'Dominican Lectionaries and Leo of Ostia's *Translatio S. Clementis*', *Archivum Fratrum Praedicatorum* 28 (1958), pp. 362–6. I am indebted to Anna Kuznetsova for this information.
79. See, for instance, H. Birnbaum, 'The Lives of Sts. Constantine-Cyril and Methodius', *TO ELLHNIKON, Studies in Honor of Speros Vryonis, Jr.*, 2, *Byzantinoslavica, Armeniaca, Islamia, the Balkans and Modern Greece*, ed. J. Stanojevich Allen, C. P. Ioannides, J. S. Langdon, S. W. Reinert (New York, 1993), pp. 3–23.
80. John VIII, ep. 22.
81. Löwe, 'Ermenrich von Passau, Gegner des Methodius. Versuch eines Persönlichkeitsbildes', pp. 327–31: A. Bauch, *Biographien der Gründungszeit, Quellen zur Geschichte der Diözese Eichstätt* (Eichstätt, 1962), p. 193. On his Fulda links see the *epistolae* to Gundram and the *oratio* and *epistola* to Rudolf prefacing the *Sermo de vita Sualonis dicti Sali*.
82. Ermenrich, *Vita Sualonis*. The date of the *Life* appears to be 839–42, Holder-Egger, MGH, SS 15, 1, p. 152. On Boniface as martyr see also *Vita Sualonis* 6. Solnhofen, the foundation of Sualo/Salo is discussed by D. Parsons, 'Some churches of the Anglo-Saxon missionaries in southern Germany: a review of the evidence', *Early Medieval Europe* 8 (1999), pp. 34, 57–62.
83. Ermenrich, *Vita Sualonis* 1; Löwe, 'Ermenrich von Passau, Gegner des Methodius. Versuch eines Persönlichkeitsbildes', pp. 329–30. Löwe is rather freer with the word 'Mission' than is warranted by the Latin – but the relevance of Ermenrich's writings for his relations with Methodius is not in question, since Christianity was not being introduced into Moravia, but organised and strengthened.
84. Ermenrich, *Epistola* 28–9, ed. E. Dümmler, MGH, Epp. 5 = Karolini Aevi 3 (Berlin, 1899): for the date, p. 535; Löwe, 'Ermenrich von Passau, Gegner des Methodius. Versuch eines Persönlichkeitsbildes', p. 330.
85. Ermenrich, *Epistola* 28.
86. Ermenrich, *Epistola* 35; Klüppel, 'Die Germania (750–950)', pp. 182–3: 'Ermenrich antwortet in seiner *Epistola ad domnum Grimoldum abbatem et archicappellanum*, die wie eine vollständige Einleitung zu einer Gallusvita zu lesen ist.' See also p. 190 on the question of whether he actually wrote the *Vita S. Galli metrica*.
87. Ermenrich, *Epistola* 36.
88. Ermenrich, *Epistola* 35.
89. Löwe, 'Ermenrich von Passau, Gegner des Methodius. Versuch eines Persönlichkeitsbildes', pp. 330–1.

90. *Annales Fuldenses*, s.a. 867; Löwe, 'Ermenrich von Passau, Gegner des Methodius. Versuch eines Persönlichkeitsbildes', pp. 333–4; Fletcher, *The Conversion of Europe*, p. 61.
91. Ermenrich, *Epistola* 17.
92. John VIII, ep. 22.
93. Ermenrich, *Vita Sualonis* 1.
94. For an edition, see B. Horák and D. Travnicek, *Descriptio civitatum ad septentrionalem plagam Danubii* (Prague, 1956); for the date and an indication of a relation to the work of Methodius, W. H. Fritze, 'Zu einer Edition des sogenannten bairischen Geographen', in *id.*, *Frühzeit zwischen Ostsee und Donau* (Berlin, 1982), pp. 127–9.
95. Vlasto, *The Entry of the Slavs into Christendom*, p. 48: 'They were not so much pioneers as consolidators of the second stage of Moravian Christianity.'
96. Vlasto, *The Entry of the Slavs into Christendom*, pp. 52–4 provides a useful survey.
97. Nicolas, ep. 27.
98. Rimbert, *Vita Anskarii* 32.
99. The sources are not entirely consistent here: see *Annales Bertiniani*, s.a. 864, *Annales Fuldenses*, s.a. 863, and Nicolas, ep. 26, p. 293. See Vlasto, *The Entry of the Slavs into Christendom*, p. 158; Wolfram, *Salzburg, Bayern, Österreich*, pp. 118–9. Over Nicolas and the Bulgarian mission in general, see R. E. Sullivan, 'Khan Boris and the conversion of Bulgaria: a case study of the impact of Christianity on a barbarian society', *Studies in Medieval and Renaissance History* 3 (1966), pp. 55–139, repr. in *id.*, *Christian Missionary Activity in the Early Middle Ages* (Aldershot, 1994).
100. Nicolas, ep. 99. See the long analysis in Sullivan, 'Khan Boris and the conversion of Bulgaria: a case study of the impact of Christianity on a barbarian society'.
101. Nicolas, ep. 140; Vlasto, *The Entry of the Slavs into Christendom*, p. 53.
102. Vlasto, *The Entry of the Slavs into Christendom*, p. 82.
103. *Epistola Theotmari*, ed. Losek, *Die Conversio Bagoariorum et Carantanorum und der Brief des Erzbischofs Theotmar von Salzburg*, MGH, p. 144.
104. *Annales Fuldenses*, s.a. 890, 891, 892.
105. Vlasto, *The Entry of the Slavs into Christendom*, p. 83.
106. *Annales Fuldenses*, s.a. 899. See aso *Notae de episcopis Pataviensibus*, p. 624.
107. See the introduction to Losek's edition of the *Epistola Theotmari*, pp. 55–81.
108. *Epistola Theotmari*, p. 138.
109. While accepting the basic authenticity of the *Epistola Theotmari*, one might still wonder whether the sentence in which this point is made was not tampered with by Bishop Pilgrim.
110. *Epistola Theotmari*, p. 140.
111. *Epistola Theotmari*, pp. 140–2, also p. 146; *Annales Fuldenses*, s.a. 871–2, 874.
112. *Epistola Theotmari*, p. 142.
113. *Epistola Theotmari*, p. 144.
114. *Epistola Theotmari*, p. 144.
115. *Epistola Theotmari*, p. 146.
116. *Epistola Theotmari*, p. 148.
117. *Epistola Theotmari*, pp. 148–50.
118. Regino, *Chronicon*, s.a. 889, ed. F. Kurze, MGH, SRG (Hanover, 1890).
119. *Epistola Theotmari*, s.a. 150.
120. Vlasto, *The Entry of the Slavs into Christendom*, pp. 82, with p. 344, n. 260, and p. 165.
121. *Epistola Theotmari*, p. 152.
122. *Annales Fuldenses*, s.a. 900.

123. *Epistola Theotmari*, p. 152.

124. *Annales Fuldenses*, s.a. 901.

125. *Epistola Theotmari*, p. 154.

126. John VIII, ep. 65; Losek, *Die Conversio Bagoriorum et Carantanorum und der Brief des Erzbischofs Theotmar von Salzburg*, p. 56.

127. ed. H. Bresslau, 'Der angebliche Brief des Erzbischofs Hatto von Mainz an Papst Johann IX', in *Festschrift für Karl Zeumer* (Weimar, 1909), pp. 27–30.

128. Losek, *Die Conversio Bagoriorum et Carantanorum und der Brief des Erzbischofs Theotmar von Salzburg*, p. 77.

129. Hatto, ed. Bresslau, p. 27. On the accession of Louis, T. Reuter, *Germany in the Middle Ages, 800–1056* (London, 1991), pp. 126–7.

130. Hatto, ed. Bresslau, p. 28.

131. Hatto, ed. Bresslau, pp. 29–30.

132. R. Holtzmann, *Geschichte der sächsischen Kaiserzeit (900–1024)* (Munich, 1941), p. 45.

133. Losek, *Die Conversio Bagoriorum et Carantanorum und der Brief des Erzbischofs Theotmar von Salzburg*, pp. 60–9.

# Chapter 9

# THE LATIN LEGENDS OF WENCESLAS

## 1. EARLY CHRISTIAN BOHEMIA

Whereas the Christian origins of Moravia have to be reconstructed by dove-tailing the information included in a whole range of sources – the *Conversio Bagoariorum et Carantanorum*, the *Lives* of Constantine and Methodius, papal letters and the letter of Theotmar – those relating to the history of early Christian Bohemia tell what is essentially the same story, despite a few significant variations, over and over again. Moreover, this same story is told in both Slavonic and Latin texts. The only significant points which lie outside this overwhelming tradition are a few chronicle entries which deal with what appears to be the earliest evidence for the acceptance of Christianity by the Bohemian aristocracy.

For the most part the entries dealing with Bohemia in the various annals written in the Frankish kingdoms concern war.[1] The *Annales Fuldenses*, however, record the visit of fourteen Bohemian *duces* to the court of Louis the German in 845. When they expressed their wish to be baptised, he arranged for the baptism.[2] Perhaps of equal importance as an indicator of one of the circumstances in which Christianity might have been spread within Bohemia is the statement in Regino of Prüm's *Chronicle*, that Arnulf conceded lordship over the Bohemians to Svatopluk of Moravia in 890.[3] Assuming that Regino is correct, the policy was reversed in 895, when the *duces* of Bohemia surrendered themselves to Arnulf.[4] Two years later they were asking for his help against the Moravians,[5] and a joint campaign with the Bavarians was mounted against the common enemy in 900.[6]

These events must provide the backdrop against which Christianity was established amongst the Bohemians. At certain points the annal entries even connect with the hagiographical traditions relating to early Christian Bohemia. Thus Borivoj, who is claimed to have been the first Christian ruler in some of the sources,[7] is plausibly identified with Goriwei, who appears as a Bohemian leader in one manuscript of the *Annales Fuldenses* under the year 872.[8] The other tradition names Spytignev, Borivoj's son and immediate successor, as the first Christian ruler of Bohemia.[9] He is one of the two leading *duces* recorded as escaping from the power of Svatopluk and surrendering to Arnulf in 895.[10]

There is a little more at stake between these two traditions than simply the name of the first Christian Bohemian leader – for some of the versions which have Borivoj as the first convert also see him as being converted by Methodius.[11] This tradition was also known to the chronicler Cosmas of Prague, writing in the twelfth century. According to Cosmas, among others, Borivoj was baptised by Methodius in 894, which is a chronological imposs- ibility, since the archbishop had died in 885.[12] In all probability this tradition is concerned to link the Christianisation of Bohemia with Slavonic rather than Bavarian influence – whatever the inaccuracy of the detail, there can be no doubt that Christianity entered Bohemia from more than one source.

Strictly speaking, the history of the initial phase of Christianisation in Bohemia has to be reconstructed from a very few fragments. The amount of evidence increases considerably when one adds to the initial phase of Christianisation the ensuing period during which Christianity was properly established in the region, since Wenceslas and his grandmother, Ludmila, martyred in 929 and 921 respectively, are the subjects of a whole cluster of texts. It is, in any case, likely that paganism had not been completely eradicated before the martyrdom of the former – indeed, pagan practices feature quite prominently in the various accounts of the saint's *passio*.[13] Moreover, although the hagiography relating to Wenceslas takes us further beyond the bounds of the history of mission than have the sources from eighth- and ninth-century Bavaria, the cult of the martyred Bohemian is of some significance for the hagiography of the subsequent missionaries, Adalbert of Prague and Bruno of Querfurt, as we shall see. The history of Wenceslas is also crucial for understanding the actual difficulties faced by Adalbert in his episcopal city.

Although it is possible to divide the accounts of the life and death of Wenceslas into Slav and Bavarian traditions, there is agreement between the different traditions over so many matters that it is reasonable to present a résumé of the fullest narrative, that of Christian, not least because the *Legenda Christiani* is variously either dependent on, or the source for, three of the Latin texts belonging to the hagiographical dossier of Wenceslas and Ludmila, *Diffundente Sole*, *Fuit in Provincia Boemorum*, and *Crescente Fide*. The chronological relationship between these texts and their additional relations to the Slavonic versions of the various legends need not concern us for the moment.

## 2. CHRISTIAN'S *VITA ET PASSIO SANCTI WENCESLAI ET SANCTE LUDMILE AVE EIUS*

Christian's account begins with the astonishing statement that the Moravian Slavs received their Christianity from Augustine,[14] which may suggest a hazy knowledge of Bede. If so, the author had little understanding of chronology for he then states that the Bulgarians were Christianised even earlier, by the Greek Cyril (Constantine), who subsequently travelled to Moravia, where he invented a new alphabet and translated the Bible, as well as the liturgy, into Slavonic. Christian's own preference is quite clearly for the Methodian tradition rather than that associated with the Bavarian Church. Having related Cyril's summons to Rome and subsequent death, the author turns to Methodius' work in Moravia, up until the moment that Svatopluk rebelled against his uncle, Rastislav – an event dated to 870 in the *Annales Fuldenses*. In a passage not dissimilar from Theotmar's account of later events in Moravia,[15] albeit describing the fate of the rival ecclesiastical party, Christian recounts the ensuing disasters, when Svatopluk disregarded Methodius and allowed his people to serve Christ and the devil.[16]

At this point Christian pauses to relate the origins of Bohemia. He explains that during a time of plague the people had consulted a Phitonissa who advised them to build the city of Prague. They then appointed a ploughman, Premysl, as their ruler, and gave him the prophetess as his wife. Thus began the Premyslid family, to which line Borivoj belonged.[17]

We are next told how Borivoj once went to his overlord, Svatopluk of Moravia. Historically, this could have taken place between 890 and 895,[18] and is therefore compatible with Cosmas' chronology for Borivoj's baptism, although the chronology rules out the ensuing involvement of Methodius.[19] At Svatopluk's court Borivoj had to eat off the floor in pagan manner, while the Christians ate at table. Seeing Borivoj so humiliated, Methodius went to speak to him, explaining that if he were a Christian he would not be so demeaned, and also prophesying that if he converted he would overcome his enemies and have many descendants. Not surprisingly, Borivoj instantly sought baptism. He returned home with a priest called Kaitch, to whom he gave a church in Hradec.[20]

The story of Borivoj at Svatopluk's court recalls that of Ingo and the Carantanian Slavs told in the *Conversio Bagoariorum et Carantanorum*, and could suggest an awareness of Salzburg traditions about mission to the Slavs.[21] There is, however, a twist in the story, in that the story of Ingo is, by implication, hostile to the Byzantine missionary, since it belongs to the justification of Salzburg's position in 870. Where the equivalent anecdote appears in the Wenceslas legends, it is employed to enhance Methodius' position.

The immediate result of Borivoj's conversion was a rebellion against him, and he had to flee to Svatopluk, where he received further instruction from Methodius. The Bohemians meanwhile appointed as their ruler a prince called Strojmir, who had been in exile among the Germans, but he was soon rejected as being unable to speak their language – a suggestive point in the context of the argument over the use of Slavonic. As a result, Borivoj's supporters were able to reinstate him. On his return he founded a church dedicated to the Virgin, and he organised the provision of priests.[22] The author's approach here, with its emphasis on church foundation and clerical provision, again suggests an awareness of the Salzburg tradition of describing mission.

At this point Christian turns his attention to Borivoj's wife. Ludmila, who had, like him, been a pagan, but who now surpassed him in her Christianity.[23] In fulfilment of Methodius' prophesy she bore her husband three sons and three daughters before he died at the age of thirty-five. He was succeeded by his eldest son, Spytignev, who continued his father's work in supporting the Church, until he too died at the age of forty.[24] Upon his death, his brother, Vratislav, seized power. The wife of the new ruler, Dragomira, came, says Christian, from a group of pagan Slavs, although it seems that this statement is a deliberate slur on her character,[25] as is the statement that she was a new Jezebel or a new Eve, the mother of Cain and Abel. This last comparison is rubbed home with the information that she herself bore two sons, Wenceslas and Boleslav. Meanwhile, in her widowhood Ludmila became a perfect almsgiver.[26]

Vratislav's reign was distinguished in Christian's eyes by the foundation of the church of St George in Prague.[27] He died aged thirty-three,[28] and was succeeded by his elder son, Wenceslas, whom he had sent to the church of Budec for a religious education.[29] Wenceslas, however, was still a minor, so he and his brother, Boleslav, were entrusted to the regency of their grandmother, Ludmila. This, however, enraged Dragomira, who plotted to have the queen-regent murdered. Ludmila, getting wind of the plot, offered to hand over all her power. When this was refused, she retired to her castle of Tetín, awaiting martyrdom.[30] The coming disaster was foreseen in a vision by Wenceslas, who understood that his grandmother would be killed and the clergy would be driven out.[31]

Even in Tetín Ludmila was not safe, since Dragomira sent Tunna and Gommon to kill her. The old queen, knowing what would happen, prayed. When her killers broke in she was already in bed. She reasoned with them, pointing out that she had been a benefactress to them. Nevertheless, they dragged her from her bed, and, although she pleaded for decapitation, they strangled her. When the murderers returned to Dragomira to report what had happened, Ludmila's servants and clergy, who had been hiding, returned to bury their mistress.[32]

Dragomira rewarded Tunna and Gommon richly for what they had done, and for a while all three ruled together. It was not long, however, before they fell out. Tunna went into exile for his own safety, but Gommon was seized and killed, as were his descendents.[33] The deaths of her killers were the first signs of Ludmila's sanctity. Meanwhile, miracles were recorded at the tomb, to the discomfort of Dragomira, who commanded that the body be removed to the church of St Michael, so that the miracles could be ascribed to the relics already in the church.[34]

Next Dragomira turned her attention to Wenceslas, whom she and her counsellors regarded as being too bookish and too like a monk. They even tried to deny any priest access to him, with the result that he had to resort to giving clergy admittance at night. Finally, Wenceslas summoned the magnates and asked what was their objection to his Biblical studies. This, among other things, split the aristocracy. Wenceslas and his followers triumphed in the ensuing conflict, and he sent his mother into temporary exile.[35] He immediately arranged for the translation of Ludmila's body from Tetín to Prague. When the coffin was opened the body was found to be intact – news which was brought to Wenceslas while he was still asleep. Ludmila was then reburied. According to Christian, Bishop Tuto of Regensburg excused himself from performing the ceremony, and sent a *coepiscopus* instead,[36] whereas the Latin *Legend of Ludmila* says that Tuto himself did officiate.[37] Given Christian's acceptance of the conversion of Borivoj by Methodius, his statement that Tuto offered his excuses is a further indication of reservations about the Bavarian episcopate. A year after the translation a miracle was recorded at the tomb.[38]

What follows in the *Legenda Christiani* is a remarkable description of extreme Christian kingship, a picture which is also supported by the other sources, although some place elements of the description in the period of Wenceslas' minority.[39] Wenceslas hated the death-penalty, and absented himself when it had to be imposed. He destroyed prisons and gallows. At the same time he helped widows, orphans and priests. In his generosity he even supplied his retinue with clothing as well as weapons. His personal piety was apparent in that he went barefoot in Lent, and wore a hair shirt under his fine clothes. If he ever drank too much he gave his best garment to a priest the next day. He himself made the bread used in the mass, harvesting his own wheat.[40] Likewise, he gathered his own grapes to make wine. While others still made offerings to idols, he destroyed their shrines. As a result of all this, priests flocked from Bavaria and Swabia to him, bringing books with them, and he rewarded them. Although he was married, he was chaste. He was also a stern critic of others.

Wenceslas determined to emulate his father and build a church in Prague. For approval of his plan he approached Tuto of Regensburg – to whose diocese Prague belonged – and was encouraged to proceed. Christian, like Gumpold, and indeed like the early Slavonic versions of the *Life* of Wenceslas, states that from the first the church was to be dedicated to St Vitus, whose cult was centred on Corvey in Saxony,[41] although it has been argued that the original intention was to dedicate the church to St Emmeram because the actual dedication took place on 22 September, St Emmeram's day.[42]

Having obtained Bishop Tuto's approval, Wenceslas commenced on the building of St Vitus' church. Meanwhile, he decided to abdicate in favour of his brother, Boleslav, and to become a monk in Rome. Only the fact that the building of his church was not finished held him back. This delay, however, infuriated Boleslav, who now decided to murder his brother.[43] He therefore invited Wenceslas to the consecration to SS. Cosmas and Damian of a church that he himself had built. Although Wenceslas knew of the plot, he accepted the invitation. Miraculously, Boleslav's men were unable to kill him during the banquet, as arranged. Instead, the murder was deferred until the next morning, when Boleslav attacked Wenceslas as he was going to Matins. The assailant, however, proved too weak on his own, and had to call on his henchmen to help. Wenceslas was martyred on 28 September 929. It was left to his mother to bury him.[44]

The death of Wenceslas marked the beginning of the persecution of his friends and of the clergy[45] – almost as a doublet to the aftermath of the murder of Ludmila. Miracles immediately occurred: it proved impossible to clean the blood away from the place of martyrdom.[46] The killers were struck down by divine vengeance.[47] After three years a divine revelation commanded that Wenceslas should be translated to Prague. Christian's account diverges from others at this point, over the question of whether Boleslav was involved in the translation. According to Christian, the ruler was informed of the revelation, and felt that he had to cooperate, but commanded that the move should take place at night, on pain of death.[48] Gumpold, whose account is similar to that of the Bavarian recension of the *Crescente Fide*, says that the translation was carried out secretly, without Boleslav knowing.[49] In both versions it took a miracle for the translation to be effected in the hours of darkness. On opening the coffin, the body was found to be intact – except for the wound inflicted by Boleslav.[50] After the burial there was a profusion of miracles, a large proportion of which were concerned with the freeing of prisoners.[51]

## 3. THE SOURCES

Leaving aside the impenetrable question of how accurate are the narratives of the martyrdoms of Ludmila and Wenceslas, the issue that has been the main subject of scholarly attention is the exact chronology of the sources and their relationship one with another. This problem is made all the more intractable in that none of the supposedly early Slavonic texts are preserved in their original linguistic form. The earliest versions of the Old Church Slavonic *Life of Wenceslas*, for instance, survive only in Croat manuscripts of the fourteenth to fifteenth centuries and Russian Church Slavonic manuscripts of the sixteenth to seventeenth centuries.[52] Despite this, some scholars have thought it possible not just to assign the underlying text to the tenth century, but even to a precise year. To the scholar who is not a Slavonic philologist such precision seems optimistic, although the fact that some versions of the legend conclude before the translation of the martyr's body to Prague does suggest that an account of the life of Wenceslas was written in the three years that the body remained at Stará Boleslav.[53]

The Latin sources are a little more tractable, not least because two of them were written by dateable individuals. First, there is the *Passio Vencezlavi*, whose preface states that it was commissioned by the emperor Otto II (967/ 73–83) from Bishop Gumpold of Mantua.[54] Second, there is the *Passio Wenzeslai Regis* of Laurentius of Montecassino, which must belong to the 1020s, although there is an inexplicable tendency among Slavicists to date it to the period 989–97.[55] Less certain is the date of the third text, the *Legenda Christiani*, whose author, Christian, claims to be the uncle of Bishop Adalbert of Prague, to whom he dedicates the work.[56] Since Adalbert abandoned Prague for the second and last time in 995, this ought to provide a *terminus ante quem* for Christian's work. The *Legenda Christiani*, which does not survive in any manuscript earlier than *c.* 1340, has, however, been seen as a later forgery, and has been assigned a much later date.[57] There is, nevertheless, one indication that the work is likely to be earlier than 1006: a manuscript of Gumpold's *Passio*, which was made for the wife of Boleslav II, Emma, who died in that year,[58] has an illustration which seems to reflect Christian's version of the narrative rather than Gumpold's.[59] It seems, therefore, that the *Legenda Christiani* was either written shortly before 995, or that it was a very early forgery, being composed in the ensuing decade.

Harder to date than these texts are two in particular which need to be put in some relation with them, since both Gumpold and Christian either used them, or were the source for them. Arguably, the earliest is the first Latin account of Wenceslas' martyrdom, the *Crescente Fide*, which survives in two recensions, one usually assigned to Bavaria, the other to Bohemia. Since the Bavarian version survives in an eleventh-century manuscript, and since this seems to be a secondary version of an earlier text, the likelihood is that the original dated from the tenth century, and was a source for Gumpold and Christian.[60] It may well have been based on a Slavonic original. More problematic is the text known by its first words *Fuit in Provincia Boemorum*, which is really a *Passio* of Ludmila. Again this may have been a source for Christian, but it could on the other hand have been derived from his work.[61]

With all this uncertainty it is best to concentrate on those works which are relatively securely dated, and whose context of composition can be inferred. This means beginning with Gumpold's *Passio Vencezlavi*, which of all the early texts has, perhaps, attracted the least attention, despite the fact that in manuscript terms it was the most read. As Vlasto comments – perhaps accurately, but without taking the implication to heart – 'The most popular, but not the best literary work.'[62] Since it was addressed to Otto II, however, it is useful to sketch in the relations of the Bohemians and Saxons in the tenth century.

## 4. SAXONY AND BOHEMIA

Although Bohemia was never central to the interests of the Saxon kings of the tenth century, it was, nevertheless, territory that concerned them, not least because of its proximity to Bavaria, which always presented a threat to the senior branch of the Ottonian family. Further, because the Bohemians had links with other Slavonic peoples to the north – one need only consider Vrastislav's marriage to Dragomira,[63] and later that of Boleslav I's daughter, Dobrava, to the Polish leader, Miesko[64] – they impinged on the Ottonian management of the eastern frontier of Saxony. Strategically, it was therefore important to exercise control over Bohemia. As a result, it is not surprising to find a string of references to the region and its people in the historical writings of both Widukind of Corvey and Thietmar of Merseburg.

Writing of 928 Widukind remarks that Henry I led his army to Prague, where he received the submission of King Wenceslas, who became tributary. He adds that the latter was a *fidelis* of the Saxon king and remained so throughout his life.[65] One might compare this with Christian's assertion that Henry was a friend of the martyr.[66] It is possible that one of the points of contention between Wenceslas and his brother was that the former was more pro-Saxon.[67] Relations between Saxony and Bohemia, however, may not have changed completely immediately after the king's murder in 929 – the church that the martyr had begun but had not completed was still dedicated to St Vitus a year later – but Boleslav was certainly hostile to the Saxons after Otto I's accession in 936. His subsequent attack on a Slav prinicipality to the north of Bohemia, which was subject to the Saxons, prompted Otto to send troops. This war, remarks Widukind, lasted until the fourth year of Otto's rule (939/40): thereafter Boleslav became and remained a faithful servant of the Saxon king.[68] Thietmar adds that Otto made Boleslav subservient to his brother, Henry of Bavaria.[69] In asserting that Boleslav remained faithful to Otto, Widukind was being ingenuous. The faithful service was ensured by hostage taking,[70] and disloyalty on Boleslav's part was punished by a further expedition against Prague in 950.[71]

The association between Boleslav and the Bavarian *duces* was to be an issue of continuing importance, and the Bohemian ruler next appears in Widukind as carrying news of the Hungarian invasion in 955 from Duke Henry to Otto. The Bohemians subsequently fought on the Saxon side at the battle of the Lech,[72] and Boleslav II was to be found at Otto the Great's court in 973, shortly before the emperor died, perhaps in connection with the pope's final approval of Prague as a bishopric.[73] Matters were less healthy, though, once Henry's son, Henry II (the Quarrelsome) had become duke of Bavaria, and was contesting Otto II's claim to the German throne. In 976 Otto deprived his cousin of the duchy of Bavaria and Henry therefore fled to Bohemia, to the court of Boleslav II (*c.* 967–99). Otto's assault on Bohemia, according to Thietmar, profited neither side.[74] After Otto II's death in 983, Henry of Bavaria was supported, once again, by Boleslav II in his challenge to the young Otto III.[75]

## 5. GUMPOLD AND OTTO II

With this background it is difficult to avoid the conclusion that Otto had some agenda in commissioning a work about Wenceslas. The martyr was, after all, Boleslav II's uncle, and he had been killed by the ruler's father. However much the two Boleslavs attempted a damage limitation exercise by accepting the cult of Wenceslas, there can be no doubt that it was, by implication, an embarrassment for them – comparison might easily be made with Edward the Martyr in England.[76] Most of the texts which deal with Wenceslas' translation to Prague suggest that it was done against the will of Boleslav I – even Christian, who says that the ruler knew about it in advance.[77] Further, the story of the martyrdom would later be used against Boleslav II in his conflict with Adalbert of Prague.[78] Moreover, since Boleslav was one of the main supporters of Henry the Quarrelsome, who attempted to prevent the successions both of Otto II and Otto III, it would appear that there was little love lost between Boleslav and the senior branch of the Ottonian house. If Gumpold's version of the *Passio* is to be dated after 973 (and that is not certain, as we shall see), Otto II can scarcely have been unaware that the commission of a work on Wenceslas had implications for two of the leading opponents of his own rule. If it belongs to the years between 967 and 973,[79] in other words to the period between Otto's elevation to imperial office and his father's death, then it may have helped to sour relations between Otto II and Boleslav in advance.

Gumpold turned to a source that was already in existence. Whether or not he saw the Bavarian recension of the *Crescente Fide* that has come down to us is not entirely certain. But he had access either to that or to a version of it. Indeed, its close dependence on apparently earlier texts is doubtless one reason why so little has been made of Gumpold's *Passio*. It is, however, possible to detect certain particular emphases in Gumpold's work which would have been appropriate for an imperial commission. At the simplest level one might note the (somewhat optimistic) references to the overlordship of Henry I[80] and Otto I over Bohemia.[81]

It is likely that Wenceslas himself was pious to the point of being otherworldly, and that this was indeed one of the reasons for his murder.[82] Certainly, the sources regularly stress that he behaved like a cleric, and that he was criticised for this, especially by his mother.[83] Yet Gumpold makes little of this criticism.[84] Indeed, he omits the question posed by the queen mother in both surviving versions of the *Crescente fide*: 'What should we do, since he, who ought to be king, has been perverted by clerics and has become a monk?'[85] Instead, the bishop of Mantua seems to be concerned to explore the image of Christian kingship set out by Wenceslas. He does this within the same framework as the Bavarian *Crescente Fide*, although at much greater length, and thus with more nuanced emphasis.

Gumpold deals with the narrative aspects of the story relatively quickly, and spends comparatively longer in commenting on the saint's virtues. Wenceslas practised the standard good works of a Christian,[86] but his piety was remarkable. Gumpold notes the saint's close association with clerics, as well as his concern to draw his semi-Christian people away from pagan practices.[87] The saint's attempt to persuade his subjects to convert is, indeed, given considerable emphasis. All this is listed before the brief and rather allusive mention of Ludmila's murder and Dragomira's seizure of power.[88] Like other authors, Gumpold comments on the saint's nocturnal visits to churches, during the period in which he was deprived of power, and his preparation of bread and wine for the mass,[89] and he states, as do both versions of the *Crescente Fide* and the *Legenda Christiani*, that Wenceslas wanted to become a monk.[90]

In a number of ways, however, Gumpold's precise emphases seem to be different from those of other hagiographers – this is particularly the case in his stress on the style of Wenceslas' rule. That the rule caused problems Gumpold immediately admits: one should not be surprised that a ruler who concentrated primarily on heavenly matters should be afflicted with various hardships.[91] Nevertheless, while Gumpold acknowledges that Wenceslas rarely let secular affairs get in the way of his piety,[92] he does not imply that this led him to neglect his worldly duties. He was careful to legislate. Unlike the *Crescente Fide*,[93] Gumpold returns to the question of law on more than one occasion,[94] notably – as in other sources – over Wenceslas' hostility to the death penalty,[95] and his destruction of gallows.[96] As soon as Wenceslas regains his position he returns, in Gumpold's account, to law, and in particular to the question of parricide – a term which clearly stretched to include the murder of a relative, and thus harked back to the murder of Ludmila and forward to that of Wenceslas himself.[97] In the bishop of Mantua's version of the martyrdom the saint explicitly attempts to stop Boleslav committing fratricide.[98] One might wonder what the implication of fratricide was for the conflicts between Otto the Great and Otto II on the one hand, and their jealous relatives on the other. Gumpold admits that the rule of Wenceslas was strange, a *regimen curiosum*.[99] Unusually among the Latin hagiographers, however, Gumpold does not comment explicitly on Wenceslas' generosity to the army.[100] Yet, overall, his is clearly intended to be a positive description of Wenceslas' rulership.

It is difficult not to conclude from all this that Gumpold saw in Wenceslas a model for Christian rulership, despite the fact that it ended in murder – it showed extreme piety to be compatible with action, which, of course, included attempts to convert pagans. Since Boleslav's wickedness is attributed to the machinations of the devil,[101] one might conclude that this in itself was proof of the quality of Wenceslas' government. Boleslav's rule, of course, appears as little more than the exercise of tyranny, for Gumpold, like the author of the Bavarian recension of the *Crescente Fide*, and like Christian, concludes his work with a number of miracles, a significant proportion of which deal with the freeing of prisoners.[102]

The idea that Gumpold was setting down a mirror of princes may be supported by a number of points in his work. First, the prologue makes much of the need for study – indeed, it goes far beyond any standard hagiographical statement that the subject of the *Life* which follows is worthy of emulation. It touches on the art of war, geometry, poetry, philosophy, literature. The *Passio Vencezlavi* might well be seen as an educational text for a prince. This would explain the author's constant stress on the fact that the saint was only young. He was a *beatissimus iuvenis* when he came to power.[103] When he regained power he was just out of his juvenile years – and Gumpold gives Wenceslas a speech in which he deals with his coming of age, quoting Paul's First Letter to the Corinthians (13, 11): 'When I was a child, I spake as a child, I understood as a child, I thought as a child: but when I became a man, I put away childish things.' The *Passio Vencezlavi* could, then, be a mirror of princes, written for a young ruler – perhaps for the young Otto II, if it were written before 973,[104] or possibly at Otto's behest as a model for the young Otto III. Even if the text was written as instruction for his father, Otto III surely learnt some of its lessons: one might note his hostility to fratricide, which led him to depose Laidulf of Capua in 999.[105] Further, like Wenceslas, Otto III thought of becoming a monk.[106] That Gumpold continued to be read in the highest of circles is clear from the evidence of the earliest surviving manuscript, dedicated to Emma, wife of Boleslav II, himself the son of Wenceslas' killer.[107]

# 6. ADALBERT OF PRAGUE AND THE CULT OF WENCESLAS

Otto II brings us face to face with Saxon interest in Wenceslas. That interest may have been fuelled by the young Bohemian aristocrat Vojtech, who, in c. 972, was sent for his education to Magdeburg, where he was to receive the name Adalbert.[108] In 983 he was to become the second bishop of Prague, and thus guardian of the cult of Wenceslas. Adalbert of Prague has, indeed, been thought to have played a major part in the development of the cult. He is said to have been responsible for the formal canonisation of Wenceslas[109] – but there seems to be no evidence that such a process ever took place, and it would, in any case, have been quite unnecessary in the tenth century. He has also been credited with a translation of Wenceslas' body, although this depends exclusively on evidence provided by Laurentius of Montecassino, who seems to have attributed the original translation of the body from Stará Boleslav to Prague, which took place in 932 to the episcopate of Adalbert,[110] that is between 983 and 997. As for the homily on the translation of Wenceslas, which was once attributed to Adalbert, it is clear that it cannot have been written by him.[111]

One other supposed indication that Adalbert promoted the cult of Wenceslas is certainly illusory. It has usually been assumed that he in some way inspired Laurentius of Montecassino's *Passio Wenzeslai Regis*, on the grounds that Adalbert himself spent time at Montecassino and could have provided Laurentius with the information in his hagiographical work.[112] Unfortunately, Laurentius was probably too young to have met Adalbert, and his version of Wenceslas' martyrdom was certainly not written until the third decade of the eleventh century.[113] However, it would still have been possible for Adalbert to have interested the community of Montecassino in the cult of Wenceslas – and for Laurentius to have been left with the task of writing up a work of hagiography. On the other hand, Laurentius also mentions a Saxon monk of Montecassino, called Benedict, who had witnessed a miracle in Prague.[114] He is perhaps a more likely source for Laurentius' sometimes confused information.

The fact that Adalbert is the dedicatee of Christian's *Vita vel Passio sancti Wenceslai et sancte Ludmile ave eius* – if it is authentic – has more plausibly been seen as the best evidence for the bishop's interest in the cult.[115] Regrettably, Christian's work, even assuming it to be authentic, does not help us to determine whether or not Adalbert was involved in the promotion of the cult of the martyred ruler. Nevertheless, if the work really were written for Adalbert by a relative, as the prologue claims, and if it is indicative of his commitment to the cult of the martyr, it must have had significant implications for the bishop's relations with Boleslav II, the Premyslid ruler at the time of his episcopate. Mere reiteration of the standard picture of Boleslav must have been offensive to the murderer's son. Moreover, Adalbert, as a member of a family, the Slavniks, which presented a challenge to the ruling Premyslid dynasty, was potentially a hostile figure for Boleslav II – and if he did champion the cult of Wenceslas, it cannot have helped relations between the two families.

The best evidence that Adalbert and his family were associated with the cult of Wenceslas in fact comes from the two early *vitae* devoted to the bishop of Prague. That ascribed to John Canaparius describes Prague as the city of Wenceslas, and refers to the king's martyrdom and to miracles which took place at the martyr's tomb.[116] Bruno of Querfurt adds yet another indication of an association between Adalbert and the martyred ruler, for he goes out of his way to make comparison between Boleslav II's treatment of the bishop and his brothers, and Boleslav I's treatment of Wenceslas. Indeed, Adalbert's brothers were massacred on the vigil of St Wenceslas, and their attackers are said to have shouted, as they moved in for the kill, 'If your saint is Wenceslas, ours is Boleslav'[117] – a story, which if true, suggests that there were groups within Bohemia which did not have any reverence for their martyred ruler. On the other hand, while Boleslav II may have thought nothing of Wenceslas, his wife, Emma, certainly did: as already mentioned, she was the recipient of the earliest surviving manuscript of Gumpold's version of the *Passio* – which suggests conflicting attitudes towards the memory of Wenceslas even within the ruling family.[118] Emma may have found in Boleslav I's fratricide a grisly reminder of the attempt by her own son, Boleslav III, to murder one brother and emasculate another. We shall return to the implications of the views of Boleslav II's followers for an understanding of Adalbert. Laurentius' *Passio Wenceslai Regis*, however, deserves a little more consideration.

## 7. THE *PASSIO WENCESLAI REGIS* OF LAURENTIUS OF MONTECASSINO

Laurentius cannot have heard about Wenceslas directly from Adalbert, but he certainly had access to some traditions about the saint, for he covers much that is to be found in the early accounts of the martyr, even though the detail in his own account is often inaccurate: he may also have had access to the *Life of Adalbert* attributed to John Canaparius.[119] At the same time, like Gumpold, he wrote a work which would be relevant for his audience, and thus shows yet another way in which a martyred ruler could be exploited.

From the start Laurentius makes it clear that he has been commissioned to write the text so that Wenceslas, whose light shone in Prague, might also shine in Montecassino.[120] This is to be a work of hagiography for monks, and it is, therefore, appropriately divided into *lectiones*. The first *lectio* announces that the successors of the apostles have now preached in almost the whole world. The second moves on into a historical narrative, albeit a somewhat confused one. Prague is introduced as a rich place filled with savage men. Its king, Wenceslas' father, is, however, correctly named as 'Bratesclabus', in other words Vrastislav. The saint's childhood is then covered: his discipline, his education in divine learning: he did not play like other children, but learnt divine dogma – a hagiographical *topos*.[121] The third *lectio* leads into allegorical consideration of divine law, baptism and foreknowledge, while the fourth deals with the saint's virtues, his consequent popularity, and a request made to his father that he, rather than his brother, should rule.

In the next *lectio*[122] Wenceslas' virtues are stressed yet further: his ability to rule his temper, his humility and humanity. The frequency of his church attendance astonished the clergy. In church he listened to the *Passiones* of the martyrs, whom he desired to follow. This is contrasted with his brother's deviousness, and his inability to work with him, occasioned by the devil. Despite this, Wenceslas gave Boleslav the city of 'Volleslabus' (Stará Boleslav) on his request. This did not assuage the younger brother's jealousy, and he now considered killing Wenceslas and seizing the throne. This is contrasted with the saint's almsgiving, and his dislike of the death-penalty.[123] Laurentius, however, adds that there were those who disapproved of a king who scarcely ever exacted capital punishment. The magnates were further angered by his ceasing to provide banquets on his birthday, as his father had done, and his feeding the poor instead[124] – a point not made explicitly in other Latin texts, although both versions of the *Crescente Fide* deal with Wenceslas' refusal to eat sacrificial pork in the company of his mother's supporters,[125] while Gumpold and Christian tell of his avoidance of pagan ceremonies.[126] The Bohemian version of the *Crescente Fide* also states that he censured drunkards.[127] According to Laurentius, it was his ending of royal birthday celebrations which prompted some to complain that Wenceslas wanted the monastic rather than the royal life, and to tell Boleslav that they wished to have him as king because of his *probitas* and *strenuitas*.[128] Further, they were afraid that Wenceslas would waste all the wealth of the kingdom through his charity, and thought they should act quickly. As a result, they formed a plot whereby Boleslav should invite Wenceslas to the annual feast of SS. Cosmas and Damian. On delivering the invitation, the would-be murderer embraced his brother, who agreed to attend the feast if Boleslav had set aside his youthful indiscretions.[129] This leads Laurentius to muse on the inhumanity of brothers, before describing Wenceslas' arrival at Boleslav's house.[130] The description of the martyrdom, and of Wenceslas' own concern that Boleslav himself should not be responsible for killing him, follows.[131] Laurentius then adds that Wenceslas appeared to an old lady, revealing to her the whereabouts of his hand, which had been cut off. When she put it with the body, it was miraculously rejoined.[132] A similar story is to be found in Christian, but there the lady in question is Wenceslas' sister, Pribislava, and the severed part of the body, the saint's ear.[133]

At this moment Laurentius wrongly attributes the *translatio* of the body to Prague to Adalbert. He also says that he has heard of a miracle which took place at the time – which he regards as being in his own day, a point which suggests that he has no idea of the true chronology: indeed, he claims to have had his information about the translation (which took place nearly a century before the time of writing) from a native Slav, *relatu cuiusdam fidelissimi praefati regni Sclavorum indigenae*,[134] which is effectively impossible. As the body reached Prague, the horses drawing it stopped, and would not move until Boleslav had thrown himself on the body of his brother, asking forgiveness – an episode quite at odds with what all the other sources have to say. The horses were then unyoked, but still the body could not be moved, even by many oxen, and only when the clergy came and prayed could it be shifted. At that moment, the body, which eight horses and twenty oxen could not move, was transported by a single ox. Laurentius was clearly concerned to show that approval of a cult was in the hands of the clergy alone. In Prague, the body was placed in a silver shrine, inside which the saint's nails continued to grow – a miracle which in other versions of the *Life* of Wenceslas is associated with the body of his servant, Podiven.[135]

Laurentius, thus, apparently had access to the same fund of information about Wenceslas as is contained in other hagiographical texts, but either he or his sources altered the story and the implications in certain ways. Boleslav's penitence is a new feature, as is the intervention of the clergy before the corpse could be moved. Laurentius is happy to portray Wenceslas as a would-be monk. Gumpold, it seems, had set out to show that Wenceslas' life-style was compatible with kingship. Laurentius had no qualms about the conflict of secular and religious life-styles, and indeed makes that conflict central to the martyrdom. In an odd way, despite the fact that his claims about sources are false, and that his account is in certain respects provably wrong, Laurentius may take us closer to the realities of the martyrdom of Wenceslas than does either Christian or Gumpold.

## Notes

1. *Annales Fuldenses*, s.a. 848, 849, 856, 869, 871, 873, 880; *Annales Bertiniani*, s.a. 873. See also Thietmar of Merseburg, *Chronicon* I 4, on the martyrdom of Bishop Arno of Würzburg, on his return from an expedition to Bohemia.

2. *Annales Fuldenses*, s.a. 845.

3. Regino, *Chronicon*, s.a. 890.

4. *Annales Fuldenses*, s.a. 895.

5. *Annales Fuldenses*, s.a. 897.

6. *Annales Fuldenses*, s.a. 900.

7. *Crescente Fide* (Bohemian recension) 1; *Diffundente Sole* 4–8; *Fuit in Provincia Boemorum* 1; *Legenda Christiani* 2.

8. See Vlasto, *The First Entry of the Slavs into Christendom*, p. 345, n. 5; also T. Reuter, *The Annals of Fulda* (Manchester, 1992), p. 68, n. 5.

9. *Crescente Fide* (Bavarian recension), p. 183; Gumpold, *Passio sancti Vencezlavi martyris* 2.

10. *Annales Fuldenses*, s.a. 895.

11. *Diffundente Sole* 1–6; *Legenda Christiani* 2.

12. Cosmas, *Chronica Boemorum*, I 10, 14, ed. B. Bretholz, MGH, SRG, n.s. 2 (Berlin, 1923); Vlasto, *The Entry of the Slavs into Christendom*, pp. 86–7.

13. *Crescente Fide* (Bohemian) 4; *Crescente Fide* (Bavarian), p. 185; Gumpold, *Passio Vencezlavi* 7; *Legenda Christiani* 6.

14. *Legenda Christiani* 1.

15. *Epistola Theotmari*, pp. 148–52.

16. *Legenda Christiani* 1.

17. *Legenda Christiani* 2; see also *Diffundente Sole* 4. For similar Slavonic origin legends see L. Slupecki, *Slavonic Pagan Sanctuaries*, pp. 185–97.

18. Regino, *Chronicon*, s.a. 890; *Annales Fuldenses*, s.a. 895.

19. Cosmas, *Chronica Boemorum* 1 10, 14; Vlasto, *The Entry of the Slavs into Christendom*, pp. 86–7.

20. *Legenda Christiani* 2; *Diffundente Sole* 5–6.

21. *Legenda Christiani* 2; *Diffundente Sole* 5; *Conversio Bagoariorum et Carantanorum* 7. One might note that *Diffundente Sole* claims that Borivoj had his satraps with him: the use of the word recalls passages in Bede, Hygeburg and the *Vita Lebuini Antiquior*; see above, Ch. 5.

22. *Legenda Christiani* 2; *Diffundente Sole* 7–8.

23. *Legenda Christiani* 3; *Diffundente Sole* 4, 8; *Fuit in Provincia Boemorum* 1.

24. *Legenda Christiani* 3; *Diffundente Sole* 9.

25. *Legenda Christiani* 3; Vlasto, *The Entry of the Slavs into Christendom*, p. 93.

26. *Legenda Christiani* 3; *Fuit in Provincia Boemorum* 3.

27. *Legenda Christiani* 3; *Diffundente Sole* 9; *Crescente Fide* (Bohemian) 1; *Crescente Fide* (Bavarian) p. 183; Gumpold, *Passio Vencezlavi* 2.

28. *Legenda Christiani* 3; *Fuit in Provincia Boemorum* 3.

29. *Legenda Christiani* 3; *Crescente Fide* (Bohemian) 1; *Crescente Fide* (Bavarian), p. 183; Gumpold, *Passio Vencezlavi* 4.

30. *Legenda Christiani* 3; *Fuit in Provincia Boemorum* 3–5.

31. *Legenda Christiani* 3; *Crescente Fide* (Bohemian) 3–4; Gumpold, *Passio Vencezlavi* 9–12.

32. *Legenda Christiani* 4; *Fuit in Provincia Boemorum* 5–8.

33. *Legenda Christiani* 4; *Fuit in Provincia Boemorum* 9.

34. *Legenda Christiani* 4; *Fuit in Provincia Boemorum* 10.

35. *Legenda Christiani* 5.

36. *Legenda Christiani* 5.

37. *Fuit in Provincia Boemorum* 13.

38. *Legenda Christiani* 5; *Fuit in Provincia Boemorum* 14.

39. *Legenda Christiani* 6; *Crescente Fide* (Bohemian) 5; *Crescente Fide* (Bavarian), pp. 183–4, 186; Gumpold, *Passio Vencezlavi* 13, see also 8.

40. This might be compared with Theodulf of Orléans *Capitula ad presbyteros parochiae suae* 5, ed. P. Brommer, MGH, Capitula Episcoporum 1 (Hanover, 1984), where priests are urged to be responsible for the making of communion bread. See R. McKitterick, *The Frankish Church and the Carolingian Reforms, 789–895* (London, 1977), pp. 52–7.

41. For St Vitus and Corvey, Widukind, *Res Gestae Saxonicae* I 33–4, III 2.

42. *Legenda Christiani* 6; *Crescente Fide* (Bavarian), p. 186; Gumpold, *Passio Vencezlavi* 6. Translations of the relevant passages of the Slavonic *Lives* are to be found in M. Kantor, *The Origins of Christianity in Bohemia* (Evanston, 1990), pp. 62, 79–80. On the Emmeram tradition, *ibid.* p. 267, n. 22; Vlasto, *The Entry of the Slavs into Christendom*, p. 94, and H. Mayr-Harting, *Ottonian Book Illumination*, vol. 2 (London, 1991), pp. 173. Whether or not one account overrides the consistent evidence of the other *Lives* of Wenceslas is a problem, and one might wonder whether the choice of the day of dedication was intended not to transfer the dedication from one saint to the other, but rather to create a link with an additional saint.

43. *Legenda Christiani* 6; *Crescente Fide* (Bohemian) 6; *Crescente Fide* (Bohemian), p. 186; Gumpold, *Passio Vencezlavi* 6.

44. *Legenda Christiani* 7; *Crescente Fide* (Bohemian) 7–8; *Crescente Fide* (Bavarian), p. 187; Gumpold, *Passio Venzelavi* 18–20, although Christian alone attributes the burial to Dragomira. The year of the martyrdom has been the subject of debate.

45. *Legenda Christiani* 8; *Crescente Fide* (Bohemian) 9; *Crescente Fide* (Bavarian), p. 187; Gumpold, *Passio Venzeslavi* 20.

46. *Legenda Christiani* 8; *Crescente Fide* (Bohemian) 9; *Crescente Fide* (Bavarian), p. 187; Gumpold, *Passio Venzeslavi* 21.

47. *Legenda Christiani* 8; *Crescente Fide* (Bohemian) 9; *Crescente Fide* (Bavarian), pp. 187–8; Gumpold, *Passio Venzeslavi* 22.

48. *Legenda Christiani* 8.

49. *Crescente Fide* (Bavarian), p. 188; Gumpold, *Passio Venzeslavi* 23.

50. *Legenda Christiani* 8; *Crescente Fide* (Bavarian), p. 188; Gumpold, *Passio Venzeslavi* 23.

51. *Legenda Christiani* 9–10; *Crescente Fide* (Bavarian), pp. 188–90; Gumpold, *Passio Venzeslavi* 24–30. On prison miracles as a type, see F. Graus, 'Die Gewalt bei den Anfängen des Feudalismus und die "Gefangenenbefreiungen" der merowingische Hagiographie', *Jahrbuch für Wirtschaftsgeschichte* 1 (1961), pp. 61–156.

52. Vlasto, *The Entry of the Slavs into Christendom*, p. 91; see also Kantor, *The Origins of Christianity in Bohemia*, pp. 15–16.

53. This also holds true for the Bohemian version of *Crescente Fide*.

54. Gumpold, *Passio Venzeslavi*, pref., where Otto is called '*victoriossimus imperatoris augustus Otto secundus*', which could imply any time between Otto's coronation as emperor during his father's lifetime in 967 and his own death in 983. One might guess that the absence of any reference to the bishopric of Prague, which was created in 973, and had as its first bishop a Saxon, that the date of composition must be before 973. Mayr-Harting, *Ottonian Book Illumination*, vol. 2, p. 172, limits the dates to 967–73.

55. See Vlasto, *The Entry of the Slavs into Christendom*, p. 90; Kantor, *The Origins of Christianity in Bohemia*, pp. 16–17. The actual date of composition was established by W. Holtzmann, 'Laurentius von Amalfi, ein Lehrer Hildebrands', *Studi Gregoriani* 1 (1947), p. 234.

56. *Legenda Christiani*, prol. That Christian was Adalbert's uncle may seem unlikely, and yet it may be significant here that Adalbert was appointed to the diocese of Prague when he was still under the canonical age to become a bishop: see Vlasto, *The Entry of the Slavs into Christendom*, p. 102.

57. Kantor, *The Origins of Christianity in Bohemia*, pp. 30–46, provides a survey of the changing assessments of Christian's work.

58. On the manuscript and its date and context, see Mayr-Harting, *Ottonian Book Illumination*, vol. 2, pp. 172–4.

59. Kantor, *The Origins of Christianity in Bohemia*, p. 18, confuses the issue, assuming that Christian was influenced by the illustration, but p. 191, in a caption to a photograph of the scene in question, argues that the image depends on Christian.

60. Vlasto, *The Entry of the Slavs into Christendom*, p. 90; Kantor, *The Origins of Christianity in Bohemia*, p. 16.

61. Vlasto, *The Entry of the Slavs into Christendom*, p. 92; Kantor, *The Origins of Christianity in Bohemia*, p. 17.

62. Vlasto, *The Entry of the Slavs into Christendom*, p. 91. For some reason Kantor chose not to translate it in *The Origins of Christianity in Bohemia*.

63. *Legenda Christiani* 3; Vlasto, *The Entry of the Slavs into Christendom*, p. 93.

64. Widukind, *Res Gestae Saxonicae* III 69; Thietmar, *Chronicon* IV 55.

65. For the date, *Adalberti continuatio Reginonis*, s.a. 928, ed. A. Bau and R. Rau, *Quellen zur Geschichte der sächsischen Kaiserzeit* (Darmstadt, 1971); Widukind, *Res Gestae Saxonicae* I 35–6. For the Bohemians being tributary to Henry I see also Thietmar, *Chronicon* I 10.

66. *Legenda Christiani* 7.

67. I share the view of Mayr-Harting, *Ottonian Book Illumination*, vol. 2, pp. 172–3, that not too much should be made of this.

68. Widukind, *Res Gestae Saxonicae* II 3. Widukind's association of the murder of Wenceslas with the war against Boleslav prompted generations of historians to misdate the martyrdom by six years.

69. Thietmar, *Chronicon*, II 2.

70. Widukind, *Res Gestae Saxonicae* II 40.

71. Widukind, *Res Gestae Saxonicae* III 3; *Adalberti continuatio Reginonis*, s.a. 950.

72. Widukind, *Res Gestae Saxonicae* III 44.

73. Thietmar, *Chronicon* II 31; Vlasto, *The Entry of the Slavs into Christendom*, p. 99.

74. Thietmar, *Chronicon* III 7 (5). To this should be added Thietmar, *Chronicon* III 18 (11).

75. Thietmar, *Chronicon* IV 2 (2), 5 (4).

76. See D. W. Rollason, *Saints and Relics in Anglo-Saxon England* (Oxford, 1989), pp. 142–4. Another comparison might be made with Boris and Gleb in Russia: see S. Franklin and J. Shepard, *The Emergence of Rus, 750–1200* (London, 1996), pp. 185, 215.

77. An exception is *Crescente Fide* (Bavarian), p. 188.

78. Bruno of Querfurt, *Passio sancti Adalberti episcopi et martyris* 21, ed. G. H. Pertz, MGH, SS 4 (Hanover, 1841).

79. M. Manitius, *Geschichte der lateinischen Literatur des Mittelalters*, 2 (Munich, 1923), p. 182, dates Gumpold's appointment as bishop of Mantua to 967, and the writing of the *Passio Vencezlavi* to 968–73. Although much cited, the entry of Manitius on Gumpold has little else to offer, and does not deal with the question of the bishop's sources.

80. Gumpold, *Passio Vencezlavi* 2.

81. Gumpold, *Passio Vencezlavi* 4.

82. Vlasto, *The Entry of the Slavs into Christendom*, p. 96.

83. *Crescente Fide* (Bohemian) 3; *Crescente Fide* (Bavarian), p. 185; *Legenda Christiani* 5.
84. Pace Vlasto, *The Entry of the Slavs into Christendom*, p. 96.
85. *Crescente Fide* (Bavarian), p. 185; *Crescente Fide* (Bohemian) 3.
86. Gumpold, *Passio Vencezlavi* 5.
87. Gumpold, *Passio Vencezlavi* 7.
88. Gumpold, *Passio Vencezlavi* 10–12. To understand Gumpold's narrative at this point it is necessary to turn to one of the other accounts of the same episodes.
89. Gumpold, *Passio Vencezlavi* 8.
90. Gumpold, *Passio Vencezlavi* 16; *Crescente Fide* (Bohemian) 6; *Crescente Fide* (Bavarian), p. 186; *Legenda Christiani* 6.
91. Gumpold, *Passio Vencezlavi* 5.
92. Gumpold, *Passio Vencezlavi* 8 (*saecularibus quamvis ob regimen negociis haud raro fuit interceptus*), 14.
93. *Crescente Fide* (Bavarian), p. 184; *Crescente Fide* (Bohemian) 2.
94. See in general, Gumpold, *Passio Vencezlavi* 5.
95. Gumpold, *Passio Vencezlavi* 6; see *Crescente Fide* (Bavarian), pp. 183–4.
96. Gumpold, *Passio Vencezlavi* 7; see *Crescente Fide* (Bavarian), p. 184.
97. Gumpold, *Passio Vencezlavi* 13.
98. Gumpold, *Passio Vencezlavi* 19.
99. Gumpold, *Passio Vencezlavi* 14. Vlasto, *The Entry of the Slavs into Christendom*, p. 96, seems to be referring to this passage. Gumpold is particularly allusive at this point.
100. *Crescente Fide* (Bavarian), p. 184; *Legenda Christiani* 6. Compare, Gumpold, *Passio Vencezlavi* 5.
101. Gumpold, *Passio Vencezlavi* 15.
102. Gumpold, *Passio Vencezlavi* 24–5, 27, 29; *Crescente Fide* (Bavarian), pp. 188–90; *Legenda Christiani* 10.
103. Gumpold, *Passio Vencezlavi* 6.
104. See above n. 53.
105. *Chronica monasterii Casinensis* II 24, ed. H. Hoffmann, MGH SS 34 (Hanover, 1980).
106. Bruno, *Vita Quinque Fratrum Poloniae* 2, ed. R. Kade, MGH, SS 15, 2 (Hanover, 1888)
107. Mayr-Harting, *Ottonian Book Illumination*, vol. 2, pp. 172–4. Whether or not the manuscript was addressed to her while in exile in Germany is unknown; Thietmar, *Chronicon* V 23 (15), 29 (18).
108. John Canaparius, *Vita Adalberti* 3, ed. G. H. Pertz, MGH, SS 4 (Hanover, 1841); Bruno, *Vita Adalberti* 4.
109. Vlasto, *The Entry of the Slavs into Christendom*, p. 101.
110. Laurentius of Montecassino, *Passio Wenzeslai Regis*, lect. 12, ed. F. Newton, MGH, Die deutschen Geschichtsquellen des Mittelalters 500–1500, 7 (Weimar, 1973).
111. ed. J. Peckar, *Die Wenzels- und Ludmila-Legenden und die Echtheit Christians* (Prague, 1906), pp. 385–8.
112. Vlasto, *The Entry of the Slavs into Christendom*, p. 90, states the standard view.
113. Laurentius, *Passio Wenzeslai Regis*; Holtzmann, 'Laurentius von Amalfi, ein Lehrer Hildebrands', p. 234.
114. Laurentius, Passio *Wenzeslai Regis*, epilogue.
115. Vlasto, *The Entry of the Slavs into Christendom*, p. 101.
116. Canaparius, *Vita Adalberti* 8.
117. Bruno, *Passio Adalberti* 21.
118. Mayr-Harting, *Ottonian Book Illumination*, vol. 2, pp. 172–4. Mayr-Harting points to the fact that Emma's son, Boleslav III, attempted to murder his brothers. See Thietmar,

*Chronicon* V 23 (15), 29 (18) for Emma's exile with her other sons: she may well have found parallels between the actions of Boleslav I and III.

119. Compare Canaparius, *Vita Adalberti* 21, '*decursis infantiae annis*', with Laurentius, *Passio Wenzeslai Regis*, lectio 2.

120. Laurentius, *Passio Wenzeslai Regis*, prol.. For the language of the *Passio*, Holtzmann, 'Laurentius von Amalfi, ein Lehrer Hildebrands', pp. 225–33.

121. See, for example, Bede, *Vita Cuthberti* 1.

122. Laurentius, *Passio Wenzeslai Regis*, lect. 5.

123. Laurentius, *Passio Wenzeslai Regis*, lect. 6; compare *Crescente Fide* (Bohemian) 2; *Crescente Fide* (Bavarian), p. 184; *Legenda Christiani* 6; Gumpold, *Passio Vencezlavi* 6. Laurentius' account is, however, subtly different, with a different choice of Biblical quotation.

124. Laurentius, *Passio Wenzeslai Regis*, lect. 7.

125. *Crescente Fide* (Bohemian) 4; *Crescente Fide* (Bavarian), p. 185.

126. Gumpold, *Passio Vencezlavi* 7; *Legenda Christiani* 6.

127. *Crescente Fide* (Bohemian) 5.

128. Laurentius, *Passio Wenzeslai Regis*, lect. 7.

129. Laurentius, *Passio Wenzeslai Regis*, lect. 8.

130. Laurentius, *Passio Wenzeslai Regis*, lect. 9.

131. Laurentius, *Passio Wenzeslai Regis*, lect. 10–11.

132. Laurentius, *Passio Wenzeslai Regis*, lect. 11.

133. *Legenda Christiani* 8.

134. Laurentius, *Passio Wenzeslai Regis*, lect. 12.

135. Gumpold, *Passio Vencezlavi* 26; *Legenda Christiani* 9.

# Chapter 10

# ADALBERT OF PRAGUE

## 1. THE CAREER OF ADALBERT OF PRAGUE

In dealing with the views of Salzburg we moved away from the *Lives* of missionary saints, and while consideration of Wenceslas has involved a return to hagiography, it has not involved a return to the history of mission, strictly speaking. The last years of the tenth century and the first of the eleventh, however, saw the re-emergence of mission-related hagiography comparable to that associated with Liudger and Anskar. The two towering figures are Adalbert of Prague and Bruno of Querfurt, both of whom worked as missionaries among the Hungarians and Prussians, while Bruno's work took him yet further east, beyond the Russian state to the world of the Petschenegs.

The career of Adalbert of Prague is well documented, not least because he is the subject of two major hagiographical texts. The first, the Roman *Life*, is thought to have been written in 999/1000 at the request of Otto III, by John Canaparius,[1] who met the martyr while he was a monk at the monastery of SS. Boniface and Alexius in Rome.[2] The second *Life* is by Bruno of Querfurt, who seems to have written a first draft of his *Passio Adalberti* in 1004, revising it in 1008, while he was waiting in Poland for an opportunity to evangelise the Prussians.[3] An account of Adalbert's career is most simply provided through a résumé of the two *Lives*.

Adalbert, or Vojtech as he was originally called, was born into the Slavnik family, one of the leading noble families of Bohemia, in *c.* 956.[4] He was offered to the Church as a child, because of illness,[5] and received an education in Bohemia[6] – which he apparently did not like, and was consequently beaten by his father[7] – before he was sent for further education in Magdeburg.[8] The archbishop of the time, Adalbert, confirmed him, and it was from him that the future martyr took his name.[9] It may also be significant for the saint's development that Adalbert of Magdeburg had been consecrated as a missionary bishop in Russia in 962,[10] and that he may well have written the brief account of his mission which is included in the additions to the *Chronicle* of Regino of Prüm.[11] Not that the mission was a success. According to the bishop, 'being unable to achieve anything in those matters for which he had been sent, and seeing himself vainly tired out, he returned, and, with certain of his own men having been killed on the return journey, he himself scarcely escaped with much labour'.

Adalbert/Vojtech's master at Magdeburg was Ochtrich,[12] who was much disliked by the archbishop, apparently because of differences of view over asceticism: the master of the school appears to have had a propensity for the convivial life.[13] Archbishop Adalbert indeed explicitly argued that Ochtrich should not succeed him, but despite his arguments, this is exactly what happened when the archbishop died in 981. Nevertheless, Ochtrich was not to take up the vacant post. He was pre-empted by Bishop Giseler of Merseburg, who wanted the post himself, and ultimately received it. As a result of this appointment the see of Merseburg lapsed until 1004[14] – a point of some importance historiographically, because the fate of the diocese is at the heart of Thietmar's *Chronicle*, and was held by the chronicler to be a cause of many of the disasters that hit the Ottonian state.[15] Meanwhile, having failed to gain the archdiocese of Magdeburg, Ochtrich fell sick in Benevento, where he supposedly had a vision of the first prior of his old church, which he understood to be a criticism of his neglect of the community. He died soon after.[16]

Ochtrich's departure from Magdeburg seems to have been the signal for Adalbert to return to Prague, where he served (another) Thietmar, the first bishop to be appointed to the new Bohemian diocese. Within a year, however, Thietmar was dead, supposedly dying tormented by visions: Adalbert was one of those who witnessed his torments, and what he saw led him to greater asceticism.[17] The death of the bishop also paved the way for Adalbert's own appointment to the bishopric: the saint's hagiographers speak of his election, although it may well have been the result of a political deal between the ruling Premyslid family and the Slavniks – despite the fact that Bruno claims to have read an eye-witness account of the event.[18] Adalbert was under age, and needed papal permission before he could take up the see.[19] This was almost immediately forthcoming, and the young bishop was invested by Otto II at Verona in 983.[20] One wonders to what extent Otto's awareness of the Bohemian Church at this moment was dominated by Gumpold's *Life of Wenceslas*. One also wonders to what extent the *Legenda Christiani*, if genuine, played a role in introducing Adalbert to his new diocese – given that he himself had been educated outside the country, at Merseburg.

Mention of the emperor prompts both Canaparius and Bruno to offer short discussions of Otto, giving radically different assessments of him. The former – who seems to have been answering an imperial commission – praises Otto II as better than his father, while later, in discussing Adalbert's relations with Otto III, he inserts what Althoff has called *ein kurzgefaßter Fürstenspiegel* [a mini mirror of princes].[21] Perhaps the *Vita Adalberti* was to

Otto III what Gumpold's *Life of Wenceslas* was to his father. Unlike Canaparius, Bruno saw Otto II as a disaster for Germany – partly because, like his cousin, Thietmar, he regarded the abolition of the see of Merseburg, caused by Giseler's translation to Magdeburg, as a catastrophe.[22]

For six years Adalbert carried out his pastoral duties in Prague. He organised the Church's income according to canonical tradition. At the same time he followed the ascetic life, and showed a concern for prisoners and captives,[23] which calls to mind the *Lives* of Wenceslas and especially the miracle stories relating to the period after the martyr's burial in Prague.[24] Adalbert was particularly angry at the fact that Jews sold Christian slaves at such high prices that he could not ransom them. As a result, Jews were, not surprisingly, the butt of his sermons, as were polygamy, marriage within the prohibited degrees, clerical marriage, and a general confusion of feast and fast days. Saddened at his failure to make any impact on the city, he decided to leave in 989.[25]

Adalbert intended to go on pilgrimage to Jerusalem, but he went first to Rome, where the dowager empress Theophanu was still lamenting the death of her husband, Otto II, six years after the event. Hearing of Adalbert's intentions, she gave him silver for his journey, and asked him to pray for Otto's soul.[26] In fact, he gave the money to the poor. And in any case, having reached Montecassino, he was dissuaded by the abbot from continuing on his journey.[27] He decided against staying at Montecassino, however, and after visiting the influential ascetic Nilus, he returned to Rome, where he joined the community of SS. Bonifatius and Alexius.[28] There he lived a notably pious life, which was probably observed at first hand by Canaparius, who paints a different picture, involving demonic assault, from the quiet sanctity recorded by Bruno.[29] Since Canaparius was present at the time, his view of the saint troubled by demons may reflect tensions caused by the bishop's stay in the monastery, which seems to be recorded in the *Miracula sancti Alexii*, where a visitor called Adalbert is anything but a welcome figure.[30]

Adalbert's time in Rome was not to last. Prague was without its bishop, and either the Bohemians themselves, as in Bruno's account, or the metropolitan of the region, the archbishop of Mainz, in Canaparius', demanded his return. Certainly, there is a political context for Adalbert's return to Prague, for Boleslav II was currently in conflict with the Polish leader and needed the support of the Slavniks.[31] The chief negotiator in securing the bishop's return was Boleslav's brother, Radla. Against his will, Adalbert agreed on condition that his flock would reform itself.[32] The moment that he arrived back in Prague – a city which took *voluptas pro lege*, pleasure as law, in Bruno's neat phrase[33] – he witnessed a Sunday market, and realised that no reform had or would take place. The final straw came when a woman was accused of committing adultery with a priest. Her relatives wanted to decapitate her, but she fled to the bishop. He hid her in the church of St George, but her pursuers caught her and killed her – in Canaparius' account, actually on the altar.[34]

Adalbert decided to leave Prague for good. In 995 he headed back to Rome – according to Canaparius, directly,[35] but, according to Bruno, first sending messengers to the newly converted Hungarians offering his services.[36] This was an offer, again according to Bruno, which he would repeat some years later.[37] On this first occasion, however, he does seem to have gone to help strengthen the Church in Hungary himself. Hungarian tradition claims that Adalbert actually baptised King Géza as well as his infant son, Stephen, the future saint, and also established many churches.[38] If any of this were the case one would have to admit that there is something very odd in Bruno's silence over the matter, since the hagiographer was himself to work in Hungary[39] – and in that he seems to have taken Adalbert as a model in many respects,[40] it would be more than curious if he passed over this achievement without comment. Bruno's actual words suggest that Adalbert made some impression on the Hungarians – 'having diverted them a little from their error he imposed the shade of Christianity' [*quibus et ab errore suo parum mutatis umbram christianitatis impressit*] – but he goes no further.[41] Thietmar of Merseburg's account of Géza's Christianity, suggests that the king's own conversion was only skin-deep: although energetic in his enforcement of the new religion, he continued to sacrifice to his old gods alongside the new one, and when challenged by his bishop over this, he justified himself on the grounds that he was rich enough to act the way he did.[42] It may well be that Hartwig, in his *Life of Stephen*, exaggerates Adalbert's role.[43] The bishop's disciples, however, were to play a major part in the Christianisation of Hungary, after his martyrdom[44] – and they may have ensured that his reputation outshone his actual achievements.

On his return to Rome, Adalbert rejoined the community of SS. Bonifatius and Alexius, much to the delight of the inmates, according to Canaparius and Bruno[45] – although the author of the *Miracula Alexii* apparently thought otherwise.[46] There he threw himself into the particular blend of Greek and Latin monasticism, which was the hallmark of the house.[47] Bruno, who was later to join the monastery for a brief while, noted the galaxy of spiritual leaders there. Canaparius, on the other hand, recorded a vision seen by the saint, of two orders in the sky, one purple and one white, symbolising Adalbert's purity and coming martyrdom – Bruno's account of the same vision is held back for a number of chapters.[48] Meanwhile, Otto III, whom Canaparius praised even more than he praised his father, had come to Rome for the enthronement of a new pope, and for his own coronation (996). In his entourage was the archbishop of Mainz, Willigisus, who, once again, drew attention to Adalbert's absence from Prague. Realising that a return to Bohemia was likely to prove difficult, Adalbert instead asked that he should be given the option of preaching to the pagans.[49] He set off north in the company of the emperor.[50] Canaparius relates how he lectured Otto on spiritual matters, and how he secretly cleaned the shoes of the courtiers. Once again he relates a vision experienced by Adalbert, this time foretelling his martyrdom.[51] The shoe-cleaning and the vision Bruno associates with the saint's final visit to the emperor.[52] Adalbert then took a detour to visit the shrines of Martin, Denis, Benedict and Maurus, asking for their support,[53] before returning to see Otto for the last time.

He finally set off for Bohemia, but before he arrived it became absolutely clear that a return to Prague was out of the question, for Boleslav had arranged the murder of all but one of Adalbert's brothers – the fortunate survivor being at the time with the Polish ruler, Boleslaw Chrobry.[54] The saint, therefore, headed for the Polish court, and from there ascertained, formally, that he would not be welcome in Prague.[55] It was at this moment – according to Bruno – that he wrote a second time to King Géza of Hungary, offering his services once again, but it appears that his letter was altered to imply a proposal to Géza's wife, described elsewhere as a formidably alcoholic lady,[56] and nothing came of the matter.[57] Only now did he resolve to make use of the apostolic licence to preach to the pagans, which he had received in Rome – it is Bruno rather than Canaparius who is specific on the point, and, as we shall see, possession of such a licence was a matter which clearly concerned the Saxon hagiographer a great deal.[58] Adalbert, therefore, discussed with Boleslaw as to where he should carry out his mission. The king advised against the Liutizi, which is perhaps not surprising, since they had been allies of the Bohemians against the Poles in 990.[59] Instead, he suggested the Prussians, providing the saint with transport and support as far as Gdansk.[60] Canaparius neatly characterises the agreed object of mission as a people 'whose god is the belly and avarice linked to death' [*quorum deus venter est et avaricia iuncta cum morte*].[61]

Having reached Gdansk, Adalbert and his companions, who included his half-brother, Gaudentius, began preaching and baptising, but they soon met with considerable hostility, and were first beaten up,[62] and then, after a respite of five days, they were seized, and Adalbert was singled out and killed.[63] In Bruno's account, the saint was terrified at the time of his martyrdom. The detailed events, as recounted by both Canaparius and Bruno, will concern us later.

## 2. THE BEGINNINGS OF THE CULT

An account of Adalbert which continues beyond the saint's martyrdom is provided by Thietmar of Merseburg.[64] He briefly relates Adalbert's days in

Magdeburg, as well as his departure from Prague, and his life under the 'Rule of Abbot Boniface' in Rome, before recording the saint's martyrdom. Like Canaparius and Bruno, Thietmar knows of a vision of a chalice reserved for Adalbert alone – but, unlike the other two, he states that it was the saint who had the dream. Since he was Bruno's cousin,[65] one might have expected him to have read his relative's *Passio Adalberti*, but this, and the fact that he misplaces the killing of the saint chronologically, suggests that he was dependent rather on hearsay. Having related the martyrdom, Thietmar then states that the killers threw the body into the sea and placed the head on a pole. When Boleslaw heard of this, he bought the body and head. Meanwhile, Otto III, hearing of what had happened, ordered the composition of hymns in the martyr's honour. Thietmar says that Otto was in Rome at the time, but he has collapsed the chronology, for the martyrdom took place in 997, when the emperor was still in Germany.

When Otto returned to Rome, however, he did promote the saint's cult with a number of church dedications.[66] This may have provided a context for the commissioning of the *Vita Adalberti* by John Canaparius.[67] Otto's interest had a number of sources of inspiration. He had known Adalbert, and clearly revered him.[68] He was also committed to the expansion of Christendom to the east of the Saxon frontier, seeing it, perhaps, as an alternative to military confrontation.[69]

Meanwhile, Boleslaw had Adalbert's body moved to Gniezno, which was now established as the centre of a new archbishopric, with the first incumbent being Radim, whom we have already met as Gaudentius, Adalbert's half-brother, who was with him at the time of the martyrdom.[70] Then, in the year 1000, Otto paid a visit to the shrine, approaching the site barefoot.[71] The tomb was opened in the emperor's presence, and from it he took various relics, which he was to distribute to a number of churches, in Aachen, Ravenna, Liège and the Reichenau: most notably, he took the arm of the saint, which he deposited in a church on the Isola di San Bartolomeo in Rome.[72]

## 3. ADALBERT

Before considering the important question of the differences between the accounts of Adalbert's martyrdom in the works of Canaparius and Bruno, it is useful to see what else can be learnt of the saint himself.[73] At one stage this would have been an easier question to answer than it is now, since the number of works which were written by or have been ascribed to the bishop of Prague has shrunk over recent years. In addition to a *Passio* of the Nicomedian martyr Gorgonius,[74] and a homily on saint Alexius,[75] they used to include a sermon on the translation of Wenceslas.[76] This last work cannot have been written by Adalbert, and the ascription depended on the bishop's supposed responsibility for the royal martyr's translation, a mistaken interpretation derived from the erroneous account of Laurentius of Montecassino.[77] The other two works, however, may well be by Adalbert, and are worthy of some consideration.

The *Passio* of Gorgonius which is contained in a letter of Adalbert addressed to the bishop of Minden, is a standard martyr account, albeit a bloodthirsty one. The preface prays that we might deserve to be *consortes* with the martyrs,[78] a fate which would happen very literally to Adalbert. The scene is then set in the city of Nicomedia during the persecutions of Diocletian's reign, when father betrayed son and brother, brother:[79] one wonders whether fraternal conflict called to mind the martyrdom of Wenceslas. Despite the persecution, Gorgonius and Dorotheus made no attempt to disguise their religion, being *cultores Dei* and *praedicatores*. They attacked the worship of idols.[80] Having been arrested, they were moved to apostatise neither by tortures,[81] nor by the blandishments of Diocletian.[82] This led to an increase in the brutality of the tortures applied – the descriptions are precise – but the two saints continued to pray.[83] Ultimately, they were executed by hanging.[84] Their bodies were thrown to the dogs, but were found intact by Christians, who buried them.[85] Later, the body of Gorgonius was moved from Nicomedia to Rome.[86] It was subsequently secured by Chrodegang of Metz, who translated it to Gorze, from where relics reached Minden.[87]

Since Gorgonius was a Greek, martyred in Nicomedia, and since his body had once rested in the Via Latina in Rome, his cult was probably of interest to the community of SS. Bonifatius and Alexius, which had strong Greek interests.[88] The tale of Gorgonius and Dorotheus was thus part of the religious culture to which Adalbert belonged during his sojourns in Rome. He may, however, have come across it earlier – for the cult of Gorgonius was well known in the *Reich* because of the translation of the body to Gorze, and the subsequent distribution of relics to Minden:[89] hence the addressee of Adalbert's letter. The letter and the accompanying *Passio Gorgonii* must indicate some interest in the cult on the part of Adalbert himself, and suggests, at the very least, that he had spent time contemplating the martyr's ability to outface torture and pain – which in the case of Gorgonius was particularly brutal – as well as the ultimate fate of martyrdom. All these issues would be relevant in the course of Adalbert's Prussian mission.

The homily on Alexius raises similar methodological questions. In writing it, the author – apparently Adalbert – was working within a standard format. Indeed, the vast majority of the text is drawn from Bede's *Homily* on Benedict Biscop.[90] It is, however, worth looking beyond the homily to the *Life of Alexius* itself. Alexius was one of the patrons of the Roman monastery where Adalbert stayed, the monastery supposedly occupying the site of the house of the saint's father. Moreover, the *vita* was written in the community of SS. Bonifatius and Alexius, probably not long before the Slavnik's arrival in Rome in 989, since the relics of the saint are first attested there only two years earlier, which is when the cult appears to have been introduced to the West.[91] Further, the *Miracula Alexii* may suggest that Adalbert himself went too far in emulating the saint's humility, even distributing relics, much to the fury of some members of the community.[92] For this reason, although Adalbert was the author not of the *Vita Alexii* itself, but only of a homily on the saint, it is worth pausing over the contents of the *Life*.[93]

Alexius was the child of Euphemianus and Aglaes[94] – he was supposedly brought up on the site of the monastery of SS. Bonifatius and Alexius. He was given a good education, and then betrothed. He determined, however, to avoid marriage, and went to Edessa as a pauper.[95] Although he was searched for, no one could find him. The saint remained there as a beggar in the atrium of a church for seventeen years, until his presence was revealed by God. He then determined to return to Rome.[96] His father did not recognise him, and the servants despised him.[97] After a further seventeen years, living unrecognised in the atrium of his father's house, the saint called for paper, wrote his life-story, and died. God then revealed his identity:[98] Euphemianus rushed to him, to find his son already dead.[99] None but the pope could take the paper from his hand. When the document was read, the saint's father collapsed,[100] and his mother threw herself on the corpse.[101] The pope enshrined the body.[102]

It is not difficult to see that Adalbert, himself driven out of his native land, would have found much that was familiar in this story, and that he would have been drawn to the saint's renunciation of everything, his permanent pilgrimage, his constancy, his facing up to temptation, his acceptance of being despised by his father's servants, and above all his patience. One might even hazard that the strange secret shoe-cleaning episodes, in the *Lives* by Canaparius and Bruno, when Adalbert was accompanying Otto III,[103] were inspired by the figure of Alexius, unnoticed in the atrium of his father's house. As already mentioned, there is also the possibility that Adalbert went rather too far for the community of SS. Bonifatius and Alexius in copying the former saint's enthusiasm for poverty: according to the *Miracula sancti Alexii*, written before 1012, a certain *floccipendens Adelbertus abbas* went round distributing the saint's relics, for which action, we are told, he deservedly died.[104] Assuming, as seems probable, that the abbot in question was the bishop of Prague, the story shows, not only the extremes to which he was prepared to go, but also hostility to him even in the monastic community to which he belonged.

The *Life of Gorgonius*, the *Homily* on Alexius and indeed the *Vita Alexii*, even though it was not written by Adalbert himself, speak of cultural and spiritual influences which weighed on the Slavnik in Rome. It would be perverse not to ask whether Christian's (or indeed any other) account of Wenceslas seemed to echo Adalbert's experiences in Prague. Leaving aside the question of the hostility between Boleslav and the Slavnik family, the more general question of the conflict between a Christian vision of society and the reality of life in Prague, expressed in the *Lives* of Wenceslas, was also an issue for Adalbert. The problems faced by Wenceslas in his attempt to Christianise society can easily be paralleled in the accounts of the two periods in which Adalbert tried to serve as bishop in Prague.[105] One moral reformer was clearly a possible model for another. Essentially, Wenceslas and Adalbert shared a Christian vision of society which was in conflict with the more secular visions of both Boleslav I and II.

## 4. ADALBERT AND HIS BIOGRAPHERS

The texts attributed to Adalbert and the *Life of Wenceslas* which claims to have been dedicated to him, together with the *Lives* written by John Canaparius, inmate and then abbot of SS. Alexius and Bonifatius,[106] and by the missionary, Bruno of Querfurt, allow us to come to some understanding of the career and personality of Adalbert himself. On the other hand, the two earliest *vitae* concerned with the saint differ subtly one from the other, and there is much to be gained by comparing them, and noting some of the more obvious points where Bruno's account of the martyr differs from the work of Canaparius.

Since the order of Bruno's narrative is very nearly the same as that given by Canaparius, it is practically certain that Bruno had read the earlier *Life*. This makes the differences between the two texts all the more important. The most obvious difference lies in the attitudes of the two writers towards Otto II. Whereas the Roman *Life* is enthusiastic about the emperor, Bruno is distinctly critical: his work has rightly been seen by Wenskus and others as a critique of much Ottonian policy, particularly the growing concerns of the Saxon emperors with Italy.[107] The distinction is scarcely surprising: Canaparius seems to have been an Italian favourable to Otto III, and appears to have been writing at the request of the emperor. Bruno, on the other hand, was a member of the Saxon aristocracy, even a relative of the Ottonians,[108] and although he had been a close associate of Otto, he wrote after the emperor's death. If he had any particular audience in mind when writing the *Passio Adalberti* it is likely to have been Henry II,[109] an emperor with whose policies he largely agreed[110] – although not with regard to Bohemia, where Henry supported the Premyslid dynasty,[111] or to Poland, as we shall see.

There are, however, other, more subtle differences between the accounts of Adalbert provided by Canaparius and Bruno. The latter seems to have had a greater interest in the history of Bohemia, and a greater appreciation of the significance of the martyrdom of Wenceslas for Adalbert's family, the Slavniks. In talking of Adalbert's return to Prague after his consecration as bishop, Canaparius notes simply that the city was that of Wenceslas, who had been martyred by his brother.[112] In the equivalent passage Bruno has nothing to say about Wenceslas: but he does refer back to the king's martyrdom while relating the massacre of Slavniks on the orders of the Premyslid Boleslav II in 996.[113] He sees in Boleslav's killing of Adalbert's brothers an echo of Boleslav I's assassination of Wenceslas, as we have seen, describing the martyrdom as an *exemplum*, and making the murderers shout 'If your saint is Wenceslas, ours is Boleslav'. Further, his depiction of the actual death of Adalbert's brothers, persuaded to flee to a church by Boleslav II's brother, Radla – who has already appeared as the man who enticed Adalbert back to Prague in 994[114] – might echo the death of Wenceslas at the church of Stará Boleslav.[115] Bruno also implies a thematic connection between Wenceslas and Adalbert in his other hagiographical work, the *Life of the Five Brothers*, where he defines Prague as the city where Boleslav I killed his brother, and from which the bishop was driven out.[116]

Not surprisingly, Bruno, coming from Querfurt, knew more about Central Europe than did Canaparius, and he therefore pays more attention to certain details of Adalbert's activities there. While Canaparius has nothing to say about Adalbert's interest in the evangelisation of the Hungarians, Bruno deals with it on two occasions, after the saint's second departure from Prague, in c. 995 and again in 997.[117] Bruno's concern to stress Adalbert's association with the Hungarians should be set alongside the same hagiographer's letter to Henry II, where he reveals that he himself worked among the Hungarians:[118] one might ask whether in emphasising Adalbert's work among that people in the *Vita Adalberti* Bruno was associating his own work with that of his subject, whom he clearly revered.

These points of detail are as nothing compared with some of the questions raised by a comparison between the *Lives* of Adalbert by Canaparius and Bruno in their closing chapters. According to both authors, once Adalbert reached Gdansk, he set about baptising. The ship, which Boleslaw had provided for the missionaries, then departed, leaving the saint and two companions, his half-brother, Gaudentius and the priest, Benedict, on a small island. There they were met with instant hostility, and Adalbert himself was attacked with an oar: he collapsed and the manuscript he was holding fell to the ground.[119] From this point on Canaparius and Bruno have slightly, but nevertheless significantly, different accounts. According to the former, Adalbert and his two companions moved on to a villa, where the saint tried to explain their mission, only to be met with a reaction no less hostile than before, because of their alien lifestyle. As a result, they withdrew for five days.[120] In the meantime, Canaparius in Rome had a vision which Nilus interpreted as foretelling Adalbert's martyrdom. So too Gaudentius had a vision of a chalice from which he was prevented from drinking, because all the wine was reserved for Adalbert.[121] On the next day, having sung the psalms, Gaudentius celebrated mass. Adalbert then fell asleep. At this point the three were seized by a group of pagans and chained. Adalbert tried to comfort the other two. A pagan priest named Sicco stepped forward to be the first to stab the saint. Others followed, and Adalbert, transfixed with seven spear wounds, died as if crucified. The pagans finally cut off his head and dismembered him.[122]

Bruno's account is longer, and has more detail, not least in terms of his consideration of the psychology involved.[123] After the first attack in which Adalbert had been hit with an oar, the saint and his companions travelled on until they came to a market. There they were surrounded by a crowd of dog-headed beings,[124] who demanded to know who they were and why they were there. Adalbert explained that they had come from Poland to save them. The pagans then claimed that it was because of such men that the harvests were bad, and told them to leave.[125] The rebuff led Adalbert to take stock of their style of work, and to reconsider whether he and his companions should not integrate themselves into society a little more, before attempting evangelisation. The three then set off to go to the Liutizi, whose language at least they understood.[126]

Bruno recounts the visions of Canaparius and the prophesy of Nilus, before returning to the three missionaries, who by this time were in a boat. Adalbert was terrified by the sound of the waves, which he took to be that of a sea-monster.[127] He was still frightened when Gaudentius recounted his vision of the reserved chalice.[128] At dawn the next day Gaudentius celebrated mass, and they then travelled further before sleeping. At this point they were seized by soldiers. A number of barbarian idolators arrived, including one whose brother had been killed by the Poles. The three Christians were chained. Although Adalbert had always wanted martyrdom, he was terrified. Bruno comments that this was in no way surprising, and considers the nature and importance of fear,[129] before discussing the washing away of sin through martyrdom.[130] He then returns to the pallid bishop, who was led up the hill, and pierced with seven wounds, which, Bruno explains, represented Christ's seven gifts of grace.[131] Again it is Sicco who strikes first, but he is not described as a priest. Adalbert lifted his arms as if crucified, and died.[132] His two companions were spared, but the martyr's head was cut off, and both head and body were sold to Boleslaw.[133]

Bruno's account is at the same time more detailed in its social and psychological observation, and more explicit in its symbolism. To take the last point first, Canaparius' presentation of the martyrdom is iconic: Adalbert is described as standing as if crucified, and the reference to his two companions standing next to him is presumably meant to recall that Christ was crucified between two thieves, although of course Canaparius cannot pursue the image too far because the martyr's companions survived and they were hardly equivalent to the thieves of the New Testament. So too the passion of Christ is recalled in Bruno's account, by setting the martyrdom on a hill, and by giving the martyr the question 'Quid vis pater?', a clear allusion to Christ on the Mount of Olives.[134] Bruno, however, is more explicit than Canaparius in dealing with the symbolism of the saint's death, in that, when he finally describes the martyrdom, he takes time to explain the meaning of the seven wounds.

Despite the symbolic setting, Bruno also goes out of his way to depict the killers as 'real' people. For Canaparius, the man who strikes the first blow, Sicco, is a something of a stock pagan leader, being a priest and a dux.[135] Bruno describes the assassins as a group of barbarians led by Sicco, but him he calls dux et magister, and not priest – the absence of the phrase sacerdos idolorum is surely significant.[136] This figure may also be the same as a man mentioned two chapters earlier, whose brother had been killed by the Poles.[137] Whether he is or not, the martyrdom is implied to be in part a revenge killing – as in Bruno's Vita Quinque Fratrum there is an element of social realism.

It is not just social realism that is added. There is also psychological verisimilitude. The effect of the seizure of the saint and his companions is to cause in Adalbert an attack of panic, and when he is finally led off alone to be killed he is white with fear.[138] It is only after describing and discussing Adalbert's fear that Bruno returns to the symbolism of the seven wounds by which Adalbert was killed.

Since eye-witness accounts of the death of Adalbert were circulating at the Polish court at the time that Bruno was waiting to go to Prussia, it is quite possible that his description is accurate: and indeed his description of the martyrdom begins with the words: Aiunt qui in illo agone fuerant . . . [They who were present at the passion say . . . ].[139] Further, Adalbert's sense of fear in Bruno's version of the martyrdom might be set alongside the implications of the Passio of Gorgonius, which suggest that its author had at least thought about the issues of torture and a martyr's death while still in Rome. On the other hand, it is worth asking why Bruno decided to make so much of Adalbert's terror as he was led to execution.

Bruno's own attitude towards danger is somewhat difficult to gauge: in the Vita Quinque Fratrum he portrays himself as a spineless individual, whose failure to risk danger and get from the pope a licence to preach for Benedict and his companions actually caused their murder at the hands of thieves. By comparison, he is not known to have shown any fear in his later missionary escapades. His letter to Henry II is positively defiant about the issue of danger,[140] and according to Wibert, he willingly entered into an ordeal by fire at the order of the king of Prussia shortly before his own martyrdom, to prove the superiority of the Christian God.[141] It is possible then that Bruno was both giving an accurate view of Adalbert's final terror in the face of martyrdom, and also, at the same time, contemplating his own reaction in the face of death.

More important still is another aspect of the closing chapters of Bruno's account of the *Life of Adalbert*, the discussion of missionary strategy, which certainly reflects the hagiographer's interest, although it is less clear that it reflects the actual attitudes of Adalbert. And here there is also an interesting comparison to be made with the account by Canaparius. According to the Roman author, when Adalbert explained his mission to the crowd assembled at the villa, after the first setback experienced by the missionaries, the pagans, who were snarling like dogs, *canino rictu*, threatened him again, saying,

> A single law and one order of life commands us and all this kingdom of which we are subjects: you, however, are of another and unknown law: unless you leave tonight you will be decapitated tomorrow.

Adalbert and his companions took the hint and withdrew.[142] But, as John Canaparius back in Rome learnt in a vision, the martyrdom was imminent.[143]

Canaparius' account is fascinating, not least for his attempt to understand the pagans: yet ultimately the picture given may have been inspired by the New Testament: the unknown law is surely based on the unknown God of the Acts of the Apostles.[144] Bruno's pagans react rather differently. For a start they actually have dog's heads: *circumstant subito caelicolam virum longo agmine capita canum*.[145] This curiously has a touch of authenticity, for there are plenty of references to the presence of *cynocephali* in the Baltic region, and they may in part be explained by the dog-masks found at Haithabu: that is the legend of the *cynocephali* could have had its origin in the wearing of dog masks, perhaps for cultic reasons.[146] According to Bruno, in response to their questions, Adalbert explained that he came from the land of the Poles, over which Boleslaw ruled and that he had come to snatch the Prussians from the devil. The presence of Boleslaw's name, which is absent from the equivalent passage in Canaparius, is certainly significant, not least because Bruno thought highly of the Polish monarch. Equally notable, the response of the pagans is more basic than that invented by Canaparius, and perhaps more compelling:

On account of such men our land will not yield crops, trees will not yield fruit, new animals are not born and old die. Therefore go far from our boundaries: if you do not set off back quickly, you will suffer a bad death, struck by cruel tortures.[147]

Yet more interesting, however, is Adalbert's response, as set down by Bruno. Having retired with his companions, he said to them,

Oppressed by great adversity, what counsel shall we take? I do not know where to turn. Our clothing and a horror of what we are wearing harms the minds of the pagans not a little, as it seems to me. So, if you agree, let us change our clerical garb, let us allow our hair to grow and hang down, and let us allow the stubble of our beards to grow. Then perhaps unrecognised we have a better chance of saving them. Having become similar to them, we may live like them, speak like them and live among them. Working with our own hands we may earn our bread like the apostles, and we may turn over secretly in our minds the order of the Psalms. Meanwhile with the pity of the Saviour supporting us, there may be something in this art and deception, for opinion to be deceived, and surely an opportunity for evangelisation will come. Why? Because, pious and faithful God, we will increase the great treasure of discovered souls, or pouring out our sweet lives for the most sweet Christ, we will die a desired death.[148]

In this remarkable speech Adalbert considers adopting a new missionary strategy, of living among the people and adopting their dress and life-style to win them over. It is a change of strategy every bit as intelligent and important as Gregory the Great's alteration of missionary tactics towards the Anglo-Saxons in 601.[149] The problem is whether the idea really was Adalbert's, or whether it was Bruno's, and that he put it into the mouth of one of his role models. It is necessary to turn to the history of Bruno himself.

## Notes

1. On Canaparius as the author, a point which was questioned by Voigt, see R. Wenskus, *Studien zur historisch-politischen Gedankenwelt Bruns von Querfurt* (Cologne, 1956), p. 82; on the text of Canaparius, *ibid.*, pp. 7–37. See also A. Gieysztor, '*Sanctus et gloriosissimus martyr Christi Adalbertus*: un état et une église missionnaires aux alentours de l'an mille', *La conversione al cristianesimo nell'Europa dell'Alto Medioevo*, Settimane di Studio 14 (Spoleto, 1967), p. 614.
2. For the date, Pertz, *Monumenta Germaniae Historica, Scriptores*, 4, p. 575. See Vlasto, *The Entry of the Slavs into Christendom*, p. 101.
3. ed. G. H. Pertz, *Monumenta Germaniae Historica, Scriptores*, 4, pp. 596–612; Wenskus, *Studien zur historisch-politischen Gedankenwelt Bruns von Querfurt*, p. 3; for the text of Bruno's work, *ibid.*, p. 13. Also Gieysztor, '*Sanctus et gloriosissimus martyr Christi Adalbertus*: un état et une église missionnaires aux alentours de l'an mille', p. 614. For a third, short *Passio* written perhaps *c.* 1025 at Gniezno, *ibid.*, 614.
4. Canaparius, *Vita Adalberti* 1, 2; Bruno, *Passio Adalberti* 1. There is a useful summary of Adalbert's life in Gieysztor, '*Sanctus et gloriosissimus martyr Christi Adalbertus*: un état et une église missionnaires aux alentours de l'an mille', pp. 615–36.

5. Canaparius, *Vita Adalberti* 2; Bruno, *Passio Adalberti* 2.

6. Canaparius, *Vita Adalberti* 3; Bruno, *Passio Adalberti* 3.

7. Bruno, *Passio Adalberti* 3.

8. Canaparius, *Vita Adalberti* 3; Bruno, *Passio Adalberti* 4; Thietmar, *Chronicon* IV 28 (19).

9. Canaparius, *Vita Adalberti* 3; Bruno, *Passio Adalberti* 4. On Adalbert of Magdeburg, see Thietmar, *Chronicon* II 22, 28 (18), III 11 (8) – 12.

10. Thietmar, *Chronicon* II 22.

11. *Adalberti continuatio Reginonis*, s.a. 962.

12. Canaparius, *Vita Adalberti* 3–6; Bruno, *Passio Adalberti* 5–6.

13. Thietmar, *Chronicon* III 12.

14. Thietmar, *Chronicon* VI 1.

15. Thietmar, *Chronicon*, IV 10.

16. Thietmar, *Chronicon* III 12 – 15; Bruno's account differs – he simply says that Ochtrich went to join the *capella regis: Passio Adalberti* 6.

17. Canaparius, *Vita Adalberti* 6; Bruno, *Passio Adalberti* 7.

18. Canaparius, *Vita Adalberti* 7; Bruno, *Passio Adalberti* 8.

19. Vlasto, *The Entry of the Slavs into Christendom*, p. 102.

20. Canaparius, *Vita Adalberti* 8; Bruno, *Passio Adalberti* 9.

21. Canaparius, *Vita Adalberti* 23; G. Althoff, *Otto III* (Darmstadt, 1996), p. 98.

22. Bruno, *Passio Adalberti* 10, 12; Thietmar, *Chronicon*, IV 10. In general on Bruno's critique of Otto II, Wenskus, *Studien zu historisch-politischen Gedankenwelt Bruns von Querfurt.*

23. Canaparius, *Vita Adalberti* 9–10; Bruno, *Passio Adalberti* 11.

24. See *Legenda Christiani* 9, 10.

25. Canaparius, *Vita Adalberti* 10–13; Bruno, *Passio Adalberti* 11.

26. Canaparius, *Vita Adalberti* 14; Bruno, *Passio Adalberti* 12.

27. Canaparius, *Vita Adalberti* 14; Bruno, *Passio Adalberti* 13.

28. Canaparius, *Vita Adalberti* 15–16; Bruno, *Passio Adalberti* 13–14. There is a useful survey of Adalbert's time in Rome in B. Hamilton, 'The monastery of S. Alessio and the religious and intellectual renaissance of tenth-century Rome', *Studies in Medieval and Renaissance History* 2 (1965), pp. 285–8, 290, 293, reprinted in *id.*, *Monastic Reform, Catharism and the Crusades 900–1300* (London, 1979).

29. Canaparius, *Vita Adalberti* 17; Bruno, *Passio Adalberti* 14.

30. *Miracula sancti Alexii* 3, ed. G. H. Pertz, MGH, SS 4 (Hanover, 1841).

31. For the political context of Adalbert's return – and in particular Boleslav's involvement in Poland, Gieysztor, '*Sanctus et gloriosissimus martyr Christi Adalbertus*: un état et une église missionnaires aux alentours de l'an mille', pp. 621–2.

32. Canaparius, *Vita Adalberti* 18; Bruno, *Passio Adalberti* 15. One might note the similarity to Laurentius of Montecassino, *Passio Wenzeslai Regis*, lect. 8.

33. Bruno, *Passio Adalberti* 15.

34. Canaparius, *Vita Adalberti* 19; Bruno, *Passio Adalberti* 16.

35. Canaparius, *Vita Adalberti* 20.

36. Bruno, *Passio Adalberti* 16.

37. Bruno, *Passio Adalberti* 23.

38. Hartwig, *Vita sancti Stephani* 3–4, ed. E. Bartoniek, in I. Szentpétery, *Scriptores Rerum Hungaricarum*, 2 (Budapest, 1938), *Acta Sanctorum* Sept 2nd, vol. 1, p. 563. See now the translation by N. Behrend, in T. Head (ed.), *Medieval Hagiography: An Anthology* (New York, 2000).

39. Bruno, ep. to Henry II, p. 689.

40. Gieysztor, '*Sanctus et gloriosissimus martyr Christi Adalbertus*: un état et une église missionnaires aux alentours de l'an mille', p. 637.

41. Vlasto, *The Entry of the Slavs into Christendom*, pp. 103–4, sees no problem. R. Grzesik, 'Die Ungarnmission des hl. Adalberts', in B. Nagy and M. Sebök, *The Man of Many Devices, Who Wandered Full Many Ways* (Budapest, 1999), pp. 230–40, provides a detailed reconstruction from the available evidence, and also accepts the tradition that Adalbert baptised Stephen.

42. Thietmar, *Chronicon* VIII 4. Thietmar calls the king Deuvix.

43. Thus Behrend, in her translation of Hartwig, p. 397, n. 5: 'Although he visited the Hungarian court, his missionary activities there were not at all on the scale depicted in the *Life*.'

44. Hartwig, *Vita sancti Stephani* 7, with Behrend's notes, p. 397, nn. 5, 14.

45. Canaparius, *Vita Adalberti* 20; Bruno, *Passio Adalberti* 17.

46. *Miracula sancti Alexii* 3.

47. B. Hamilton, 'The monastery of S. Alessio and the religious and intellectual renaissance in tenth-century Rome', pp. 265–310.

48. Bruno, *Passio Adalberti* 21.

49. Canaparius, *Vita Adalberti* 21–2; Bruno, *Passio Adalberti* 18.

50. Canaparius, *Vita Adalberti* 23; Bruno, *Passio Adalberti* 19.

51. Canaparius, Vita Adalberti 23–4.

52. Bruno, Passio Adalberti 20.

53. Canaparius, *Vita Adalberti* 25; Bruno, *Passio Adalberti* 19.

54. Canaparius, *Vita Adalberti* 25; Bruno, *Passio Adalberti* 20–1. For the surviving brother's subsequent history, Thietmar, *Chronicon* VI 12 (9); Cosmas, *Chronica Boemorum*, I 29.

55. Canaparius, *Vita Adalberti* 26; Bruno, *Passio Adalberti* 22.

56. Thietmar, *Chronicon* VIII 4.

57. Bruno, *Passio Adalberti* 23. On Géza's wife, Beleknegni, and on the rather half-hearted Christianity of Géza himself, see also Thietmar, *Chronicon* VIII 4. On the possibility that Adalbert's contacts with the Hungarians had political implications, and presented a threat to the Premyslids, see Grzesik, 'Die Ungarnmission des hl. Adalberts', p. 235.

58. Bruno, *Passio Adalberti* 24. On Bruno's involvement in obtaining a papal licence for Benedict and John see Ch. 11, below.

59. Thietmar, *Chronicon* IV 11 (9).

60. Canaparius, *Vita Adalberti* 27; Bruno, *Passio Adalberti* 24.

61. Canaparius, *Vita Adalberti* 27. Gieysztor, '*Sanctus et gloriosissimus martyr Christi Adalbertus*: un état et une église missionnaires aux alentours de l'an mille', pp. 632–3 points to the importance of the trading site at Truso/Druzno.

62. Canaparius, *Vita Adalberti* 28; Bruno, *Passio Adalberti* 24–5.

63. Canaparius, *Vita Adalberti* 29–30; Bruno, *Passio Adalberti* 25–33.

64. Thietmar, *Chronicon* IV 28 (19).

65. Thietmar, *Chronicon* VI 94 (58)–95.

66. Vlasto, *The Entry of the Slavs into Christendom*, p. 105. Hamilton, 'The monastery of S. Alessio and the religious and intellectual renaissance of tenth-century Rome', pp. 294–5.

67. Gieysztor, '*Sanctus et gloriosissimus martyr Christi Adalbertus*: un état et une église missionnaires aux alentours de l'an mille', p. 614. This is, however, only a hypothesis.

68. Althoff, *Otto III*, pp. 96–9.

69. Despite the obvious political message it had at the time it was written, F. Dvornik, 'The first phase of the Drang nach Osten', *Cambridge Historical Journal* 7 (1943), pp. 129–45, remains a compelling interpretation. See also Hamilton, 'The monastery of S. Alessio and the religious and intellectual renaissance of tenth-century Rome', pp. 295–300.

70. Hamilton, 'The monastery of S. Alessio and the religious and intellectual renaissance of tenth-century Rome', p. 299.

71. Thietmar, *Chronicon* IV 47 (29).

72. *De translatione Adalberti*, ed. G. H. Waitz, MGH, SS 15, 2 (Hanover, 1888), p. 708; Vlasto, *The Entry of the Slavs into Christendom*, p. 105; K. Görich, 'Otto III. öffnet das Karlsgrab in Aachen', *Herrschaftsrepräsentation im ottonischen Sachsen*, ed. G. Althoff and E. Schubert, Vorträge und Forschungen 46 (Sigmaringen, 1998), pp. 406–9.

73. For the approach that follows I am indebted to Pit'ha, *Cechy a Jejich Svatí*, pp. 30–54.

74. *Passio Gorgonii*, = *Magnum summopere*, ed. C. Suysken, AASS, Sept 9th, vol. 3 (Paris, 1868), pp. 340–2. I have been unable to consult the edition published by Hoddick in *Das Münstermaifelder Legendar* (1928).

75. ed. M. Sprissler, *Das rythmische Gedicht 'Pater Deus Ingenite' und das altfranzösische Alexiuslied* (Münster 1966), pp. 102–6.

76. ed. Pekar, *Die Wenzels- und Ludmila- Legenden und die Echtheit Christians*, pp. 385–88.

77. Laurentius, *Passio Sancti Wenzeslai Regis*, lect. 12.

78. *Passio Gorgonii* 1.

79. *Passio Gorgonii* 2.

80. *Passio Gorgonii* 3.

81. *Passio Gorgonii* 4.

82. *Passio Gorgonii* 5.

83. *Passio Gorgonii* 6–9.

84. *Passio Gorgonii* 10.

85. *Passio Gorgonii* 11.

86. *Passio Gorgonii* 12.

87. *Passio Gorgonii* 13.

88. Hamilton, 'The monastery of S. Alessio and the religious and intellectual renaissance of tenth-century Rome'. See also B. Hamilton, 'The city of Rome and the Eastern Churches in the tenth century', *Orientalia Christiana Periodica* 27 (1961), pp. 5–26, reprinted in *id., Monastic Reform, Catharism and the Crusades (900–1300)*.

89. *Passio Gorgonii* 13. For the *translatio* to Gorze, see *Translatio Gorgonii*, ed. C. Suysken, AASS, Sept 9th, vol. 3 (Paris, 1868), pp. 343–55.

90. Sprissler, *Das rythmische Gedicht 'Pater Deus Ingenite' und das altfranzösische Alexiuslied*, pp. 102–6.

91. Hamilton, 'The city of Rome and the Eastern Churches in the tenth century', p. 15; Hamilton, 'The monastery of S. Alessio and the religious and intellectual renaissance of tenth-century Rome', pp. 269–72. On the presence of Adalbert in the community, *ibid.*, pp. 285–8.

92. *Miracula Alexii* 3.

93. *Vita Alexii*, ed. J. Pin, AASS, July 17th, vol. 4 (Paris, 1868), pp. 251–78. For the *Vita Alexii*, Hamilton, 'The Monastery of S. Alessio and the religious and intellectual renaissance of tenth-century Rome', pp. 269–80.

94. *Vita Alexii* 1.

95. *Vita Alexii* 3.

96. *Vita Alexii* 5.

97. *Vita Alexii* 6.
98. *Vita Alexii* 7.
99. *Vita Alexii* 8.
100. *Vita Alexii* 9.
101. *Vita Alexii* 10.
102. *Vita Alexii* 11.
103. Canaparius, *Vita Adalberti* 23; Bruno, *Passio Adalberti* 20.
104. *Miracula Alexii* 3.
105. Compare *Legenda Christiani* 6 with Canaparius, *Vita Adalberti* 9–12, 18–20, and Bruno, *Passio Adalberti* 11, 15–16.
106. For Canaparius, see *Miracula Alexii* 2. See also Hamilton, 'The monastery of S. Alessio and the religious and intellectual renaissance of tenth-century Rome', pp. 290–1, 300–1.
107. Wenskus, *Studien zur historisch-politischen Gedankenwelt Bruns von Querfurt.*
108. Petrus Damiani, *Vita Romualdi* 27, ed. G. Tabacco, Fonti per la storia d'Italia 94 (Rome, 1957).
109. Wenskus, *Studien zur historisch-politischen Gedankenwelt Bruns von Querfurt*, pp. 89, 90.
110. Wenskus, *Studien zur historisch-politischen Gedankenwelt Bruns von Querfurt*, pp. 126, 187.
111. Wenskus, *Studien zur historisch-politischen Gedankenwelt Bruns von Querfurt*, pp. 188–9.
112. Canaparius, *Vita Adalberti*, 8.
113. Bruno, *Passio Adalberti* 21.
114. Bruno, *Passio Adalberti* 15.
115. e.g. *Crescente Fide*, (Bohemian) 8.
116. Bruno, *Vita Quinque Fratrum* 11. See also 13 for a further connection between the *Vita Quinque Fratrum* and Adalbert.
117. Bruno, *Passio Adalberti*, 16. Compare Hartwig, *Vita Stephani* 3–4.
118. Bruno, *Epistola ad Heinricum II Imperatorem*, pp. 689, 690.
119. Canaparius, *Vita Adalberti* 28; Bruno, *Passio Adalberti* 24–5.
120. Canaparius, *Vita Adalberti* 28.
121. Canaparius, *Vita Adalberti* 29.
122. Canaparius, *Vita Adalberti* 30.
123. In general on Bruno's greater psychological sense, as compared with Canaparius, Wenskus, *Studien zu historisch-politischen Gedankenwelt Bruns von Querfurt*, p. 72.
124. Bruno, *Passio Adalberti* 25, has the words '*capita canum*', which seem less like a simile than Canaparius, *Vita Adalberti* 28, '*canino rictu*'.
125. Bruno, *Passio Adalberti* 25.
126. Bruno, *Passio Adalberti* 26.
127. Bruno, *Passio Adalberti* 27–8.
128. Bruno, *Passio Adalberti* 29.
129. Bruno, *Passio Adalberti* 30.
130. Bruno, *Passio Adalberti* 31.
131. Bruno, *Passio Adalberti* 32.
132. Bruno, *Passio Adalberti* 33.
133. Bruno, *Passio Adalberti* 34.
134. Bruno, *Passio Adalberti* 32; see also the comparison of Adalbert and his companions with *latrones* in Bruno, *Passio Adalberti* 30.
135. Canaparius, *Vita Adalberti* 30.
136. Bruno, *Passio Adalberti* 33.

137. Bruno, *Passio Adalberti* 31.
138. Bruno, *Passio Adalberti* 32.
139. Bruno, *Passio Adalberti* 32. Gieysztor, '*Sanctus et gloriosissimus martyr Christi Adalbertus*: un état et une église missionnaires aux alentours de l'an mille', p. 614 suggests that Bruno had access to information from Radla and Vilicon of Prague. He also notes, p. 637, that Bruno would have met Gaudentius-Radim at the court of Otto III.
140. Bruno, *Epistola ad Heinricum II Imperatorem*, p. 689.
141. Wibert, *Hystoria de predicatione Episcopi Brunonis cum suis capellanis in prussia et martyrio eorum*, ed. G. H. Pertz, MGH, SS 4 (Hanover, 1841), pp. 579–80.
142. Canaparius, *Vita Adalberti*, 28.
143. Canaparius, *Vita Adalberti*, 29.
144. Acts 17, 23.
145. Bruno, *Passio Adalberti* 25.
146. Wood, 'Christians and pagans in ninth-century Scandinavia', pp. 64–6.
147. Bruno, *Passio Adalberti*, 25.
148. Bruno, *Passio Adalberti*, 26. On this passage see I. N. Wood, 'Pagans and holy men 600–800', in P. Ní Chatháin and M. Richter, *Irland und die Christenheit* (Stuttgart, 1987), pp. 358–9.
149. See especially R. A. Markus, 'Gregory the Great and a papal missionary strategy', *Studies in Church History* 6, *The Mission of the Church and the Propagation of the Faith*, ed. G. J. Cuming (Cambridge, 1960), pp. 29–38, reprinted in R. A. Markus, *From Augustine to Gregory the Great* (London, 1983).

# Chapter 11

# BRUNO OF QUERFURT

## 1. THE SOURCES FOR BRUNO OF QUERFURT

Unlike the majority of the saints who have concerned us so far, Bruno of Querfurt was the subject of no major *vita* in the years directly after his death in 1009,[1] although there is a very short account of his martyrdom, which claims to have been dictated by Wibert, who was supposedly present at the time.[2] Whilst Bruno and the rest of his companions were killed, Wibert's eyes were torn out, but he lived to tell the tale. He seems to have related it in order to win support, perhaps for further missions: 'since then I have travelled round numerous provinces on pilgrimage for God, calling on male and female saints for help for the Christians'. His concluding request for patronage and for the remission of the sins of all Christians, could suggest, however, that for him personally the future was bleak.

While there is no major work of hagiography devoted to Bruno, there are brief accounts of the martyr's life in texts concerned with other matters, and it is possible to reconstruct his career in some detail.[3] Thietmar of Merseburg, who was the son of Bruno's cousin, provides a short account of the saint in his *Chronicle*,[4] while Peter Damian includes a more extensive excursus on Bruno in his *Life of Romuald of Benevento*, written around 1042.[5] Despite the lack of a large-scale *vita*, it is clear that Bruno was regarded as a saint from the moment of his martyrdom.

More important than these texts, however, are Bruno's own works, which bring us closer to the heart of mission than perhaps any writings of the Early Middle Ages. We have already considered Bruno's *Life of Adalbert* – and we shall return to it again – but there is also a second work of hagiography, the *Vita Quinque Fratrum*, or more fully the *Life and Passion of Saints Benedict, John and their Companions*,[6] and finally there is a letter addressed by Bruno to the emperor Henry II, and written in 1008. The letter is a blistering attack on Henry's policy towards the Slavs, but it also includes a quite remarkable account of Bruno's own missionary work among the Petschenegs.[7] Bruno's writings are more important for understanding mission and its hagiography, than are the writings about him.

## 2. SAXONY, POLAND AND BOHEMIA IN THE LIFETIME OF BRUNO

We have already considered the importance of Bohemia to the German *Reich* up to the death of Otto II in 983. Thereafter, matters were complicated by the rise in the importance of Poland. To understand Bruno's work, and his critique of Henry II, it is necessary to sketch in the increasingly powerful and complex world to the east of the *Reich*. Here it is particularly interesting to follow the account provided by Thietmar, since, although he was a relative of Bruno, he also had widely differing views on the Polish problem: the two men make an interesting contrast.[8]

The earliest of the Polish leaders of the Piast dynasty to make an impact on Thietmar, is Miesko, who first appears as being made tributary to Otto I in 963.[9] At that time he was a pagan, but he converted to Christianity soon after, following his marriage to the daughter of the Bohemian Boleslav I, Dobrava, who made concessions over her observance of Lent in order to induce him to accept her religion.[10] Despite some conflict with the German margrave, Hodo, Miesko remained a *fidelis* of Otto,[11] and, along with Boleslav II of Bohemia, attended the emperor at Quedlinburg ten years later.[12] Thietmar has nothing to say about Miesko, or the Poles, in his account of the reign of Otto II, although in his excursus on the Piast ruler he does relate Miesko's second marriage, to the daughter of the margrave of the Saxon Nordmark, Oda, who was at the time a nun. This caused something of a stir in *c.* 978, but was allowed to stand for diplomatic reasons. Interestingly, Oda was instrumental in freeing prisoners and throwing opening prisons,[13] which may suggest the influence of Wenceslas' style of rulership. In addition, Bruno, in his *Vita Adalberti*, relates that Miesko defeated the emperor, adding the rather mysterious word *arte*, 'by cunning', to describe the victory.[14]

On Otto's death, Miesko, like Boleslav II, threw in his lot with the duke of Bavaria, Henry the Quarrelsome, and not with the emperor's son, the young Otto III.[15] Connections between Henry and Boleslav continued to be important for as long as the Bavarian duke claimed the throne of the *Reich*: he visited Bohemia in 984.[16] All three, however, submitted to Otto at Quedlinburg later in the same year.[17] Thereafter, the Polish and Bohemian leaders fell out, despite the fact that Miesko had married Boleslav II's sister, Dobrava,[18] and had consequently converted to Christianity.[19] In 990 Boleslav allied with the north Slavonic Liutizi against the Poles, while Miesko appealed to the Empress Theophanu, who was acting as regent for her son, Otto III. Saxon intervention led Miesko and Boleslav to make peace, but the latter still indulged in some plundering on his return to Bohemia.[20]

For the rest of Otto III's reign the Poles, first under the leadership of Miesko and then, after 992, under his son, Boleslaw Chrobry,[21] tended to be in league with the emperor.[22] When Adalbert of Prague was killed in 997, Boleslaw retrieved the body, while Otto helped to disseminate the cult, not least by visiting the martyr's shrine at Gniezno in 1000.[23]

This policy of friendship with Poland was reversed with the accession of Henry II in 1002.[24] Early in his reign the new emperor made Boleslav III, who had ruled over Bohemia since 999, his close friend, by blandishment and threat [*ad amicum familiarem blandiciis ac minis adipiscitur*].[25] By contrast, Boleslaw Chrobry began to assert his independence, taking over territory on the German frontier.[26] His independence was, for Thietmar, one mark of his inferiority to his father, Miesko.[27]

Not that Boleslav III of Bohemia was, in any way, a commendable character. He had one brother castrated, and tried to drown another, before exiling the two of them, together with his mother – Emma, whom we have met as the recipient of the earliest surviving manuscript of Gumpold's *Passio Vencezlavi*.[28] It must have seemed as if family history was trying to repeat itself. As a result, the Bohemians called in Vladivoj – perhaps a half-brother of Boleslaw Chrobry – and he presented himself to Henry, who gave him Bohemia to hold as a benefice. Yet he proved to be no better than his predecessor: as Thietmar commented, he could not last for an hour without a drink. Boleslav himself fled to the margrave, Henry, who handed him on to his cousin, Boleslaw Chrobry.[29] When Vladivoj died, he reinstated Boleslav as ruler of Bohemia.[30]

Boleslav, however, did not regain the support of his people. Far from it: when he saw that they were given over to execrable rites,[31] he embarked on the liquidation of the nobility. As a result, the Bohemians appealed to Boleslaw Chrobry. He overthrew his cousin, had him blinded, and claimed the country for himself.[32] Henry offered to allow Boleslaw to keep his acquisitions, if he would submit to the Empire. Boleslaw simply ignored the offer.[33]

One probable reason for Boleslaw's silence was his involvement in the rebellion of Henry of Schweinfurt, who now tried to oust Henry II.[34] Although the rebel was a relative of Thietmar, the historian makes no attempt to exonerate him,[35] but he does note the wicked influence of Boleslaw Chrobry.[36] It was to the latter, who was fighting in Bohemia, that Henry of Schweinfurt fled in 1003, when he knew all was lost.[37] The emperor retaliated by attacking the Milzi, a Slavonic tribe which was subordinate to Boleslaw. At this point Henry of Schweinfurt handed himself over to his imperial namesake.[38]

Henry II did not forgive Boleslaw for his independence of mind or for the support he had given Henry of Schweinfurt. After a campaign in Italy, he set off to punish the Poles in 1004. Because the rivers were in flood he headed not for Poland, but for Bohemia, taking Boleslaw by surprise, and defeating him.[39] Meanwhile, he made use of a surviving brother of the Bohemian Boleslav III, Jaromir, who was established in his place, and who remained a reliable ally of the emperor. In the course of Boleslaw's flight from Bohemia, Adalbert of Prague's one surviving brother, Sobieslaw, was killed.[40] Boleslaw subsequently had to abandon territory in the face of a combined onslaught from Henry II and Jaromir.[41]

The following year, in 1005, Henry again campaigned against the Poles, with the support of Jaromir and the Bohemians, and at this point he even joined forces with the pagan Liutizi.[42] This alliance of Christian Empire and pagan tribesmen against the Christian Poles was to be at the heart of Bruno of Querfurt's critique of Henry II.[43] Even Thietmar, who, unlike Bruno, has little but distrust of and scorn for Boleslaw, and considerable praise for Henry, seems to have balked at this, inserting at this moment a lengthy excursus on the paganism of the Liutizi.[44] The excursus was surely meant as a critique of the emperor's actions. In the ensuing war Boleslaw had to ask for peace, although Henry's forces also suffered considerable losses.[45]

Boleslaw clearly smarted at the losses, and in 1007 the Liutizi and the people of Wolin, together with Jaromir, informed Henry that the Pole was building up support with bribes and kind words – and they threatened to withdraw from their alliance with the emperor if he did not make preparations against Boleslaw. Even Thietmar saw this as bad counsel: nevertheless, Henry broke the peace, prompting counterattacks by Boleslaw, who managed to force various towns into submission to himself.[46]

It was against this background that Bruno of Querfurt arrived in Poland and moved on thence to the Prussians, among whom he was martyred in 1009 – although, curiously, Thietmar only remembered to insert an account of his cousin's martyrdom after he had dealt with the year 1013.[47] A year after Bruno's death, in 1010, the Poles and the Saxons were back at war, with Boleslaw sending troops across the Elbe and Henry and Jaromir of Bohemia counterattacking.[48] There was war again in 1012,[49] and when Boleslaw asked for peace it proved impossible to reach agreement.[50] Matters, moreover, were complicated when Jaromir was driven out of Bohemia by his brother, Odalrich, and had to flee to Boleslaw as a relative.[51] In any case Henry II refused to reinstate Jaromir.[52]

Despite some military success,[53] Boleslaw and his son, Miesko, were keen to make peace with Henry,[54] and Miesko even swore to keep faith with the emperor at Magdeburg early in 1013. Henry was, nevertheless, furious that a group of magnates went to visit Boleslaw without his permission.[55] After this contretemps, however, Boleslaw himself turned up with hostages, to become a vassal of the emperor.[56] No doubt the reason for this meekness was his desire for Henry's support against the Russians. Nevertheless, the subservience was temporary, and when Henry demanded his presence on an expedition to Italy, he sent his excuses to the pope, explaining that he feared treachery on Henry's part.[57] The emperor demanded an apology, albeit without success, on his return.[58]

Meanwhile, events in Bohemia were again complicating matters. Odalrich had embarked on the extermination of those he thought were in league with Jaromir.[59] At the same time Boleslaw sent Miesko to Odalrich to negotiate an alliance against the emperor. Odalrich responded by imprisoning Miesko and executing his companions. Henry then demanded that Miesko be passed on to him, which Odalrich did after some objection. When Boleslaw asked Henry to return his son he was, not surprisingly, summoned to Merseburg.[60] For once he attended an imperial summons, and received Miesko back, on condition that he would abide by the promises he had made – which, according to Thietmar, he did not.[61] In 1015 Henry gathered an army at Magdeburg to chastise Boleslaw.[62] He sent messengers to Miesko to tell him to remember his promises, but although Miesko promised to try to persuade his father to submit, he explained that he would have to defend his country.[63] Despite initial Saxon and Bavarian successes against the Poles,[64] Henry's army was trapped at Diadesi, and suffered substantial and important losses.[65] Thietmar does not stop to remark that Boleslaw's negotiator at this point, Abbot Antonius of Meseritz, was a pupil of his own cousin, Bruno of Querfurt.

At the same time, Boleslaw's Moravian allies inflicted a major defeat on Henry's Bavarian troops, after which the Pole sent to the emperor to ask for peace.[66] Henry, however, marched on Nimptsch, with an army which included Bohemians and pagan Liutizi, who tried out the Christian God by setting up a cross, but to no avail.[67] They were also to lose an image of their goddess as they crossed a swollen river, on their return journey home.[68] Meanwhile, both Miesko and the Moravians took advantage of Odalrich of Bohemia's absence to attack Bohemia.[69] Boleslaw, who had had considerable successes in the war, was by now more keen than ever to make peace, for he and his family were under threat from the Russian ruler, Iaroslav.[70]

In 1018, peace was finally made between Henry and Boleslaw, and the peace was confirmed by an uncanonical marriage between the Pole and the daughter of the margrave Ekkehard,[71] a marriage which calls forth a lengthy excursus by Thietmar on the marriage customs of the Poles.[72] Again, the excursus clearly has a critical purpose. Boleslaw's sexual appetites are the cause of more than one aside by the chronicler, who even calls him 'the old fornicator'.[73]

Boleslaw's renewed interest in Russia in 1017, following the death of Vladimir of Kiev two years earlier,[74] must have brought considerable relief to Henry, who had agreed to the Pole's planned campaign, and allowed his own magnates to take part[75] – even though Boleslaw refused to attend the emperor's court almost immediately,[76] and continued to do so.[77] The reason for Boleslaw's interest in Russia is straightforward: his daughter had married one of Vladimir's sons, Sviatopolk, and he thus had hopes of being the father-in-law of the ruler of Kiev.[78]

Boleslaw's involvement in Russia prompts a number of lengthy digressions from Thietmar. Sviatopolk had fallen foul of his father, who thought that he was plotting against him. As a result, Vladimir had his son and daughter-in-law imprisoned, which, not surprisingly, enraged Boleslaw. But the Russian ruler died and Sviatopolk escaped to Boleslaw, although his wife remained in prison.[79] Subsequently, in 1018, Boleslaw supported Sviatopolk's bid to take the throne from his brother, Iaroslav, winning a major battle, and forcing the latter to retreat. Boleslaw and Sviatopolk took Kiev.[80] Boleslaw then demanded the return of his daughter from Iaroslav.[81]

Thietmar's narrative effectively ends at this point, and the author himself died in 1018. Henry II was to last until 1024 and Boleslaw a year longer. Bruno of Querfurt had, however, died nine years before his cousin stopped writing his *Chronicle*.

## 3. THE CAREER OF BRUNO OF QUERFURT[82]

Bruno himself was born around 974. He was educated, along with his cousin, Thietmar of Merseburg, in Magdeburg.[83] From there he joined the court of Otto III – to whom he is said to have been distantly related – as a chaplain at some point before 998.[84] It was probably in the company of Otto, who took up residence on the Aventine when in Rome, that he visited the monastery of SS. Boniface and Alexius, shortly after the martyrdom of Adalbert, and what he heard and saw prompted him to join the community.[85] He announced that he was to be another Boniface – referring not to the Roman martyr, perhaps, but to the Anglo-Saxon.[86] He became an extreme ascetic, fasting and living on fruit and roots, according to Damian,[87] and living by the work of his own hands, *de opere suo*, according to Thietmar.[88] Bruno joined Romuald of Benevento's eremitical community at Pereum outside Ravenna.[89]

It was in the company of Romuald that he met two monks, John and Benedict: indeed, Romuald had wanted Otto III make the latter abbot of the new foundation of Pereum.[90] Meanwhile, the emperor, in addition to involving himself in the monastery, was also talking of mission to the Slavs: a goal which fired Bruno, and which he, in turn, suggested to Benedict. It is probable that the emperor's interest in mission at this precise time had been encouraged by his memory of Adalbert: John Canaparius had just written his *Vita Adalberti*, apparently at Otto's request, and a church in the monastery of the Pereum was dedicated to the martyr.[91] Bruno's own enthusiasm for the missionary project was all the greater because he could not abide the swamps which surrounded Ravenna.[92]

The coterie associated with Otto at Pereum was, in any case, breaking up. Romuald himself left towards the end of 1001, upset by some scandal, and probably aggravated by the emperor's increasing dependence on him.[93] Otto himself sent Benedict and John on their mission, apparently in response to a request for preachers from Boleslaw Chrobry.[94] The departure of the former seems to have been emotionally devastating for Bruno, but it was agreed that he should follow his friends to the mission field, indeed, he promised to secure for them a papal licence to preach to the pagans, and he was advised to learn Slavonic in the meantime.[95]

In the event the crises that enveloped Italy at the end of Otto's life, and following his death in 1002, as well as problems in the Slav world, were such as to leave Bruno incapable first of collecting a licence and then of delivering it within any reasonable timespan, for, having finally obtained the document, he travelled to Regensburg, but then diverted to Hungary.[96] In the meantime, Benedict, John and their companions were killed by robbers while waiting in Poland for permission to preach in 1003. Bruno blamed himself for their fate.[97]

On his journey north Bruno had with him not just the fatally delayed licence, but also the *pallium*, which had been given to him by the pope, together with a request that he should be consecrated by Tagino of Magdeburg, as a missionary bishop.[98] The intended area of his mission seems to have been Poland, but at this moment Boleslaw had no wish to accept a bishop from Henry II's Magdeburg, and so Bruno returned to Hungary, where he did indeed evangelise.[99] Soon after, however, he had an encounter with Henry II's brother, another Bruno, who was on an embassy at the Hungarian court, and the saint appears to have been pressurised into leaving: he set off for Russia.[100] There, he asked Vladimir's support for a mission to the Petschenegs, and although the Russian tried to dissuade him, he went to work among them, with some success.[101]

In 1007 Bruno left the Petschenegs and Russia to return to Poland. He immediately befriended Boleslaw, who became a considerable benefactor.[102] On the other hand, relations between Henry and Boleslaw were degenerating once again – and Henry was even resorting to a renewal of alliances with the pagan Liutizi.[103] Bruno's horror at the prospect of an alliance between the Christian Empire and pagans against Christian Poland prompted his writing to Henry II a letter which offered a devastating critique of the emperor's Slav policy, together with an account of the saint's own missionary work.[104] At more or less the same time, while in Poland, Bruno revised

232

his account of Adalbert's life and also wrote the *Vita Quinque Fratrum*.[105] At the start of the next year he set out for Prussia. There, despite – perhaps even because of – initial success, he was killed, on 9 March 1009.[106] As with the body of Adalbert, so with those of Bruno and his companions: they were ransomed by Boleslaw.[107]

## 4. THE *LIFE OF THE FIVE BROTHERS*

In many respects Bruno embodied a particular ascetic and missionary commitment associated with the court of Otto III, which was necessarily hostile to those aspects of Henry II's policies which concerned Boleslaw and the Poles.[108] Dvornik commented that the '*Life of the Five Brothers* is so interesting, just because it reveals how stubbornly Otto's devotees fought against endless odds to carry out their master's dreams'.[109] Yet Bruno's hostility to aspects of Henry's policies has also to be weighed against the praise meted out to the emperor in the *Vita Adalberti*.[110] Further, his enthusiasm for the missionary concerns of Henry's predecessor contrasts directly with his hostility to the Italian policies of Otto II and Otto III, and his more general critique of Otto III in the *Life of the Five Brothers*.[111]

Bruno's *Vita Quinque Fratrum* is more than a rearguard statement of Otto III's missionary policy in Poland and beyond: it is also more than a critique of Otto II and Otto III.[112] One point which distinguishes Bruno's picture of Adalbert from that of John Canaparius is its psychological realism.[113] The same psychological depth is a dominant feature of the *Life of the Five Brothers*. It is worth looking in some detail at this text, even though it will mean revisiting Bruno's own career.

The *Vita Quinque Fratrum* begins with an outcry by Bruno, asking for divine help in writing. Although requests for God's aid are effectively *topoi*, Bruno sounds genuinely overwhelmed, and what he goes on to write suggests that the cry is heartfelt. Bruno then turns to the history of Benedict, a Beneventan, who entered the eremitical life,[114] and who joined John, an old man who was living as a hermit at Montecassino.[115] John had already been influenced by Romuald of Benevento, particularly in his teaching of the *Collationes* of John Cassian. The influence was increased when Romuald abandoned the monastery at Classe, over which he had been placed by Otto, and joined Benedict and John at Montecassino.[116] There the newcomer befriended Benedict, and the three of them then moved on to Rome – after Romuald had nearly died.[117] Rome, however, was not to their taste, and so they transferred to Pereum, outside Ravenna, where Otto III founded a new monastic community. At Pereum they were regularly visited by the emperor, who himself was contemplating entry into the monastic life.[118]

233

Otto's backing for the community at Pereum prompted murmurings about Romuald's avarice – which Bruno clearly did not believe in, although he does admit to the ascetic's desire to offend everyone: *quod displicere hominibus per studium querebat.* Yet, while Romuald was closely involved in the foundation at Pereum, he had no desire to be abbot, and he told Otto to appoint Benedict instead. This was not what Benedict wanted, however, and he persuaded Bruno to approach the emperor, while he himself undertook to assuage Romuald. The latter accepted Benedict's point of view, but still had him flagellated, naked, in the imperial council, for being disobedient – one of many indications of Romuald's impossible nature.[119]

In addition to his monastic interests, Otto was also concerned to send missionaries to work among the Slavs. Bruno suggested such work to Benedict, adding that he would be ready to join – not least because he found the landscape and climate of Ravenna unconducive to work. Despite the suggestion, they remained for a while with Otto, who had embarked on building a marble rotunda to commemorate Adalbert of Prague.[120]

After a year the basilica was completed. Romuald, who was upset by a scandal involving two of his disciples, departed for Istria, while Otto finally sent Benedict and John off on their Slav mission.[121] The parting of Bruno and Benedict appears to have been an emotional affair,[122] which the hagiographer heightens by describing a vision seen by Benedict not unlike that seen by Gaudentius shortly before Adalbert of Prague's martyrdom.[123] Finally, Bruno promised to secure a licence from the pope for Benedict and John to preach to the pagans, and to learn Slavonic.[124] The two missionaries then set off north to Boleslaw.[125]

Otto had, meanwhile, decided to punish Rome for the revolts against him in 1001. However, he was struck down by illness and died in 1002. The death of Otto prompts Bruno to an assessment of the emperor, which effectively concludes that he was a fine ruler pursuing the wrong policy, and that he should have concentrated on problems in Germany.[126] Despite Otto's weaknesses, Bruno clearly had considerable affection for him.[127] So too did Benedict, John and, above all, Boleslaw.[128]

In Bruno's reading, Otto's death led to chaos. He claims that the situation was such that he could not obtain a licence for Benedict and John, which left them wondering why he had not come with the necessary document.[129] For the next section of his work Bruno effectively alternates between describing his fear and guilt and the bewilderment and boredom of Benedict and John, who were worried that they would die without fighting God's cause.

Bruno's fears were increased by the murder of a friend of his, Rothulf, in Rimini – but this time the danger actually prompted him to go to Rome and secure the longed-for licence. Having reached Regensburg, however, he turned aside to go to Hungary – in part at least because of the problematic relations between Henry II and the Slavs.[130] Memory of the delay once again prompts Bruno to an analysis of his own failings.

Meanwhile, Benedict was becoming increasingly impatient. He had learnt Slavonic, and, like John, had adopted the local style of dress. They also had their heads shaved, to fit in with the pagans[131] – a variant of the policy which Bruno also attributed to Adalbert of Prague shortly before his martyrdom.[132] In his impatience Benedict decided to discover what had happened to Bruno, and set out with ten pounds of silver, which Boleslaw had given him to dissuade him from his objective,[133] leaving John to look after the hermitage they had established among the Poles. Benedict got as far as Prague before discovering that it was too dangerous to proceed. He returned to John, angry at not reaching Bruno.

Once Benedict had returned to the hermitage, Boleslaw allowed one of their companions to set off to obtain the papal licence and to find Bruno.[134] Benedict and John, meanwhile, lived a perfect ascetic life, in which they were joined by two Slav brothers, Isaac and Matthew, and by some helpers, including a cook called Christinus.[135] Nevertheless, they came increasingly to worry about both Bruno and their emissary to Rome, and at the same time to lament the tedium of waiting for permission to preach.[136] Bruno lists question after question which occurred to them: why could they not preach to the pagans? why, if they could do nothing, had they learnt Slavonic, changed their style of dress, and so on?

News of the ten pounds of silver that Boleslaw had given Benedict had, however, leaked out, and a gang of Christian thieves plotted to steal it from the would-be missionaries, though, unbeknown to the criminals, it had actually been returned. They attacked by night, and despite John's attempts to reason with them, they killed first him and then Benedict. Bruno compared the 'Brothers' to Adalbert of Prague.[137] Issac shouted out, but then accepted his martyrdom with joy, blessing his killers, which momentarily nonplussed them. They then struck Matthew outside the church. Finally Christinus, the cook, was killed trying to defend himself. The five martyrs Bruno compared to the five wounds of Christ. It is difficult not to recall, at this moment, his discussion of the seven wounds inflicted on Adalbert.[138]

The thieves, meanwhile, could find nothing, so they divided up a missal between them – this may have been an object of some value for the community's manuscripts had come from Otto III. They also took the altar covering, and relics. Finally, they set fire to the church, hoping to disguise their crime. But the church would not burn, and the bodies of the five martyrs were plain for all to see. The next day the locals discovered the corpses, telling the bishop as soon as they were able.[139] Bruno describes the position of the bodies and their subsequent burial – the precision perhaps

235

reflecting the hagiographer's own trauma at the loss of Benedict. Christinus was originally buried outside the church, because he alone had defended himself, but a heavy fall of rain led to his body being placed with the others, thus ensuring that there was no distinction between the martyrs.[140] The text concludes with the accounts of a considerable number of miracles – but although these are certainly contemporary, they are so different in style from the main body of the work, that they may have been added as an afterthought.[141]

The *Life of the Five Brothers* undoubtedly contains a critique of policies of both Otto III and Henry II; it may also contain a description of Otto's missionary ideal. It is, however, a more extraordinary work than such comments suggest. From the moment that Benedict and John leave for Poland, until the beginning of the narrative of the martyrdom itself, the work is dominated by the bewilderment and tedium of the martyrs and by the fears and guilt of Bruno. The work is an astonishing study in psychology – both that of the martyrs and of the author, and the tedium of the former serves to enhance the guilt of the latter. Nor are the opening and closing narratives devoid of psychological detail or of personal involvement on Bruno's part: he was instrumental in the sending of the mission, and his friendship with Benedict seems to have been out of the ordinary. The *Vita Quinque Fratrum* is, in short, a sustained confession of (admittedly indirect) complicity in the deaths of the five martyrs, and, as such, is psychological autobiography of a sort that is not supposed to have been written between the end of the fourth century and the mid-eleventh.[142] Despite its implied critique of Henry, which gives one indication of an intended audience, it should surely be read as a personal work, and it may be significant that it only survives in one manuscript.[143]

## 5. THE LETTER TO HENRY II

Bruno's third, and shortest, work is equally autobiographical, albeit in a rather more traditional way – for the author is clearly defending himself against criticism for his association with Boleslaw, and attacking Henry's policies through consideration of his own missionary experiences.[144]

Bruno begins his address to Henry with professions of respect, and hope for the monarch's success. He thanks the emperor for the concern which he showed for his safety while he was still in Hungary, but relies on God and St Peter for his protection. He then turns to the missionary work which he has carried out since leaving Hungary.

He went first to the Russians, where he was detained for a month, because the ruler (Vladimir) did not want him to work among the Petschenegs, regarding them as irrational. According to Vladimir, Bruno would achieve nothing except a miserable death. When he saw that the missionary could not be shaken from his purpose, he took him to the frontier, which was fortified – an observation which is supported archaeologically.[145] For two days Vladimir and Bruno sized up the situation, each encamped on a different hilltop. Bruno, carrying a cross and singing hymns to St Peter, was not frightened by what he saw. Vladimir explained that, were Bruno to be killed, it would redound to the Russian's shame, but the missionary explained that God had opened the path to the pagans for him, as He had opened that of Paradise to Vladimir. At this point the king gave up trying to dissuade Bruno from his objective.

Bruno then tells Henry of his experiences among the Petschenegs. For two days he and his companions were left alone: on the third they were led to execution, but then released safe and sound. On the following Sunday they reached a more populous area, and were left to continue as they were until a council had been called. This took place on a subsequent Sunday, when the missionaries were threatened and even tortured, until their tor-turers realised that they had come to bring benefits. Thereafter they were allowed to evangelise, which they did for five months, visiting the people of three-quarters of the territory, and dealing with messengers from the fourth quarter. As a result, they converted about thirty people, and they brought peace between the Petschenegs and the Russians.

Bruno next explains to Henry that he has now turned his mind to the Prussians. By way of showing that anything was possible, he notes that even the Black Hungarians have been converted, despite the sins of the Chris-tians, and he attributes all success to God and St Peter, with the help of the blood of the saints. He nevertheless thanks Henry for what he has done for him, and for his concerns, but he also criticises the emperor's anger at his departure for the land of the Prussians, and he remarks that no one should harbour hate. At the same time he asserts his personal desire to live, because of the mountain of his own sins.

Bruno goes on to address the question of his association with Boleslaw, and his great affection for him. He explains that this is not a slight against Henry, and that he wants to win the Pole to Henry's side. But he turns the tables on the emperor, asking whether it is good to persecute Christians and be on friendly terms with the pagans – referring to Henry's support for the Liutizi against the Poles. He balances Christ and Belial, light and dark, St Maurice and the demon Zuarasi(ci)[146] – a comparison which has particu-lar resonance in that the standard of St Maurice was an object which was on occasion carried into battle by the Ottonians.[147] Bruno moves on to the question of the sacrifice of Christians to pagan totems – something that Thietmar mentions in his account of the involvement of the Liutizi in Henry's wars.[148] Would it not be better, Bruno remarks, to have the Christian

Boleslaw as a *fidelis*, and to be able to collect tribute and convert the pagan with his help? With this in mind he urges Henry not to persecute the Polish ruler. Which is better, fighting against pagans for the sake of Christianity, or fighting Christians for the sake of secular honour?

Bruno then invokes the help that Henry could receive from St Peter, or St Adalbert, or even five recent martyrs – that is the Five Brothers – at whose shrine miracles are being performed. He comments on the justice of Henry's rule, but suggests that he should be more merciful. He would gain more by gifts than by war, especially as he is fighting on three fronts.

Bruno admits that the question of political alignment is none of his business, but he argues that certain issues are of concern to him. First, he points out that although Boleslaw wants to help him evangelise the Prussians, he is hamstrung by war. He also remarks that God has not commanded the emperor to fight the Liutizi just because they are pagans and idolators, but He does expect the ruler to compel them to come in. This would increase the Church, lead to the baptism of pagans, and bring peace to the Christians – all of which would bring the ruler honour. As it is, the emperor does not have a *fidelis* in Boleslaw, nor the Polish ruler in the emperor. Whereas there were men who were in a position to convert the pagans in the days of Constantine and Charlemagne, there are none such now. Indeed, the Christians are being persecuted.

Bruno urges Henry to give the Christians peace, and to fight for Christianity against the pagans, for this would serve him well at the Last Judgement. This, he says, would win over Boleslaw. Just as Miesko was on good terms with the dead emperor, so his son, Boleslaw, should be on good terms with Henry.

He then tells Henry that he has sent a bishop of his, along with the noble monk Rodbert, to evangelise the Swedes (*Svigi*), and that news has arrived that the leader (*senior*) of the *Svigi* has been baptised, and that a thousand *homines* and seven *plebes* – perhaps communities – have received the same grace. Although some wanted to kill them, they all returned with the bishop on time. Bruno promises to inform Henry further, when he has better information.[149]

He concludes by emphasising his support for Henry, and he asks for the blessings of God and St Peter. He also exhorts the emperor to assist in the Christianisation of the Liutizi and the Prussians, as a pious king should. Finally, he wishes long life to the emperor.

Bruno's letter to Henry is many things. It is a piece of political justification in a very awkward situation. It is an exhortation to peace between the Saxons and the Poles, and an encouragement to the emperor to support evangelisation. In pursuit of such arguments it marshals recent history – notably the martyrdoms of Adalbert and the Five Brothers – and yet more contemporary history – briefly, that of the monk Rodbert, and at greater length that of Bruno himself. It thus comes once again into the category of autobiography.

## 6. BRUNO AND MISSION

Bruno was clearly a committed missionary – and he thought long and hard about his calling. We have already seen that one of the differences between his account of the last days of Adalbert and that of Canaparius is that Bruno gives the martyr a long speech on the weakness of the missionary strategy that he and his companions had adopted: they looked too distinctive, and should, therefore, abandon their ecclesiastical clothing, grow their hair and beards, and try to pass as locals. They should live by the work of their own hands – which would not look out of the ordinary, but would at the same time echo the Biblical notion of self-sufficiency.[150] By this deception, says Adalbert, an opportunity for mission might be opened up.[151]

Whether or not these ideas really were expressed by the bishop of Prague, we have no means of telling. Similar points are, however, made by Bruno with regard to Benedict and John, who dressed as locals and shaved their heads to blend in with their intended audience.[152] Clearly, there is a difference in hairstyle between that advocated by Adalbert and that adopted by Benedict and John, but the strategy is the same – and we can scarcely doubt that it was one of which Bruno approved, even if it did not originate with him.

We do have some other indications that he was sensitive to the impact of dress on his audience. Peter Damian, in his rather confused narrative, relates that when Bruno turned up at the Russian (probably a mistake for Prussian) court, he was wearing rags, which led the ruler to think he was a beggar. Thereupon, Bruno went to his lodging and put on his pontifical vestments – which led the king to comment on the bishop's vanity and to challenge him to walk between two lines of blazing timber, which he did, still wearing his vestments. As a result, he converted the king, but was subsequently killed, according to Damian, by the king's brother.[153] The story, as it stands, is misplaced, because Vladimir was already a Christian, and Bruno was not martyred in Russia. At the very least Damian has confused Russia with Prussia. Certainly Wibert, who claims to have witnessed Bruno's martyrdom, describes it in terms not dissimilar to those set down by Damian.

According to Wibert, once among the Prussians, Bruno and his companions were led to the king, Nethimir. The saint asked for an idol to be brought, and he threw it into the fire. The enraged king then ordered that Bruno himself should be thrown into the fire. Bruno, who was wearing his episcopal vestments, commanded that his chair be set in the fire, and he sat on it, while his chaplains chanted seven psalms. Not surprisingly, conversions followed.[154]

Along with dress, language is a recurrent, albeit not consistent, factor in Bruno's evaluation of the missionary strategy – he says nothing, for instance, about how he communicated with the Hungarians or Petschenegs. His concern with language is, however, present in the *Life of Adalbert*: he emphasises the saint's mastery of three languages.[155] Further, according to Bruno, when Adalbert met resistance among the Prussians, he resolved to work among the Liutizi, whose language he knew.[156] Bruno's interest in language is yet more apparent in the exhortation made by Benedict, that he should learn Slavonic,[157] and in his stress on the acquisition of the language by both Benedict and John.[158]

Bruno's hagiography, therefore, deals with strategies for mission. It also deals with his awareness of the psychological stress placed on missionaries. There is his picture of the tedium experienced by Benedict and John as they waited to get out into the field – tedium which Bruno himself experienced while he waited for an opportunity to work among the Prussians. There is, in addition, his awareness of the impact of fear on the actions of a would-be missionary: fear had paralysed him, and prevented him from securing the licence for Benedict and John;[159] and there is his portrait of Adalbert's terror, immediately before his martyrdom, which has no counterpart in the account of John Canaparius.[160] His own fear he seems to have mastered in his remarkable insistence in working among the Petschenegs, despite the objections of Vladimir,[161] and finally in his ordeal by fire.[162] Bruno, at least as much as Patrick and Rimbert, takes us to the psychological stresses and triumphs of the missionary.

## Notes

1. Later texts are listed in *Bibliotheca Hagiographica Latina Antiquae et Mediae Aetatis, Novum Supplementum*, ed. H. Fros (Brussels, 1986), p. 170.
2. Wibert, *Hystoriae de predicatione Episcopi Brunonis cum suis capellanis in Prussia et martyrio eorum*, pp. 579–80. See Gieysztor, 'Sanctus et gloriosissimus martyr Christi Adalbertus: un état et une église missionnaires aux alentours de l'an mille', p. 642, for the problem of its authenticity.
3. The chief account continues to be H. G. Voigt, *Bruno von Querfurt* (Stuttgart, 1907). For a detailed account of Bruno's ideology, Wenskus, *Studien zur historisch-politischen Gedankenwelt Bruns von Querfurt*.
4. Thietmar, *Chronicon* VI 94 (58) – 95.
5. Petrus Damiani, *Vita Romualdi* 26–7; for the date of composition, see Tabacco's edition, pp. liv–v.
6. *Vita quinque fratrum*, ed. Kade.
7. Bruno, ep. to Henry, ed. von Giesebrecht.

8. For an assessment of the relations between the *Reich*, the Poles and Bohemia, see F. Dvornik, *The Making of Central and Eastern Europe* (London, 1949). For the need to juxtapose Bruno and Thietmar, Wenskus, *Studien zur historisch-politischen Gedankenwelt Bruns von Querfurt*, p. 5.

9. Thietmar, *Chronicon* II 14.

10. Thietmar, *Chronicon* IV 55 (35) – 56.

11. Thietmar, *Chronicon* II 29.

12. Thietmar, *Chronicon* II 31.

13. Thietmar, *Chronicon* II 57 (36).

14. Bruno, *Vita Adalberti* 10.

15. Thietmar, *Chronicon* IV 2 (2) – 9 (7).

16. Thietmar, *Chronicon* IV 5 (4).

17. Thietmar, *Chronicon* IV 9 (7).

18. Thietmar, *Chronicon* IV 55 (35). For the chronology, Vlasto, *The Entry of the Slavs into Christendom*, pp. 115–7.

19. Thietmar, *Chronicon* IV 56.

20. Thietmar, *Chronicon* IV 11 (9) – 13.

21. Thietmar, *Chronicon* IV 57 (36) – 58 (37).

22. See F. Dvornik, 'The first phase of the Drang nach Osten', pp. 129–45; also *id.*, *The Making of Central and Eastern Europe*, pp. 142–8.

23. Thietmar, *Chronicon* IV 28 (19), 44 (28) – 46. See K. Görich, 'Otto III. öffnet das Karlsgrab in Aachen', pp. 406–9.

24. For Henry's policies, Dvornik, *The Making of Central and Eastern Europe*, pp. 185–213.

25. Thietmar, *Chronicon* V 7 (5), 11 (7).

26. Thietmar, *Chronicon* V 9 (6) – 10, 18 (10).

27. Thietmar, *Chronicon* V 9 (6).

28. Mayr-Harting, *Ottonian Book Illumination*, vol. 2, pp. 172–4.

29. Thietmar, *Chronicon* V 23 (15).

30. Thietmar, *Chronicon* V 29 (18).

31. Thietmar, *Chronicon* V 29 (18) – not necessarily an allusion to paganism: perhaps a comment on the use of Slavonic liturgy.

32. Thietmar, *Chronicon* V 30.

33. Thietmar, *Chronicon* V 31 (19).

34. Thietmar, *Chronicon* V 32 (20).

35. Thietmar, *Chronicon* V 32 (20).

36. Thietmar, *Chronicon* V 33, 36 (22) – 37.

37. Thietmar, *Chronicon* V 38 (23).

38. Thietmar, *Chronicon* VI 2.

39. Thietmar, *Chronicon* VI 10.

40. Thietmar, *Chronicon* VI 11 – 12 (9).

41. Thietmar, *Chronicon* VI 14 (11) – 15.

42. Thietmar, *Chronicon* VI 19 (14), 22 (16).

43. Bruno, ep. to Henry; see Dvornik, *The Making of Central and Eastern Europe*, pp. 202–4.

44. Thietmar, *Chronicon* VI 23 (17) – 25 (18).

45. Thietmar, *Chronicon* VI 26 (19) – 27 (20).

46. Thietmar, *Chronicon* VI 33 (24) – 34.

47. Thietmar, *Chronicon* VI 94 (58) – 95.

48. Thietmar, *Chronicon* VI 54 (38) – 59 (19), 67.

49. Thietmar, *Chronicon* VI 67.

50. Thietmar, *Chronicon* VI 69 (45).
51. Thietmar, *Chronicon* VI 71.
52. Thietmar, *Chronicon* VI 83 (50).
53. Thietmar, *Chronicon* VI 80 (48)
54. Thietmar, *Chronicon* VI 89 (54).
55. Thietmar, *Chronicon* VI 90.
56. Thietmar, *Chronicon* VI 91 (55).
57. Thietmar, *Chronicon* VI 92.
58. Thietmar, *Chronicon* VII 4 (5), 9.
59. Thietmar, *Chronicon* VI 99 (60).
60. Thietmar, *Chronicon* VII 10 (7) – 11.
61. Thietmar, *Chronicon* VII 12 (8).
62. Thietmar, *Chronicon* VII 16.
63. Thietmar, *Chronicon* VII 17.
64. Thietmar, *Chronicon* VII 18 (12) – 19.
65. Thietmar, *Chronicon* VII 20 – 22 (14).
66. Thietmar, *Chronicon* VII 57 (42).
67. Thietmar, *Chronicon* VII 59 (44) – 61.
68. Thietmar, *Chronicon* VII 64 (47).
69. Thietmar, *Chronicon* VII 59 (44), 61.
70. Thietmar, *Chronicon* VII 65 (48).
71. Thietmar, *Chronicon* VIII 1 (1).
72. Thietmar, *Chronicon* VIII 2 (2) – 3.
73. Thietmar, *Chronicon* VIII 32.
74. S. Franklin and J. Shepard, *The Emergence of Rus 750–1200* (London, 1996), pp. 186–7.
75. Thietmar, *Chronicon* VII 50 (35).
76. Thietmar, *Chronicon* VII 51 (36).
77. Thietmar, *Chronicon* VII 73.
78. Thietmar, *Chronicon* VII 72 (52); Franklin and Shepard, *The Emergence of Rus 750–1200*, p. 168.
79. Thietmar, *Chronicon* VII 73.
80. Thietmar, *Chronicon* VIII 31 (16) – 32.
81. Thietmar, *Chronicon* VIII 33.
82. There are short accounts in Wenskus, *Studien zur historisch-politischen Gedanken-welt Bruns von Querfurt*, pp. 2–3; Dvornik, *The Making of Central and Eastern Europe*, pp. 196–204; Vlasto, *The Entry of the Slavs into Christendom*, p. 274; and Gieysztor, 'Sanctus et gloriosissimus martyr Christi Adalbertus: un état et une église missionnaires aux alentours de l'an mille', pp. 636–43. Otherwise, there is the much longer account of Voigt, *Bruno von Querfurt*.
83. Thietmar, *Chronicon* VI 94 (58).
84. Damian, *Vita Romualdi* 27.
85. Bruno, *Vita Adalberti* 17.
86. Damian, *Vita Romualdi* 27, with Tabacco, ed., p. 56, n. 8.
87. Damian, *Vita Romualdi* 27.
88. Thietmar, *Chronicon* VI 94 (58).
89. Damian, *Vita Romualdi* 26. There is a useful commentary on Romuald and his circle in B. Hamilton, 'S. Pierre Damien et les mouvements monastiques de son temps', *Studi Gregoriani* 10 (1975), pp. 179–95, reprinted in *id., Monastic Reform, Catharism and the Crusades, 900–1300*.

90. Bruno, *Vita Quinque Fratrum* 2.
91. Damian, *Vita Romualdi* 30.
92. Bruno, *Vita Quinque Fratrum* 2.
93. Bruno, *Vita Quinque Fratrum* 3; Hamilton, 'S. Pierre Damien et les mouvements monastiques de son temps', p. 193.
94. Damian, *Vita Romualdi* 28. On Boleslaw's interest in the Pereum see Dvornik, *The Making of Central and Eastern Europe*, p. 199.
95. Bruno, *Vita Quinque Fratrum* 4–5.
96. Bruno, *Vita Quinque Fratrum* 10.
97. Bruno, *Vita Quinque Fratrum* 10, 13.
98. Thietmar, *Chronicon* VI 95 (58). See also Damian, *Vita Romualdi* 27 for his collection of the *pallium*.
99. Bruno, ep. to Henry.
100. Bruno, ep. to Henry. See Dvornik's interpretation, *The Making of Central and Eastern Europe*, p. 201.
101. Bruno, ep to Henry. Damian, *Vita Romualdi* 27 is hopelessly confused at this point, apparently mixing up information on Bruno's martyrdom among the Prussians with his dealings with the Russian ruler.
102. Thietmar, *Chronicon* 94 (58).
103. Thietmar, *Chronicon* VI 33 (24) – 34.
104. Bruno, ep. to Henry.
105. Wenskus, *Studien zu historisch-politischen Gedankenwelt Bruns von Querfurt*, p. 3.
106. Wibert, *Hystoriae de predicatione Episcopi Brunonis cum suis capellanis in Prussia et martyrio eorum*.
107. Thietmar, *Chronicon* VI 95.
108. Dvornik, *The Making of Central and Eastern Europe*, p. 200. Gieysztor, 'Sanctus et gloriosissimus martyr Christi Adalbertus: un état et une église missionnaires aux alentours de l'an mille', pp. 637–8.
109. Dvornik, *The Making of Central and Eastern Europe*, p. 200.
110. Bruno, *Vita Adalberti* 12.
111. Bruno, *Vita Adalberti* 9, 10–12; Bruno, *Vita Quinque Fratrum* 7; Wenskus, *Studien zu historisch-politischen Gedankenwelt Bruns von Querfurt*.
112. Wenskus, *Studien zu historisch-politischen Gedankenwelt Bruns von Querfurt*.
113. Wenskus, *Studien zu historisch-politischen Gedankenwelt Bruns von Querfurt*, p. 72.
114. Bruno, *Vita Quinque Fratrum* 1.
115. Bruno, *Vita Quinque Fratrum* 2.
116. Bruno, *Vita Quinque Fratrum* 2; compare Damian, *Vita Romualdi* 22, 26.
117. Bruno, *Vita Quinque Fratrum* 2; compare Damian, *Vita Romualdi* 23–6.
118. Bruno, *Vita Quinque Fratrum* 2.
119. Bruno, *Vita Quinque Fratrum* 2. Every chapter of Petrus Damiani, *Vita Romualdi*, illustrates how difficult Romuald was.
120. Bruno, *Vita Quinque Fratrum* 2.
121. Bruno, *Vita Quinque Fratrum* 3.
122. Bruno, *Vita Quinque Fratrum* 3–5.
123. Compare Bruno, *Vita Quinque Fratrum* 4 with *id.*, *Vita Adalberti* 29.
124. Bruno, *Vita Quinque Fratrum* 5.
125. Bruno, *Vita Quinque Fratrum* 6.
126. Bruno, *Vita Quinque Fratrum* 7. See Wenskus, *Studien zur historisch-politischen Gedankenwelt Bruns von Querfurt*.

127. Dvornik, *The Making of Central and Eastern Europe*, p. 211: 'one cannot read the account of his last moments by Bruno in his *Life of the Five Brothers* without emotion'.
128. Bruno, *Vita Quinque Fratrum* 8.
129. Bruno, *Vita Quinque Fratrum* 9.
130. Bruno, *Vita Quinque Fratrum* 10.
131. Bruno, *Vita Quinque Fratrum* 10.
132. Bruno, *Vita Adalberti* 26.
133. Bruno, *Vita Quinque Fratrum* 11; Bruno's comments on the silver in 10 and 11 are contradictory, and perhaps reflect his own sense of trauma over the sequel.
134. Bruno, *Vita Quinque Fratrum* 12.
135. Bruno, *Vita Quinque Fratrum* 13.
136. Bruno, *Vita Quinque Fratrum* 13.
137. Bruno, *Vita Quinque Fratrum* 13.
138. Bruno, *Passio Adalberti* 32.
139. Bruno, *Vita Quinque Fratrum* 13.
140. Bruno, *Vita Quinque Fratrum* 13–14.
141. Bruno, *Vita Quinque Fratrum* 15–31.
142. C. Morris, *The Discovery of the Individual 1050–1200* (London, 1972), pp. 79–86. One can only conclude that Professor Morris did not look at some of the missionary hagiography of previous centuries.
143. Kade, MGH, SS 15, 2, p. 710.
144. There is a reasonably full discussion in Dvornik, *The Making of Central and Eastern Europe*, pp. 202–4.
145. For Vladimir's walls, Franklin and Shepard, *The Emergence of Rus 750–1200*, p. 172.
146. On this god see also Thietmar, *Chronicon* VI 25.
147. K. J. Leyser, 'The Battle at the Lech, 955', *History* 50 (1965), pp. 1–25, reprinted in *id.*, *Medieval Germany and its Neighbours 900–1250* (London, 1982), p. 66.
148. Thietmar, *Chronicon* VII 64 (47).
149. On this mission see Gieysztor, '*Sanctus et gloriosissimus martyr Christi Adalbertus*: un état et une église missionnaires aux alentours de l'an mille', p. 640.
150. See below, Ch. 12 for the relevant Biblical passages.
151. Bruno, *Passio Adalberti*, 26. On this passage see Wood, 'Pagans and holy men 600–800', pp. 358–9.
152. Bruno, *Vita Quinque Fratrum* 10.
153. Damian, *Vita Romualdi* 27.
154. Wibert, *Hystoriae de predicatione Episcopi Brunonis cum suis capellanis in Prussia et martyrio eorum*.
155. Bruno, *Vita Adalberti* 5.
156. Bruno, *Vita Adalberti* 26.
157. Bruno, *Vita Quinque Fratrum* 5.
158. Bruno, *Vita Quinque Fratrum* 10, 13.
159. Bruno, *Vita Quinque Fratrum* 9–10.
160. Bruno, *Vita Adalberti* 31–2.
161. Bruno, ep. to Henry.
162. Wibert, *Hystoriae de predicatione Episcopi Brunonis cum suis capellanis in Prussia et martyrio eorum*.

# PART 4

## CONCLUSION

# Chapter 12

# THE MISSIONARY, THE 'FAMILIAR' AND THE 'OTHER'

## 1. 'MISSIONARY HAGIOGRAPHY'

The history of mission, as opposed to that of Christianisation, in the Early Middle Ages has largely to be reconstructed from hagiography. Fortunately, there are a good number of *vitae* of 'missionaries', particularly from the eighth and ninth centuries. Yet the existence of a large number of texts carries with it additional problems. The hagiography relating to missionaries, and particularly to the so-called 'Anglo-Saxon missionaries' active on the continent, forms a group of interlinked chains of saints' *Lives*, the more recent of which draw on previous texts, gaining authority from them, adding to them or subverting them. At the head of the most extensive of these chains – that concerned with the Christianisation of Frisia and Saxony – lie Willibald's *Life of Boniface* and Alcuin's *Life of Willibrord* – while behind Alcuin and many of the other works of hagiography lies Bede's *Historia Ecclesiastica*. The *Life of Boniface* is also central to Bavarian hagiography of the eighth century. A further cluster of texts surrounds Adalbert of Prague and Bruno of Querfurt. To see the full import of each work of hagiography – and especially those of the eighth and ninth centuries – it is necessary to recognise its place in the chains of *Lives* to which it is linked – noting the extent to which it is either adding to or rejecting a previously stated position.

   Yet, while the hagiography of missionaries in this period is interconnected, it does not amount to an isolable literary or devotional form. There is nothing that one can call a genre of missionary hagiography. To begin with, the subject matter is more varied than the single term 'missionary' suggests. Indeed, there is no classical or medieval Latin word *missionarius*: the category of 'missionary' is not an early medieval one, but rather a modern catch-all, in which religious figures of various kinds have been enshrined. Of course, texts can and do ignore differences between their subjects, but the *vitae* themselves are far more varied in form and content than a single classification would suggest.[1] They are united by being connected one to another, through citation and reminiscence, but (except in specific instances) not by form – other than the general one of hagiography – or even intent. For all the citations of previous 'missionary' hagiography, the intentions of the hagiographers were varied, as were the expectations of their audiences.

The notions of 'missionary hagiography' and even of 'the missionary' are constructs which may be very useful categories in certain contexts, but they should also be recognised for what they are. The categories should certainly not get in the way of an analysis of the precise nature of the career of the individual 'missionary', or of the individual requirements of his or her hagiographer, and of the intended audience of the resulting *vita*.

## 2. AUDIENCES AND INTENTIONS

The hagiographers we have considered varied widely in their intentions and in the audience or rather audiences – for they did not limit themselves to one – which they were addressing. At the highest social limit, Gumpold's *Passio Vencezlavi* was written for Otto II, and seems to have been something of a mirror of princes. Strictly speaking, of course, none of the Wenceslas *Lives* are concerned with a missionary – although they are concerned with a king's attempt to deepen the Christianity of a society. For royal involvement in the composition of hagiography of a missionary saint, one can still turn to the *Vita* of Adalbert of Prague by John Canaparius, which seems to have been commissioned by Otto III. One section of it has been described as a *Fürstenspiegel*.[2] It is, moreover, likely that the *Life* by Canaparius influenced Otto in his views of the need for missions to the Slavs and beyond.

Other texts about saints who have been seen as missionaries also connect with royal or imperial policy, although not necessarily with missionary policy. Factional propaganda in favour of the Carolingians creeps into Willibald's *Vita Bonifatii*, where the Thuringian leaders, Heden and Theobald, are portrayed as semi-pagan.[3] Similar impressions are given of the family of Gozbert, in Würzburg, by the author of the *Passio Kiliani*,[4] while the Agilolfings in Arbeo's *Lives* of Emmeram and Corbinian have serious moral failings.[5] The Bavarians themselves are described as mixing idolatory and the mass.[6] Together, the criticisms of the ruling dynasties of Hesse, Thuringia and Bavaria amount to a demonising of the opponents of the Carolingians – and the demonisation has been remarkably successful down to modern times. Although Willibald wrote for Bishops Lull of Mainz and Megingoz of Würzburg, while Arbeo wrote at the request of Bishop Virgil of Salzburg, given these political critiques, it is possible that both hagiographers expected their works to reach a wider audience, which included secular leaders.

Bishops also had political concerns which are reflected in the texts associated with mission: most obviously there is the *Conversio Bagoariorum et Carantanorum*, prepared by or for Bishop Adalwin of Salzburg at the time of the trial of Methodius. In addition, there is the letter of Adalwin's successor,

Theotmar. These, of course, are not *vitae*, although the *Conversio* includes hagiographical elements, notably in its accounts of Rupert[7] and of the priest Ingo.[8] Further, as we have seen, the pattern of writing up the history of the Church of Salzburg may have derived in some way from one developed in Ireland, and most obviously exemplified in Tírechán's *Life of Patrick*.

The *Conversio* is concerned chiefly with jurisdiction, as are a number of other pieces of eighth- and ninth-century hagiography. Willibald's *Life of Boniface* seems to have been concerned, among other things, to promote the importance of the saint as diocesan founder – an image which does not appear to have been popular in Bavaria. Certainly, the jurisdiction of the archbishops of Mainz was something that concerned Eigil in his *Life of Sturm*, although there the crucial point was to deny the authority of the archbishops over the monastery of Fulda. Ecclesiastical jurisdiction is yet more central to Rimbert's *Life of Anskar*, where documentation for the amalgamation of the dioceses of Hamburg and Bremen lies at the very heart of the text.[9]

The earliest surviving manuscript of Rimbert's work may have been a presentation copy, written for Bishop Solomon of Konstanz, who played a crucial role in securing papal approval for the amalgamation of the two dioceses.[10] Yet Rimbert dedicated the *Vita Anskarii* to the monastery of Corbie. His work was to be more than a work about jurisdiction: it has strong monastic concerns. A large number of *Lives* of saints who have been categorised as missionaries are addressed to monks or monastic communities. Alongside the *Vita Anskarii* are Alcuin's *Vita Willibrordi*, Eigil's *Life of Sturm*, and the *Vita Rimberti*. Of course, monks could be missionaries, and while Alcuin's named audience is that of the abbot and community of Echternach, it is fairly clear that he was addressing this group as potential missionaries, and, indeed, that he was supplying them with a model for missionary work.

Alcuin is the earliest hagiographer who can be identified as making mission the central issue of a piece of hagiography – although he may have been foreshadowed by one or other *Life of Amandus* in so doing. He was not, though, a missionary himself. Some of the hagiography he inspired, on the other hand, was written by missionaries, most notably the *Life of Gregory* by Liudger. The *Life of Anskar* by Rimbert, and the *Life of Adalbert* by Bruno of Querfurt share the same strengths. These texts, in which mission is described by individuals active in the field, bring us face to face with missionary experience. In one case, Liudger's *Life of Gregory*, the author seems to have used a work of hagiography to deal with his own concerns, and in so doing created a rather curious text which in parts comes closer to fantasy than to history, but which might better be seen as being a displaced autobiography of Liudger himself. In Rimbert's *Life of Anskar* there appears to be no such slippage between the interests of the author and those of the subject, although those interests reflect Anskar's later years rather than the period of his initial successes. The closest association of author and subject matter, however, comes in the works of Bruno of Querfurt. Comparison between his *Passio* of Adalbert of Prague and the *vita* written by John Canaparius, which he had read, shows him exploring certain concerns which crop up in his other writings, but which are either absent from or less pronounced in the earlier account. These concerns may well have been Adalbert's, and they were certainly Bruno's. The *Life of the Five Brothers* comes yet closer to being the autobiography of a missionary, since the hagiographer alternates between describing his fears and the anguish of Benedict and John. Bruno's letter to Henry goes one degree further, and provides a fully fledged account of mission in the first person.

The personal involvement in mission of a number of our hagiographers means that we can come close to understanding some of the emotional and psychological problems experienced by missionaries in the field. Moreover, this evidence can be expanded by consideration of other of our hagiographical texts, and of a number of non-hagiographical works, which help to define the cultural perceptions with which the missionaries were working.

## 3. THE 'OTHER': IMAGINED AND REAL

Christians were brought up to think that there might be pagans living amongst them. Hagiographical and canonical texts speak of paganism surviving within the borders of the Frankish and Anglo-Saxon kingdoms, and certain superstitious practices clearly did survive in those regions. Nevertheless, there is a strong case for interpreting much of what is described as pagan in those regions as being syncretism, deviant Christianity or even simply political propaganda.[11] In newly converted states, on the other hand, there probably was considerable pagan survival. Gumpold shows Wenceslas avoiding pagan ceremonies.[12] According to John Canaparius, many who were called Christian in Slavonia actually lived as pagans.[13] Similar confusion of paganism and Christianity is noted by Bruno of Querfurt in Hungary.[14] Such a comment on a Christian country is not far from that of Widukind, who described the Danes, before the conversion of Harald Bluetooth, and thus before the official Christianisation of his people, as having long been Christian, but worshipping idols.[15] A state just before Christianisation might not be so different, the household of the ruler apart, from a state just after. And in marital practices, at least, even rulers – perhaps rulers in particular – continued to ignore the Christian canons.

Although the continuance, real or supposed, of some pagan practice within Christian regions, ought to have meant that paganism was not completely unknown to the Christians, there were those who regarded the pagan world beyond the frontiers as being alien – although others, including merchants, may well have thought otherwise. Augustine famously came close to abandoning his mission to Kent because of fear of the unknown – in the imagination of the missionaries sent by Gregory, the English were a barbarous, savage and unbelieving people who spoke a language they could not understand.[16] When Anskar offered to join Harald Klak in 826, he was understood to be going to work among the unknown and the barbarians, *cum ignotis ac barbaris*, according to Rimbert.[17] His willingness to go was supposedly a matter of surprise – although it is said to have caused less consternation than did the willingness of Autbert, who was of noble birth, to accompany him: young aristocrats should not go as evangelists to pagan kingdoms. Yet the mission which they were prepared to undertake was only to the kingdom of the Danes, which bordered the Carolingian Empire. Mission to the Swedes is categorised by Rimbert, using a phrase of Jeremiah, as going to the ends of the earth.[18] Mission to the world's end automatically carried apocalyptic overtones, for Matthew 24, 14 announces: 'And this gospel of the kingdom shall be preached in all the world for a witness unto all nations; and then shall the end come.'

Mission in a pagan country was, therefore, thought of as involving a confrontation with the 'Other'. Sometimes what was envisaged was an armchair exercise of the sort embarked on by the author of the *Vita Altera Bonifatii* in describing the population of northern Frisia.[19] Yet encounters with the 'Other' were not just literary fantasies. Before becoming bishop of Passau, Ermenrich could consider the pagan gods as part of an intellectual exercise, and could analyse the word *Vulgáres* simply in terms of having the same stress pattern as *Amazónes* – a standard rule in barbarian nomenclature, *in barbaris nominibus*, he claims.[20] Yet he became bishop of a diocese which had pastoral responsibilities among the Moravians, and was sent on a mission to the Bulgars.

The alien nature of pagans might be unpleasant, but innocuous. The Slavs whom Sturm came across as he went in search of the perfect site for his monastery were merely naked and smelly.[21] They, however, were discovered in Carolingian territory. Pagans in their own territories could be terrifying. Bruno of Querfurt described the Petschenegs, among whom he had worked, and for whom he had negotiated peace with the Russian ruler Vladimir, as the worst and cruellest of peoples.[22]

Such terms do not convey the extent to which some areas of mission were thought to differ from the Christian world. Here it may well be that Germanic, and even Slavonic society, was less alien to missionaries, than was that of the Prussians.[23] In the account of John Canaparius, the Prussians snarled at Adalbert as if they were dogs.[24] According to Bruno, some were indeed dog-headed.[25] He also records that Adalbert was frightened by what he took to be the sound of a sea-monster.[26] By the time he revised his version of the *Passio Adalberti* in 1008 Bruno was already in Poland, and had probably heard accounts of what had been witnessed by Adalbert's companion and half-brother, Gaudentius, who had been archbishop of Gniezno from 1000 to 1006.[27] His statement is, therefore, that of a man close to good sources of information, and about to enter the very mission field where Adalbert had been martyred. It is not the fantasy of someone dreaming of aliens he will never meet.

Yet dog-headed men are not confined to Prussia: they are a recurrent feature of writings about the Baltic and beyond. They were probably used as bogeymen, with tales of their existence being circulated to frighten enemies.[28] On the other hand there may have been groups of individuals who were known as *cynocephali*,[29] and they may have distinguished themselves by wearing dog-masks, such as those found in the harbour at Haithabu.[30] While the masks may have been used by a specific group of men, the term seems to have been applied more generally: in Notker's *Gesta Karoli* the term *cynocephalus* is used by Charlemagne to refer to the Danes.[31] The longest, and most important discussion of the *cynocephali*, is by Ratramnus of Corbie, who had been asked by Rimbert whether they had souls or not.[32] The latter had heard that he was likely to come across such beings in the course of his missionary work, and wanted to know whether or not they should be saved. Ratramnus replied by rejecting Isidore's classification of the *cynocephali* on the strength of the information passed to him by Rimbert. Since the latter had heard that they lived according to custom in *villae* or villages, that they practised arable agriculture and that they wore clothes, they were clearly rational. In any case, since St Christopher had been a *cynocephalus* it was clear that they were human.

This letter is certainly not a farrago of nonsense. Ratramnus is responding to what he considers to be good information, from a man who thought he would meet a *cynocephalus* at any moment. In his reply to Rimbert he used what are recognisably the same as modern anthropological categories of the cultivated and the natural to decide whether a *cynocephalus* was man or beast. Indeed, because it was physically part human and part dog, the monster itself was an ideal subject on which to hang a discussion of the limits of humanity – and that is clearly what both Rimbert and Ratramnus were concerned with: when did the 'Other' become so alien that there was no need to include it in the field of mission?

Ratramnus came to the conclusion that the *cynocephali* were human. The eighth-century author known as Aethicus Ister was not so sure. He also describes the society in which they live, but ultimately categorises them in terms which recall the Abominations of Leviticus.[33] The *Cosmography* of

Aethicus has been regarded as a comic attack on Boniface by Virgil of Salzburg.[34] The identification of the work as comic is probably erroneous – although the author may well have had a sense of humour: there appear to be citations of his work in the hagiography of Arbeo of Freising,[35] and Aethicus was thought to be spiritual enough to be quoted on the Hereford altarpiece of the thirteenth century known as the *Mappa Mundi*.[36] The attribution of the *Cosmography* to Virgil is also questionable. Yet the work was certainly circulating in Bavaria in Virgil's time,[37] and it may be connected in some way with Boniface's claim that Virgil had been arguing that there was another world and other men under the earth.[38] It may also have prompted the equally curious claim, in the *Life* of the Byzantine missionary Constantine, that German clergy believed that men with large heads lived under the earth.[39] One way of interpreting the *Cosmography* of Aethicus Ister, together with the criticisms levelled against Virgil by Boniface and against the German clergy by Constantine, is to see them all as relating to the same underlying issue as that discussed by Ratramnus: where were the limits of humanity?

If one reads these fragments of information in this way, it becomes clear that the missionaries thought that they were working in territory inhabited by beings who stood on either side of the divide between man and beast. Such regions were truly alien, and it is no wonder that Rimbert sought guidance from Ratramnus. Of course, the missionaries usually dealt with rather more normal beings, but it is important to recognise that they were prepared to come face to face with some very marginal creatures.

## 4. PAGANISMS AND SUPERSTITIONS

Pagans were constructed in the minds of the missionaries as the 'Other'. Getting far beyond these subjective constructions is rarely possible. Although we have already considered the varied nature of the paganisms that confronted Christians, it is useful to bring together some of the detail we have encountered in previous chapters. Germanic paganism has often been reconstructed from those myths which were set down in writing in Iceland in the thirteenth century by Snorri Sturluson.[40] As a result, a good deal is known of the myths associated with Donar, Wodan and Frija (and their variants). Yet although many of the stories Snorri records are undoubtedly of great antiquity, it is dangerous to assume that knowledge of them was spread over the whole Germanic world – although Snorri presents a pantheon, it is probably made up of gods and goddesses whose cults originated at different times and in different places. One cannot conclude from thirteenth-century evidence that there was a pan-Germanic religion. Some

253

gods remained of regional significance, even into the eighth century: thus the cult of Fosite, which is better represented in our sources than any other, seems to have been confined to Helgoland – and Fosite himself is otherwise unknown.[41] The cults of other gods seem to have been more widely spread in geographical terms, but they may not have been revered by all classes of the population: Wodan may well have been primarily a god of warriors. Chronology, geography and even social division are factors which need to be kept under consideration when assessing the existence of religious beliefs.[42] Similar cautions are necessary when assessing the beliefs of the pagan Slavs.[43] Further, even if one does have a record of the myths or beliefs of a people, there is also a problem in determining the precise function of those beliefs within religious practice.

Little is known of the religious practices associated with any cult, at least between the fifth and the ninth centuries. Cult sites are rarely associated with particular gods in our sources – that of Fosite is unusual.[44] Temples are also rare in the literary record concerning Germanic paganism, although there are a number of references to *fana*, shrines, which were presumably of no great size.[45] Archaeology has also failed to prove the existence of large temples in the Germanic area – but there is abundant archaeological evidence for Slav temples from the Carolingian period onwards, which suggests that the negative evidence is of some significance.

The exceptions in the literary record may have very specific explanations. Thus Bede does talk of at least two temples in Anglo-Saxon England,[46] and in doing so he seems to be backed up by the evidence of Gregory the Great.[47] The fact that there are no equivalent descriptions for the region east of the Rhine may suggest that the Anglo-Saxons developed the use of temples in Britain because of the presence of churches, and even of Roman temples. Perhaps significantly, one of the temples mentioned by Bede, that used by Rædwald, had a altar dedicated to Christ and another for offerings to demons.[48] Otherwise, one has to wait for Adam of Bremen's description, written in the late eleventh century, of the great temple dedicated to Thor (Donar), Wodan and Frikko (identified with Frija) at Uppsala.[49] To what extent his description is accurate is wide open to question: archaeology has so far provided no support, and Adam is known to have let ecclesiastical bias distort his judgement over other issues.[50] Besides, even if Uppsala did boast a great temple in the eleventh century, this may have been inspired by Slavonic buildings or even Christian churches: it might tell us nothing of Germanic religion in the Carolingian period or earlier.

It is, however, unquestionable that there were sacred places, although these seem to have been natural features, groves and springs, rather than buildings.[51] Most famously there is Jupiter's oak at Geismar.[52] In Frisia paganism, or sacrifice at least, seems to have been closely associated with water, and tides[53] – not surprising, perhaps, in view of the landscape, but an indication of how much local natural features may have dominated religious practice. There were also idols[54] – although those which have come from bog finds tend to belong to the pre-Roman Iron Age,[55] while the later figures tend to be what one might call statuettes.[56]

As with temples, so it is with priests. There is a distinct lack of priestly figures in the literary sources, with the exception of the histories of Bede[57] and Adam,[58] although their existence is implied by linguistics.[59] That there were some major public cults is, however, indicated by Thietmar, who records an annual sacrifice of ninety-nine men, horses, dogs and cocks at Lejre on Sjælland, to appease the infernal gods. This practice supposedly continued up until the time of the German king Henry I.[60] The description is not unlike that of Adam's account of the goings on at Uppsala, albeit without the temple or the priests. Mention of sacrifice does occur in other sources, and Boniface even speaks of Christians selling slaves to pagans for sacrifice.[61]

More common than sacrifice in the written record are references to public acts of lot-casting, for instance to determine the fate of those responsible for the desecration of religious sites,[62] or to discover whether or not the gods favoured a particular enterprise.[63] For these rituals there must have been presiding figures who effectively took on a priestly function: in the *Vita Willibrordi* this role was taken by Radbod.[64] It may be that there was no significant priesthood in the Germanic world, because religious functions fell automatically to political leaders or heads of households. This was probably the case in Iceland, where temples seem to have been integral to farm complexes.[65]

Much more common than references to public cults are those of rituals performed within the home, especially superstitious practices intended to secure health, good harvests and the like. Such superstitious acts are the butt of endless ecclesiastical legislation, whereas there is little or no condemnation of public pagan cults. The implication seems to be, not surprisingly, that public paganism collapsed very early in the process of Christianisation – certainly once a region ceased to be ruled by pagans – but that private superstition proved very much harder to extirpate.[66] Indeed the 'handlist' of pagan practices produced within Bonifatian circles, the *Indiculus superstitionum et paganiarum*,[67] is a list of practices performed within the Christian world, and it includes sacrifices to Christian saints – suggesting at this level of belief very considerable syncretism.[68]

The evidence for Slavonic paganism up to the eleventh century contrasts dramatically with what is known of Germanic religion. Although much of the literary documentation for pagan sites and practices among the Slavs relates either to the missions of Otto of Bamberg or to the Baltic crusades,

Thietmar included an extensive account of the paganism of the Liutizi, in the context of their alliance with Henry II against the Poles in 1005.[69] In particular, he describes the city, *urbs*, of Riedegost, which appears in Adam of Bremen as Rethra.[70] The place was surrounded by a triangular wall with three towers. On two sides lay a sacred forest, on the third was the sea. The only building inside was a wooden temple, decorated on the outside with images of gods. Inside there were idols, notably of Zuarasici. There too the military banners of the people were kept.[71] The temple was guarded by *ministri*, appointed by the locals, who cast lots, which were then trampled on by a sacred white horse, in order to determine sacrifices and other major actions.[72] Although other temples and idols were to be found elsewhere in the domains of the Liutizi, that at Riedegost was the chief one, and it was there that offerings – including human and animal sacrifices – were made to the gods after war.[73]

There is nothing in any early description of Germanic paganism to equal this, although there are similar accounts for other sites in the Slavonic world, most notably for the temple at Arkona on Rügen.[74] Further, such literary accounts are fully backed up by archaeological finds,[75] which include very extensive temple complexes and major cult objects. All this must suggest that in its public manifestations the paganism of the Slavs was entirely unlike that of the Germanic peoples – except, perhaps in its latest, eleventh century, phases – and that religion and religious practices played a somewhat different role within Slavonic social and political structures. Existence of substantial temples with appointed guardians alone must have required the allocation of major resources – and must have created strongly entrenched interests. It is not, perhaps, surprising that the Christianisation of the Northern Slavs, at least, followed a very different pattern from that of the Germanic peoples, necessitating a series of violent crusades. Why Bohemian and Polish paganism should have collapsed so peacefully, and so early, is an unanswerable point – although presumably neither had developed in the same way as had that of the Liutizi, before their close encounter with Christianity.

## 5. STRATEGIES OF MISSION

Paganism was, therefore, many things, and it must have required many strategies to combat it. These were determined at the most basic level by the political situation. Was Christianisation being enforced in the context of war? In this case the destruction of pagan cult sites could be a military aim. Were missions being encouraged by a ruler already inclining towards conversion? Or was the missionary out on a limb, alone in potentially hostile territory?

In the Early Middle Ages missionaries rarely involved themselves in military action. As a result, their main task tended to involve persuasion. Alcuin, and those who followed his approach, stressed the need for preaching. Exactly what was preached is unclear, although we do have a letter from Daniel of Winchester telling Boniface how to argue with pagans: first show that, even by their own reckoning, their gods had a beginning: then turn to the question of the benefits they convey, before asking how it is that Christians can cast down their idols without being punished.[76] The sermon attributed to Eligius of Noyon suggests that a certain amount of basic Christian doctrine was also expounded, at least in mission areas within the Frankish kingdom.[77] Ratramnus' response to Rimbert apart, our evidence for the discussion and formulation of missionary practice suggests a relatively prosaic approach to the pagan – and indeed Ratramnus is nothing if not level-headed in his discussion of the *cynocephali*. After teaching came baptism, which involved a catechism forswearing the pagan gods.[78] The extent to which preaching and baptism were combined with or came after a display of force depended on the circumstances in which the evangelisation took place.

Preaching must normally have been in the vernacular: certainly the surviving baptismal oaths are. Language, however, is rarely mentioned as an issue, although Gregory the Great took care to ensure that Augustine had interpreters with him when he went to England.[79] Bede also mentions that King Oswald initially helped interpret for Aidan,[80] while the reason given for splitting up the diocese of Agilbert of Wessex was that, as a Frank, he was unintelligible to the king.[81] Language was, of course, a major issue between Methodius and his critics, but only with regard to the language of the mass, not to that of preaching. German clerics were well aware of the need to preach in the vernacular. The importance of fluency in Slavonic is fully stated by Bruno of Querfurt: Benedict and John went out of their way to learn the language, and encouraged Bruno to do so as well.[82] Boso of Merseburg had already attempted to teach in Slavonic, but ended up making a mockery of the *Kyrie Eleison*, since he was understood as saying that the alder stands in a bush.[83] Adalbert of Prague was a native Slavonic speaker – although this did not help him among the Prussians, who were Balts rather than Slavs, and indeed he is said to have resolved to abandon the Prussian mission in favour of a mission to the Liutizi, whose language he could understand, but was killed before he could do anything about it.[84]

Mastery of the local language and the preparation of material for preaching were issues that a missionary could address in advance, but new issues were inevitably thrown up in the course of mission. Gregory the Great had to advise Augustine on a series of issues, including the treatment of pagan temples.[85] The issues raised by Augustine were thorny, and they prompted

257

some hard thinking on the part of Gregory,[86] but they were not life and death matters, since Æthelbehrt had sanctioned the mission, even if he had not himself already converted. Augustine was not working in a hostile environment.

## 6. STRATEGIES OF SURVIVAL, NEW AND FAMILIAR

The situation faced by Adalbert of Prague was somewhat different. Working among the Prussians, he was in a totally alien environment, which terrified him. At the same time he himself stuck out like a sore thumb. When he and his companions arrived in Prussia they were quickly identified as being from another world, dressed in strange clothes and practising unheard-of rituals: *ex alio orbe, ignoto habitu et inaudito cultu*.[87] As outsiders, they were criticised as being the cause of natural disasters.[88] What is particularly interesting about this is that it marks an attempt to understand pagan thought in a more subtle way than did Daniel of Winchester when he told Boniface to turn pagan statements about the genealogies of their gods into opportunities to show that they had a beginning and were thus secondary beings.[89] In giving the Prussians a speech in which they criticised the Christians, Bruno was going one step further than Rimbert had done, when he put words into the mouth of a Swede, who had supposedly been at a gathering of gods who gave him this message:

> You have long had us as favourable to you, and you held the land where you live, in abundance, with our help, in peace and prosperity for a long time. You offered sacrifices and due obligations to us, and your services were pleasing to us. But now you take away the accustomed sacrifices and make spontaneous offerings more sluggishly, and what displeases us more, you introduce another god over us. If you wish us to be favourable to you, increase the sacrifices you have left undone and make more offerings. Do not accept the cult of another god whose teachings are contrary to us, and do not act in his service. On the other hand, if you wish to have more gods, and we are not sufficient for you, we have unanimously accepted your one-time king Eric into our college, that he may be one in the number of gods.[90]

This quite extraordinary speech, whose closing offer may sound to us a little comic, is an attempt by a missionary to understand the thought processes of pagans who did not accept the Christian message.

Adalbert's reaction in an equivalent situation was, according to Bruno, to reconsider his missionary style, and to suggest that he and his companions should abandon their clerical garb and adopt the local hairstyle. They should earn their own keep, and thus integrate themselves into society. This would supposedly make their work easier.[91] With this in mind, Adalbert determined to set off for the Liutizi, among whom it would be easier for him and his companions to pass themselves off as natives, *mutata veste et habitu*, because they had not already set eyes on them, and because in any case he could speak their language.[92]

The ideas expressed by Bruno are not in Canaparius' version of the *Passio Adalberti*, and they may be the hagiographer's own theory – although, equally, they may have been reported to him while he was in Poland. Certainly, they reflect strategies that Bruno considers elsewhere. He reports that Benedict and John decided to go native in preparation for their Prussian mission: they learnt Slavonic, shaved their heads, and wore clothing appropriate to secular males, so as not to put the pagans off.[93] Whether the policy would have worked is another matter: Peter Damian states that when Bruno himself turned up at the court of the king of the Russians in rags he was laughed at, but when he put on vestments he was thought to be vain.[94] Damian certainly mistakes the setting in which Bruno was working, but he may be right to identify clothing as an issue at the time of the saint's martyrdom. Wibert, who claims to have been present with Bruno in Prussia, states that the saint underwent an ordeal by fire wearing his vestments.[95]

Clothing and lifestyle could pull in different ways. Going native could be seen as living the simple life of the early Church. When Bruno makes Adalbert claim that they should feed themselves by the work of their own hands, he acknowledges the apostolic model: *laborando quoque manibus propriis, victum quaeremus ad instar apostolorum*.[96] The reference is to I Corinthians 4, 12: 'And labour, working with our own hands'. It is a recurrent image in the history of mission. Bede presents the life-style of Augustine and his companions at Canterbury in exactly the same manner.[97] The same image is associated with Amandus.[98] Willibald describes Boniface likewise,[99] as does Liudger in his account of the work of Boniface and Gregory.[100] The anonymous author of the *Life of Cuthbert* links such manual labour with Paul's Second Letter to the Thessalonians, 3, 10: 'For even when we were with you, this we commanded you, that if any would not work, neither should he eat.'[101] In discussing Anskar's commitment to manual work, Rimbert, on the other hand, cites I Thessalonians 4, 11: 'And that ye study to be quiet, and to do your own business, and to work with your own hands, as we commanded you'.[102] And there was another model for the practice in the Rule of St Benedict, which is cited by Willibald in his *Life of Boniface*.[103]

The life-style of the early Christian communities was a model which was cited regularly within both monastic and missionary circles, and from Adalbert's point of view it may well have seemed to be practical. Nevertheless, missionaries could not live in exactly the same way as the native populations around them. However much they tried to disguise the fact, they were aliens, and scarcely had access to the same resources of land, food, or support from kin. In any case, the Christians could not simply adopt a life-style indistinguishable from that of the pagans around them because of the demands of their own religion. In Bruno's account Adalbert, having set out the need to live off one's own work, added that he and his companions should meditate on the psalms secretly: *absconsa mente revolvimus censum psalmorum*.[104] Such contemplation could be carried out without anyone noticing. So too could prayer, and Patrick, for one, prayed regularly when first in Ireland.[105] But a priest ought also to celebrate mass. While the apostolic life-style might have seemed to allow the missionary to go native, ritual requirements meant that the Christian was almost inevitably distinctive.

It is notable how often ritual or ritual objects occur in descriptions of martyrdoms or in the run-up to them. Bede states that what alerted the pagans to the fact that the Hewalds practised a different religion was the simple point that they were continually singing psalms and praying, and that each day they celebrated mass, having with them liturgical vessels and a makeshift altar. Having noticed these practices, the pagans murdered them, before they could influence the local satrap.[106] Boniface was killed, prior to a ceremony of mass baptism, supposedly holding a book.[107] More certainly, the manuscripts with him were scattered in the mud by his killers.[108] Both John Canaparius and Bruno note that Adalbert had taken communion shortly before his martyrdom,[109] but they also note that, when he was first attacked by the Prussians, he dropped a manuscript.[110] Bruno tells us himself, that while waiting on the borders of Russia to evangelise the Petschenegs, he carried a cross and sang hymns to St Peter.[111] According to Wibert, he subsequently insisted on undergoing an ordeal by fire in full vestments, sitting on his *cathedra*.[112]

Rituals and ritual objects seem to have provided flashpoints which were a cause of martyrdom. Of course, the association may have been made by the hagiographer, for martyrdom was itself sacramental. Nevertheless, liturgical objects and religious rituals may well have been of particular importance to the missionaries themselves. It is as if they were fragments of the regular life they knew at home, to which they clung when in an alien environment. Augustine and his companions are famously supposed to have entered Canterbury carrying a cross and singing an anthem.[113] Lebuin is said to have appeared at Marklo wearing full vestments.[114] Anskar is noted as celebrating mass just before a major meeting to determine whether he would be able to work in Sweden.[115] Books recur regularly in accounts of the work of missionaries, actual and supposed.[116] A considerable list can be set along-side those already mentioned from the course of martyr narratives. There are the books and vestments which were buried with Kilian.[117] Willehad is noted as having copied the Epistles of Peter while at Echternach.[118] Books recur in Liudger's *Life of Gregory*,[119] and the hagiographer himself is associated with manuscripts and their production.[120] Anskar was devastated at the loss, in the course of the sack of Hamburg, of the library which had been given to him by the emperor Louis the Pious.[121] In Birka, a manuscript, which was stolen after the martyrdom of the priest Nithard, was the cause of disaster among the thief's family.[122] And there is the missal of the Five Brothers, one of a number of manuscripts given to them by Otto III, which was divided between their killers.[123] All this can, no doubt, be seen as a reflection of the manuscript culture of the Carolingian and Ottonian periods, but set in the missionary context it seems to be more than that. Boniface wrote to Abbess Eadburga, asking her for a copy of the Epistles of Peter, written in gold, both to impress the pagans and to keep the apostle's words ever before him.[124] Boniface was working at the time within the bounds of Frankish influence. For those further from home Bibles and liturgical books – like the ritual of the mass, and, indeed, like prayer – linked their owners with the Christian societies they had left, and thus provided reassurance in an alien world. They added to the feeling of living the life of the early Church.

## 7. VISIONS AS SPIRITUAL CONSOLATION

Books, liturgical objects, rituals and prayer all provided psychological aids for the missionary – yet more was needed to alleviate the stress of work in the field. Just as books recur in our sources, so too do visions.[125] This is already apparent in the *Confessio* of Patrick, where they punctuate the major moments in the development of the saint's vocation. He has a vision telling him to escape from Ireland,[126] another in the course of his escape,[127] and a third instructing him to return to the Forest of Foclut to evangelise his erstwhile neighbours.[128] According to Jonas of Bobbio, Columbanus decided not to pursue the idea of evangelising the Slavs after experiencing a vision in which an angel appeared to him, and showed him a globe marked with desert areas.[129] Closer to the experience of Patrick, almost every stage of Anskar's career was marked by a vision, according to Rimbert,[130] and since one which the saint took to foretell his martyrdom appeared at first sight not to have been fulfilled, it seems likely that the saint genuinely did have the visions set down by the hagiographer.[131] Further, Rimbert's own hagiographer insists that the saint was guided both by Anskar's visions and his own.[132]

The visions of Patrick, Anskar and Rimbert have, on the whole, a consolatory function, and even the vision which Anskar took to predict his martyrdom was regarded by the saint as a consolation. Visions also punctuate the *Lives* of Ludmila and Wenceslas, and while they do not concern a call to mission, they do foretell martyrdom[133] – although here the image is rather less reassuring than in the case of Anskar, since the death of Ludmila was also a prelude to persecution. The emphasis on martyrdom is equally strong in the visions associated with Adalbert of Prague. Leaving aside the tormented dream of his predecessor in the see of Prague,[134] and a vision exposing the sin of Otto II in destroying the see of Merseburg,[135] the majority of the visions recorded by John Canaparius and Bruno relate to the martyrdom of the saint, or deaths in his family. The vast majority were experienced by Adalbert himself,[136] but one was seen by Gaudentius[137] and another by Canaparius in Rome.[138] The dreams and visions of the two *Passiones* of Adalbert have a literary function, in that they forewarn the reader of the glorious martyrdom to come. On the other hand they can also be read as indicative of the stresses of the missionary life.

## 8. THE SHIFT IN THE MIRACULOUS

Visions were usually souces of consolation for missionaries, even though those of martyrdom may not always seem to be so: for the saint martyrdom was a reward, however unpleasant the prior physical pain. Another source of consolation was the miraculous – yet here the pressure of events changed the way in which miracles were understood, and indeed the expectations which they raised.

Gregory the Great had been very clear that conversion and the miraculous went hand in hand.[139] In this he was basing himself on Paul's First Letter to the Corinthians, 14, 22: 'Wherefore tongues are for a sign, not to them that believe, but to them that believe not: but prophesying serveth not for them that believe not, but for them which believe.'[140] Miracles could help in the destruction of idols, and they had a greater role to play in strengthening the faith of new converts than in reassuring established believers.[141] In arguing this he was not asserting that conversion itself was a miracle, although that was also a point of view that he held.[142] Since Gregory set out his opinion in the years immediately prior to Augustine's mission to England it is not surprising that the new archbishop of Canterbury was soon reporting on the occurrence of wonder-working.[143] The pope was clearly not surprised by his reports, but told Augustine to be quiet about the miracles, for fear of vainglory.[144]

Gregory set out what was to be a basic assumption about the role of the miraculous up to the time of Bede and beyond. Alcuin took what was essentially a Gregorian stance, in the very heart of the *Vita Willibrordi*, in describing the miraculous as less important than preaching, but nevertheless as being worthy of note.[145] In this he was followed almost verbatim by Altfrid in his *Vita Liudgeri*.[146] Yet those miracles in the *Life of Willibrord* which relate to Christianisation – as opposed to the miracles relating to the established Christian landscape of the Moselle – tend not to prompt conversion so much as to protect God's agents when under threat from pagans.[147] Liudger seems to have had a similar understanding.[148] In this respect one miracle recorded by Altfrid, that of the cure and conversion of the blind bard, Bernlef, is rather closer to the Gregorian model.[149]

In general, however, this was clearly under some strain. Rimbert certainly failed to follow the model set out by Gregory the Great. While there are miracle stories in the *Vita Anskarii*, they do not concern the saint himself. For the most part they relate to the Christian community left in Birka after one of the pagan backlashes,[150] although in terms of the working of the casting of lots, they also acted in such a way as to influence the action of pagans.[151] Thus the Christian *praefectus*, Herigar, outdid the pagan leaders in a competition reminiscent of Elijah and the prophets of Baal.[152] He was also the beneficiary of a miraculous cure. One Christian lady, who left Birka to give alms in Dorestad, found her purse miraculously replenished.[153] In a miracle closer to the divine vengeance stories of Alcuin, a codex stolen after the death of the priest Nithard wrought havoc on the thief's family.[154]

That the function of the miraculous was now more closely associated with the consolation of those under stress is made even more apparent in Anskar's own account of the miracles which took place at Willehad's tomb around the year 860. The hagiographer prefaces his work with a statement that numerous miracles had been worked in the current period of disaster caused by pagan onslaughts, and he sees the events as encouraging people to return to their homes despite the devastation.[155]

From being an aspect of the process of Christianisation the miraculous had become necessary consolation for those Christians under threat. It is difficult not to conclude that the changing function of miracles was related to setbacks to Christianisation which occurred in the late eighth and ninth centuries, not least those associated with the Saxons and the Vikings. While Christianity was expanding, its successes could be associated with the workings of the divine. When it was under threat, those same workings were directed at reassuring the Christians. In a sense, the miraculous was analogous to the vision, which provided solace for the individual missionary, especially for the missionary who sought martyrdom. Rimbert's allocation of visions to Anskar on the one hand and miracles to the Christian community in Birka on the other, are two sides of the same coin.

Exactly where one places the interpretation of miracles offered in the *Vita Altera Bonifatii* depends on the date given to the text in its current state, and the closing section of the text could belong to a secondary recension. Although the author admits to the occurrence of miracles, he originally omitted any discussion of them, much to the fury of his readers.[156] As a result of the complaints, he responded that the apostles worked signs and prodigies, but that conversion was worked internally: *Signa quidem et prodigia fecerunt apostoli; sed intus erat qui operabatur, intus qui moderabatur quique ydolatras et incredulos trahent ad fidem.*[157] His interest was in the cure of the inner man, and he resolutely refused to provide his audience with the information that they wanted.

## 9. CONFESSIONAL WRITING

It may be that the act of writing should also be included in this context of stress and the need for consolation. Missionaries wrote works both of hagiography and of autobiography – and some certainly did so under stress. Patrick clearly felt that he needed to justify himself in writing the *Confessio*, which is a personal document as much as it is a public statement. So too, Bruno went out of his way to acknowledge his own faults in the *Life of the Five Brothers* – which was not a work destined for much, if any, public circulation. The letter to Henry II comes nearest to providing a public autobiography.

The sixth to eighth centuries, when missions on the whole were successful, boast little in the way of autobiography or indeed writing of any sort by missionaries – although it is striking that Gregory of Tours claims that most of his account of Vulfolaic's missionary activity is composed in the stylite's own words,[158] while Jonas of Bobbio provides an account of his own work with Amandus in the dedicatory letter of the *Vita Columbani*.[159] After Patrick one has apparently to wait until the early ninth century before there is an account of mission by a missionary, and the result, Liudger's *Life of Gregory*, is interesting in that the narrative does not seem to be an accurate account of the work of either Boniface or Gregory: instead it looks more like a peg on which Liudger hung his own concerns. Rimbert appears to have written a more accurate account of Anskar – at least in terms of his later years – but at that time he was the saint's pupil, and as his successor he inherited many of his concerns.

There is nothing tidy about the hagiography of mission. It cannot be categorised as a single genre, even though there is a literary relationship between a number of the *vitae* in question: rather it is the gathering of texts around figures that modern scholarship have interpreted as missionaries. As a result, it is not surprising that the aims of the various hagiographical texts differ widely: some are concerned with episcopal jurisdiction, some with monasticism and some even with the lifestyle appropriate for kings. Together these make up the documentation from which a history of mission has to be constructed. Nevertheless, it does seem significant that there are a number of texts which have autobiographical elements. It also seems significant that most of these texts were written under conditions of stress. Quite apart from the difficulties caused by the resurgence of paganism under the Saxons in the late eighth century, or the Vikings in the ninth, it is clear that missionary activity in alien regions was itself stressful. In those texts which are, or which come close to being, autobiographical, we perhaps come as near as is possible to seeing an early medieval individual confronted by the unknown. Despite the filters of *topoi* and genre we get a glimpse of the missionary life.

## 10. HAGIOGRAPHY AND THE HISTORY OF MISSION

The history of mission has to be written largely from the *Lives* of saints, but, as we have seen, those *Lives* were never intended as history. Each hagiographical text has its own purpose, and sometimes that purpose involved misrepresentation. Some narratives are clearly fraudulent: some *vitae* have made their subjects look more like missionaries than they were, and over the last century some modern interpreters have compounded the problems.

It has been necessary to look at each text in order, so as to clarify, as far as possible, the work of individual saints. We have, as a result, reconstructed a number of short missionary histories. At the same time, consideration of the purposes of hagiographical texts has allowed us to investigate aspects of the history of mission outside the standard grand narrative. We have seen how missionary activity came to the fore as a historical and hagiographical topic only with Bede's composition of the *Historia Ecclesiastica*. We have also seen how attitudes towards mission changed, and we have considered individuals whose writings have taken us closer to an understanding of what it was to be a missionary in the Early Middle Ages. While we have lost some parts of the grand narrative, we have gained an understanding of the complexity of early medieval mission and of the ways it was represented by hagiographers.

Yet if hagiography is our main source for the history of mission, we should not be deluded into thinking that it presents a full account of the process of Christianisation. Its focus is on saints, but the work of saints is only one element in the Christianisation of Europe. Sometimes saints played a part very early on in the process: Adalbert and Bruno may have been among the very first to introduce Christianity to Prussia – and they met with an extremely hostile reaction. Usually, however, an awareness of Christianity seems to have spread along other channels: through trading contacts and more general cultural seepage. Missionaries tended to follow such contacts. In many cases their missions had a political context. Missions to Scandinavia followed communication between Danish and Swedish rulers and the Carolingians. The contexts for the conversions of the leaders of Carinthia, Moravia and Bohemia seem also to have been political. In such cases missionaries would have been requested and sent, and Christianisation would have been largely from the top down. When Christianisation followed war and conquest, so too it must have been imposed from above – and again the Christianisers, now frequently bishops rather than true missionaries to the pagans, would have been appointed by the powers that be.

Yet, not all missionaries were emissaries of others: a remarkable number were following their own vocations. Indeed, there appear to have been moments when a missionary vocation was in vogue, particularly among the Anglo-Saxons of the late seventh and eighth centuries, but also in the mid-seventh century among the disciples of Columbanus. Mission would return to vogue at the court of Otto III. Sometimes, although not always, the would-be missionary sought approval from the pope – one might give Willibrord, Boniface, Corbinian, Adalbert and Bruno as examples. Yet the popes themselves were rarely prime movers in setting up missions, with the exception of Celestine in the fifth century, and Gregory the Great in the sixth. Other would-be missionaries sought permission from lesser ecclesiastics. Lebuin went to Gregory of Utrecht and Willehad to a Northumbrian council. Interestingly, neither of them began their work by approaching Charlemagne for permission to evangelise the Frisians – although in previous generations Willibrord had approached Pippin II and Boniface had sought the backing of Charles Martel. And, once in the mission field, not all missionaries headed for the top: although Lebuin sought relatively powerful friends who could protect him, the power that they had seems to have been localised.

Finally, if the last stages of Christianisation were controlled by bishops, organising dioceses, enforcing canon law, and trying to ensure that old superstitions were eradicated from Christian practice, the workers at the coalface were small-time priests, few of whom had the charisma or subsequent reputation of Ingo. Many such figures must have been very lowly, and not infrequently they must have been incompetent – local priests who have long been nameless: it was, indeed, the work of such men that Boniface came across in Thuringia, Hesse and Bavaria. Yet collectively they had a huge impact: the language of Germanic Christianity suggests that the evangelisation of much of the area to the immediate east of the Rhine was carried out by unnamed Franks, before ever the so-called missionaries arrived. No single model will account for the Christianisation of Europe. Equally, no single *vita* sets out standard missionary practice, and no single missionary saint can be called representative.

# Notes

1. On the general question of hagiographic variety in the period, Wood, 'The use and abuse of Latin hagiography', in Chrysos and Wood (eds), *East and West: Modes of Communication*, pp. 93–109.
2. Althoff, *Otto III*, p. 98.
3. Willibald, *Vita Bonifatii* 6.
4. *Passio Kiliani* 3.
5. Arbeo, *Passio Haimhrammi* 9; *Vita Corbiniani* 24, 26.
6. Arbeo, *Passio Haimhrammi* 7.
7. *Conversio Bagoariorum et Carantanorum* 1.
8. *Conversio Bagoariorum et Carantanorum* 7.
9. Rimbert, *Vita Anskarii* 23.
10. Rimbert, *Vita Anskarii* 23.
11. For an assessment of Merovingian 'paganism', see Y. Hen, *Culture and Religion in Merovingian Gaul, AD 481–751*, pp. 154–206.
12. Gumpold, *Passio sancti Vencezlavi martyris* 7.
13. Canaparius, *Vita Adalberti* 1.
14. Bruno, *Vita Adalberti* 23.
15. Widukind, *Res Gestae Saxonicae* III 65.
16. Bede, *Historia Ecclesiatica* I 23.
17. Rimbert, *Vita Anskarii* 7.
18. Rimbert, *Vita Anskarii* 25; Jeremiah 26, 14.
19. *Vita Altera Bonifatii* 8–9.
20. Ermenrich, ep. to Grimbold 17.
21. Eigil, *Vita Sturmi* 8.
22. Bruno, ep. to Henry, p. 690.
23. For the generally good reception accorded to missionaries in the Germanic world see Wood, 'Pagans and holy men, 600–800', pp. 349–51.
24. Canaparius, *Passio Adalberti* 28.
25. Bruno, *Passio Adalberti* 25.
26. Bruno, *Passio Adalberti* 28.
27. Gieysztor, '*Sanctus et gloriosissimus martyr Christi Adalbertus*: un état et une église missionnaires aux alentours de l'an mille', pp. 614, 637.
28. See Paul the Deacon, *Historia Langobardorum* I 11. On what follows, see Wood, 'Christians and pagans in ninth-century Scandinavia', pp. 63–8.
29. O. Höfler, *Kultische Geheimbunde der Germanen* (Frankfurt, 1934), pp. 62–3.
30. I. Hägg, *Die Textilfunde aus dem Hafen von Haithabu*, Ausgrabungen in Haithabu 20 (Neumünster, 1984), pp. 69–72.
31. Notker, *Gesta Karoli* II 13.
32. Ratramnus, ep. 12. See the discussion in Wood, 'Christians and pagans in ninth-century Scandinavia', pp. 64–6.
33. Aethicus Ister, *Cosmographia*, ed. O. Prinz, MGH, Quellen zur Geistesgeschichte des Mittelalters 14 (Munich, 1993), pp. 114–5: 'He describes the northern island Munitia. Considering the dog-headed men excessively, with famous investigation, they have the likeness of a dog's head, but their other limbs are human in form; their hands and feet are like those of the other type of men; they are greater in height; their aspect is savage; and monsters are unheard of among them. The peoples who are their neighbours call them male Canaanites, for their women do not present a likeness to them. A polluted people, whom no history discusses except this philosopher.

The people of *Germania*, especially those who administer taxes and their tradesmen, say that they often travel by sea to their island, and that they call that people Canaanite. Those foreigners travel (*incendunt* for *incedunt*) with bare legs; they preserve their hair, anointing it with oil giving off an excessive greasy smell; they lead the most foul life, eating unlawful meat of unclean quadrupeds, mice, moles and so forth. They have no worthy houses, but beams with woven tents, in wooded and out-of-the-way places, marshes and reedy spots, with numerous herds and flocks of birds and many sheep. Worshipping demons and auguries, they have no king; they make use of lead (reading *stannum* for *stagnum*) rather than silver, saying that lead is softer and clearer than silver, for it is not found in those regions unless it is brought from elsewhere. Gold is found on their shores; fruit does not grow nor vegetables; there is plenty of milk, but little honey. All this the philosopher described in pagan fashion.' Compare Leviticus 11: 27, 29.

34. H. Löwe, *Ein literarischer Widersacher des Bonifatius. Virgil von Salzburg und die Kosmographie des Aethicus Ister*, Abhandlungen der Akademie der Wissenschaften und der Literatur Mainz, Geistes- und sozialwissenschaftliche Klasse 11, 1951 (Wiesbaden, 1952).

35. Glaser, 'Bischof Arbeo von Freising als Gegenstand der neueren Forschung', pp. 25–6.

36. P. D. A. Harvey, *Mappa Mundi, the Hereford World Map* (London, 1996), pp. 45–7.

37. W. Stelzer, 'Ein Alt-Salzburger Fragment der Kosmographie des Aethicus Ister aus dem 8. Jahrhundert', *Mitteilungen des Instituts für Österreichische Geschichtsforschung* 100 (1992), pp. 132–49.

38. Boniface, ep. 80

39. *Vita Constantini* 15.

40. For Scandinavian paganism, see the intermittently sceptical survey by Meulengracht Sørensen, 'Religions old and new', in P. Sawyer (ed.), *The Oxford Illustrated History of the Vikings* (Oxford, 1997), pp. 202–24.

41. Alcuin, *Vita Willibrordi* 10; Altfrid, *Vita Liudgeri* 1, 19, 22.

42. See, for instance, the scholarly appraisal of the evidence in K. Helm, *Altgermanische Religionsgeschichte*, 2, *Die nachrömische Zeit*, 2, *Die Westgermanen* (Heidelberg, 1953).

43. For a survey see Z. Vána, *The World of the Ancient Slavs* (Prague, 1983), pp. 83–100; for a more detailed coverage of the archaeology, see Slupecki, *Slavonic Pagan Sanctuaries*.

44. Alcuin, *Vita Willibrordi* 10; Altfrid, *Vita Liudgeri* 1, 19, 22.

45. Wood, 'Pagan religions and superstitions east of the Rhine from the fifth to the ninth century', in G. Ausenda (ed.), *After Empire: Towards an Ethnology of Europe's Barbarians* (Woodbridge, 1995) pp. 260–1.

46. Bede, *Historia Ecclesiastica* II 13, 16.

47. Bede, *Historia Ecclesiastica* I 30.

48. Bede, *Historia Ecclesiastica* II 16; Wood, 'Pagan religions and superstitions east of the Rhine from the fifth to the ninth century', p. 261.

49. Adam, *Gesta Hammaburgensis Ecclesiae Pontificum* IV 26–7. One should note the phonological problems in equating Frikko and Frija.

50. Meulengracht Sørensen, 'Religions old and new', pp. 203, 215 notes the problems, without integrating them into his interpretation.

51. Wood, 'Pagan religions and superstitions east of the Rhine from the fifth to the ninth century', p. 261.

52. Willibald, *Vita Bonifatii* 6.

53. *Vita Vulframni* 8.

54. Wood, 'Pagan religions and superstitions east of the Rhine from the fifth to the ninth century', p. 262.

55. M. Müller-Wille, *Opferkulte der Germanen und Slawen* (Darmstadt, 1999), pp. 26–8.

56. See the illustrations in Müller-Wille, *Opferkulte der Germanen und Slawen*, p. 69.

57. Bede, *Historia Ecclesiastica* II 13; Wood, 'Pagan religions and superstitions east of the Rhine from the fifth to the ninth century', pp. 261–4.

58. Adam, *Gesta Hammaburgensis Ecclesiae Pontificum* IV 26–7.

59. Wood, 'Pagan religions and superstitions east of the Rhine from the fifth to the ninth century', p. 263.

60. Thietmar, *Chronicon* I 17. See Müller-Wille, *Opferkulte der Germanen und Slawen*, pp. 76–7 for plans of the site.

61. Boniface, ep. 20.

62. Alcuin, *Vita Willibrordi* 11; Wood, 'Pagan religions and superstitions east of the Rhine from the fifth to the ninth century', p. 265.

63. Rimbert, *Vita Anskarii* 27, 30.

64. Alcuin, *Vita Willibrordi* 11; Wood, 'Pagan religions and superstitions east of the Rhine from the fifth to the ninth century', p. 265.

65. Jochens, 'Late and peaceful: Iceland's conversion through arbitration in 1000', p. 628; Meulengracht Sørensen, 'Religions old and new', pp. 213–4.

66. Wood, 'Pagan religions and superstitions east of the Rhine from the fifth to the ninth century', pp. 266–7.

67. *Indiculus superstitionum et paganiarum*, ed. Dierkens.

68. The complex mixture of pagan and Christian beliefs is treated in V. Flint, *The Rise of Magic in Early Medieval Europe* (Oxford, 1991).

69. Thietmar, *Chronicon* VI 23–5.

70. Adam, *Gesta Hammaburgensis Ecclesiae Pontificum* II 21 (18). See Slupecki, *Slavonic Pagan Sanctuaries*, pp. 51–69.

71. Thietmar, *Chronicon* VI 23.

72. Thietmar, *Chronicon* VI 24.

73. Thietmar, *Chronicon* VI 25.

74. Slupecki, *Slavonic Pagan Sanctuaries*, pp. 24–44. See also Coblenz, ed., *825 Jahre Christianisierung Rügens*.

75. See Slupecki, *Slavonic Pagan Sanctuaries*, passim. Müller-Wille, *Opferkulte der Germanen und Slawen*, pp. 81–9.

76. Boniface, ep. 23.

77. Eligius, *Praedicatio*, ed. B. Krusch, MGH, SRM 4 (Hanover). See Hen, *Culture and Religion in Merovingian Gaul, AD 481–751*, p. 197.

78. *Interrogationes et responsiones baptismales*, ed. A. Boretius, MGH, Legum 2, Capitularia Regum Francorum 1 (Hanover, 1883), p. 222.

79. Gregory I, *Register* VI 49, ed. P. Ewald and L. Hartmann, MGH, Epistolae 1–2 (Hanover, 1887–99); Bede, *Historia Ecclesiastica* I 25.

80. Bede, *Historia Ecclesiastica* III 3. For a similar story in the eleventh century, when the Slav ruler, Gottschalk, interpreted for missionaries, see Adam of Bremen, *Gesta Hammaburgensis Ecclesiae Pontificum* III 20 (19).

81. Bede, *Historia Ecclesiastica* III 7.

82. Bruno, *Vita Quinque Fratrum* 5, 10.

83. Thietmar, *Chronicon* II 37.

84. Bruno, *Passio Adalberti* 26.

85. Bede, *Historia Ecclesiastica* I 27; on these responses see R. Meens, 'A background to Augustine's mission to Anglo-Saxon England', *Anglo-Saxon England* 23 (1994), pp. 5–17.

86. Markus, 'Gregory the Great and a papal missionary strategy'.
87. Bruno, *Passio Adalberti* 24; compare Canaparius, *Passio Adalberti* 28.
88. Bruno, *Passio Adalberti* 25.
89. Boniface, ep. 11.
90. Rimbert, *Vita Anskarii* 26.
91. Bruno, *Passio Adalberti* 26.
92. Bruno, *Passio Adalberti* 26.
93. Bruno, *Vita Quinque Fratrum* 10.
94. Damian, *Vita Romualdi* 27.
95. Wibert, *Hystoriae de predicatione Episcopi Brunonis cum suis capellanis in Prussia et martyrio eorum.*
96. Bruno, *Passio Adalberti* 26. For Bruno himself see also Thietmar, *Chronicon* VI 94 (58).
97. Bede, *Historia Ecclesiastica* I 26; see also the comments in Bede, *Vita Cuthberti* 16.
98. *Vita Amandi* 13.
99. Willibald, *Vita Bonifatii* 6. Compare also Willibald, *Vita Bonifatii* 8, citing Acts 4, 32.
100. Liudger, *Vita Gregorii* 2.
101. Anon., *Vita Cuthberti* III 5.
102. Rimbert, *Vita Anskarii* 33.
103. Willibald, *Vita Bonifatii* 2. See also Eigil, *Vita Sturmi* 13.
104. Bruno, *Passio Adalberti* 26.
105. Patrick, *Confessio* 16.
106. Bede, *Historia Ecclesiastica* V 10.
107. *Vita Altera Bonifatii* 16.
108. Willibald, *Vita Bonifatii* 8.
109. Canaparius, *Passio Adalberti* 30; Bruno, *Passio Adalberti* 30.
110. Canaparius, *Passio Adalberti* 28; Bruno, *Passio Adalberti* 25.
111. Bruno, ep. to Henry.
112. Wibert, *Hystoriae de predicatione Episcopi Brunonis cum suis capellanis in Prussia et martyrio eorum.*
113. Bede, *Historia Ecclesiastica* I 25. On the historicity of the episode see, however, Wood, 'Augustine's journey', pp. 37–8.
114. *Vita Lebuini Antiquior* 6.
115. Rimbert, *Vita Anskarii* 27.
116. C. de Hamel, *A History of Illuminated Manuscripts* (Oxford, 1986), pp. 11–37, discusses what the author terms 'Books for missionaries', but the majority of the books he deals with are not associated with those who worked in pagan societies.
117. *Passio Kiliani* 10–11.
118. *Vita Willehadi* 7.
119. Liudger, *Vita Gregorii* 8, 14.
120. Altfrid, Vita Liudgeri I 8, 12, 30. Also *799 Kunst und Kultur der Karolingerzeit, Karl der Große und Papst Leo III. in Paderborn*, 2, pp. 469–71, 479–91.
121. Rimbert, *Vita Anskarii* 16. For Anskar's books see also *ibid.*, 10, 35, 41.
122. Rimbert, *Vita Anskarii* 18.
123. *Vita Quinque Fratrum* 13.
124. Boniface, ep. 35.
125. Dutton, *The Politics of Dreaming in the Carolingian Empire*, pp. 51–3, discusses Anskar's visions, but otherwise leaves aside the link between visionary experiences and mission.
126. Patrick, *Confessio* 17.

127. Patrick, *Confessio* 20.
128. Patrick, *Confessio* 23.
129. Jonas, *Vita Columbani* I 27.
130. Rimbert, *Vita Anskarii* 2, 3, 4, 5, 9, 25, 27, 29, 32, 35, 36, 38, 40, 42; Lammers, 'Ansgar, visionäre Erlebnisformen und Missionsauftrag'.
131. Rimbert, *Vita Anskarii* 25, 40.
132. *Vita Rimberti* 19; see also Anskar's visions in *Vita Rimberti* 5, 6, 11 and Rimbert's in *Vita Rimberti* 7, 8, 11, 22, 24.
133. *Legenda Christiani* 3; *Crescente Fide* (Bohemian) 3–4; Gumpold, *Passio Vencezlavi* 9–12.
134. Canaparius, *Passio Adalberti* 6; Bruno, *Passio Adalberti* 7. See Gieysztor, 'Sanctus et gloriosissimuus martyr Christi Adalbertus: un état et une église missionnaires aux alentours de l'an mille', p. 618: 'les résurgences oniriques pourraient faire l'objet de la psychanalyse'.
135. Bruno, *Passio Adalberti* 12.
136. Canaparius, *Passio Adalberti* 20, 24; Bruno, *Passio Adalberti* 20–1.
137. Canaparius, *Passio Adalberti* 29; Bruno, *Passio Adalberti* 29.
138. Canaparius, *Passio Adalberti* 29; Bruno, *Passio Adalberti* 27.
139. W. D. McCready, *Signs of Sanctity: Miracles in the Thought of Gregory the Great* (Toronto, 1989), pp. 17, 20, 22, 35–8, 47, 57. For what follows see also Wood, 'The mission of Augustine of Canterbury to the English', pp. 13–15.
140. See Gregory, *Homiliae in Evangelia* I, 4, 3; II, 29, 4, Patrologia Latina 76; *id.*, *Moralia in Job* 27, 18 (36), ed. M. Adriaen, Corpus Christianorum Series Latinorum 143 (1979–85).
141. McCready, *Signs of Sanctity: Miracles in the Thought of Gregory the Great*, pp. 36, 38, 47, 58.
142. Gregory, *Homiliae in Evangelia* II, 29, 4; *id.*, *Dialogues*, III, 17, 7, ed. A. de Vogüé, Sources Chrétiennes 251, 260, 265 (Paris, 1978–80).
143. Gregory, *Register* XI 36.
144. Gregory, *Register* XI 36. See also VIII 29, XI 48 and Bede, *Historia Ecclesiatica* II 3.
145. Alcuin, *Vita Willibrordi* 14.
146. Altfrid, *Vita Liudgeri* I 25.
147. Alcuin, *Vita Willibrordi* 11, 14.
148. Liudger, *Vita Gregorii* 12.
149. Altfrid, *Vita Liudgeri* I 25–6.
150. Rimbert, *Vita Anskarii* 18–20.
151. Rimbert, *Vita Anskarii* 19, 27, 30.
152. Rimbert, *Vita Anskarii* 19.
153. Rimbert, *Vita Anskarii* 20.
154. Rimbert, *Vita Anskarii* 18.
155. Anskar, *Vita Willehadi*, praef. (=1).
156. *Vita Altera Bonifatii* 18.
157. *Vita Altera Bonifatii* 19.
158. Gregory, *Decem Libri Historiarum* VIII 15.
159. Jonas, *Vita Columbani*, ep. This is not the only autobiographical element in the work: see also II 5, 23.

# BIBLIOGRAPHY OF WORKS CITED

## ABBREVIATIONS

AASS    Acta Sanctorum
MGH     Monumenta Germaniae Historica
AA      Auctores Antiquissimi
SRG     Scriptores Rerum Germanicarum in usum scholarum editi
SRM     Scriptores Rerum Merovingicarum

## PRIMARY SOURCES

*Acta Aunemundi*, ed. P. F. Chifflet, AASS, Sept 28th, vol. 7 (Paris, 1867), pp. 694–6: trans. P. Fouracre and R. Gerberding, *Late Merovingian France, History and Hagiography 640–720* (Manchester, 1996).

Adalbert of Prague, *Homilia in natali sancti Alexii confessoris*, ed. M. Sprissler, *Das rythmische Gedicht 'Pater Deus Ingenite' und das altfranzösische Alexiuslied* (Münster, 1966).

Adalbert of Prague, *Passio Gorgonii, Magnum summopere*, ed. C. Suysken, AASS, Sept 9th, vol. 3 (Paris, 1868), pp. 340–2.

'Adalbert of Prague', *Sermo in translatione Wenezlai*, ed. J. Peckar, *Die Wenzels- und Ludmila-Legenden und die Echtheit Christians* (Prague, 1906).

*Adalberti continuatio Reginonis*, ed. A. Bau and R. Rau, *Quellen zur Geschichte der sächsischen Kaiserzeit* (Darmstadt, 1971).

Adam of Bremen, *Gesta Hammaburgensis Ecclesiae Pontificum*, ed. W. Trillmich, *Quellen des 9. und 11. Jahrhunderts zur Geschichte der hamburgischen Kirche und des Reiches* (Darmstadt, 1961).

Aethicus Ister, *Cosmographia*, ed. O. Prinz, MGH, Quellen zur Geistesgeschichte des Mittelalters 14 (Munich, 1993).

Alcuin, *Epistolae*, ed E. Dümmler, *Monumenta Germaniae Historica, Epistolae IV, Karolini Aevi* 2 (Berlin, 1895); see also F. Unterkircher, *Alkuin-Briefe und andere Traktate*, Codices Selecti Phototypice Impressi 20 (Graz, 1969).

Alcuin, *Versus de sanctis Euboricensis ecclesiae*, ed. P. Godman, *Alcuin, The Bishops, Kings and Saints of York* (Oxford, 1982).

Alcuin, *Vita Richarii*, ed. B. Krusch, MGH, SRM 4 (Hanover, 1902).

Alcuin, *Vita Vedasti*, ed. B. Krusch, MGH, SRM 7 (Hanover, 1920).

Alcuin, *Vita Willibrordi* (*opus geminatum*, i.e. the full programme), ed A. Poncelet, AASS Nov 7th, vol. 3 (Brussels, 1910), pp. 435–57.

Alcuin, *Vita Willibrordi* (prose), ed. W. Levison, MGH, SRM 7 (Hanover, 1920); also H.-J. Reischmann, *Willibrord – Apostel der Friesen* (Sigmaringendorf, 1989).

Alcuin, *Vita Willibrordi* (verse), ed. E. Dümmler, MGH, Poetae Latini aevi Carolini 1 (Berlin, 1881).

Altfrid, *Vita Liudgeri*, ed. W. Diekamp, *Die Vitae Sancti Liudgeri* (Münster, 1881).

Anastasius Bibliothecarius, *Epistolae*, ed. E. Perels and G. Laehr, MGH, Epistolae 7, Karolini Aevi 5 (Munich, 1978).

*Anglo-Saxon Chronicle*, ed. C. Plummer and J. Earle, *Two of the Saxon Chronicles Parallel* (Oxford, 1892–9).

*Annales Bertiniani*, ed. G. Waitz, MGH, SRG (Hanover, 1883): trans. J. L. Nelson, *The Annals of St-Bertin* (Manchester, 1991).

*Annales qui dicuntur Einhardi*, ed. F. Kurze, MGH, SRG (Hanover, 1895).

*Annales Fuldenses*, ed. F. Kurze, MGH, SRG (Hanover, 1891): trans. T. Reuter, *The Annals of Fulda* (Manchester, 1992).

*Annales Laureshamenses*, s.a. 792, ed. G. H. Pertz, MGH, SS 1 (Hanover, 1826).

*Annales Mosellani*, ed. G. H. Pertz, MGH, SS 1 (Hanover, 1826).

*Annales Petaviani*, ed. G. H. Pertz, MGH, SS 1 (Hanover, 1826).

*Annales Regni Francorum*, ed. F. Kurze, MGH, SRG (Hanover, 1895).

*Annales Xantenses*, ed. B. von Simson, MGH, SRG (Hanover, 1909).

Anskar, *Miracula Willehadi*, ed. A. Poncelet, AASS, Nov 8th, vol. 3 (Brussels, 1910), pp. 847–51.

Arbeo of Freising, *Vita Haimhrammi*, ed. B. Krusch, *Arbeonis Episcopi Frisingensis Vitae Sanctorum Haimhrammi et Corbiniani*, MGH, SRG (Hanover, 1920): also ed. B. Bischoff, *Leben und Leiden des hl. Emmeram* (Munich, 1953).

Arbeo of Freising, *Vita Corbiniani*, ed. B. Krusch, *Arbeonis episcopi Frisingensis vitae sanctorum Haimhrammi et Corbiniani*, MGH, SRG (Hanover, 1920): also ed. F. Brunhölzl, *Vita Corbiniani. Bischof Arbeo von Freising und die Lebensgeschichte des Hl. Korbinian* (Munich, 1983).

Astronomer, *Vita Hludowici*, ed. R. Rau, *Quellen zur karolingischen Reichsgeschichte* 1 (Darmstadt, 1968).

Bede, *Historia Ecclesiastica Gentis Anglorum*, ed. C. Plummer, *Baedae Opera Historica* (Oxford, 1896).

Bede, *In primam partem Samuelis Libri IIII*, ed. D. Hurst, Corpus Christianorum Series Latina 119 (Turnhout, 1962).

Bede, *Vita Cuthberti*, ed. B. Colgrave, *Two Lives of Saint Cuthbert* (Cambridge, 1940).

Bobolenus, *Vita Germani Grandivallensis*, ed. B. Krusch, MGH, SRM 5 (Hanover, 1910).

Boniface, *Epistolae*, ed. M. Tangl, *S. Bonifatii et Lulli Epistolae*, MGH, Epistolae selectae in usum scholarum 1 (Berlin, 1916); also, partially, ed. R. Buchner, *Briefe des Bonifatius: Willibalds Leben des Bonifatius* (Darmstadt, 1968).

*Breves Notitiae*, ed. F. Losek, '*Notitia Arnonis* und *Breves Notitiae*', in *Mitteilungen der Gesellschaft für Salzburger Landeskunde* 130 (1990), pp. 5–191.

Bruno of Querfurt, *Epistola ad Heinricum II Imperatorem*, ed. W. von Giesebrecht, *Geschichte der deutschen Kaiserzeit*, 4th edn. vol. 2 (Leipzig, 1875), pp. 689–92.

Bruno of Querfurt, *Passio sancti Adalberti episcopi et martyris*, ed. G. H. Pertz, MGH, SS 4 (Hanover, 1841).

Bruno of Querfurt, *Vita quinque fratrum Poloniae*, ed. R. Kade, MGH, SS 15, 2 (Hanover, 1888).

*Calendar of St Willibrord*, ed. H. W. Wilson, Henry Bradshaw Society 55 (London, 1918).

John Canaparius, *Vita Adalberti*, ed. G. H. Pertz, MGH, SS 4 (Hanover, 1841).

Candidus, *Vita Eigilis*, ed. G. Waitz, MGH, SS 15, 1 (Hanover, 1887).

*Capitulare Saxonicum*, ed. A. Boretius, *Capitularia Regum Francorum* 1, MGH, Leges, sectio 2 (Hanover, 1883).

Capitulatio *de partibus Saxoniae*, ed. A. Boretius, *Capitularia Regum Francorum* 1, *MGH*, Leges, sectio 2 (Hanover, 1883).

Christian, *Legenda Christiani*, ed. J. Pekar, *Die Wenzels- und Ludmila-Legenden und die Echtheit Christians* (Prague, 1906): trans. M. Kantor, *The Origins of Christianity in Bohemia* (Evanston, 1990), pp. 163–203.

*Chronica monasterii Casinensis*, ed. H. Hoffmann, MGH, SS 34 (Hanover, 1980).

Columbanus, ed. G. S. M Walker, *Sancti Columbani Opera* (Dublin, 1970).

*Concilia Aevi Karolini*, ed. A. Weminghoff, MGH, Leges 3, Concilia 2 (Hanover, 1906–8).

*Conversio Bagoariorum et Carantanorum*, ed. F. Losek, *Die Conversio Bagoariorum et Carantanorum und der Brief des Erzbischofs Theotmar von Salzburg*, MGH, Studien und Texte 15 (Hanover, 1997). Also ed. H. Wolfram, *Conversio Bagoariorum et Carantanorum: Das Weißbuch der Salzburger Kirche über die erfolgreiche Mission in Karantanien und Pannonien* (Vienna, 1979).

Cosmas of Prague, *Chronica Boemorum*, ed. B. Bretholz, MGH, SRG n.s. 2 (Berlin, 1923).

*Crescente Fide* (Bavarian recension), ed. J. Truhar, Fontes rerum Bohemicarum 1 (Prague, 1873), pp. 183–90.

*Crescente Fide* (Bohemian recension), ed. V. Chaloupecky, *Svatovaclavsky Sbornik* II 2, *Prameny X. Stoleti* (Prague, 1939), pp. 495–501: trans. M. Kantor, *The Origins of Christianity in Bohemia* (Evanston, 1990), pp. 143–53.

*De Conversione Saxonum*, ed. S. A. Rabe, *Faith, Art and Politics at Saint-Riquier: the Symbolic Vision of Angilbert* (Philadelphia, 1995), pp. 54–74.

*Descriptio civitatum ad septentrionalem plagam Danubii*, ed. B. Horák and D. Travnicek (Prague, 1956).

*De translatione Adalberti*, ed. G. H. Waitz, MGH, SS 15, 2 (Hanover, 1888).

*Die Traditionen des Hochstifts Freising*, ed. T. Bitterauf, 1 (Munich, 1905).

*Diffundente Sole*, ed. V. Chaloupecky, *Svatovaclavsky Sbornik* II 2, *Prameny X. Stoleti* (Prague, 1939), pp. 486–92: trans. M. Kantor, *The Origins of Christianity in Bohemia* (Evanston, 1990), pp. 245–51.

*Diplomata Karolinorum* 1, ed. E. Mühlbacher, MGH, Diplomata (Hanover, 1906).

Eigil, *Vita Sturmi*, ed. P. Engelbert, *Die Vita Sturmi des Eigil von Fulda, literarkritisch-historische Untersuchung und Edition* (Marburg, 1968): trans. C. H. Talbot, in T. F. X. Noble and T. Head, *Soldiers of Christ: Saints and Saints' Lives from Late Antiquity and the Early Middle Ages* (Philadelphia, 1995).

Eligius, *Praedicatio*, ed. B. Krusch, MGH, SRM 4 (Hanover, 1902).

Ermenrich of Passau, *Epistola ad domnum Grimoldum abbatem et archicappellanum*, ed. E. Dümmler, MGH, Epp. 5 = Karolini Aevi 3 (Berlin, 1899).

Ermenrich of Passau, *Sermo de vita Sualonis dicti Sali*, ed. O. Holder-Egger, MGH, SS 15, 1 (Hanover, 1887): also ed. A. Bauch, *Quellen zur Geschichte der Diözese Eichstätt*, I *Biographien der Gründungszeit* (Eichstätt, 1962).

Ermoldus Nigellus, *In honorem Hludovici Pii*, ed. E. Faral, *Ermold le Noir – Poème sur Louis le Pieux* (Paris, 1932).

Eugippius, *Vita Severini*, ed. P. Régerat, *Eugippe, Vie de saint Séverin*, Sources Chrétiennes 374 (Paris, 1991).

Fredegar IV and *continuationes*, ed. J. M. Wallace-Hadrill, *The Fourth Book of the Chronicle of Fredegar* (London, 1960).

*Fuit in Provincia Boemorum* 1, ed. V. Chaloupecky, *Svatovaclavsky Sbornik* II 2, *Prameny X. Stoleti* (Prague, 1939), pp. 467–81: trans. M. Kantor, *The Origins of Christianity in Bohemia* (Evanston, 1990), pp. 155–62.

Gaeraldus, *Waltarius*, ed. A. K. Bate (Reading, 1978).

*Gesta Hrodberti*, ed. W. Levison, MGH, SRM 6 (Hanover, 1913).

*Gesta sanctorum patrum Fontenallensis coenobii*, ed. F. Lohier and J. Laporte (Rouen and Paris, 1931).

Gregory I, *Dialogues*, ed. A de Vogüé, Sources Chrétiennes 251, 260, 265 (Paris, 1978–80).

Gregory I, *Homiliae in Evangelia*, Patrologia Latina 76.

Gregory I, *Moralia in Job*, ed. M. Adriaen, Corpus Christianorum Series Latinorum 143 (1979–85).

Gregory I, *Register*, ed. P. Ewald and L. Hartmann, MGH, Epistolae 1–2 (Hanover, 1887–99).

Gregory II, *Literae decretales*, ed. J. Merkel, MGH, Leges in folio 3 (Hanover, 1863), pp. 451–4.

Gregory of Tours, *Decem Libri Historiarum*, ed. B. Krusch and W. Levison, MGH, SRM 1, 1 (Hanover, 1951).

Gregory of Tours, *Liber in Gloria Martyrum*, ed. B. Krusch, MGH, SRM 1, 2 (Hanover, 1885).

Gregory of Tours, *Liber Vitae Patrum*, ed. B. Krusch, MGH, SRM 1, 2 (Hanover, 1885).

Gumpold, *Passio sancti Vencezlavi martyris*, ed. F. J. Zoubek, Fontes rerum Bohemicarum 1 (Prague, 1973), pp. 146–66.

Hartwig, *Vita sancti Stephani*, ed. E. Bartoniek, in I. Szentpétery, *Scriptores Rerum Hungaricarum*, 2 (Budapest, 1938), pp. 401–40: trans. N. Behrend, in T. Head (ed.), *Medieval Hagiography: An Anthology* (New York, 2000), pp. 375–98.

Hatto of Mainz, *Epistolae*, ed. H. Bresslau, 'Der angebliche Brief des Erzbischofs Hatto von Mainz an Papst Johann IX', in *Festschrift für Karl Zeumer* (Weimar, 1909), pp. 9–30.

Hygeburg, *Vita Willibaldi*, ed. O. Holder-Egger, MGH, SS 15, 1 (Hanover, 1887); also ed. A. Bauch, *Quellen zur Geschichte der Diözese Eichstätt*, I *Biographien der Gründungszeit* (Eichstätt, 1962): trans. C. H. Talbot, in T. F. X. Noble and

T. Head, *Soldiers of Christ: Saints and Saints' Lives from Late Antiquity and the Early Middle Ages* (Philadelphia, 1995).

Hygeburg, *Vita Wynnebaldi*, ed. O. Holder-Egger, MGH SS, 15, 1 (Hanover, 1887): A. Bauch, *Quellen zur Geschichte der Diözese Eichstätt*, I *Biographien der Gründungszeit* (Eichstätt, 1962).

*Indiculus superstitionum et paganiarum*, ed. A. Dierkens, 'Superstitions, christianisme et paganisme à la fin de l'époque mérovingienne', in H. Hasquin (ed.), *Magie, sorcellerie, parapsychologie* (Brussels, 1985), pp. 9–26.

*Interrogationes et responsiones baptismales*, ed. A. Boretius, MGH, Legum 2, Capitularia Regum Francorum 1 (Hanover, 1883).

*Islendingabók Landnámabók*, ed. J. Benediktsson (Reykjavik, 1968).

John VIII, *Epistolae*, ed. E. Caspar, MGH, Epp. 7 = Karolini Aevi 5 (Berlin, 1928).

Jonas, *Vita Columbani*, ed. B. Krusch, MGH, SRM 4 (Hanover, 1902): reprinted in B. Krusch, *Ionae Vitae Sanctorum Columbani, Vedastis, Iohannis*, MGH, SRG (Hanover, 1905).

Jonas, *Vita Vedastis*, ed. B. Krusch, MGH, SRM 3 (Hanover, 1896): reprinted in B. Krusch, *Ionae Vitae Sanctorum Columbani, Vedastis, Iohannis*, MGH, SRG (Hanover, 1905).

Laurentius of Montecassino, *Passio Sancti Wenzeslai Regis*, ed. F. Newton, MGH, Die deutschen Geschichtsquellen des Mittelalters 500–1500, 7 (Weimar, 1973).

*Leges Baiuwariorum*, ed. E. von Schwind, MGH, Leges 5, 2 (Hanover, 1926).

*Liber Aureus Epternacensis*, ed. C. Wampach, *Geschichte der Grundherrschaft Echternach im Frühmittelalter* 1, 2, Quellenband (Luxembourg, 1930).

*Liber Historiae Francorum*, ed. B. Krusch, MGH, SRM 2 (Hanover, 1885).

*Liber Pontificalis*, ed. L. Duchesne, *Le Liber Pontificalis* (Paris, 1886–92).

Liudger, *Vita Gregorii*, ed. O. Holder-Egger, MGH SS 15, 1 (Hanover, 1887).

Lupus of Ferrières, *Vita Wigberti*, ed. O. Holder-Egger, MGH, SS 15, 1 (Hanover, 1887).

Milo, *Vita Amandi*, ed. B. Krusch, MGH, SRM 5 (Hanover, 1910).

*Miracula sancti Alexii*, ed. G. H. Pertz, MGH, SS 4 (Hanover, 1841).

Nicolas I, *Epistolae*, ed. E. Perels, MGH, Epp 6 (Berlin, 1892).

*Notae de episcopis Pataviensibus*, ed. G. Waitz, MGH, SS 25 (1880), pp. 623–4.

*Notitia Arnonis*, ed. F. Losek, '*Notitia Arnonis* und *Breves Notitiae*', in *Mitteilungen der Gesellschaft für Salzburger Landeskunde* 130 (1990), pp. 5–191.

Notker, *Gesta Karoli Magni Imperatoris*, ed. H. F. Haefele, MGH, SRG 12 (Berlin, 1962).

Otloh, *Vita Bonifatii*, ed. W. Levison, *Vitae sancti Bonifatii archiepiscopi Moguntini*, MGH, SRG 57 (Hanover, 1905).

*Passio Kiliani*, ed. W. Levison, MGH, SRM 5 (Hanover, 1910).

*Passio Leudegarii I*, ed. B. Krusch, MGH, SRM 5 (Hanover, 1910): trans. P. Fouracre and R. Gerberding, *Late Merovingian France, History and Hagiography 640–720* (Manchester, 1996).

*Passio sanctorum Herenaei episcopi, Andochii presbiteri, Benigni presbiteri, Tyrsi diaconi, Felicis negotiatoris*, ed. J. van der Straeten, 'Les actes des martyrs d'Aurélian en Bourgogne: le texte de Farfa', *Analecta Bollandiana* 79 (1961), pp. 447–68;

introduction in *id.*, 'Les actes des martyrs d'Aurélian en Bourgogne: étude littéraire', *Analecta Bollandiana* 79 (1961), pp. 115–44.

Patrick, *Confessio* and *Epistola ad milites Corotici*, ed. D. R. Howlett, *The Book of Letters of Saint Patrick the Bishop* (Blackrock, 1994).

Paul the Deacon, *Historia Langobardorum*, ed. G. Waitz, MGH, SRG (Hanover, 1878).

Petrus Damiani, *Vita Romualdi*, ed. G. Tabacco, Fonti per la storia d'Italia 94 (Rome, 1957).

Prosper, *Chronicle*, ed. T. Mommsen, Chronica Minora 1 MGH, AA 9 (Berlin, 1892).

Radbod of Utrecht, *Homilia de sancto Lebuino*, PL 132, cols. 553–8.

Radbod of Utrecht, *Libellus de miraculo sancti Martini*, ed. O. Holder-Egger, MGH, SS 15 2 (Hanover, 1888).

Radbod of Utrecht, *Sermo de Swithberto*, PL 132, cols. 547–50.

Ratramnus of Corbie, *epistolae*, ed. E. Dümmler, *Epistolae Variorum*, in MGH, Epistolae 6 (Karolini Aevi 4) (Berlin, 1925).

Regino, *Chronicon*, ed. F. Kurze, MGH, SRG (Hanover, 1890).

Rimbert, *Vita Anskarii*, ed. W. Trillmich, *Quellen des 9. und 11. Jahrhunderts zur Geschichte der Hamburgischen Kirche und des Reiches* (Darmstadt, 1961).

Rudolf of Fulda, *Vita Leobae*, ed. G. Waitz, MGH, SS 15, 1 (Hanover, 1887): trans. C. H. Talbot, in T. F. X. Noble and T. Head, *Soldiers of Christ: Saints and Saints' Lives From Late Antiquity and the Early Middle Ages* (Philadelphia, 1995).

Rudolf of Fulda/Meginhart of Fulda, *Translatio sancti Alexandri*, ed. B. Krusch, 'Die Übertragung des H. Alexander von Rom nach Wildeshausen durch den Enkel Widukings 851: Das älteste niedersächsische Geschichtsdenkmal', *Nachrichten von der Gesellschaft der Wissenschaften zu Göttingen* aus dem Jahre 1933, Philologisch-Historische Klasse (Berlin, Weidmann, 1933), pp. 405–36.

Stephanus, *Vita Wilfridi*, ed. B. Colgrave, *The Life of Bishop Wilfrid by Eddius Stephanus* (Cambridge, 1927).

Sulpicius Severus, *Vita Martini*, ed. J. Fontaine, *Sulpice Sévère, Vie de Saint Martin*, Sources Chrétiennes 133–5 (Paris, 1967–9).

Thegan, *Vita Hludowici*, ed. R. Rau, *Quellen zur karolingischen Reichsgeschichte* 1 (Darmstadt, 1968).

Theodulf of Orléans, *Capitula ad presbyteros parochiae suae*, ed. P. Brommer, MGH, Capitula Episcoporum 1 (Hanover, 1984), pp. 103–42.

Theotmar, *Epistola*, ed. F. Losek, *Die Conversio Bagoariorum et Carantanorum und der Brief des Erzbischofs Theotmar von Salzburg*, MGH, Studien und Texte 15 (Hanover, 1997).

Thietmar of Merseburg, *Chronicon* IV 55, ed. W. Trillmich (Darmstadt, 1957).

Thio(t)frid, *Vita Willibrordi*, ed. A. Poncelet, AASS, Nov. 7th, vol. 3 (Brussels, 1910), pp. 459–500.

Tírechán, ed. L. Bieler, *The Patrician Texts in the Book of Armagh* (Dublin, 1979).

*Translatio Gorgonii*, ed. C. Suysken, AASS, Sept 9th, vol. 3 (Paris, 1868), pp. 343–55.

*Urkundenbuch des Klosters Fulda* 1, ed. E. E. Stengel (Marburg, 1958).

*Vita Agili*, ed. J. Stilting, AASS, August 30th, vol. 6 (Paris, 1868), pp. 574–87.

*Vita Alexii*, ed. J. Pin, AASS, July 17th, vol. 4 (Paris, 1868), pp. 251–78.

*Vita Altera Bonifatii*, ed. W. Levison, *Vitae sancti Bonifatii*, MGH, SRG 57 (Hanover, 1905).

*Vita Amandi*, ed. B. Krusch, MGH, SRM 5 (Hanover, 1910): trans. J. N. Hillgarth, *Christianity and Paganism, 350–750: the conversion of Western Europe* (Philadelphia, 1986).

*Vita Aredii*, ed. B. Krusch, MGH, SRM 3 (Hanover, 1896).

*Vita Balthildis*, ed. B. Krusch, MGH, SRM 2 (Hanover, 1888): trans. P. Fouracre and R. Gerberding, *Late Merovingian France, History and Hagiography 640–720* (Manchester, 1996).

*Vita Constantini*, ed. A. Vaillant, *Textes Vieux-Slaves*, 2 vols. (Paris, 1968).

*Vita Constantini-Cyrilla cum translatione S. Clementis*, ed. D. Bartonkova, L. Havlik, J. Ludvikovsky, Z. Masarik and R. Vecerka, *Magnae Moraviae Fontes Historici* 2 (Brun, 1967), pp. 120–32.

*Vita Cuthberti*, ed. B. Colgrave, *Two Lives of Saint Cuthbert* (Cambridge, 1940).

*Vita Desiderii Cadurcensis*, ed. B. Krusch, MGH, SRM 4 (Hanover, 1902).

*Vita Eligii*, ed. B. Krusch, MGH, SRM 4 (Hanover, 1902).

*Vita Galli Vetustissima* 1, ed. I. Müller, 'Die älteste Gallus-vita', *Zeitschrift für schweizerische Kirchengeschichte* 66 (1972), pp. 209–49.

*Vita Lebuini Antiqua*, ed. O. Hofmeister, MGH, SS 30, 2 (Leipzig, 1934).

*Vita Liutbirgae*, ed. O. Menzel, *Das Leben des Liutbirg*, Deutsches Mittelalter, Kritische Studientexte des Reichsinstituts für ältere deutsche Geschichtskunde, MGH 3 (Leipzig, 1937).

*Vita Methodii*, ed. A. Vaillant, *Textes vieux-slaves*, 2 vols (Paris, 1968).

*Vita Richarii*, ed. B. Krusch, MGH, SRM 7 (Hanover, 1920).

*Vita Rimberti*, ed. G. Waitz, MGH, SRG 55 (Hanover, 1884).

*Vita Samsonis*, ed. P. Flobert, *La vie ancienne de saint Samson de Dol* (Paris, 1997).

*Vita Secunda Liudgeri*, ed. W. Diekamp, *Die Vitae Sancti Liudgeri* (Münster, 1881).

*Vita Vulframni*, ed. W. Levison, MGH, SRM 5 (Hanover, 1910).

*Vita Willehadi*, ed. A. Poncelet, AASS, Nov 8th, vol. 3 (Brussels, 1910), pp. 842–6; also A. Röpke, *Das Leben des heiligen Willehad Bischof von Bremen und die Beschreibung der Wunder an seinem Grabe* (Bremen, 1982).

Wampach, C., *Geschichte der Grundherrschaft Echternach im Frühmittelalter*, 1, 2 (Luxemburg, 1930).

Wetti, *Vita Galli*, ed. B. Krusch, MGH, SRM 4 (Hanover, 1902).

Wibert, *Hystoria de predicatione Episcopi Brunonis cum suis capellanis in Prussia et martyrio eorum*, ed. G. H. Pertz, MGH, SS 4 (Hanover, 1841), pp. 579–80.

Widukind, *Res Gestae Saxonicae*, ed. A. Bauer and R. Rau, *Quellen zur Geschichte der sächsischen Kaiserzeit* (Darmstadt, 1971).

Willibald, *Vita Bonifatii*, ed. W. Levison, *Vitae sancti Bonifatii archiepiscopi Moguntini*, MGH, SRG 57 (Hanover, 1905); also ed. R. Buchner, *Briefe des Bonifatius: Willibalds Leben des Bonifatius* (Darmstadt, 1968): trans. T. Head, in T. F. X. Noble and T. Head, *Soldiers of Christ: Saints and Saints' Lives from Late Antiquity and the Early Middle Ages* (Philadelphia, 1995).

# SECONDARY WORKS

Airlie, S., 'Narratives of triumph and rituals of submission: Charlemagne's mastering of Bavaria', *Transactions of the Royal Historical Society*, 6th series, 9 (1999), pp. 93–119.

Althoff, G., *Otto III* (Darmstadt, 1996).

Ambrosiani, B. and Clarke, H. (eds), *Investigations in the Black Earth*, Birka Studies 1 (Stockholm, 1992).

Angenendt, A., *Monachi peregrini: Studien zu Pirmin und den monastischen Vorstellungen des frühen Mittelalters* (Munich, 1972).

Angenendt, A., 'The conversion of the Anglo-Saxons considered against the background of the early medieval mission', *Angli e sassoni al di qua e al di là de mare*, Settimane di studio del centro italiano di studi sull'alto medioevo 32 (Spoleto, 1986), pp. 747–92.

Becher, M., *Eid und Herrschaft. Untersuchungen zum Herrscherethos Karls des Großen* (Sigmaringen, 1993).

Becher, M., '*Non habent regem idem Antiqui Saxones* . . . Verfassung und Ethnogenese in Sachsen während des 8. Jahrhunderts', *Studien zur Sachsenforschung* 12 (Oldenburg, 1999), pp. 1–32.

Berschin, W., *Biographie und Epochenstil im lateinischen Mittelalter* II, *Merowingische Biographie Italien, Spanien und die Inseln im frühen Mittelalter,* Quellen und Untersuchungen zur lateinischen Philologie des Mittelalters Band IX (Stuttgart, 1988).

Berschin, W., *Biographie und Epochenstil im lateinischen Mittelalter* III, *Karolingische Biographie 750–920 n. Chr.,* Quellen und Untersuchungen zur lateinischen Philologie des Mittelalters Band X (Stuttgart, 1991).

Bieler, L., *The Patrician Texts in the Book of Armagh* (Dublin, 1979).

Birnbaum, H., 'The Lives of Sts. Constantine-Cyril and Methodius', *TO ELLHNIKON, Studies in Honor of Speros Vryonis, Jr.*, 2, *Byzantinoslavica, Armeniaca, Islamica, the Balkans and Modern Greece*, ed. J. Stanojevich Allen, C. P. Ioannides, J. S. Langdon, S. W. Reinert (New York, 1993), pp. 3–23.

Bowlus, C., *Franks, Moravians and Magyars: the Struggle for the Middle Danube 788–907* (Philadelphia, 1995).

Boyle, L., 'Dominican Lectionaries and Leo of Ostia's *Translatio S. Clementis*', *Archivum Fratrum Praedictorum* 28 (1958), pp. 362–94.

Brown, P. R. L., 'Aspects of the Christianization of the Roman aristocracy', *Journal of Roman Studies* 51 (1961), pp. 1–11, reprinted in *id.*, *Religion and Society in the Age of Saint Augustine* (London, 1972), pp. 161–82.

Brown, P. R. L., *The Rise of Western Christendom* (Oxford, 1996); 2nd edn., with notes (Oxford, 1997).

Büttner, H., 'Mission und Kirchenorganisation des Frankenreiches bis zum Tode Karls des Großen', in W. Braunfels (ed.), *Karl der Große: Lebenswerk und Nachleben*, 1, *Persönlichkeit und Geschichte*, ed. H. Beumann, 3rd edn. (Düsseldorf, 1967), pp. 454–87.

Campbell, J., 'The first century of Christianity in England', *Ampleforth Journal* 71 (1971), pp. 12–29, repr. in *id.*, *Essays in Anglo-Saxon History* (London, 1986), pp. 49–67.

Carasso-Kok, M., 'Le diocèse d'Utrecht, 900–1200', in G. Philippart, *Hagiographies*, 2, Corpus Christianorum (Turnhout, 1996), pp. 373–411.

Charles-Edwards, T. M., 'Palladius, Prosper, and Leo the Great: mission and primatial authority', in D. N. Dumville (ed.), *Saint Patrick, A.D. 493–1993* (Woodbridge, 1993), pp. 1–12.

Christiansen, E., *The Northern Crusades* (London, 1980).

Coblenz, K. (ed.), *825 Jahre Christianisierung Rügens* (Altenkirchen, 1993).

Collins, R., *Charlemagne* (London, 1998).

de Gaiffier, B., 'L'auteur de la Vie de S. Amand BHL 335,' *Analecta Bollandiana* 97 (1979), p. 308.

de Hamel, C., *A History of Illuminated Manuscripts* (Oxford, 1986).

de Moreau, E., *Saint Amand: apôtre de la Belgique et du Nord de la France* (Louvain, 1927).

Deug-Su, I., *L'Opera agiographica di Alcuino* (Spoleto, 1983).

Dumville, D. N., 'The death date of St Patrick', in D. N. Dumville (ed.), *Saint Patrick, A.D. 493–1993* (Woodbridge, 1993), pp. 29–33.

Dutton, P. E., *The Politics of Dreaming in the Carolingian Empire* (Lincoln, Nebraska, 1994).

Dvornik, F., 'The first phase of the Drang nach Osten', *Cambridge Historical Journal* 7 (1943), pp. 129–45.

Dvornik, F., *The Making of Central and Eastern Europe* (London, 1949).

Ewig, E., 'Milo et eiusmodi similes', *Sankt Bonifatius. Gedenkengabe zum zwölfhundertsten Todestag* (Fulda, 1953), pp. 412–440; reprinted in *id.*, *Spätantikes und fränkisches Gallien* 2 (Munich, 1979), pp. 189–219.

Ewig, E., 'Die christliche Mission bei den Franken und im Merowingerreich', in D. Baker (ed.), *Miscellania Historiae Ecclesiasticae* 3 (Louvain, 1970), pp. 24–52.

Fletcher, R. A., 'An *Epistola Formata* from León', *Bulletin of the Institute of Historical Research* 45 (1972), pp. 122–8.

Fletcher, R. A., *The Conversion of Europe: From Paganism to Christianity 371–1386 AD* (London, 1997).

Flint, V., *The Rise of Magic in Early Medieval Europe* (Oxford, 1991).

Franklin, S. and Shepard, J., *The Emergence of Rus 750–1200* (London, 1996).

Fritze, W. H., '*Universalis gentium confessio*. Formeln, Träger und Wege universalmissionarischen Denkens im. 7. Jahrhundert', *Frühmittelalterliche Studien* 3 (1969), pp. 78–130.

Fritze, W. H., *Frühzeit zwischen Ostsee und Donau* (Berlin, 1982).

Fritze, W. H., *Untersuchungen zur frühslawischen und frühfränkischen Geschichte bis ins 7. Jahrhundert* (Frankfurt am Main, 1994).

Fros, H. (ed.), *Bibliotheca Hagiographica Latina Antiquae et Mediae Aetatis, Novum Supplementum* (Brussels, 1986).

Ganz, D., 'The debate on predestination', in M. Gibson and J. L. Nelson (eds), *Charles the Bald, Court and Kingdom*, 2nd edn. (London, 1990), pp. 283–302.

Garnsey, P. and Saller, R., *The Roman Empire: Economy, Society and Culture* (London, 1987).

Gerberding, R., *The Rise of the Carolingians and the Liber Historiae Francorum* (Oxford, 1987).

Gieysztor, A., '*Sanctus et gloriosissimus martyr Christi Adalbertus*: un état et une église missionnaires aux alentours de l'an mille', *La conversione al cristianesimo nell'Europa dell'Alto Medioevo*, Settimane di Studio 14 (Spoleto, 1967), pp. 611–47.

Glaser, H., 'Bischof Arbeo von Freising als Gegenstand der neueren Forschung', in H. Glaser, F. Brunhölzl and S. Benker, *Vita Corbiniani: Bischof Arbeo von Freising und die Lebensgeschichte des hl. Korbinian* (Munich, 1983), pp. 11–76.

Godman, P. (ed.), *Alcuin, The Bishops, Kings and Saints of York* (Oxford, 1982).

Goffart, W., *The Narrators of Barbarian History (A.D. 550–800)* (Princeton, 1988).

Goldberg, E. J., 'Popular revolt, dynastic politics and aristocratic factionalism in the Early Middle Ages: the Saxon Stellinga reconsidered', *Speculum* 70 (1995), pp. 467–501.

Görich, K., 'Otto III. öffnet das Karlsgrab in Aachen', *Herrschaftsrepräsentation im ottonischen Sachsen*, ed. G. Althoff and E. Schubert, Vorträge und Forschungen 46 (Sigmaringen, 1998), pp. 381–430.

Grant, A., 'The construction of the early Scottish state', in J. R. Maddicott and D. M. Palliser, *The Medieval State* (London, 2000), pp. 47–71.

Graus, F., 'Die Gewalt bei den Anfängen des Feudalismus und die "Gefangenenbefreiungen" der merowingische Hagiographie', *Jahrbuch für Wirtschaftsgeschichte* 1 (1961), pp. 61–156.

Graus, F., *Volk, Herrsher und heilige im Reich der Merowinger* (Prague, 1965).

Green, D. H., *Language and History in the Early Germanic World* (Cambridge, 1998).

Griffe, E., *La Gaule chrétienne à l'époque romaine*, vol. 1, 2nd edn., (Paris, 1964).

Grzesik, R., 'Die Ungarnmission des hl. Adalberts', in B. Nagy and M. Sebök, *The Man of Many Devices, Who Wandered Full Many Ways* (Budapest, 1999), pp. 230–40.

Hägg, I., *Die Textilfunde aus dem Hafen von Haithabu*, Ausgrabungen in Haithabu 20 (Neumünster, 1984).

Hamilton, B., 'The city of Rome and the Eastern Churches in the tenth century', *Orientalia Christiana Periodica* 27 (1961), pp. 5–26, reprinted in *id.*, *Monastic Reform, Catharism and the Crusades (900–1300)* (London, 1979).

Hamilton, B., 'The monastery of S. Alessio and the religious and intellectual renaissance in tenth-century Rome', *Studies in Medieval and Renaissance History* 2 (1965), pp. 265–310, reprinted in *id.*, *Monastic Reform, Catharism and the Crusades 900–1300* (London, 1979).

Hamilton, B., 'S. Pierre Damien et les mouvements monastiques de son temps', *Studi Gregoriani* 10 (1975), pp. 179–95, reprinted in *id.*, *Monastic Reform, Catharism and the Crusades, 900–1300* (London, 1979).

Harvey, P. D. A., *Mappa Mundi, the Hereford World Map* (London, 1996).

Hauck, K., *Apostolischer Geist im Genus sacerdotale des Liudgeriden* (Essen, 1986).

Heather, P., 'The crossing of the Danube and the Gothic conversion', *Greek, Roman and Byzantine Studies* 27 (1986), pp. 289–318.

Heather, P. and Matthews, J. F., *The Goths in the Fourth Century* (Liverpool, 1991).

Helm, K., *Altgermanische Religionsgeschichte*, 2, *Die nachrömische Zeit*, 2, *Die Westgermanen* (Heidelberg, 1953).

Hen, Y. *Culture and Religion in Merovingian Gaul, AD 481–751* (Leiden, 1995).

Herbert, M., *Iona, Kells and Derry* (Oxford, 1988).

Higham, N., *The Convert Kings* (Manchester, 1997).

Hillgarth, J. N., *Christianity and Paganism, 350–750: the Conversion of Western Europe* (Philadelphia, 1986).

Höfler, O., *Kultische Geheimbunde der Germanen* (Frankfurt, 1934).

Hollis, S., *Anglo-Saxon Women and the Church* (Woodbridge, 1992).

Holtzmann, R., *Geschichte der sächsischen Kaiserzeit (900–1024)* (Munich, 1941).

Holtzmann, W., 'Laurentius von Amalfi, ein Lehrer Hildebrands', *Studi Gregoriani* 1 (1947), pp. 207–36.

Jahn, J., 'Virgil, Arbeo und Cozroh: Verfassungsgeschichtliche Beobachtungen an bairischen Quellen des 8. Jahrhunderts', in *Mitteilungen der Gesellschaft für Salzburger Landeskunde* 130 (1990), pp. 201–91.

Jahn, J., 'Hausmeier und Herzöge. Bemerkungen zur agilolfingisch-karolingischen Rivalität bis zum Tode Karl Martels', in J. Jarnut, U. Nonn and M. Richter, *Karl Martel in seiner Zeit* (Sigmaringen, 1994), pp. 317–44.

Jochens, J., 'Late and peaceful: Iceland's conversion through arbitration in 1000', *Speculum* 74 (1999), pp. 620–55.

Johanek, P., 'Der Ausbau der sächsischen Kirchenorganisation', in C. Stiegemann and M. Wemhoff (ed.), *Kunst und Kultur der Karolingerzeit* (Mainz, 1999), Bd. 2, pp. 494–506.

Kantor, M., *The Origins of Christianity in Bohemia* (Evanston, 1990).

King, P. D., *Charlemagne: Translated Sources* (Lancaster, 1987).

Klüppel, T., 'Die Germania (750–950)', in G. Philippart (ed.), *Hagiographies*, 2, Corpus Christianorum (Turnhout, 1996), pp. 161–209.

Lammers, W., 'Ansgar, visionäre Erlebnisformen und Missionsauftrag', in C. Bauer, L. Böhm and M. Müller (eds), *Speculum Historiale* (Munich, 1965), pp. 541–58.

Lane Fox, R., *Pagans and Christians* (London, 1987).

Lebecq, S., 'Le baptême manqué du roi Radbod', in O. Redon and B. Rosenberger (eds), *Les assises du pouvoir: temps médiévaux, territoires africains* (St-Denis, 1994), pp. 141–50.

Levison, L., *England and the Continent in the Eighth Century* (Oxford, 1946).

Leyser, K. J., 'The Battle at the Lech, 955', *History* 50 (1965), pp. 1–25, reprinted in *id.*, *Medieval Germany and its Neighbours 900–1250* (London, 1982), p. 66.

Löwe, H., 'Arbeo von Freising: eine Studie zu Religiosität und Bildung im 8. Jahrhundert', *Rheinische Vierteljahrsblätter* 15/16 (1950/1), pp. 87–120, reprinted in *id.*, *Von Cassiodor zu Dante: Ausgewählte Aufsätze zur Geschichtschreibung und politischen Ideenwelt des Mittelalters* (Berlin, 1973), pp. 75–110.

Löwe, H., *Ein literarischer Widersacher des Bonifatius. Virgil von Salzburg und die Kosmographie des Aethicus Ister*, Abhandlungen der Akademie der Wissenschaften und der Literatur Mainz, Geistes- und sozialwissenschaftliche Klasse 11, 1951 (Wiesbaden, 1952).

Löwe, H., 'Liudger als Zeitkritiker', *Historisches Jahrbuch* 74 (1955), pp. 79–91, reprinted in Löwe, *Von Cassiodor zu Dante: Ausgewählte Aufsätze zur Geschichtschreibung und politischen Ideenwelt des Mittelalters* (Berlin, 1973), pp. 111–22.

Löwe, H., 'Ermenrich von Passau, Gegner des Methodius. Versuch eines Persönlichkeitsbildes', *Mitteilungen der Gesellschaft für Salzburger Landeskunde* 126 (1986), pp. 221–41, reprinted in *id.*, *Religiosität und Bildung im frühen Mittelalter* (Stuttgart, 1994), pp. 327–47.

MacMullen, R., *Christianizing the Roman Empire A.D. 100–400* (Yale, 1984).

Manitius, M., *Geschichte der lateinischen Literatur des Mittelalters*, 2 (Munich, 1923).

Markus, R. A., 'Gregory the Great and a papal missionary strategy'. *Studies in Church History* 6, *The Mission of the Church and the Propagation of the Faith*, ed. G. J. Cuming (Cambridge, 1960), pp. 29–38: reprinted in R. A. Markus, *From Augustine to Gregory the Great* (London, 1983).

Markus, R. A., *Christianity in the Roman World* (London, 1974).

Mayr-Harting, H. M. E., *Ottonian Book Illumination*, 2 vols. (London, 1991).

McCready, W. D., *Signs of Sanctity: Miracles in the Thought of Gregory the Great* (Toronto, 1989).

McKitterick, R., *The Frankish Church and the Carolingian Reforms, 789–895* (London, 1977).

McKitterick, R., *Anglo-Saxon Missionaries in Germany*, Eighth Brixworth Lecture, Vaughan Paper 36 (Leicester, 1991).

Meens, R., 'Willibrords boeteboek?', *Tijdschrift voor Geschiedenis* 106 (1993), pp. 163–78.

Meens, R., 'A background to Augustine's mission to Anglo-Saxon England', *Anglo-Saxon England* 23 (1994), pp. 5–17.

Meens, R., 'Christentum und Heidentum aus der Sicht Willibrords? Überlegungen zum *Paenitentiale Oxoniense II*', in M. Polfer, *Die Christianisierung der Region zwischen Maas und Mosel und die Gründung der Abtei Echternach (5.–9. Jahrhundert)* (forthcoming).

Meulengracht Sørensen, P., 'Religions old and new', in P. Sawyer (ed.), *The Oxford Illustrated History of the Vikings* (Oxford, 1997), pp. 202–24.

Mordek, H., 'Die Hedenen als politische Kraft im austrasischen Frankenreich', in J. Jarnut, U. Nonn and M. Richter (eds), *Karl Martell in seiner Zeit* (Sigmaringen, 1994), pp. 345–66.

Morris, C., *The Discovery of the Individual 1050–1200* (London, 1972).

Müller, I., 'Die älteste Gallus-vita', *Zeitschrift für schweizerische Kirchengeschichte* 66 (1972), pp. 209–49.

Müller-Wille, M., *Opferkulte der Germanen und Slawen* (Darmstadt, 1999).

Netzer, N., *Cultural Interplay in the Eighth Century: the Trier Gospels and the Making of a Scriptorium at Echternach* (Cambridge, 1994).

Niemeyer, G., 'Die Herkunft der Vita Willehadi', *Deutsches Archiv* 12 (1956), pp. 17–35.

Noble, T. F. X., 'Lupus of Ferrières in his Carolingian context', in A. C. Murray (ed.), *After Rome's Fall: Narrators and Sources of Early Medieval History* (Toronto, 1998), pp. 232–50.

Parkes, M. B., *The Scriptorium of Wearmouth-Jarrow*, Jarrow Lecture 1982.

Parsons, D., 'Sites and monuments of the Anglo-Saxon mission in central Germany', *Archaeological Journal* 140 (1983), pp. 280–321.

Parsons, D., 'Some churches of the Anglo-Saxon missionaries in southern Germany: a review of the evidence', *Early Medieval Europe* 8 (1999), pp. 31–67.

Pit'ha, P., *Cechy a Jejich Svatí* (Prague, 1992).

Pohl, W., *Die Awaren. Ein Steppenvolk in Mitteleuropa* (Munich, 1988).

Price, R. M., 'The holy man and Christianisation from the apocryphal gospels to St Stephen of Perm', in J. Howard-Johnston and P. A. Hayward (eds), *The Cult of the Saints in Late Antiquity and the Early Middle Ages* (Oxford, 1999), pp. 215–38.

Price, S., 'From noble funerals to divine cult: the consecration of Roman Emperors', in D. Cannadine and S. Price, *Rituals of Royalty: Power and Ceremonial in Traditional Societies* (Cambridge, 1987), pp. 56–105.

Rabe, S. A., *Faith, Art and Politics at Saint-Riquier: the Symbolic Vision of Angilbert* (Philadelphia, 1995).

Reuter, T., 'Saint Boniface and Europe', in T. Reuter (ed.), *The Greatest Englishman: Essays on St Boniface and the Church at Credition* (Exeter, 1980), pp. 71–94.

Reuter, T., *Germany in the Middle Ages, 800–1056* (London, 1991).

Riedmann, J., 'Unbekannte frühkarolingische Handschriftenfragmente in der Bibliothek des Tiroler Landesmuseums Ferdinandeum', *Mitteilungen des Instituts für Österreichische Geschichtsforschung* 84 (1976), pp. 262–89.

Riedmann, J., 'Die ältesten Handschriftenfragmente in der Bibliothek des Museums Ferdinandeum', *Veröffentlichungen des Tiroler Landesmuseums Ferdinandeum* 56 (1976), pp. 129–39.

Rohr, C., 'Hagiographie als historische Quelle: Ereignisgeschichte und Wunderberichte in der *Vita Columbani* des Ionas von Bobbio', *Mitteilungen des Instituts für Österreichische Geschichtsforschung* 103 (1995), pp. 229–64.

Rollason, D. W., *Saints and Relics in Anglo-Saxon England* (Oxford, 1989).

Sawyer, B., 'Scandinavian conversion histories', in B. Sawyer, P. H. Sawyer and I. N. Wood (eds), *The Christianization of Scandinavia* (Alingsås, 1987), pp. 88–110.

Sawyer, P. H., 'The process of Scandinavian Christianization in the tenth and eleventh centuries', in B. Sawyer, P. H. Sawyer and I. N. Wood (eds), *The Christianization of Scandinavia* (Alingsås, 1987), pp. 68–87.

Schäferdiek, K. (ed.), *Kirchengeschichte als Missionsgeschichte, 2, 1: Die Kirche des früheren Mittelalters* (Münster, 1978).

Schieffer, T., *Winfrid-Bonifatius und die christliche Grundlegung Europas* (Freiburg, 1954).

Schröer, A., 'Das Datum der Bischofsweihe Liudgers von Münster', *Historisches Jahrbuch* 76 (1957), pp. 106–17.

Senger, B., *Liudger, Leben und Werk* (Münster, 1984).

Sims-Williams, P., *Religion and Literature in Western England, 600–800* (Cambridge, 1990).

Slupecki, L., *Slavonic Pagan Sanctuaries* (Warsaw, 1994).

Smith, J. M. H., 'The hagiography of Hucbald of Saint-Amand', *Studi Medievali* 35 (1994), pp. 517–42.

Springer, M., 'Was Lebuins Lebensbeschreibung über die Verfassung Sachsens wirklich sagt oder warum man sich mit einselnen Wörter beschäftigen muß', *Studien zur Sachsenforschung* 12 (Oldenburg, 1999), pp. 223–39.

Stancliffe, C., 'From town to country: the Christianisation of the Touraine 370–600', *Studies in Church History* 16 (1979), pp. 43–59.

Stancliffe, C., *Saint Martin and his Hagiographer: History and Miracle in Sulpicius Severus* (Oxford, 1983).

Stelzer, W., 'Ein Alt-Salzburger Fragment der Kosmographie des Aethicus Ister', *Mitteilungen des Instituts für Österreichische Geschichtsforschung* 100 (1992), pp. 132–49.

Stiegemann, C., and M. Wemhoff, M. (eds), *799 Kunst und Kultur der Karolingerzeit, Karl der Große und Papst Leo III. in Paderborn*, 3 vols. (Mainz, 1999).

Sugar, P. F. (ed.), *A History of Hungary* (Bloomington, 1990).

Sullivan, R. E., 'The Carolingian missionary and the pagan', *Speculum* 28 (1953), pp. 705–40, repr. in *id.*, *Christian Missionary Activity in the Early Middle Ages* (Aldershot, 1994).

Sullivan, R. E., 'Carolingian missionary theories', *Catholic Historical Review* 42 (1956), pp. 273–95, repr. in *id.*, *Christian Missionary Activity in the Early Middle Ages* (Aldershot, 1994).

Sullivan, R. E., 'Khan Boris and the conversion of Bulgaria: a case study of the impact of Christianity on a barbarian society', *Studies in Medieval and Renaissance History* 3 (1966), pp. 55–139, repr. in *id.*, *Christian Missionary Activity in the Early Middle Ages* (Aldershot, 1994).

Thacker, A., '*Peculiaris patronus noster*: the saint as patron of the state in the Early Middle Ages', in J. R. Maddicott and D. M. Palliser, *The Medieval State* (London, 2000), pp. 1–24.

Thomas, C., *Christianity in Roman Britain to A.D. 500* (London, 1981), pp. 271–4.

Thompson, E. A., 'Christianity and the northern barbarians', in A. Momigliano (ed.), *The Conflict between Paganism and Christianity in the Fourth Century* (Oxford, 1963), pp. 56–78.

Thompson, E. A., *The Visigoths in the Time of Ulfila* (Oxford, 1966).

Townsend, D., 'Alcuin's Willibrord, Wilhelm Levison, and the MGH', in R. Frank (ed.), *The Politics of Editing Medieval Texts* (New York, 1993), pp. 107–30.

Unterkircher, F., *Alkuin-Briefe und andere Traktate*, Codices Selecti Phototypice Impressi 20 (Graz, 1969).

Vána, Z., *The World of the Ancient Slavs* (Prague, 1983).

van der Straeten, J., 'Les actes des martyrs d'Aurélian en Bourgogne: étude littéraire', *Analecta Bollandiana* 79 (1961), pp. 115–44.

van der Straeten, J., 'Les actes des martyrs d'Aurélian en Bourgogne: le texte de Farfa', *Analecta Bollandiana* 79 (1961), pp. 447–68.

Van Es, W. A., and Hessing, W. A. M., *Romeinen, Friezen en Franken* (Den Haag, 1994).

Verhulst, A., and Declercq, G., 'L'action et le souvenir de saint Amand en Europe centrale. À propos de la découverte d'une *Vita Amandi antiqua*', in M. Van Uytfanghe and R. Demeulenaere, *Aevum inter Utrumque, Mélanges offerts à Gabriel Sanders* (Den Haag, 1991), pp. 503–26.

Verwers, W. J. H., 'Wijk bij Duurstede-Dorestad', in W. A. Van Es and W. A. M. Hessing, *Romeinem, Friezen en Franken* (Den Haag, 1994), pp. 234–8.

Vlasto, A. P., *The Entry of the Slavs into Christendom* (Cambridge, 1970).

Voigt, H. G., *Bruno von Querfurt* (Stuttgart, 1907).

von Padberg, L., *Heilige und Familie: Studien zur Bedeutung familiengebundener Aspekte in den Viten des Verwandten- und Schülerkreises um Willibrord, Bonifatius und Liudger* (Münster, 1981).

von Padberg, L., *Mission und Christianisierung. Formen und Folgen bei Angelsachsen und Franken im 7. und 8. Jahrhundert* (Stuttgart, 1995).

Wallace-Hadrill, J. M., *The Frankish Church* (Oxford, 1983).

Wenskus, R., *Studien zur historisch-politischen Gedankenwelt Bruns von Querfurt* (Cologne, 1956).

Wickham, C., 'European forests in the Early Middle Ages: landscape, and land clearance', *L'ambiente vegetale nell'alto medioevo*, Settimane di studio sull'alto medioevo 37 (Spoleto, 1990), pp. 479–548.

Wolfram, H., 'Virgil of St Peter's at Salzburg', in P. Ní Chatháin and M. Richter, *Irland und die Christenheit* (Stuttgart, 1987), pp. 415–20.

Wolfram, H., *Die Geburt Mitteleuropas* (Vienna, 1987).

Wolfram, H., *Grenzen und Räume* (Vienna, 1995).

Wolfram, H., *Salzburg, Bayern, Österreich. Die Conversio Bagoariorum et Carantanorum und die Quellen ihrer Zeit* (Vienna, 1995).

Wood, I. N., 'The conversion of the barbarian peoples', in G. Barraclough (ed.), *The Christian World* (London, 1981), pp. 85–98.

Wood, I. N., 'The *Vita Columbani* and Merovingian hagiography', *Peritia* 1 (1982), pp. 63–80.

Wood, I. N., 'Christians and pagans in ninth-century Scandinavia', in B. Sawyer, P. H. Sawyer and I. N. Wood (eds), *The Christianization of Scandinavia* (Alingsås, 1987), pp. 36–67.

Wood, I. N., 'Pagans and holy men 600–800', in P. Ní Chatháin and M. Richter, *Irland und die Christenheit* (1987), pp. 347–61.

Wood, I. N., 'Forgery in Merovingian hagiography', in MGH Schriften 33, *Fälschungen im Mittelalter* 5 (Hanover, 1988), pp. 369–84.

Wood, I. N., 'Saint-Wandrille and its hagiography', in I. N. Wood and G. A. Loud (eds), *Church and Chronicle in the Middle Ages* (London, 1991), pp. 1–14.

Wood, I. N., *The Merovingian Kingdoms 450–751* (London, 1994).

Wood, I. N., 'The mission of Augustine of Canterbury to the English', *Speculum* 69 (1994), pp. 1–17.

Wood, I. N., 'Pagan religions and superstitions east of the Rhine from the fifth to the ninth century', in G. Ausenda (ed.), *After Empire: Towards an Ethnology of Europe's Barbarians* (Woodbridge, 1995), pp. 253–79.

Wood, I. N., 'Augustine's journey', *Canterbury Cathedral Chronicle* 92 (1998), pp. 28–44.

Wood, I. N., 'The frontiers of Western Europe: developments east of the Rhine in the sixth century', in R. Hodges and W. Bowden (eds), *The Sixth Century: Production, Distribution and Demand* (Leiden, 1998), pp. 231–53.

Wood, I. N., 'Jonas, the Merovingians, and Pope Honorius: *Diplomata* and the *Vita Columbani*', in A. C. Murray (ed.), *After Rome's Fall: Narrators and Sources of Early Medieval History* (Toronto, 1998), pp. 99–120.

Wood, I. N., 'The use and abuse of Latin hagiography', in E. Chrysos and I. N. Wood (eds), *East and West: Modes of Communication* (Leiden, 1999), pp. 93–109.

Wood, I. N., 'Augustine and Aidan: bureaucrat and charismatic?', in C. de Dreuille (ed.), *L'Église et la mission au VIe siècle* (Paris, 2000), pp. 148–79.

Wood, I. N., 'An absence of saints? The evidence for the Christianisation of Saxony' (forthcoming).

Wood, I. N., 'Beyond satraps and ostriches: political and social structures of the Saxons in the early Carolingian period' (forthcoming).

Wood, I. N., 'Cults, churches and conversion histories in the Auvergne and Burgundy 400–1000' (forthcoming).

Zöllner, E., 'Die Herrkunft der Agilolfinger', *Mitteilungen des Instituts für Österreichische Geschichtsforschung* 59 (1951), pp. 245–64.

# MAPS

The Christianisation of Europe, 400–1000

From Patrick to Bede

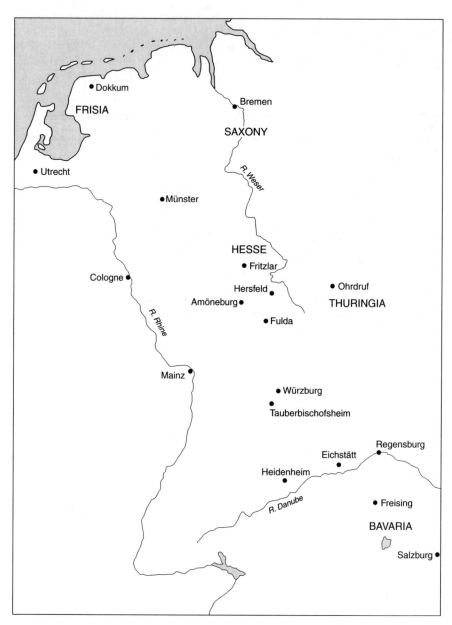

Boniface, Mainz and Fulda

Alcuin and Echternach

Utrecht and Münster

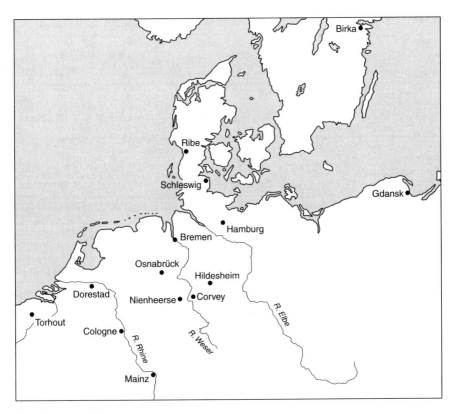

Hamburg and Bremen

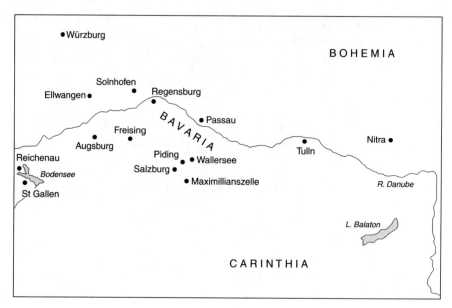

Salzburg and Freising in the eighth century

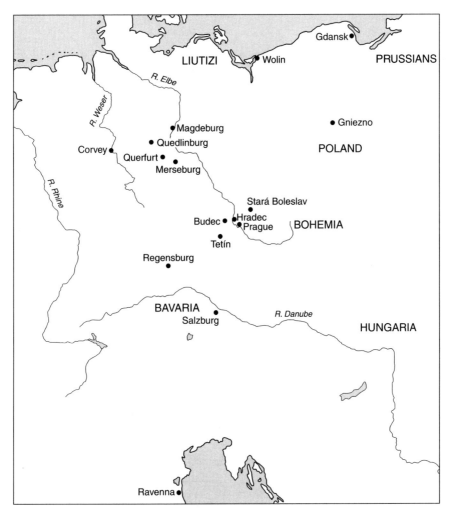

The latin legends of Wenceslas, Adalbert of Prague, Bruno of Querfurt

# INDEX